THE NEW CAMBRIDGE SHAKESPEARE

HAMLET, PRINCE OF DENMARK

THE NEW CAMBRIDGE SHAKESPEARE

Romeo and Juliet, edited by G. Blakemore Evans
The Taming of the Shrew, edited by Ann Thompson
Othello, edited by Norman Sanders
King Richard II, edited by Andrew Gurr
A Midsummer Night's Dream, edited by R. A. Foakes
Hamlet, edited by Philip Edwards
Twelfth Night, edited by Elizabeth Story Donno
All's Well That Ends Well, edited by Russell Fraser
The Merchant of Venice, edited by M. M. Mahood
Much Ado About Nothing, edited by F. H. Mares
The Comedy of Errors, edited by T. S. Dorsch
Julius Caesar, edited by Marvin Spevack

HAMLET, PRINCE OF DENMARK

Edited by
PHILIP EDWARDS
King Alfred Professor of English Literature
University of Liverpool

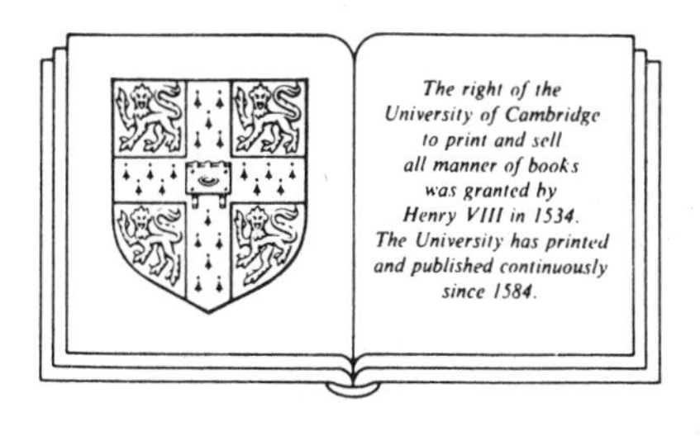

CAMBRIDGE UNIVERSITY PRESS
Cambridge
New York   Port Chester
Melbourne   Sydney

Published by the Press Syndicate of the University of Cambridge
The Pitt Building, Trumpington Street, Cambridge CB2 1RP
40 West 20th Street, New York, NY 10011, USA
10 Stamford Road, Oakleigh, Melbourne 3166, Australia

First published 1985
Reprinted 1988 (twice) 1989

Printed in Great Britain by
the University Press, Cambridge

Library of Congress catalogue card number: 84-17517

British Library Cataloguing in Publication Data
Shakespeare, William
Hamlet, Prince of Denmark. – (The New
Cambridge Shakespeare)
I. Title II. Edwards, Philip III. Series
822'.3'3 PR2807
ISBN 0 521 22151 X hard covers
ISBN 0 521 29366 9 paperback

UP

THE NEW CAMBRIDGE SHAKESPEARE

The *New Cambridge Shakespeare* succeeds *The New Shakespeare* which began publication in 1921 under the general editorship of Sir Arthur Quiller-Couch and John Dover Wilson, and was completed in the 1960s, with the assistance of G. I. Duthie, Alice Walker, Peter Ure and J. C. Maxwell. *The New Shakespeare* itself followed upon *The Cambridge Shakespeare*, 1863–6, edited by W. G. Clark, J. Glover and W. A. Wright.

The New Shakespeare won high esteem both for its scholarship and for its design, but shifts of critical taste and insight, recent Shakespearean research, and a changing sense of what is important in our understanding of the plays, have made it necessary to re-edit and redesign, not merely to revise, the series.

The *New Cambridge Shakespeare* aims to be of value to a new generation of playgoers and readers who wish to enjoy fuller access to Shakespeare's poetic and dramatic art. While offering ample academic guidance, it reflects current critical interests and is more attentive than some earlier editions have been to the realisation of the plays on the stage, and to their social and cultural settings. The text of each play has been freshly edited, with textual data made available to those users who wish to know why and how one published text differs from another. Although modernised, the edition conserves forms that appear to be expressive and characteristically Shakespearean, and it does not attempt to disguise the fact that the plays were written in a language other than that of our own time.

Illustrations are usually integrated into the critical and historical discussion of the play and include some reconstructions of early performances by C. Walter Hodges. Some editors have also made use of the advice and experience of Maurice Daniels, for many years a member of the Royal Shakespeare Company.

Each volume is addressed to the needs and problems of a particular text, and each therefore differs in style and emphasis from others in the series.

PHILIP BROCKBANK
General Editor

What is he that builds stronger than either the mason, the shipwright, or the carpenter?

To the memory of my great-grandfather

ROBERT EDWARDS
1829–1908

Sexton of St John's Church, Rhydymwyn, Clwyd

CONTENTS

ILLUSTRATIONS

PREFACE

The vastness of the commentary on *Hamlet* gives an editor of the play a rather special freedom. Even if he could read them all, he could not accommodate within the covers of a book an account of the multitude of theories and ideas generated by the play; and to attempt to sum up even the enduring contributions would so overload the work that it would defeat the main purpose of an edition, which is to make an author's work more accessible. This edition of *Hamlet* is selective in its account of what has gone before, and the view of the play presented in the Introduction, the Commentary – and the text – is personal without I hope being idiosyncratic. Everything that I consider essential to the meaning of the play I have endeavoured to discuss; where I consider problems insoluble, or not central, I have avoided prolonged debate.

The text of *Hamlet* presents great difficulties, and any discussion of it affects and is affected by our understanding of the play. I have not therefore been able to separate my account of the text from the main part of the introduction, as is the custom in this series. In trying to offer help towards the understanding of this great and perplexing play, it is essential to make clear at the outset that there is more than one *Hamlet* we might be talking about.

Most of the work for this edition was completed before the appearance of Harold Jenkins's masterly edition in the New Arden series in the spring of 1982. It has nevertheless been of immense benefit to have his work before me since that time, as my commentary frequently acknowledges. All students of *Hamlet* are in debt to Harold Jenkins for the results of his patient and exacting research.

Some of the material in the critical account of the play in the Introduction appears also in an essay, 'Tragic balance in *Hamlet*', in *Shakespeare Survey 36* (1983); I am grateful to the editor of *Shakespeare Survey* for accepting this overlap.

In acknowledging assistance in this edition of *Hamlet*, I ought to start with John Waterhouse in 1942 and Allardyce Nicoll in 1945, from whom I learned so much about the play. In recent times, my greatest debt is to Kenneth Muir, an untiring lender of books, a patient listener, and a generous adviser. John Jowett gave me great help in checking parts of my typescript, and in sifting through recent writings on the play. I am grateful to Joan Welford for typing the Commentary.

This edition was prepared during a period of rather heavy administrative duties in the University of Liverpool. I am most grateful to the University for two periods of leave, and to the University of Otago, the British Academy and the Huntington Library for enabling me to make the most of them.

P.E.

University of Liverpool, 1984

ABBREVIATIONS AND SHORT TITLES

All quotations and line references to plays other than *Hamlet* are to G. Blakemore Evans (ed.), *The Riverside Shakespeare*, 1974.

Adams	*Hamlet*, ed. Joseph Quincy Adams, 1929
N. Alexander	*Hamlet*, ed. Nigel Alexander, 1973 (Macmillan Shakespeare)
P. Alexander	*William Shakespeare, The Complete Works*, ed. Peter Alexander, 1951
Bullough	Geoffrey Bullough (ed.), *Narrative and Dramatic Sources of Shakespeare*, 8 vols., 1957–75
Cambridge	*The Works of William Shakespeare*, ed. William George Clark, J. Glover and William Aldis Wright, 1863–6, viii; 2nd edn, 1891–2, VII (Cambridge Shakespeare)
Capell	*Mr William Shakespeare, His Comedies, Histories and Tragedies*, ed. Edward Capell, 1767–8, X
Clark and Wright	*Hamlet Prince of Denmark*, ed. William George Clark and William Aldis Wright, 1872 (Clarendon Press Shakespeare)
Collier	*The Works of William Shakespeare*, ed. J. Payne Collier, 1842–4, VII
conj.	conjectured
Dowden	*The Tragedy of Hamlet*, ed. Edward Dowden, 1899 (Arden Shakespeare)
Duthie	George Ian Duthie, *The 'Bad' Quarto of 'Hamlet': A Critical Study*, 1941
Dyce	*The Works of William Shakespeare*, ed. Alexander Dyce, 1857, V
F	*Mr William Shakespeares Comedies, Histories, and Tragedies*, 1623 (First Folio) [see Introduction, p. 9]
Hanmer	*The Works of Shakespear*, ed. Sir Thomas Hanmer, 1743–4, VI
Hoy	*Hamlet*, ed. Cyrus Hoy, 1963 (Norton Critical Editions)
Jenkins	*Hamlet*, ed. Harold Jenkins, 1982 (Arden Shakespeare)
Johnson	*The Plays of William Shakespeare*, ed. Samuel Johnson, 1765, VIII
Kittredge	*Hamlet*, ed. George Lyman Kittredge, 1939
Knight	*The Pictorial Edition of the Works of Shakspere*, ed. Charles Knight, 1838–43, I, 'Tragedies'
MacDonald	*The Tragedie of Hamlet*, ed. George MacDonald, 1885
Malone	*The Plays and Poems of William Shakespeare*, ed. Edmond Malone, 1790, IX
MLN	*Modern Language Notes*
MSH	J. Dover Wilson, *The Manuscript of Shakespeare's 'Hamlet'*, 2 vols., 1934; reprinted 1963
N & Q	*Notes and Queries*
NV	*Hamlet*, ed. Horace Howard Furness, 2 vols., 1877; reprinted 1963 (A New Variorum Edition of Shakespeare)
OED	*The Oxford English Dictionary*, 1884–1928, reprinted 1933
PMLA	*Publications of the Modern Language Association of America*
Pope	*The Works of Shakespear*, ed. Alexander Pope, 1723–5, VI
Pope²	*The Works of Shakespear*, ed. Alexander Pope, 2nd edn, 1728, VIII
Q1	*The Tragicall Historie of Hamlet Prince of Denmarke*, by William Shakespeare, 1603 (first quarto)

Q2	*The Tragicall Historie of Hamlet, Prince of Denmarke,* by William Shakespeare, 1604, 1605 (second quarto)
Q 1611, Q 1676	Quarto editions of those dates
RES	*Review of English Studies*
Ridley	*Hamlet,* ed. M. R. Ridley, 1934 (New Temple Shakespeare)
Rowe	*The Works of Mr William Shakespear*, ed. Nicholas Rowe, 1709, V
Schmidt	Alexander Schmidt, *Shakespeare-Lexicon*, 2 vols., 1874–5; 2nd edn, 1886
SD	stage direction
SH	speech heading
Spencer	*Hamlet*, ed. T. J. B. Spencer, 1980 (New Penguin Shakespeare)
SQ	*Shakespeare Quarterly*
Staunton	*The Plays of Shakespeare*, ed. Howard Staunton, 1858–60, reissued 1866, III
Steevens	*The Plays of William Shakespeare,* ed. Samuel Johnson and George Steevens, 1773, X
Steevens[2]	*The Plays of William Shakespeare*, ed. Samuel Johnson and George Steevens, 2nd edn, 1778, X
Steevens[3]	*The Plays of William Shakespeare*, ed. Samuel Johnson and George Steevens, 4th edn, 1793, XV
Sternfeld	F. W. Sternfeld, *Music in Shakespearean Tragedy*, 1963
Theobald	Lewis Theobald, *Shakespeare Restored,* 1726
Theobald[2]	*The Works of Shakespeare,* ed. Lewis Theobald, 1733, VII
Theobald[3]	*The Works of Shakespeare,* ed. Lewis Theobald, 1740, VIII
Tilley	Morris Palmer Tilley, *A Dictionary of the Proverbs in England in the Sixteenth and Seventeenth Centuries,* 1950 [references are to numbered proverbs]
TLS	*The Times Literary Supplement*
Verity	*The Tragedy of Hamlet*, ed. A. W. Verity, 1904
Walker	William Sydney Walker, *A Critical Examination of the Text of Shakespeare*, 3 vols., 1860
Warburton	*The Works of Shakespear*, ed. William Warburton, 1747, VIII
White	*The Works of William Shakespeare*, ed. Richard Grant White, 1857–66, XI
Wilson	*Hamlet*, ed. J. Dover Wilson, 1934; 2nd edn, 1936, reprinted 1968 (New Shakespeare)

INTRODUCTION

Source and date

The basic though not the immediate source of *Hamlet* is a twelfth-century story of Amleth in Saxo Grammaticus's *Historiae Danicae*, which was first put into print in 1514.[1] It is remarkable how much of the primitive legend survives through the successive redactions into Shakespeare's masterpiece. Amleth's father, who has defeated the king of Norway in a duel, is murdered by his brother Feng, who takes his brother's widow, Gerutha, to wife. The murder is not secret. To protect himself and avert suspicion from his plans, Amleth starts acting as an idiot, but his speeches are such a perplexing mixture of shrewdness and craziness that tests are devised for him. One test is to see if he will react normally to a 'fair woman' who is put in his way. He does, but he swears her to secrecy. Then a friend of Feng suggests they should get Amleth and his mother together while he conceals himself in the chamber to listen to them. Amleth discovers the eavesdropper, kills him, dismembers the body and feeds it to the pigs. He returns to the lamenting mother and bitterly attacks her for forgetting her first husband and marrying Feng. Feng now sends Amleth to Britain with two retainers who carry a secret letter to the king requesting the death of Amleth. Amleth gets the letter, substitutes his companions' name for his own – and adds the suggestion that the king should give his daughter in marriage to Amleth. After a time in Britain, Amleth returns home and finds his own obsequies being carried out. He overcomes the courtiers, sets fire to the palace, and kills Feng in his bed, thus exacting 'the vengeance, now long overdue, for his father's murder'. 'O valiant Amleth, and worthy of immortal fame!' says Saxo. Amleth now lies low, uncertain how the populace will take what he has done, but boldly emerges to make a fine speech of justification. 'It is I who have wiped off my country's shame; I who have quenched my mother's dishonour; I who have beaten back oppression...It is I who have stripped you of slavery, and clothed you with freedom...I who have deposed the despot and triumphed over the butcher.' Amleth is made king, and has other adventures before meeting his death in battle.

Here is a success story and no tragedy, but here also is the story of old Fortinbras and old Hamlet, of fratricide and the queen's remarriage, of Hamlet's assumed madness and his riddling talk, of Ophelia being used to test him, of Polonius's eavesdropping and death and the contemptuous treatment of his corpse, of Hamlet's objurgation of Gertrude, of Rosencrantz and Guildenstern accompanying Hamlet to England with a secret commission to have him killed, and the cunning alteration of the commission. Even the germ of the exchange of weapons in the final affray is there.

[1] Oliver Elton's translation of the Latin text is given in Bullough, VII (1973), 60–79.

Between Saxo Grammaticus and *Hamlet* lies a French version of Saxo's story by François de Belleforest, published in his *Histoires Tragiques* in 1570 (followed by many later editions). It does not appear that the Hamlet story was translated into English until 1608. Belleforest is most conscious of the unchristian savagery of the tale and pointedly remarks that it all happened in pre-Christian times. His account is long, wordy and sententious, but in the incidents of the story he follows the stark version of Saxo closely except in two important respects relating to the queen. She and Feng, or Fengon as he now is, have an adulterous liaison before the king is murdered; Fengon 'used her as his concubine'. Secondly, after Hamlet has convinced his mother of the error of her ways (following the death of the eavesdropper), the queen encourages Hamlet in his vengeance, promises to keep his secret, and hopes to see him enjoy his right as king of Denmark. None of this collaboration between Gertrude and Hamlet is in Shakespeare's play, but it does feature in the first quarto, which we shall be looking at shortly.

As for Hamlet's revenge, Belleforest does not acclaim it as enthusiastically as Saxo does, and clearly recognises that some justification is needed. Hamlet argues that his vengeance is neither felony nor treason, but the punishment of a disloyal subject by a sovereign prince (Bullough, VII, 100). And on the death of Fengon, Belleforest states that this is an occasion when vengeance becomes justice, an act of piety and affection, a punishment of treason and murder.

The most important changes which appear in *Hamlet* are as follows:

1 The murder becomes secret;
2 A ghost tells Hamlet of the murder and urges revenge;
3 Laertes and young Fortinbras are introduced;
4 Ophelia's role is extended and elevated;
5 The players and their play are introduced;
6 Hamlet dies as he kills the king.

To be added to this list is a more general change of great significance. The setting of the story is moved from the pre-Christian times where Belleforest deliberately placed it to a courtly, modern-seeming period, in which, though England still pays tribute to Denmark, renaissance young men travel to and fro to complete their education in universities or in Paris.

How many of these changes did Shakespeare himself originate? It is impossible to say, because of our ignorance about the Elizabethan *Hamlet* which preceded Shakespeare's. The earliest reference to this play is in a scornful attack by Thomas Nashe on the Senecan dramatists of the day in 1589. 'English Seneca read by candlelight yields many good sentences, as *Blood is a beggar* and so forth, and if you entreat him fair in a frosty morning he will afford you whole Hamlets, I should say handfuls, of tragical speeches.'[1] Five years later, at the end of the disastrous plague period of 1592–4, Philip Henslowe recorded a short season of plays at Newington Butts (south of the Thames) shared by the Lord Admiral's men and the emerging company of the Lord Chamberlain's men, Shakespeare's company, during which, on 9 June

[1] Preface to Greene's *Menaphon*; Nashe, *Works*, ed. McKerrow, 1904–10, III, 315.

1594, a play of *Hamlet* was performed.[1] In 1596, Thomas Lodge wrote of one who 'walks for the most part in black under cover of gravity, and looks as pale as the vizard of the ghost who cried so miserably at the Theatre like an oyster-wife, *Hamlet, revenge!*'[2]

It may be that this old play was not immediately supplanted and driven from the stage when Shakespeare wrote his version. One of the characters in Dekker's *Satiromastix* (written late in the year 1601) says 'My name's Hamlet revenge; thou hast been at Paris Garden, hast not?' (4.1.121–2); the reference is probably to the older play. The authorship of the earlier play (often called the Ur-*Hamlet*) is not known. Nashe's attack of 1589 on the 'sort of shifting companions' who bleed the English translations of Seneca dry in order to create their dismal tragedies seems to include three glancing references to Thomas Kyd, the author of *The Spanish Tragedy*. These men 'leave the trade of Noverint, whereto they were born', which fits Kyd because his father was a 'noverint' or scrivener; Nashe speaks of 'the Kid in Aesop'; and the phrase 'those that thrust Elysium into hell' may well refer to *The Spanish Tragedy*. But even if Kyd was one of the Senecans whom Nashe was abusing it does not necessarily follow that Nashe meant he was the author of the early *Hamlet*. He may have been. The relationship between Shakespeare's *Hamlet* and Kyd's *Spanish Tragedy* is close and profoundly important. How far that relationship developed through Shakespeare reworking a Kydean *Hamlet* is impossible to say. *The Spanish Tragedy* is about the revenge of a father for his murdered son, and includes the presence on stage of the ghost of a dead man, the hero's madness, and a crucial play-within-the-play. The Ur-*Hamlet*, which was about the revenge of a son for his murdered father, had a ghost urging Hamlet to take revenge, and must have included the assumed madness of the hero, which is among the irreducible constituents of the old story. It seems more likely that the old *Hamlet* would have preceded *The Spanish Tragedy* than vice versa.[3] They were probably companion plays, the successor very conscious of the predecessor, whether Kyd wrote both plays or not. For the Hamlet story there is a quite definite literary source, as we have seen; for *The Spanish Tragedy* there is no known source. If one play copies another, and one is based on a known source and the other isn't, there is a strong argument that the play with a source is the earlier. On this argument, the 'madness' of Hamlet in the old play, being part of the traditional story, would be the original, and the madness of Hieronimo in *The Spanish Tragedy* would be the copy. So we may say that Kyd or one of his fellow-dramatists wrote an early version of *Hamlet*, that Kyd capitalised on its success in *The Spanish Tragedy*, which borrowed many of its features, and that Shakespeare, writing a new version of *Hamlet* which seems very attentive to Kyd's handling of revenge, is influenced by the two similar earlier plays.

Returning then to our question of what changes in the traditional Hamlet story were Shakespeare's, we see that he did not introduce the Ghost. A ghost urging Hamlet to take revenge was an elemental part of the old play; it was what everyone

[1] *Henslowe's Diary*, ed. R. A. Foakes and R. T. Rickert, 1961, p. 21.
[2] *Wits Miserie*, 1596, signature H4^v (text reads 'miserally').
[3] Argued by E. E. Stoll in *Modern Philology* 35 (1937–8), 32–3.

remembered. (This one hard fact we have about the contents of the old play may have been, I shall argue, the feature which attracted Shakespeare to it.) Apart from this, if it is the case that *The Spanish Tragedy* cashed in on the success of the old *Hamlet* and imitated it, then there is a strong possibility not only that the old *Hamlet* had its play-within-the-play, but that it had its Laertes too; for the generation of a second revenge action in the middle of the play is the way *The Spanish Tragedy* works. (In *The Spanish Tragedy*, Hieronimo's vengeance for Horatio is a second motif within the prior revenge scheme of Andrea against Balthasar, which it completes. In *Hamlet*, Laertes' vengeance for Polonius is a second motif within the prior revenge of Hamlet against Claudius; it is only through the completion of Laertes' revenge that Hamlet is brought to the completion of his.)

As for the setting of the play within a renaissance court, one certainly cannot assume that it was Shakespeare who made the transformation. The contrast between the modernity of the characters and the archaic cry of a ghost for revenge is of supreme importance in *Hamlet*, but *The Spanish Tragedy* also accommodates a primitive blood-feud within the setting of a renaissance court and here also it may indicate the nature of the old *Hamlet*.

When did Shakespeare write his *Hamlet*? 'The Revenge of Hamlet Prince [of] Denmark as it was lately acted by the Lord Chamberlain his men' was entered for publication in July 1602 (see p. 9). A very faulty unauthorised text of the play, 'by William Shake-speare', which was published in 1603 (the first quarto), suggests that by then the play had been on the stage for quite some time. Within the play itself, the reference to the great popularity of the children's acting companies as against the adult players (2.2.313–33) is always accepted as a direct reference by Shakespeare to the 'war of the theatres' in London around 1601 and the success of the revived children's companies. The details of this 'war of the theatres' are very vague and shadowy.[1] There is a slanging match with Jonson on one side and Marston and Dekker on the other. Jonson's *Poetaster*, performed by the Chapel boys in 1601, probably in the spring, contains a well-known remark about the professional men-actors. They think of hiring Demetrius (Dekker) and say:

> O, it will get us a huge deal of money, Captain, and we have need on't; for this winter has made us all poorer than so many starved snakes. Nobody comes at us, not a gentleman nor a – (3.4.327–30)

It may well be that a crisis for the men's companies in 1600–1 is what the *Hamlet* passage refers to. This passage is found only in the Folio text; it is one of the most striking omissions from the text of the 'good' quarto of 1604/5. It is my view that Shakespeare added this passage to his original draft as a kind of afterthought before he submitted his manuscript to his colleagues (see p. 19).[2] I think that as he was

[1] See E. K. Chambers, *The Elizabethan Stage*, 1923, I, 379–82; II, 19–21, 41–3. Suspicion that the whole affair was a 'contrived situation' for publicity purposes is expressed by Reavley Gair, *The Children of Paul's*, 1982, p. 134.

[2] Not quite the same thing as the 'later insertion' suggested by E. A. J. Honigmann, 'The date of *Hamlet*', *Shakespeare Survey* 9 (1956), 27–9.

finishing his play the success of the children and the plight of his own company suggested to Shakespeare an amplification of what he had already written about the Players turning up in Elsinore because of the troubled times in Denmark and a decline in their reputation (see the notes to 2.2.308–9 and following). If we could be sure of dating the height of the stage-quarrel in mid 1601 we should have a fairly precise date for Shakespeare finishing his play.

A reference which has been much discussed in dating *Hamlet* is in the marginal note made by Gabriel Harvey in his copy of Speght's Chaucer, which runs:

> The younger sort takes much delight in Shakespeares Venus, & Adonis, but his Lucrece, & his tragedy of Hamlet, Prince of Denmarke, have it in them, to please the wiser sort.[1]

The Chaucer was published in 1598 and Harvey signed his name in his copy with the date '1598'. His very long note, which is a kind of assessment of English literature in his time, refers to Spenser (died 1599) and Watson (died 1592) as with Shakespeare among 'our flourishing metricians', but mentions 'Owen's new epigrams' published in 1607. It also contains the statement, 'The Earl of Essex much commendes Albions England' – which certainly suggests that the Earl was alive; he was executed in February 1601. The sense of time is so confused in Harvey's note that it is really of little use in trying to date *Hamlet*.

E. A. J. Honigmann (see note on p. 4) rightly argued that there is very strong evidence that *Hamlet* was written later than *Julius Caesar*, which was being acted in the summer of 1599. Just before the play-within-the-play there is this exchange between Hamlet and Polonius:

> HAMLET ...My lord, you played once i'th'university, you say.
> POLONIUS That did I my lord, and was accounted a good actor.
> HAMLET And what did you enact?
> POLONIUS I did enact Julius Caesar. I was killed i'th'Capitol. Brutus killed me.
> HAMLET It was a brute part of him to kill so capital a calf there. (3.2.87–93)

Honigmann points out that it is usually assumed that John Heminges acted both the old-man parts, Caesar in the first play and Polonius in the second, and that Richard Burbage acted both Brutus and Hamlet. 'Polonius would then be speaking on the extra-dramatic level in proclaiming his murder in the part of Caesar, since Hamlet (Burbage) will soon be killing him (Heminges) once more in *Hamlet*.' There does indeed seem to be a kind of private joke here, with Heminges saying to Burbage 'Here we go again!' But there is also something much deeper – the identification of the two killers, Brutus and Hamlet. Once again, Burbage plays the part of the intellectual as well-intentioned assassin. In both *Julius Caesar* and *Hamlet*, a bookish, reflective man, honoured by his friends and associates, is summoned to a major political task requiring complete personal involvement and a violent physical assault. The assassination that is to purify Rome is quickly decided on and quickly carried out. The greater part of the play is devoted to the disastrous consequences of killing Caesar. In *Hamlet*,

[1] *Gabriel Harvey's Marginalia*, ed G. C. Moore Smith, 1913, p. 232. See the discussion by Jenkins, pp. 3–6 and 573–4, and Honigmann, 'Date of *Hamlet*', pp. 24–6.

the deed which is to purify Denmark is extraordinarily delayed; most of the play is devoted to disasters in the course of doing the deed. But both plays end in political failure. In neither Rome nor Denmark does the political future turn out as it was desired and planned by the hero. What spiritual triumph there is in both plays is muted. That *Hamlet* is a reworking of the basic underlying theme of *Julius Caesar*, namely the commitment of the philosopher-hero to violent action in order to remove an intruder from the government of the state and restore an ideal condition belonging to former times, seems to me undeniable. The unlocking of the beautifully controlled and articulated Roman play to produce the perturbed and bewildering tangle which is *Hamlet Prince of Denmark* may well seem a strange progression. It is a progression which shows up Shakespeare's sense of the increasing complexity and difficulty of the problems as he continued to think about them. Again, to move from the moral and constitutional problems of high Roman civilisation to the barbarities of nordic myth and the crudities of the Elizabethan revenge play may seem curious. Yet the resources of these less civilised traditions were perhaps what Shakespeare needed in order to take one step further the problem of commitment which both *Julius Caesar* and *Hamlet* present. In particular, the questioning of what relationship there may be between the divine will, retaliatory violence, and the achieving of justice is a constant factor in the revenge tradition as represented by Pickering's *Horestes* (1567) and *The Spanish Tragedy*. Although the supernatural has its place in *Julius Caesar*, and includes a ghost, it does not go near to suggesting an eternal world surrounding, enclosing and explaining the world of man. The figure of the summoning ghost in the old *Hamlet* (the one that cried like an oyster-wife) is what transforms the problem of *Julius Caesar* into the new guise of *Hamlet*. Because of this ghost, the decisions of men about killing are placed as Pickering and Kyd had placed them, within a vast transcendent world of shadowy figures and mysterious commands. The setting of *Hamlet* is not Elsinore but heaven, earth and hell. In the middle of *Hamlet* the actors remind us that they recently acted in the play *Julius Caesar*; they are now in a much more barbaric and untidy play which takes the problems of the earlier work into the perplexities of a spiritual dimension.

If *Hamlet* is in some sense 'inspired' by *Julius Caesar*, it also shares its period of composition with one of Shakespeare's greatest comedies, *Twelfth Night*. T. W. Craik argues that Shakespeare started writing the latter in the middle of 1601 and completed it before the end of the year (New Arden edition, 1975, pp. xxxiv–xxxv). This would fit well with the view that Shakespeare had just finished *Hamlet* when the 'war of the theatres' had come to a head, taking the production of Jonson's *Poetaster* in the spring of 1601 to represent the high point of the quarrel.

We must now look at the curious relationship between Shakespeare's *Hamlet* and Marston's *Antonio's Revenge*. This blood-bespattered and overcharged revenge-play was a main target for Jonson's ridicule in *Poetaster*, and it was probably staged in the winter of 1600–1.[1] It has many parallels with *Hamlet*. The ghost of a poisoned father appears, to tell his son of the concealed murder and urge him to take revenge.

[1] See Reavley Gair's Revels Plays edition, 1978, pp. 14–15.

Later the ghost appears in the bedroom of his errant widow, who is being wooed by the murderer. The avenging son masks his intentions by taking on the role of an idiot. The closest verbal parallel is:

> The other ghost assumed my father's shape;
> Both cried 'Revenge!' (1.3.45–6)[1]

Compare *Hamlet*, 'If it assume my noble father's person' (1.2.243) and 'the devil hath power / T'assume a pleasing shape' (2.2.552–3).

Marston's curious play – at what level of seriousness such an able and intelligent writer undertook this strained and absurd work is impossible to say – is steeped in reminiscences of *The Spanish Tragedy, Richard III, Titus Andronicus.* The play is so receptive of other men's work that in a debate about indebtedness as between Shakespeare's *Hamlet* and *Antonio's Revenge*, Marston starts at a disadvantage; and in an extended discussion Jenkins names him as the borrower (New Arden edition, pp. 7–13). But the two most recent editors of Marston's play, G. K. Hunter (Regents Renaissance series, 1966) and Reavley Gair (Revels Plays, 1978) both accept as the greater likelihood that the *Hamlet* echoes in *Antonio's Revenge* echo not Shakespeare but the old play of *Hamlet.*[2] I am sure this is right. What has influenced Marston is old-fashioned drama, ten years or so old. A Senecan *Hamlet* of the late '80s is the more likely to have helped him to his 'burly words' and melodramatic situations. Shakespeare's *Hamlet* would have manifested its influence in quite different ways. If this view is correct, we do not have to struggle for a timetable which will place *Hamlet* before *Antonio's Revenge*, while the timetable which we have been moving towards suggests the fascinating possibility that Shakespeare was actually at work on his *Hamlet* when Marston's play was staged. There is no need to think that there was much or anything that he wanted to borrow from it – unless he carried in his head the phrase 'assumed my father's shape'. The parallels between the two plays will be accounted for by both dramatists independently making use of a common source, the old play of *Hamlet.* It is not at all unlikely, however, that Shakespeare in his play was reacting strongly against the facile attitudes towards revenge found in Marston's play. In particular, Antonio's idea of an avenger's obligation to evince extreme emotion could well be the source of Hamlet's acceptance and immediate rejection of such an obligation in the 'rogue and peasant slave' soliloquy at the end of Act 2.

G. K. Hunter rightly warns us (p. xx) to resist the temptation to try to re-create the Ur-*Hamlet* from the evidence of *Antonio's Revenge.* All the same, the ghost urging the widow, in her chamber, to co-operate with their son in revenge reminds us of that element in Belleforest which as I have mentioned occurs again in the bad quarto of *Hamlet*, when the queen promises her assistance to Hamlet at the close of the closet scene. Further, the presence of the ghost on stage quietly and contentedly watching the climactic carnage that avenges him might well be an indication of an element in the old play which Shakespeare pointedly and purposefully removed (see pp. 58–9).

Any dating of *Hamlet* must be tentative. It is later than mid 1599, the date of *Julius*

[1] References are to Gair's edition (see preceding note).
[2] See J. H. Smith, L. D. Pizer, E. K. Kaufman in *SQ* 9 (1958), 493–8.

Caesar, and it is earlier than July 1602, when it was registered for publication. The strongest internal evidence is the allusion in 2.2 to the war of the theatres. This suggests a possible date of mid 1601 for the completion of the play.

The play's shape

Shakespeare's *Hamlet* appears to be a rewriting or a reworking of a well-known earlier play of unknown authorship. But what do we mean when we speak of 'Shakespeare's *Hamlet*'? The textual problem of the play is of great complexity. It may seem an exasperating coincidence that a play which is as perplexing and problematic for the critic as *Hamlet* should also have unusually severe textual difficulties, but in fact the ambiguities in the meaning of the play are closely connected with its lack of a clear and settled text. Both the prince and his play come down to us in more shapes than one. If the prince were not so mercurial the text would be more stable. It is Shakespeare's difficulty in containing Hamlet within the bounds of a play, and the theatre's difficulty in comprehending the working of Shakespeare's mind, that have led to the multiple and scarcely reconcilable variations in the play's language and structure.

Everyone who wants to understand *Hamlet*, as reader, as actor, or director, needs to understand the nature of the play's textual problems, and needs to have his or her own view of them, however tentative. Ideally, every theatre-goer should be aware of the issues, so that he or she can appreciate whose *Hamlet* is being presented; there will be much evidence in this section of the Introduction and in the section on stage history of how radically the significance of the play changes in the varying theatrical versions of the play.

In searching for a solution to the play's textual problems, we should not imagine that we are likely ever to find ourselves with a single definitive text. The study of the early texts of *Hamlet* is the study of a play in motion. Earlier editors of *Hamlet* may have thought that 'a complete and final version' of the play was the object of their search,[1] but nowadays we are more ready to accept what centuries of theatrical history tell us – that what is written for the theatre often undergoes considerable modification as it moves from the writer's desk towards performance on the stage and also during performance. We must be prepared for the possibility that the variations in the text of *Hamlet* are not alternative versions of a single original text but representations of different stages in the play's development. Then our task becomes to choose the moment at which we would try to arrest the movement of the play and say 'This is the *Hamlet* we want'; or even, if we dare, 'This is the *Hamlet* that Shakespeare most wanted.' Do we have enough evidence to describe the history of Shakespeare's *Hamlet* in its early days and put together a version of it as it existed at a given point in time, a version that we can call not a definitive text but in our view the *best* text?

It is this question which the rest of this section of the Introduction tries to answer. While it will be necessary to consider material evidence about printing and publishing

[1] See, for example, Joseph Quincy Adams's introduction to his 1929 edition.

and playhouse procedures, the reader will see that the important decisions about the text of *Hamlet* are in the end literary decisions: not a matter of technical demonstration but of literary and linguistic judgement. Just as no one can argue about *Hamlet* who is not aware of the problems of its text, so no one can argue about the text who does not have a watchful eye for the value of words and for the possible meanings of the play.

We possess three basic printed texts of *Hamlet*, and no manuscript. The first published text is dated 1603, 'The Tragicall Historie of HAMLET Prince of Denmarke. By William Shake-speare'. The title page claims this to be the play 'as it hath beene diuerse times acted' by Shakespeare's company 'in the Cittie of London: as also in the two Vniuersities of Cambridge and Oxford, and else-where'. The publishers were Nicholas Ling and John Trundell, the printer Valentine Simmes.[1] This publication, known as the first quarto (Q1), is generally recognised as a 'bad' quarto: a corrupt, unauthorised version of an abridged version of Shakespeare's play. It runs to 2,154 lines.[2] Only two copies of this publication survive.

The second publication is dated 1604 in some copies and 1605 in others. It has the same title, but carries the legend, 'Newly imprinted and enlarged to almost as much againe as it was, according to the true and perfect Coppie'. This publication, the second quarto (Q2), is not well printed, but is generally held to be based on Shakespeare's own manuscript, his 'foul-papers'; that is, the completed draft, as opposed to a fair copy, which he submitted to his company. This is the fullest of the three versions, 3,674 lines. It was printed by James Roberts for Nicholas Ling.[3] Roberts had entered the play in the Stationers' Register, as if intending to publish, as early as 16 July 1602. ('The Revenge of Hamlett Prince Denmarke as yt was latelie Acted by the Lo: Chamberleyn his servants'.)[4] A. W. Pollard believed that this was a 'blocking' entry organised by the acting company to prevent unauthorised publication.[5] If this was the case, the move was clearly a failure. Roberts may well have been securing his own right, with the company's consent, for publication at some later date. But again, it did not prevent Ling's 1603 publication, and, whatever the source of Ling's text, publication gave him rights in the play, so he shared with Roberts the venture of the authorised text in 1604.

The third basic text is that published in the posthumous *Comedies, Histories, and Tragedies* of Shakespeare in 1623, the First Folio (F). A number of passages found in the second quarto, amounting to 222 lines, are omitted, but five new passages, totalling 83 lines, are added, giving a total for the play of 3,535 lines. There are a great many variant readings, some of them trifling and some of them very important. There is no general agreement about the source of this text except that it shows the influence of the theatre.

[1] W. W. Greg, *Bibliography of the English Printed Drama*, vol. I, 1939, no. 197a. There are numerous reprints. A facsimile was published by the Scolar Press in 1969.

[2] For the length of the various texts I use the figures given by Alfred Hart in *Shakespeare and the Homilies*, 1934, pp. 124–5, 148–9.

[3] Greg, *Bibliography*, no. 197b. There is a facsimile edited by W. W. Greg (1940), and another published by the Scolar Press (1969).

[4] Greg, *Bibliography*, I, 18.

[5] *Shakespeare Folios and Quartos*, 1909, p. 73.

These three texts are not wholly independent of each other. James Roberts's compositors,[1] while they were setting the second quarto, had in front of them not only a manuscript but a copy of the bad quarto of 1603 and they frequently copied its readings in the first act and possibly elsewhere.[2] The Folio compositors[3] may likewise have made use of a copy of the second quarto, though the extent of this use is extremely uncertain.[4] There is always a problem when our texts disagree, but the agreement of two texts on a particular reading can be the result of mere copying.

There can hardly be dispute about the view, orthodox since the publication of Dover Wilson's *The Manuscript of Shakespeare's 'Hamlet'* in 1934, that the manuscript used by the printer for the second quarto (Q2) was Shakespeare's own 'foul-papers'. The sheets must have been in a rough condition and must have presented considerable difficulties to the compositors in the way of bad handwriting, deletions and insertions. There are many quite extraordinary readings, as can be seen by looking at the collation in the present edition, for example 1.2.77, 2.2.391, 3.2.325, 4.7.22, 4.7.61. I shall argue also that by the time the MS. reached the printing house, several years after Shakespeare completed it, it must have become illegible in a number of places through wear and damage.

It is evident that on half-a-dozen occasions there is a muddle in the second quarto which was caused by Shakespeare having changed his mind as he wrote but not making his erasures or deletion marks so positive or clear that the compositors understood them.[5] Here are two small examples.

2.2.73	Q2:	Giues him threescore thousand crownes in anuall fee
	F:	Giues him three thousand Crownes in Annuall Fee
2.2.493	Q2:	a speech of some dosen lines, or sixteen lines
	F:	a speech of some dosen or sixteene lines

In the first example, Shakespeare may have started to write 'three score crowns', changed it to 'three thousand crowns' but failed to delete 'score' positively enough for the Q2 compositor to take notice of it. With 'score' retained, the line is metrically overloaded. Similarly, the casual phrase 'some dozen or sixteen lines' seems to have come after the false start of 'some dozen lines', but the first 'lines' has not been properly deleted.

It looks as though Shakespeare hesitated a good deal over the Player Queen's speeches in 3.2, perhaps not finding it easy to get exactly the right kind of prosy sententiousness without becoming positively tedious. Two of the couplets found in the second quarto are omitted in the Folio (3.2.152–3 and 199–200) and I think

[1] For the division of the texts between two compositors, see J. R. Brown, *Studies in Bibliography* 7 (1955), 17–40.

[2] *MSH*, pp. 158–62; Greg, *Shakespeare's First Folio*, 1955, pp. 315–16; A. Walker, *Textual Problems of the First Folio*, 1953, p. 121; F. T. Bowers, *Studies in Bibliography* 8 (1956), 39–66; Jenkins, pp. 46–52.

[3] C. Hinman, *Printing...of the First Folio*, 1963, II, 208–75; updated in Jenkins, pp. 53–4.

[4] Jenkins summarises the previous debate in his discussion, pp. 65–73.

[5] Several Shakespearean texts contain material which clearly was meant to be deleted, e.g. *Love's Labour's Lost* and *Romeo and Juliet*. See Greg, *Shakespeare's First Folio*, pp. 110, 220.

Shakespeare had marked them for excision. Concerning two more of the prosy couplets there is definite evidence of Shakespeare's hesitation.[1]

3.2.148 Q2: For women feare too much, euen as they loue,
And womens feare and loue hold quantitie,
Eyther none, in neither ought, or in extremitie,

F: For womens Feare and Loue, holds quantitie,
In neither ought, or in extremity:

Evidently the first line in Q2 was given up; it is the first line of an uncompleted rhyming couplet. And evidently 'Eyther none' was meant to be deleted also; in the Folio version both sense and metre are completed. A little further on, the variants between Q2 and F again suggest that Shakespeare's corrections were not understood by the Q2 compositor.

3.2.203–4 Q2: Both heere and hence pursue me lasting strife,
If once I be a widdow, euer I be a wife.

F: Both heere, and hence, pursue me lasting strife,
If once a Widdow, euer I be Wife.

It looks as though Shakespeare cancelled the first 'I be' in the second line and the Q2 compositor nevertheless set it. All these false starts in the Player Queen's speeches suggest that Shakespeare did not find it easy to write stilted verse.[2]

The presence of unobserved deletion marks in the copy for Q2 has been widely accepted, though their possible extent has never been fully investigated.[3] The most ingenious argument that these marks existed and were ignored by the Q2 compositors was provided by Dover Wilson himself (*MSH*, p. 30) in discussing the following speech by Claudius, 4.1.39–45, which I give as it appears in the quarto, adding square brackets to indicate that part of the speech which is omitted in the Folio.

And let them know both what we meane to doe
And whats vntimely doone,
[Whose whisper ore the worlds dyameter,
As leuell as the Cannon to his blanck,
Transports his poysned shot, may misse our Name
And hit the woundlesse ayre,] ô come away,
My soule is full of discord and dismay.

The passage as it stands in Q2 is clearly incomplete, since there is a grammatical as well as a metrical gap after 'whats vntimely doone' in the second line. The passage will make sense if we fill the gap with such words as those suggested by Theobald and Capell, 'so haply slander'. As one of his 'three alternative explanations' of the puzzle, Dover Wilson suggested

that the lines in question were marked for omission in the original manuscript not by transverse lines... but by some kind of brackets or rectangular enclosure, an arm of which appeared to delete the first half-line of the passage, so that the Q2 compositor set up all but that half-line.

[1] Compare Greg, *Shakespeare's First Folio*, p. 314.
[2] Other possible examples in Q2 of false starts are mentioned in the notes to 3.2.335, 4.5.74–6 and 4.7.8.
[3] See J. M. Nosworthy, *Shakespeare's Occasional Plays*, 1965, p. 139.

It may well be that the section of the speech omitted in F, including the lost half line, was one of the passages in the play which Shakespeare 'surrendered in the actual process of composition', to use J. M. Nosworthy's phrase.[1] If Shakespeare, having got as far as 'woundlesse ayre', begins to feel (as well he might) that he is meandering, and strikes out all after 'vntimely doone', he will need to pick up the metre and complete the imperfect line he is now left with. The line as given in the Folio provides a perfect seam:

And what's vntimely done. Oh come away,

A number of cuts made in the Folio version of Hamlet's speeches to Gertrude in Act 3, Scene 4 (53–88, 158–81) may all reflect Shakespeare's own tightening of his dialogue as he wrote. With the Player Queen, Shakespeare's problem had been to strike a balance between sententiousness and vapidity; in the closet scene, we have to be made to feel that Hamlet goes on too much, and here the danger is that he will merely seem prolix. Here is the passage 3.4.68–88 (modernised), first as it appears in the Folio, and secondly as it appears in the second quarto (with brackets round the additional material).

F: You cannot call it love, for at your age
The heyday in the blood is tame, it's humble,
And waits upon the judgement; and what judgement
Would step from this to this? What devil was't
That thus hath cozened you at hoodman-blind?
O shame, where is thy blush? Rebellious hell,
If thou canst mutine in a matron's bones,
To flaming youth let virtue be as wax
And melt in her own fire. Proclaim no shame
When the compulsive ardour gives the charge,
Since frost itself as actively doth burn,
And reason panders will.

Q2: You cannot call it love, for at your age
The heyday in the blood is tame, it's humble,
And waits upon the judgement; and what judgement
Would step from this to this? [Sense sure you have,
Else could you not have motion, but sure that sense
Is apoplexed, for madness would not err,
Nor sense to ecstasy was ne'er so thralled,
But it reserved some quantity of choice
To serve in such a difference.] What devil was't
That thus hath cozened you at hoodman-blind?
[Eyes without feeling, feeling without sight,
Ears without hands or eyes, smelling sans all,
Or but a sickly part of one true sense
Could not so mope.] O shame, where is thy blush?
Rebellious hell,
If thou canst mutine in a matron's bones,

[1] Nosworthy, *Shakespeare's Occasional Plays*, p. 140.

To flaming youth let virtue be as wax
And melt in her own fire. Proclaim no shame
When the compulsive ardour gives the charge,
Since frost itself as actively doth burn,
And reason panders will.[1]

If we put the two versions together in this order, our familiarity with the fuller version is less likely to obstruct our perceiving that the speech is much more effective when the cuts have been made. Each of the two passages cut from the Folio has an uncertainty of control about it which suggests a tentative exploration from which Shakespeare pulled back. It will be noticed that if Shakespeare, as he was composing the speech, stopped at 'Could not so mope' and decided to abandon the three-and-a-half lines he had just written, he must obviously continue with a new full line, which is what we have in the Folio:

O shame, where is thy blush? Rebellious hell,

But the second quarto, by printing the excised half line *and* the new full line, is left with half a line too much.

Could not so mope, O shame, where is thy blush?
Rebellious hell,

There are very many short lines in *Hamlet*, and they are not in themselves evidence that the text has been altered. But when these short lines appear in the quarto only, in association with passages omitted from the Folio, they suggest revision. Here is the second quarto's version (modernised) of 1.4.69–79, with brackets round that part of it omitted from the Folio.

HORATIO What if it tempt you toward the flood, my lord,
Or to the dreadful summit of the cliff
That beetles o'er his base into the sea,
And there assume some other horrible form
Which might deprive your sovereignty of reason,
And draw you into madness? Think of it.
[The very place puts toys of desperation
Without more motive, into every brain
That looks so many fathoms to the sea
And hears it roar beneath.]
HAMLET It waves me still. Go on, I'll follow thee.

Here again we can imagine Shakespeare stopping himself after running on too far. The impressiveness of this speech as it appears in the Folio is the emphasis laid on Horatio's fear that the Ghost may draw Hamlet into madness. This ominous introduction of the theme of the tainted mind is much weakened by the continuation of the speech as it appears above, in which Horatio says that the place, not the Ghost, puts the idea of suicide into people's minds. Hamlet doesn't need a cliff to put thoughts of suicide into his head. If Shakespeare marked the passage within square brackets

[1] For 'panders' Q2 reads 'pardons'.

for deletion, he would need to continue with a full line, which is what we have in Hamlet's reply. But once again, by printing both the excised half line and the new full line, the second quarto leaves us with the tell-tale half line 'And hears it roar beneath'. This stitching to retain the verse pattern is not always so neat; in the other much-altered speech in 3.4, lines 158–81, one of the cuts leaves the very short line 'Refrain tonight' (166); but in the following cut, the half line which is left hanging, 'To the next abstinence' (168), is completed by 'Once more good night' (171).

Is it possible that other passages which appear only in the second quarto had been cancelled by Shakespeare himself and were never meant to form part of his play? In *Shakespeare's Occasional Plays*, J. M. Nosworthy argued that two major Folio cuts, usually taken to be unintelligent theatre-cuts, were in fact 'composition cuts'. They are both reflective passages preceding an entry of the Ghost, and neither of them makes full sense as it stands. The first passage, 1.1.107–25, is largely Horatio's discussion of the portents before the death of Caesar. It is not a strong or necessary speech, and few would find the play worse for its absence. The second passage (1.4.17–38) is not so easily written off, being the speech in which Hamlet after being indignant that Danish drinking habits besmirch the whole nation reflects on 'the vicious mole of nature' which ruins the reputation of otherwise worthy men. The speech ends with the notorious 'dram of eale' crux. Nosworthy writes (p. 141), 'The simplest explanation of this crux is that the sentence is unfinished, the implication being that Shakespeare lapsed into incoherence and gave up the struggle.' Nosworthy found the whole 'lengthy meditation' sententious. Dover Wilson's defence of the speech, that it was needed 'to lull the minds of his audience to rest and so startle them the more with his apparition' (*MSH*, p. 25), is not much of a compliment. Though it is often maintained that the speech has an important choric value, as regards Hamlet himself, and affords a glimpse of Shakespeare's view of tragedy, both these contentions are disputable, and I doubt whether removing the speech decreases the effectiveness of the scene or diminishes our understanding of the play. It is quite possible that these two cuts are theatre-cuts, but there is in my opinion much to be said for the view that Shakespeare was dissatisfied with them as he wrote.

Jonson said of Shakespeare, 'He flowed with that facility, that sometime it was necessary he should be stopped. *Sufflaminandus erat*.'[1] The evidence of the second quarto of *Hamlet* shows both Shakespeare's facility and his awareness of the need to curb it. It is ironic that compositors may have unwittingly preserved a good deal of material which Shakespeare decided to dispense with. If that is in fact the case, they will have provided us with immensely valuable information about Shakespeare's methods of composition, but presented an editor with the formidable problem of whether he should put back into a play what Shakespeare had decided to leave out.

Although there is at least one more passage found in the second quarto only which may have been a 'composition cut' (4.7.99–101), I want now to consider two major passages which do not appear in the Folio text but which have none of those deficiencies, structural, thematic or linguistic, which may suggest Shakespeare's

[1] *Discoveries*; in *Ben Jonson*, ed. Herford and Simpson, VIII, 1947, 583–4.

discontent with them as he wrote. These are Hamlet's speech to Gertrude at the end of the closet scene, 3.4.203–11, about Rosencrantz and Guildenstern (hoisting the engineer with his own petar), and the long fourth soliloquy (4.4), 'How all occasions do inform against me', after Hamlet has seen Fortinbras's army. These are generally held to be playhouse cuts, but there are reasons for thinking that Shakespeare himself may have removed both speeches.

Here is the first passage, in modernised form, first as in the Folio and then in the fuller quarto version.

F: HAMLET I must to England, you know that?
GERTRUDE Alack,
I had forgot. 'Tis so concluded on.
HAMLET This man shall set me packing.

Q2: HAMLET I must to England, you know that?
GERTRUDE Alack,
I had forgot. 'Tis so concluded on.
HAMLET There's letters sealed, and my two schoolfellows,
Whom I will trust as I will adders fanged,
They bear the mandate. They must sweep my way
And marshall me to knavery. Let it work,
For 'tis the sport to have the engineer
Hoist with his own petar, an't shall go hard
But I will delve one yard below their mines
And blow them at the moon. Oh 'tis most sweet
When in one line two crafts directly meet.
This man shall set me packing.

Hamlet's speech in the fuller quarto version creates many problems. In the first place, though the audience has just seen Claudius instructing Rosencrantz and Guildenstern to accompany Hamlet to England, Hamlet has been given no means of learning that they are to go with him. And the audience has still to be told (it comes at 4.3.54) that Claudius is using the voyage to England to liquidate Hamlet. There are problems graver than these, however. One is the surprise of this new conviction in Hamlet that Rosencrantz and Guildenstern are accomplices in a plot to destroy him. The second is the definiteness of Hamlet's plans. In spite of the recent re-appearance of the Ghost urging him to his main task of revenge, he here renounces the immediate prosecution of his mission, accepts the journey to England, and with cool pleasure undertakes to countermine Claudius's plots in his own good time, and to destroy Rosencrantz and Guildenstern.

The explicitness of this speech is surely remarkable. What Hamlet here outlines is what actually happens. Can Shakespeare have wanted Hamlet at this point to be so buoyantly in charge of his own destiny? It is a major factor in Hamlet's actions on board ship, as he narrates them to Horatio in 5.2, that the idea of entering the cabin of Rosencrantz and Guildenstern was a sudden inspiration, a wild rashness, in which he saw the hand of Providence. It was by means of that unplanned move that Hamlet learned of Claudius's treachery, and it was as a consequence of that knowledge that Hamlet sent Rosencrantz and Guildenstern to their deaths. George MacDonald, in his 1885 edition of the play (p. 181), suggested that it was Shakespeare's original plan that Hamlet should board the vessel looking for an opportunity to outwit his companions, but that he altered the plan 'and represents his escape as more plainly providential'. The change in Hamlet's relationship with Rosencrantz and Guildenstern, now sent to their deaths on a sudden impulse, is surely reflected in a line which is found in the Folio but not in the second quarto, and which may therefore be an addition or an insertion into the original script. In reply to Horatio's pensive words, 'So Guildenstern and Rosencrantz go to't', Hamlet (in the second quarto) impatiently replies 'They are not near my conscience', as indeed he might have some justification in saying if they were accomplices of Claudius whom Hamlet had long decided must be got out of the way. But if they are no more than repulsive sneaks, royal toadies, who are unwitting agents in the king's plot, their grim punishment is a more sensitive affair. 'Why man, they did make love to this employment', says Hamlet in the Folio, 'They are not near my conscience.' In view of other important lines in Hamlet's communication to Horatio which are also found only in the Folio (and which I shall shortly discuss), it seems very likely that Shakespeare revised this passage. If so the new line, 'Why man, they did make love to this employment', etches in Hamlet's awareness of the unspoken accusation in Horatio's remark, and his wish to exculpate himself in the new moral context for the deaths of Rosencrantz and Guildenstern.

To return to the 'engineer' speech, we may feel that the value of the curt ending given to the closet scene in the Folio, no more than a sardonic recognition of the king's plan to get him out of Denmark and a consciousness that he, Hamlet, has now given Claudius the pretext which he wanted ('This man shall set me packing'), lies not only in avoiding a commitment to a delayed revenge but also in its complete silence about any plans whatsoever. The play is not the less eloquent for this silence (see below p. 55). A great many possibilities are going through our minds about what may be going through Hamlet's. The Hamlet whose experiences and thoughts have been with us for three acts is lessened and limited by the plan and the threat which he issues in the quarto version of his speech. It it's bluster, of course, or the old 'procrastination', it would have a place in a credible total view of Hamlet, but a view I could not share. Shakespeare may have thought it best not to provide Hamlet with arguments for his acceptance of being sent off to England.

This question of his willingness to leave is at the forefront in the fourth soliloquy in 4.4, which is not given in the Folio at all. The core of the speech is self-reproach for not having done a deed which ought to have been done, and which could easily have been done. Hamlet finds his inactivity inexplicable.

Q2: Now whether it be
Bestial oblivion, or some craven scruple
Of thinking too precisely on th'event –
A thought which quartered hath but one part wisdom
And ever three parts coward – I do not know
Why yet I live to say this thing's to do,

Sith I have cause, and will, and strength, and means
To do't. (4.4.39–46)

This looks very much like an alternative to the 'engineer' speech we have been discussing. As Hamlet faces being sent to England, we are given first a demonstration of defiance and determination; then we are to see him in a state of nerveless drifting, bafflement, indecision and inactivity. Again, a credible Hamlet *can* be made out, if we postulate a violent swing of mood, from blustering threats to guilt and self-questioning. But it is also possible to see the fourth soliloquy as a second attempt, a contradictory attempt, and a weaker attempt to provide a psychological bridge for this very difficult stage of the plot, Hamlet's departure for England.

Although entire theories of the prince have been built on this speech, it is not one of the great soliloquies; much less intricate, subtle, mobile and suggestive than the two great central soliloquies, 'O what a rogue and peasant slave' and 'To be or not to be'. But, more important, it is a speech which does not know all that has gone before it. Hamlet's thoughts and emotions have become far too complicated and deep for this simple self-accusation to make any sense –

Sith I have cause, and will, and strength, and means
To do't.

No, it is insufficient and inappropriate for Act 4 of *Hamlet*. We may agree with Ernst Honigmann[1] that when Shakespeare was writing a play he would not necessarily have begun with Act 1 and gone on to the end, but might have tried out speeches or scenes which would eventually find their place in the later parts of the play. Perhaps the fourth soliloquy was such a speech. But by the time we have reached the point at which it has been placed, Hamlet has become so immense in his mystery, so unfathomable, that the speech is scarcely adequate for the speaker.[2]

It seems to me the likeliest thing in the world that in creating a hero who is a tangle of conflicting tendencies Shakespeare would have written a lot of tentative material – passages relating to aspects of *Hamlet* and his mission which needed saying but whose final placing was uncertain – and that in the end some of this material would seem redundant or wrong, and not to belong anywhere. If 'How all occasions do inform against me' comes into this category, its removal at rather a late stage in the preparation of the play was a much bigger wrench than the removal of the 'engineer' speech, because we are left with an awkward fragment of a scene, just about enough to remind us of the existence of Fortinbras.

By omitting the engineer speech and the fourth soliloquy, the Folio version leaves Hamlet silent about being sent to England, except for his taunt about Claudius's purposes – 'I see a cherub that sees them' (4.3.45). This silence throws a great deal of weight on to the explanations of his thoughts and actions which Hamlet gives to Horatio on his unlooked-for return, in 5.2, particularly about his loss of confidence in his 'deep plots' and his submission to the guidance of heaven. The heart of his

[1] *The Stability of Shakespeare's Text*, 1965, ch. 4.

[2] Compare W. Empson, '*Hamlet* when new', *Sewanee Review* 61 (1953), 15–42 and 185–205; also E. Prosser, *Hamlet and Revenge*, 1967, pp. 207–8.

explanation is a short passage which is for me the pivot of the entire play (as I explain more fully on pp. 56–8).

And is't not to be damned
To let this canker of our nature come
In further evil? (5.2.68–70)

These lines are found only in the Folio, and I find it hard to resist the conclusion that Shakespeare wrote them in at the time he cut out the two earlier speeches in 3.4 and 4.4. It is the destination to which a 'revised' Hamlet has come, and is all the evidence we need of the 'kind of fighting' in his heart between the re-appearance of the Ghost in Gertrude's room and the return to Denmark.

This vital area of the play appears in the two texts as follows (modernised and corrected):

Q2: HORATIO So Guildenstern and Rosencrantz go to't.
HAMLET They are not near my conscience. Their defeat
Does by their own insinuation grow.
'Tis dangerous when the baser nature comes
Between the pass and fell incensèd points
Of mighty opposites.
HORATIO Why, what a king is this!
HAMLET Does it not, think thee, stand me now upon –
He that hath killed my king, and whored my mother,
Popped in between th'election and my hopes,
Thrown out his angle for my proper life,
And with such cosenage – is't not perfect conscience?

Enter a COURTIER

F: HORATIO So Guildenstern and Rosencrantz go to't.
HAMLET Why man, they did make love to this employment.
They are not near my conscience. Their defeat
Doth by their own insinuation grow.
'Tis dangerous when the baser nature comes
Between the pass and fell incensèd points
Of mighty opposites.
HORATIO Why, what a king is this!
HAMLET Does it not, think'st thee, stand me now upon –
He that hath killed my king, and whored my mother,
Popped in between th'election and my hopes,
Thrown out his angle for my proper life,
And with such cosenage – is't not perfect conscience
To quit him with this arm? And is't not to be damned
To let this canker of our nature come
In further evil?
HORATIO It must be shortly known to him from England
What is the issue of the business there.
HAMLET It will be short. The interim's mine,
And a man's life no more then to say 'one'.

But I am very sorry, good Horatio,
That to Laertes I forgot myself,
For by the image of my cause, I see
The portraiture of his. I'll court his favours.
But sure the bravery of his grief did put me
Into a towering passion.

HORATIO Peace, who comes here?

Enter young OSRIC

In the second quarto version there is obviously something missing at the end, after 'conscience'. It could be that Shakespeare has struck out some words similar to the Folio's 'To quit him with this arm' and inserted the all-important longer passage which appears only in the Folio, either in the margin where they were overlooked by the Q2 compositor, or on a separate sheet or slip which, in the four years or more elapsing between the completion of the manuscript and its use in Roberts's printing house, had somehow gone astray.

This matter of a separate slip or interleaved sheet is of course the purest speculation, but it might help to explain the existence in the Folio of another passage not found in the second quarto, the 'war of the theatres' passage, 2.2.313–33 (see above, pp. 4–5). If when he was completing his play in 1601 Shakespeare had indeed added this new material to an already written Act 2, Scene 2, and written it on an additional separate sheet, it may well have become separated or lost by 1604.

I have been suggesting that Shakespeare's 'foul-papers', which were used by Roberts in setting up the 1604/5 quarto, contained a certain amount of material which Shakespeare had decided he didn't want. Whatever cancellation marks he used were not observed or not understood by Roberts's compositors. The manuscript may also have contained insertions which again were either not seen or not understood by the compositors. As a result, the second quarto supplies us with some of Shakespeare's rejected first thoughts and fails to provide us with some of Shakespeare's second thoughts.

In addition, I have suggested that some major changes affecting the part of Hamlet in the last half of the play, reflected in the omission of two major speeches in the Folio, were possibly the result of a revision by Shakespeare. When might such a revision have taken place? Perhaps at the time when it became necessary to make a fair copy of the 'foul-papers'. We can only guess what happened when Shakespeare had a new play ready for his own company. Even Shakespeare, one assumes, had to have his play accepted. It must have been read and discussed. Perhaps it was given to Shakespeare to read out an untidy and unpunctuated manuscript. For all we know, alterations may have been talked about at this stage, and the revision may have taken place then. What looks certain is that at an early stage there would be the need to prepare a fair copy. There was an important discussion of this question of fair copies by Fredson Bowers in *On Editing Shakespeare* in 1955. Theatres normally required fair copies from their playwrights. Bowers suggested that Shakespeare's privileged position may have freed him from the labour of making his own transcript, but, since a fair copy would be essential for the preparation of the actors' parts and the promptbook, we have to think it possible that the playhouse scrivener would 'make an intermediate transcript of them [the foul-papers] for consideration, revision, submission to the censor, copying of the parts, or sometimes for marking and cutting in preparation for the final prompt-book' (pp. 20–1). Again, 'A temporary manuscript to serve as a basis for the copying of the parts and for guiding rehearsal would be a practical necessity before the book-keeper was ready to engage himself to the preparation of the final prompt-book' (p. 113).

It is evident that the hypothesis of an intermediate scribal transcript of foul-papers will serve to explain the source of the text of a number of Shakespeare's plays, which exhibit the tell-tale features of neither foul-papers nor promptbooks.[1] It seems very probable that the Folio text of *Hamlet* began its life as such a transcript, a fair copy of Shakespeare's foul-papers, containing his latest revisions, before the play went into production. This was the view argued by J. M. Nosworthy in *Shakespeare's Occasional Plays*.[2] It runs counter to the view advanced with such brio by John Dover Wilson in *The Manuscript of Shakespeare's 'Hamlet'* that the Folio text was based ultimately on the theatre's promptbook. The promptbook theory never received more than cautious acceptance. Nosworthy points out that Greg was always uneasy about it. Only his respect for Dover Wilson seems to have kept him loyal to the theory.[3] A strong argument against the Folio text being based on the promptbook is its length. At 3,535 lines it is only 140 lines or so shorter than the second quarto, and as Greg said it cannot 'suggest any serious attempt to shorten the play' (*Shakespeare's First Folio*, p. 317). The average length of plays at the time was under 2,500 lines.[4] Plays varied in length, of course, and it is clear that both Shakespeare and Jonson were given to writing very long plays. Even so, there is no chance of a play of over 3,500 lines being acted in full. If it is an acting version we are looking for, it will be something nearer the length of *Macbeth*, or the first quarto of *Hamlet*.

In the next place, a text so deficient in its stage directions could never have served in the theatre. The Folio follows the second quarto in omitting very many exits, and some entrances too, and it actually leaves out some important exits which are present in the quarto. It omits some of the quarto's directions for music, for properties, for off-stage noises and on-stage actions. (The parallel lists of stage directions in Dover Wilson's *Manuscript of Shakespeare's 'Hamlet'* make a comparison of the two texts a simple matter.) It is of course true that the Folio adds to and changes the stage directions as found in the second quarto, but, essentially, the Folio's attention to staging is fitful and patchy, and its concerns for properties almost nil. A working promptbook would have regularised and filled out the mechanics of staging in a consistent manner, and this would certainly be reflected in any printed version based on it.[5]

1 E.g. *As You Like It*. See R. Knowles's introduction to the New Variorum edition, 1977, esp. pp. 331–4.
2 In his 1982 edition, Jenkins supports the idea of a 'pre-prompt' transcription; see pp. 59, 64.
3 'On the whole it seems to be a rather queer prompt-book, if prompt-book it is, that lies behind F.' (*Shakespeare's First Folio*, p. 323; see also p. 316.)
4 Hart, *Shakespeare and the Homilies*, pp. 86–9.
5 The failure in F to carry out the act and scene division beyond the beginning of Act 2 is a further argument against prompt-copy. See Greg, *The Editorial Problem in Shakespeare*, 3rd edn, 1954, pp. 35–6.

If the Folio text is not based ultimately on the promptbook of the play, it is also abundantly clear that its ultimate source is not a strict fair copy of Shakespeare's manuscript. The departures from the text of the second quarto, quite apart from the cuts already discussed, and making every allowance for the inaccuracy of the Q2 compositors, are too extensive for the phrase 'fair copy' to be allowable. Bowers's phrase 'intermediate transcript' is very helpful. A scrutiny of the differences between the stage directions in Q2 and F points us towards the special quality of the transcript that lies behind the Folio text, neither a straightforward copy of Shakespeare's manuscript nor yet a full production script developed from it.[1]

It will be quickly noticed that the variants in the stage directions and the staging which they imply are not spread evenly through the play. In the first act, though there are two alterations which I shall comment on, F tends to omit Q2's directions. Indications for 'Flourish' are generally omitted; the sound of the cannon at 1.4.6 is not mentioned; 'It spreads his arms' and 'The cock crows' are eliminated. Half way through the second act a change of attitude towards stage-business is discernible. Q2's directions are observed, altered and added to. Hamlet enters 'reading on a book' (2.2.165). At 2.2.338, Q2's 'Flourish' is recorded and expanded: 'Flourish for the Players'. By the middle of Act 3, F's attention to music is such that all Q2's directions are noticed (some of them altered), and new directions are being inserted.

By far the greater number of revisions to the stage directions occur in the last three acts. Of the 52 which are of special significance, only 19 occur up to the crucial moment of the king's exit from the play-scene (3.2), which is just slightly beyond the actual half-way point of the play. As concern with matters of staging develops in the Folio text, there is an increasing boldness in intervening and interfering with the text itself in connection with the changes. Nothing previous to 4.5.0 shows the temerity of cutting out the Gentleman who tells Gertrude about Ophelia's madness, and giving his lines (so inappropriately) to Horatio and Horatio's to Gertrude. Innovations of this kind begin a little earlier, at 4.3.0, where, by depriving Claudius of the 'two or three' who enter with him, a prepared public utterance is turned into an unsuitable worried self-communion.

It looks as though a scribe's conception of his task changed during the course of making a transcript. At the outset, he is providing a plain text on which the promptbook may be based. Flourishes are left out because the musical effects are to be decided later. But as the work of transcribing these untidy papers continues – and for all we know discussion about the staging of the play grows more detailed – the transcript begins to include proposals or decisions about the details of the staging and the size of the cast. We can suppose that the scribe is the book-keeper himself, the man responsible for preparing the promptbook and supervising the production.[2] His concern with practicalities of the theatre (including paying and costuming men and boys for walk-on parts) will become clearer if we now look at the character of the changes made in the Folio's stage directions.

[1] This was the conclusion reached by T. M. Parrott and Hardin Craig in their 'critical edition' of the second quarto, 1938, p. 50: 'not the prompt-book, but, probably, the manuscript on which the final prompt-book...was based'.

[2] For the book-keeper's duties, see Greg, *Shakespeare's First Folio*, p. 100.

In the first place, on a number of occasions the scribe was visualising what has to happen on stage more clearly than Shakespeare seems to have done. At 1.5.113, for example, Horatio and Marcellus, in pursuit of Hamlet, will need to cry 'My lord, my lord!' before and not after their entry on stage. At 2.2.489–97, Polonius cannot be left awkwardly on stage while Hamlet discusses the 'dozen or sixteen lines' with the First Player. In the graveyard scene (5.1), Hamlet and Horatio need to enter earlier, 'a farre off', in order to listen to the Clown before they comment on what he is doing.

Secondly, the scribe was intolerant of Shakespeare's vagueness about the names and functions of characters and how many there were in group entries. (It is interesting that the permissive entry of the 'two or three' kind must have had a definiteness for him.) So 'Enter the Players' becomes 'Enter foure or fiue Players' (2.2.384). 'Enter Horatio and others' becomes 'Enter Horatio with an Attendant' (4.6). 'Enter old Polonius, with his man or two' becomes 'Enter Polonius, with Reynaldo' (2.1). The scribe's need to identify and to number is very interestingly shown in the directions for the dumb-show in 3.2, with provision for 'Mutes' and 'a Fellow'. At 5.2.340, 'the Embassadors' becomes 'English Ambassador'.

The scribe's constant concern to reduce the number of minor characters throws into relief the strange lavishness, for a practical man of the theatre, with which Shakespeare produced additional characters, especially late in the play, who have little or nothing to say or do. Sometimes the reduction is quite deft, as at 4.5.111 where Laertes' militant followers, instead of entering as 'others', are made to remain shouting outside the doors. But sometimes the attempt to stanch the unending stream of supernumeraries is more damaging to the texture of the play. The Lord who invites Hamlet to the fencing match at 5.2.170 is cut out along with twelve lines of text. I have already mentioned the disfigurement caused by the removal of the 'two or three' who enter with Claudius at 4.3.0, and the removal of the Gentleman at 4.5.0. At 3.2.312 it would appear from the quarto that Shakespeare's idea was that the players should come on as a consort to play music. 'Enter the Players with Recorders' is reduced to 'Enter one with a Recorder', and the text has to be changed.

The three major entries of the full court at 1.2.0, 3.2.81 and 5.2.196 show considerable changes, with the Folio versions showing a special concern for the management of these important stage occasions, filling out the bare entries of the quarto with elaborate detail. The many alterations for the grand entry to witness the fencing contest in the final scene give an impression of being tentative and provisional (see Commentary).

If it is accepted that the changes in the stage directions in the Folio text are *notes towards a production* made while transcribing Shakespeare's foul-papers, and that the book-keeper included signals to the actors, and was ready to alter the text to accommodate his more frugal standards of numbers in the cast, then some other variants which have been taken to be 'actors' interpolations' or accretions to the text sanctioned by stage custom may also be seen as the work of the scribe.[1] At 5.1.152

[1] See *MSH*, p. 79, and Jenkins in *Studies in Bibliography* 13 (1960), 31–47.

the Gravedigger produces another skull, which he says was Yorick's. 'This?' asks Hamlet. 'E'en that', replies the Gravedigger. In Q2 Hamlet continues 'Alas poore *Yoricke*'. But in F he says 'Let me see. Alas poore *Yorick*'. Hamlet's 'Let me see' provides for the transferring of the skull from one actor to the other.

It is not in the least surprising that an experienced playhouse scrivener, accustomed to Shakespeare's script, should be able to give a more intelligent rendering of the foul-papers than the compositors in James Roberts's printing house, especially in following Shakespeare's marks for deletion and insertion. He has on many occasions preserved the true reading of the text when the second quarto has blundered.[1] Yet he would alter Shakespeare's text, as we have seen, and he too could blunder. There is at 5.1.252–6 a very bad misascription of a speech by Gertrude to Claudius. It is quintessentially a Gertrude speech, anxious, protective, sentimental, flowery, and there can be no reason except carelessness for giving it to Claudius. How do we know that this misascription in the Folio was the error of a scribe at an early date in the play's history and not the error of the Folio compositors? Because the 'bad' first quarto of 1603 also contains the erroneous ascription.

The first quarto gives us some of the strongest and clearest evidence of the nature of the manuscript which is the source of the Folio text, and helps to distinguish its various archaeological layers. Corrupt and adulterated though its text is, it demonstrates that an acting-text of *Hamlet*, based on the playhouse transcription of Shakespeare's foul-papers which we have been discussing, had become established in performance by 1603. When the Folio and the first quarto agree on readings which differ from the second quarto and are manifestly or arguably inferior to the second quarto, we may consider we have evidence of changes which the book-keeper made when copying out Shakespeare's manuscript, which changes were then transmitted to the promptbook and into performance, and so were established in the theatre-text corruptly 'reported' in the first quarto.

The invaluable tables of common and divergent readings given by Dover Wilson in *The Manuscript of Shakespeare's 'Hamlet'* show us on pp. 336–40 a number of occasions when the first quarto confirms an early weakening of Shakespeare's text. The second quarto's 'But who, a woe, had seene' (i.e. 'But who – ah woe! – had seen') was weakened to 'But who, O who, had seen' found in both the first quarto and the Folio (2.2.460). 'The Lady doth protest too much' was weakened to 'The Lady protests to[o] much.' An interesting change is at 4.7.177 where in the description of the death of Ophelia the first quarto confirms that Shakespeare's 'snatches of old laudes' (Q2) had been altered to 'snatches of old tunes' (F). Presumably the book-keeper thought 'lauds' altogether too outlandish or unfamiliar.

Once the fair copy of Shakespeare's manuscript had been made, it would be necessary to prepare from it a shorter version for acting, the promptbook, from which in turn the actors' parts would be taken. Unfortunately we have no idea what the form of this acting version was, nor whether Shakespeare was involved in creating it. If he

[1] E.g. the fretful, not the fearful porpentine (1.5.20), and scullion, not stallion (2.2.540).

knew of some of the changes already made involving some of the minor characters in the later part of the play (which have just been discussed) he cannot have approved of them. Things already seem to be going forward without his co-operation; and it seems to me very unlikely that he was closely engaged in what to some extent must have been a mutilation of his work. *Macbeth*, of which we have only a single text of about 2,500 lines, is alone among the Histories and Tragedies in giving us what looks like an acting-text. What Shakespearean riches have been lost in achieving that brevity is beyond conjecture. With *Hamlet* it is the other way round. We have two texts, one authorial of great amplitude, and one which seems to contain authorial deletions and changes and also bears signs of the play being got ready for the stage. But we have no evidence of the shape of the play as it was eventually acted on Shakespeare's stage. Why in the first place Shakespeare should on this occasion as on many others have written a play manifestly too long for theatrical presentation is a far-reaching and unsettling question.

The one link we have with *Hamlet* as acted at the Globe Theatre is the first quarto of 1603, deriving as it must from a stage version based upon the transcript which we have postulated as lying behind the Folio text. The verbal links between the transcript and the first quarto have been noted, and there is further evidence of dependence in the fact that the passages deleted by the Folio (which appear in the second quarto) are all missing from the first quarto.[1] In trying to fill the great gap in our knowledge of the history of *Hamlet*, the shape of the play as given on Shakespeare's stage, we need to look closely at the first quarto.

The first quarto is a much-abbreviated as well as a much-debased version of Shakespeare's play as we know it from the second quarto and the Folio. The standard example of its quality is the opening of the 'To be or not to be' soliloquy (here modernised):

> To be or not to be, ay there's the point;
> To die, to sleep, is that all? Ay, all.
> No, to sleep, to dream; ay marry, there it goes,
> For in that dream of death, when we awake
> And borne before an everlasting judge,
> From whence no passenger ever returned,
> The undiscovered country, at whose sight
> The happy smile, and the accursed damned...

The quality varies greatly, however, and in some parts of the play, especially near the beginning, there is an approximation to the standard text. There is little dispute that the first quarto is a 'reported' text, an attempt to put together the text of a play from memory without recourse or access to an authoritative manuscript. It is generally thought, in view of the superiority of the text whenever he is on stage, that the actor playing Marcellus, perhaps doubling as Lucianus in the play-within-the-play, was responsible for the piracy.[2]

[1] One or two phrases in Q1 seem to echo passages cut from F. It is not at all unlikely that in preparing the promptbook for the Globe some extra material from the foul-papers was added for clarification. See Chambers, *William Shakespeare*, 1930, I, 416, and Duthie, p. 273.

[2] This view was advanced by H. D. Gray in 1915 and accepted by Duthie.

While in the main the first quarto follows, to the best of its ability, an abbreviated version of the standard play, there are four substantial and interesting departures. The first is that Polonius has become Corambis. Secondly, the 'To be or not to be' soliloquy and the subsequent nunnery scene are placed earlier than in the standard text. Third, at the end of the closet scene Hamlet asks Gertrude to assist him in revenge, and she vows that

> I will conceal, consent, and do my best,
> What stratagem soe'er thou shalt devise.

The fourth change is a drastic reworking of Hamlet's return from the voyage to England. Horatio is given a new scene with the queen, in which he tells *her* the news that in the standard text Hamlet tells *him* of the king's plot on his life and the exchange of the commission which sends Rosencrantz and Guildenstern to their doom. There is no mention of the fight with the pirates.

Is it possible that these alterations represent a recognised version of Shakespeare's play as it was acted in London before 1603 when the first quarto was published? Some evidence that the shape of the first quarto was the conventional and accepted shape is provided by a curious German manuscript of 1710, now lost, which was printed in 1781: *Der bestrafte Brudermord oder Prinz Hamlet aus Dannemark* (sometimes known as *Fratricide Punished*).[1] This play may well be the descendant of a *Hamlet* taken by a travelling English company to Germany in the early seventeenth century. Details of such companies are given by E. K. Chambers in *The Elizabethan Stage* (II, 272–92), and *Hamlet* is one of the plays acted. But, writes Bullough, 'generations of actors played havoc with the original text and doubtless changed incidents as well as dialogue' (*Narrative and Dramatic Sources*, VII, 21). However, it is possible to discern that the original text, while not dependent on the first quarto of *Hamlet*, shared many of its features. In particular, Polonius is Corambus, and the nunnery scene occupies the same early position as in the first quarto. But the first quarto scene between Horatio and the queen telling of Hamlet's escape is not repeated. Instead Hamlet gives the information to Horatio himself, as in the second quarto (though the circumstances of the escape have become altered out of recognition). So it seems possible that the change of name from Polonius to Corambis or Corambus, and the earlier placing of the nunnery scene, were established features of *Hamlet* as it was being acted before 1603; but that the other features of the first quarto – the complicity of the queen with Hamlet and the reworking of the news of Hamlet's escape – are peculiar to that text. It is a plausible suggestion that the new role for the queen is not new at all, but is a recollection of the old play of *Hamlet*.[2]

The transposition of the nunnery scene in the first quarto and in *Bestrafte Brudermord* invites further discussion for the light it may be able to shed on the matter of the fluidity of the text of *Hamlet*, with which we began this section of the Introduction.

In the first quarto, when Corambis has heard Ophelia's story of Hamlet bursting

[1] See Duthie, pp. 238–70. There is a translation in Bullough, VII, 128–58.
[2] Duthie, pp. 196–206.

into her room and has decided that this is love-madness, he says 'Let's to the King', and in the following scene Ophelia enters with Corambis, though she has nothing to say while Hamlet's letter to her is read out and the 'Ophelia trap' is planned. Then Hamlet enters, with the king saying 'See where he comes, poring upon a book.' Corambis asks the queen to leave, gives Ophelia a book, and we launch into the 'To be or not to be' soliloquy and the nunnery scene. At the end of this, Hamlet goes out, Ophelia voices her distress, and the king and Corambis make their comments, all – very roughly – as in the standard text. But then Hamlet must enter again, and Corambis greets him to initiate the fishmonger scene. This runs on as usual to the 'rogue and peasant slave' soliloquy with Hamlet's resolve to test the king in a play. The 'mousetrap' play follows almost at once, after the interposition of the equivalent of only the first 35 lines of 3.1.

It has often been noted[1] that in the standard text of *Hamlet*, Polonius like Corambis tells Ophelia to accompany him to the king.

> Come, go with me, I will go see the king. (2.1.99)

> Come, go we to the king.
> This must be known. (2.1.115–16)

But when he enters in 2.2 he is alone. Did Shakespeare once toy with – even try out – the idea of bringing Hamlet on after the long lapse of time that is supposed to follow the end of the first act, to show him meditating suicide? And of following that with the attack on Ophelia, which gives continuity with the earlier attack which we have just heard about from Ophelia herself? It is curious not only that we have the signs of an intention to bring on Ophelia in 2.2 but also that there is a noticeable 'join' in 3.1 to initiate the nunnery scene. At 2.2.158, in planning the Ophelia trap, Polonius says

> You know sometimes he walks four hours together
> Here in the lobby...
> At such a time I'll loose my daughter to him.
> Be you and I behind an arras then.

At 2.2.205, however, at the end of the fishmonger scene, Polonius says

> I will leave him, and suddenly contrive the means of meeting between him and my daughter.

(This is the Folio reading: the second quarto omits most of this, and gives the obviously defective sentence: 'I will leave him and my daughter.') At 3.1.28, Claudius says

> Sweet Gertrude, leave us too,
> For we have closely sent for Hamlet hither,
> That he, as 'twere by accident, may here
> Affront Ophelia.

[1] Especially by Harley Granville Barker in his *Preface*, 1937, an important contribution to which this discussion is indebted.

In the word 'closely', the normal sense of secrecy applies to Claudius's purpose and not to sending the message; he has sent for Hamlet under pretence of something other than the real reason. When Hamlet enters, however, he is deep in meditation, communing with himself, giving no indication whatsoever that he has been sent for. This is his usual lobby walk, and he is surprised when he sees Ophelia. We can see that his entry belongs to the original scheme prepared for by Polonius's words at 2.2.158, 'sometimes he walks four hours together / Here in the lobby... / At such a time I'll loose my daughter to him.' Claudius's words are inconsistent with Hamlet's entry, and Polonius's words at 2.2.205 are inconsistent with Claudius's words. It is arguable that postponing 'To be or not to be' and the nunnery scene has led to a little gluing and patching; the defectiveness of the second quarto at 2.2.205 suggests problems with the manuscript arising from deletions or additions.

The positioning of 'To be or not to be' where it now finds itself is of profound importance for the ultimate meaning of the play (see pp. 47–8 below). Yet it is easy to see that 3.1 is not the only place it could have gone. Shakespeare may well have hesitated about what Chambers calls 'the order of the tests by which the court endeavours to ascertain the reason of Hamlet's strangeness' (*William Shakespeare*, I, 416). Once it finds its final placing, it invites incomprehension. Hamlet has been given his mission, has cursed himself for his delay, has planned to test the Ghost's veracity with a play and – now what? Back to the beginning and the strain of the very first soliloquy, wishing he were dead and cursing the conscience that stops him from doing anything. A great many critics try to rescue Shakespeare from his decision to place 'To be or not to be' where it is by denying the plain truth of what the soliloquy says, that is, that death is better than life but that we haven't the courage to kill ourselves. From Dr Johnson onwards there has always been someone who tries to pull Hamlet out of the deep pit of pessimism he is in. Here at least we might agree with Rebecca West that critics misinterpret *Hamlet* because they cannot face its bleakness.[1] Would it therefore be surprising if actors of Shakespeare's day, with perhaps a Hamlet among them, had argued that the play would go with a greater swing if, when he has decided on his plan to test both the Ghost and Claudius, Hamlet were allowed to get on with it? The leap into Ophelia's grave shows us that Hamlet was allowed to do things on the stage that Shakespeare hadn't wanted him to do (see the note to 5.1.225SD). Possibly the players, possibly Shakespeare's own fellows, pushed 'To be or not to be' and the nunnery scene back to an earlier position which Shakespeare had originally tried out but later rejected. The whole history of the development of the playing text of *Hamlet* in the theatre (which is discussed at p. 61) shows not merely abbreviation of the play but an ironing out of its complexities. The refusal of the stage to meet the challenge of the personality that Shakespeare created may have begun very early.

Our postulated fair copy of Shakespeare's manuscript, having been used to create the promptbook and the actors' parts, would be carefully preserved in case a new promptbook were ever needed. When it became desirable to supplant the inferior first quarto with its outrageous claim to be the play that Shakespeare wrote, it was

[1] *The Court and the Castle*, 1958.

Shakespeare's own manuscript, now no doubt in a very messed-up condition, that was given to the printer. Little wonder that the compositors tried to get help from a copy of the first quarto. It seems very plausible that in the three years and more since Shakespeare completed his play wear and tear had made the manuscript less legible than it was when the book-keeper took it over to make his transcript. There is one particular area of the second quarto, from 5.2.145 to 170, where omissions and errors (by comparison with the Folio) are unusually deep and extensive. For example:

5.2.146	Q2:	why is this all you call it?
	F:	why is this impon'd as you call it?
158	Q2:	Shall I deliuer you so?
	F:	Shall I redeliuer you e'en so?
161–2	Q2:	Yours doo's well to commend it himselfe
	F:	Yours, yours; hee does well to commend it himselfe
165	Q2:	A did so sir with his dugge [corrected from 'A did sir']
	F:	He did Complie with his Dugge
166	Q2:	more of the same breede
	F:	more of the same Beauy
167	Q2:	and out of an habit
	F:	and outward habite
168	Q2:	a kind of histy collection
	F:	a kinde of yesty collection
169	Q2:	prophane and trennowed opinions
	F:	fond and winnowed opinions

An interesting feature of this series of misreadings is the uncharacteristic attempt to invent and supply words, like 'breede' and 'prophane'. This last is a less wild guess than it seems. The Folio's 'fond' is itself a misreading of 'fand' (= 'fanned'). If a tattered manuscript had what seemed to be (with the common mistake of final e for final d) 'fane', the compositor may have thought he had the tail-end of 'profane'. At any rate, it very much looks as though this page of Shakespeare's manuscript had become very difficult to decipher since it had been used for the theatre transcript some years before. It seems to me unlikely that Roberts's compositors would on their own initiative supply words like 'prophane'; they would have turned to a superior for help.

There are three other places in the second quarto where I think the extraordinary distance of the variant from the much stronger Folio reading indicates that the manuscript was no longer legible and that a guess was made in the printing house to remedy the deficiency. (The variant readings are discussed in the Commentary as they occur.)

1.3.26	Q2:	As he in his particuler act and place
	F:	As he in his peculiar Sect and force
3.3.79	Q2:	Why, this is base and silly, not reuendge
	F:	Oh this is hyre and Sallery, not Reuenge

3.4.50 Q2: With heated visage
F: With tristfull visage

I have already suggested that two passages which appear in the Folio but are not found in the second quarto, namely the passage in 2.2 about the war of the theatres and the words of Hamlet in 5.2, 'Is't not to be damned...', were late additions which either became detached or were overlooked. A third omission from the second quarto is the passage 2.2.229–56 which contains the reference to Denmark being a prison. It has often been suggested that by 1604 with Anne of Denmark as the king's consort this might have seemed a sensitive passage and so was cut out. This is the best explanation; possibly the printing house was where this self-censorship took place.

If we could leave the text of *Hamlet* at this point, with only Roberts's compositors between us and Shakespeare's manuscript, and Jaggard's compositors (who set up the Folio text) between us and the book-keeper's transcript of the same manuscript, we should be fortunate indeed. It is certain, however, that the manuscript used by Jaggard for printing the Folio text was not the book-keeper's transcript itself but a careless and rather free copy of it. The copy was made sometime after 1606, and conceivably was made specially for the printing of the Folio (1623). The existence of a second scribe was argued by Dover Wilson in *The Manuscript of Shakespeare's 'Hamlet'*, and though I do not think we can accept the colourful rogue whom Dover Wilson believed he had driven into a corner (p. 56), an old actor and a fan of Burbage, who would write down what he had heard the actors say instead of relying on his copy, there can be no doubt of this agent of transmission. His existence is proved by the first quarto. When Q2 and Q1 agree in what appears to be the true reading, and they differ from F, then since Q1 has no access to the true reading except through the stage version which emanated from the book-keeper's transcript, that transcript must once have contained the true reading, and it must have been obliterated at a later stage. That 'later stage' in hundreds of minor cases must have been the setting up of the Folio text itself, but often the extent of the variation takes it far beyond a compositor's error. The tendency to substitute a word of similar sense often makes the Folio text a sort of paraphrase. Examples are 'just' for 'jump' at 1.1.65; 'day' for 'morn' at 1.1.150; 'gives' for 'lends' at 1.3.117; 'two' for 'ten' at 2.2.177; 'swathing' for 'swaddling' at 2.2.351; 'that' for 'yonder' at 3.2.339; 'claims' for 'craves' at 4.4.3; 'imperial' for 'imperious' at 5.1.180 (all these examples in modernised form). The concurrence of Q2 and Q1 in a good reading when the variant in F is also a good reading cannot prove that the F reading is a substitution by the second scribe, because the use by the Q2 compositors of a copy of Q1, particularly in the first act, can mean that the reading common to Q2 and Q1 is an error deriving from the latter. So the famous doublets in Act 1, where Q2 and Q1 agree against F, become no easier to solve. (E.g. lawless / landless, 1.1.98; sallied / solid, 1.2.129; interred / enurned, 1.4.49; waves / wafts 1.4.61; roots / rots, 1.5.33.)

A convincing demonstration can be made, by the use of the first quarto, of how

Shakespeare's language was progressively weakened during the course of the two transcriptions lying between his foul-papers and the printing of the Folio.

1.1.161	Q2:	And then they say no spirit dare sturre abraode
	Q1:	And then they say, no spirite dare walke abroade
	F:	And then (they say) no Spirit can walke abroad

The inference here is that the first scribe, the book-keeper, has made the no doubt unconscious substitution of 'walk' for 'stir' and this has found its way to the stage and thence eventually into the first quarto. The second scribe has weakened 'dare' to 'can'.

The Act to Restrain Abuses of Players of 1606 (see Chambers, *Elizabethan Stage*, IV, 338–9) forbade the use of the name of God, Jesus, the Holy Ghost or the Trinity in any play. It is clear that the second scribe made appropriate changes in his text when he remembered, but that he sometimes forgot. 'God' becomes 'Heaven' at 1.5.24 and elsewhere; 'By the mass' (2.1.50), ''Sblood' (2.2.337) and ''swounds' (2.2.528) are removed, but 'Gods bodkin' actually becomes 'Gods bodykins' (2.2.485). 'God a mercy' is smoothed to 'Gramercy' (4.5.194).

To summarise the foregoing discussion about a possible relationship between the three texts of *Hamlet*: the second quarto of 1604/5 was printed from Shakespeare's own manuscript, his 'foul-papers', as submitted to his company in 1601. This manuscript contained quite a number of passages which Shakespeare had marked for deletion. These deletion-marks were ignored or overlooked by the compositors, so that the second quarto – and consequently the received text of *Hamlet* – preserves much that Shakespeare had himself discarded. In the playhouse, an official fair copy was made of Shakespeare's no doubt untidy manuscript as a first stage towards preparing a text for the theatre. This fair copy did not include those false starts and unwanted passages which Shakespeare had marked for deletion. It also cut out two passages and added a third; these three changes can be considered as a multiple change of fundamental importance for the meaning of the play, and it is possible that the responsibility for these late changes was Shakespeare's. As the preparation of the fair copy went forward, the scribe made an increasing number of changes to his text, many of which stem from a determined effort to reduce the large number of minor and walk-on characters.

This conjectural fair copy eventually became the Folio text of 1623, but not directly. A transcript of the fair copy must have been made at some point after 1606 by a scribe with a cavalier indifference to the ethic of fidelity to one's copy. This second scribe did untold damage by casualness and rash improvement, and this damage is compounded by the usual carelessness and liberties of the Folio's compositors.

The first quarto of 1603, an abbreviated and adapted version in language which severely corrupts the original, inherits the cuts and changes made in the early playhouse transcript, and demonstrates that the transcript was in progress towards the Globe's official promptbook. It is not inconceivable that in spite of all its corruption it reflects the shortened acting version of Shakespeare's own theatre. The first quarto was used by the compositors of the second quarto, especially during the first act. It is also likely that the Folio compositors had available a copy of the second quarto.

This hypothesis of the relation between the texts may be represented by the following diagram.

The text of *Hamlet*

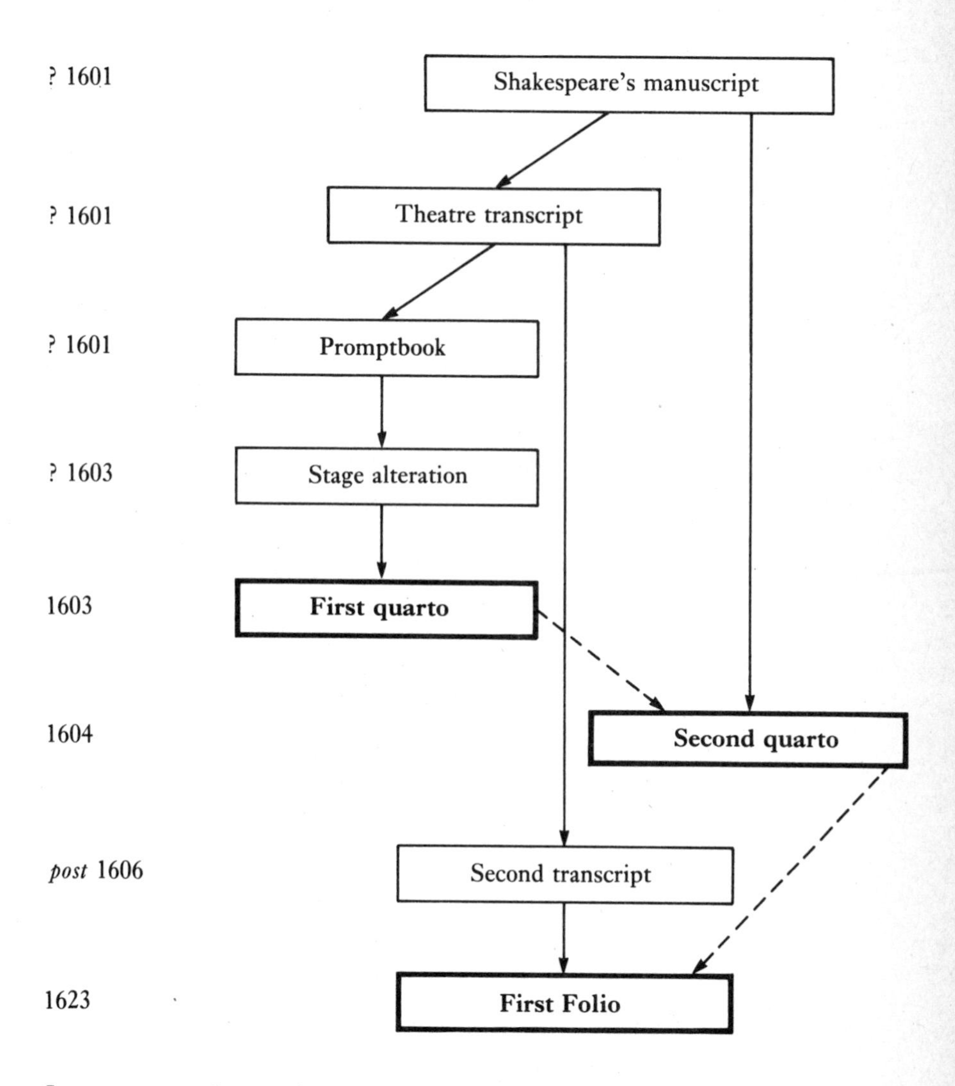

I now return to the question with which I began. What do we mean by 'Shakespeare's *Hamlet*'? I believe there was a point when Shakespeare had made many alterations to his play, mostly reflected in cutting rather than adding material, some of which he may have made after preliminary discussions with his colleagues among the

Chamberlain's men. The play then became the property of these colleagues who began to prepare it for the stage. At this point what one can only call degeneration began, and it is at this point that we should arrest and freeze the play, for it is sadly true that the nearer we get to the stage, the further we are getting from Shakespeare. This ideal version of the play does not exist in either of the two main authoritative texts, the second quarto and the Folio, but somewhere between them.

However convinced one may be that the true history of the text of *Hamlet* is of the kind that has been described in this Introduction, it is not always possible (as Hamlet found in the 'To be or not to be' soliloquy) to have the courage of one's convictions. To present readers with a lean and spare *Hamlet* lacking the 'dram of eale' speech and the soliloquy 'How all occasions do inform against me' might seem arrogance and eccentricity, even if the missing passages were supplied at the foot of the page. I have however wished to keep the different shapes of the second quarto and the Folio in front of the reader as much as possible. I have therefore marked all the second quarto passages which are cut in the Folio within square brackets. As for the main body of the text where the two early versions run parallel, the text of this edition will necessarily be an eclectic text, because neither version, in the case of any single variant, has a guaranteed superiority over the other. In some cases I have judged the Folio to be correct and in some cases the quarto.

With the stage directions, I have pursued a policy of compromise between the two texts. It is obvious (from the second quarto) that Shakespeare had not fully thought out the movements on stage and that the Folio provides necessary improvements. I have blended the two, to preserve an intimacy with Shakespeare's own pen, and also the greater clarity of the Folio's staging.

The play and the critics

It is probably safe to say that in the world's literature no single work has been so extensively written about as *Hamlet Prince of Denmark*. There are numerous histories, summaries and analyses of this great body of criticism, or parts of it, and numerous anthologies give selections from it. A brief guide to these guides will be found in the Reading List. What follows here is not an attempt to provide, even in the most summary form, a history of *Hamlet* criticism. It is a personal graph, linking together some moments in the history of the interpretation of *Hamlet* which I find important. It provides a starting point for the critical essay which follows on p. 40.

The eighteenth century was not disposed to sentimentalise Hamlet. Dr Johnson (1765) spoke of the 'useless and wanton cruelty' of his treatment of Ophelia, and of the speech in the prayer scene, when Hamlet refrains from killing Claudius for fear he will go to heaven, he said it was 'too horrible to be read or to be uttered'. The reader or the audience has a right to expect the 'poetical justice' of the punishment of Claudius, but this expectation is thwarted by the death of Ophelia, and the death of Hamlet as the price of killing the king. Hamlet indeed is 'rather an instrument than an agent', and 'makes no attempt to punish' Claudius after he has confirmation of his guilt.

Johnson's brief remarks convey his strong sense of Hamlet's failure (and the weakness seems to him as much the author's as the prince's). 'The apparition left the regions of the dead to little purpose' (NV II, 145–6).

George Steevens (1778) was strongly and unfavourably impressed by Hamlet's violence and callousness; he said it was the more necessary 'to point out the immoral tendency of his character' 'because Hamlet seems to have been hitherto regarded as a hero not undeserving the pity of the audience' (NV II, 147). But for Henry Mackenzie (1780) Hamlet was a man of exquisite sensibility and virtue 'placed in a situation in which even the amiable qualities of his mind serve but to aggravate his distress and to perplex his conduct'. Hamlet was not perfect, but from our compassion and anxiety concerning him arises that 'indescribable charm...which attracts every reader and every spectator' (NV II, 148). This is very much the tone of Goethe's famous comments in *Wilhelm Meisters Lehrjahre* (1795–6; translated into English by Carlyle, 1812). *Hamlet* essentially is a story of the inadequacy and impotence of sensitivity in the face of the stern demands of action. An oak tree has been planted in a precious vase fitted to receive beautiful flowers; as the tree's roots spread out the vase is shattered in pieces. 'A beautiful, pure, noble, and most moral nature, without the strength of nerve which makes the hero, sinks beneath a burden which it can neither bear nor throw off; every duty is holy to him, – this too hard.' Much less often quoted are some later remarks which show how completely off the mark Rebecca West was in *The Court and the Castle* (1958, pp. 64–5) in supposing that Goethe was impatient with Hamlet for not saving himself by effort and action, and in associating Goethe with the 'pelagianism' of believing that the world offers its rewards to those who really try. Quite the reverse; Goethe says that poets and historians flatter us by pretending that man's proud lot may be the single-minded accomplishment of great purposes. 'In *Hamlet* we are taught otherwise.' Purgatory is shown to have no power to bring about what it wishes and nor has man. Inscrutable Fate has its way, toppling the bad with the good, mowing down one race as the next springs up. Hamlet's impotence, therefore, is only an extreme form of a powerlessness general to mankind (NV II, 273–4).

The impotence of Hamlet as understood by Coleridge (1808–12) is quite different. His Hamlet is not a man broken under the weight of too demanding an obligation, but a man incapable of acting. 'Shakespeare wished to impress upon us the truth, that action is the chief end of existence.' Hamlet knows perfectly well what he ought to do, and he is always promising to do it, but he is constitutionally averse to action, and his energy evaporates in self-reproach. The world of the mind was more real than the external world; his passion was for the indefinite. 'Hence great, enormous, intellectual activity, and a consequent proportionate aversion to real action.' Coleridge confessed that 'I have a smack of Hamlet myself, if I may say so.'[1] The habit of identifying oneself with Hamlet, which is far from being as widespread as is sometimes supposed, is enshrined in the remark of Hazlitt (1817) that the speeches and sayings of Hamlet are 'as real as our own thoughts...It is *we* who are Hamlet' (NV II, 155).

[1] NV II, 152–5; but see more fully *Shakespearean Criticism*, ed. T. M. Raysor, 1930; 2nd edn, 1960.

To return to Germany, where so much was contributed to the study of *Hamlet*, we reach a landmark with A. W. Schlegel's *Lectures on Dramatic Art and Literature*, delivered in 1808. *Hamlet* is a 'tragedy of thought' (*Gedankentrauerspiel*). This 'thought' is not Coleridge's habit-of-contemplation, inevitably inhibiting action, but a profound scepticism which questions the value of action. Here, powerfully, is Hamlet the doubter, and not the amiable dreamer: a restless sceptic of uncertain principles.

Hamlet has no firm belief either in himself or in anything else: from expressions of religious confidence he passes over to religious doubt... The stars themselves, from the course of events, afford no answer to the questions so urgently proposed to them. A voice, commissioned as it would appear by Heaven from another world, demands vengeance for a monstrous enormity, and the demand remains without effect. The criminals are at last punished, but, as it were, by an accidental blow... The less guilty or the innocent are equally involved in the general destruction. (NV II, 279–80)

It was left for Herman Ulrici (1839) to focus Hamlet's doubts on an area which had attracted little discussion, the morality of revenge. Ulrici's work has been neglected because Bradley was so dismissive of the 'conscience theory'. 'Even though the King were trebly a fratricide,' wrote Ulrici, 'in a *Christian* sense it would still be a sin to put him to death with one's own hand, without a trial and without justice.' Of the Ghost he says, 'it cannot be a pure and heavenly spirit that wanders on earth to stimulate his son to avenge his murder'. In Hamlet, therefore, the Christian struggles with the natural man. It is his task to make the action imposed on him one that he can undertake freely and by conviction as a moral action. His 'regard for the eternal salvation of his soul... forces him to halt and consider'. However, he is betrayed less by his vindictive impulses than by his own creative energy in trying to 'shape at pleasure the general course of things'. He thus rejects the guiding hand of God, and his aspiration to be a kind of god himself is a sinful overestimate of human power. Here, I think for the first time, is the view that Hamlet errs in trying to act as Providence, a view which has been considerably developed in the twentieth century.[1]

Almost every writer and thinker of the later nineteenth century had his say about Hamlet. Friedrich Nietzsche in *The Birth of Tragedy* (1872) found that Hamlet 'speaks more superficially than he acts'; there is something deeper going on in the play than finds appropriate expression in the speeches. It is with *Hamlet* as with Greek tragedy – 'the myth... never finds an adequate objective correlative in the spoken word'.[2] At this level deeper than speech, Nietzsche saw Hamlet as an example of Dionysiac man who has pierced through the illusions by which we live and sustain ourselves and who, if forced back into 'quotidian reality', views it with detestation.

Dionysiac man might be said to resemble Hamlet; both have looked into the true nature of things; they have *understood* and are now loth to act. They realise that no action of theirs can work any change in the eternal condition of things, and they regard the imputation as ludicrous

[1] NV II, 292–3 gives brief selections from Morrison's 1846 translation of *Shakespeares Dramatische Kunst*; see further L. D. Schmitz's 1876 translation of Ulrici's third edition.

[2] Nietzsche, *Birth of Tragedy*, section 17; translated by F. Golffing, Anchor Books, 1956, p. 103. The word translated as 'objective correlative' is *Objectivation*.

> or debasing that they should set right the time which is now out of joint. Understanding kills action, for in order to act we require the veil of illusion; such is Hamlet's doctrine, not to be confounded with the cheap wisdom of John-a-Dreams, who through too much reflection, as it were a surplus of possibilities, never arrives at action. (section 7; p. 51)

In this last sentence Nietzsche dismisses the Coleridgean contemplator. It is not reflection but *understanding* which debars action: 'the apprehension of truth and its terror'. 'The truth once seen, man is aware everywhere of the ghastly absurdity of existence, comprehends the symbolism of Ophelia's fate and the wisdom of the wood sprite Silenus: nausea invades him' (pp. 51–2). (Silenus thought it was better not to be born at all or, failing that, to die as soon as possible.) Hamlet is not fixed enough in his nature for Nietzsche's portrait to have general applicability, but, as I shall argue (see p. 48), Nietzsche's words are a profound comment on the 'To be or not to be' soliloquy.

The observations of Stéphane Mallarmé on *Hamlet* first became widely known from Joyce's use of them in *Ulysses* (1922). In 1886, Mallarmé wrote of the tentativeness of Hamlet as a person (*le seigneur latent qui ne peut devenir*), and of his failure to translate potentiality into achievement, as being the very stuff of drama, which primarily concerns itself with the quarrel between men's dreams and the calamities of fortune. Mallarmé stressed Hamlet's solitariness, as an alien wherever he appeared.[1] This emphasis was resumed in some remarkable lines in an article 'Hamlet et Fortinbras' in *La Revue blanche* in 1896.[2] 'He walks about, and the book he reads is himself' (*Il se promène...lisant au livre de lui-même*). He denies others with his look. But it's not just the solitude of the contemplative man which is expressed. He is a killer. He kills without concern, and even if he does not do the killing – people die. 'The black presence of this doubter causes this poison.' (*Il tue indifféremment ou, du moins, on meurt. La noire présence du douteur cause ce poison, que tous les personnages trépassent: sans même que lui prenne toujours la peine de les percer, dans la tapisserie.*)

Mallarmé saw Hamlet by flashes, and the sinister figure whom he glimpsed seems as far removed as possible from the prince as he appears in A. C. Bradley's *Shakespearean Tragedy* of 1904. Bradley's masterly work on *Hamlet* was the most considered and extended examination which the play had up to that time received. It stands as a kind of pillar at the end of the nineteenth century, reviewing and assessing what had gone before, the last and greatest statement of a prevailing view of Hamlet (though the preceding review indicates that it had already been undermined). It is a view of Hamlet as a noble and generous youth who for reasons inexplicable to himself is unable to carry out a deed of punishment enjoined on him by divine authority. What causes this paralysis? It is not conscience, it is not the immorality of revenge, it is not the frailty of his nature nor the fatal habit of contemplation. Hamlet procrastinates, Bradley argues, because his true nature is blanketed by the melancholy ensuing from the death of his father and his mother's

[1] Mallarmé, *Crayonné au théâtre*; *Oeuvres complètes*, Gallimard, 1945, pp. 300–2.
[2] *Oeuvres complètes*, p. 1564.

remarriage. It is this affliction which inhibits the fulfilment of his purposes and makes him seek any excuse for delay.

Bradley's book as a whole was dismissive of the religious element in Shakespearean tragedy and Elizabethan drama as a whole (it was 'almost wholly secular', p. 25), but he saw *Hamlet* as something of an exception.

> While *Hamlet* certainly cannot be called in the specific sense a 'religious drama', there is in it nevertheless both a freer use of popular religious ideas, and a more decided, though always imaginative, intimation of a supreme power concerned in human evil and good, than can be found in any other of Shakespeare's tragedies. (p. 174)

It is because of the sense of Providence in the play that 'the apparent failure of Hamlet's life is not the ultimate truth concerning him'. The figure of the Ghost is 'a reminder or a symbol of the connexion of the limited world of ordinary experience with the vaster life of which it is but a partial appearance'. He 'affects imagination' not only as 'the apparition of a dead king who desires the accomplishment of *his* purposes' but as 'the messenger of divine justice'.

A. C. Bradley, like Edward Dowden (who contributed a notable edition of *Hamlet* to the old Arden series in 1899), was a professor in one of the departments of English Literature which were being created in universities new and old throughout the English-speaking world towards the end of the nineteenth century. The number of studies of *Hamlet* increased enormously as the academic study of English literature burgeoned. A great deal of attention was now given to the difficult problem of the text of the play; to its sources, to the relationship of the play with its predecessor; to its date; to the status of the first quarto; to the theatrical conventions of the revenge play; to theatre conditions and audience response; to contemporary history; to contemporary thinking about spirits, second marriages, melancholy, incest, elective monarchies, purgatory and punctuation. Yet it has to be said that with some notable exceptions like Bradley the academics have not always been the leaders of opinion on *Hamlet*, and the understanding of the play owes as much to writers and thinkers who were not professional scholars as to the scholars themselves. A good example of this is the influence of Freud, whose mere footnote on Hamlet's Oedipus complex in *The Interpretation of Dreams* in 1900 has had gigantic influence. Ernest Jones built on this in 1910 for the first of his several psychoanalytic studies of *Hamlet*, arguing that Hamlet's problems were caused by his unconscious wish to supplant his father and lie with his mother. Psychoanalytic explanations of Hamlet's delay lurk behind T. S. Eliot's lofty and capricious essay of 1919. 'The play is most certainly an artistic failure', because Shakespeare was unable to transform the intractable material he inherited from the old play and the sources into a vehicle or 'objective correlative' capable of conveying the issues and emotions which it strives to express. 'Nothing that Shakespeare can do with the plot can express Hamlet for him.' Hamlet's emotions are 'in *excess* of the facts as they appear'. Shakespeare's failure lay in trying to convert a father-and-son play about revenge into a mother-and-son play about – something else. The reason he couldn't get it into shape was the extent of his own hang-ups.

'*Hamlet*, like the sonnets, is full of some stuff that the writer could not drag to light, contemplate, or manipulate into art.'[1]

Eliot was a greater poet than John Masefield, but the essay on *Hamlet* which Masefield wrote as an introduction to the play in 1911 is more interesting and valuable than Eliot's better-known pages. Masefield saw Hamlet as the embodiment of a very special human wisdom caught between two opposing forces which were trying to complete themselves. The one force is seen in a murderous take-over of the kingdom; the other in a cry for revenge. A bloody purpose from outside life matches a bloody purpose within. Life has been wrenched from its course and an attempt has to be made to wrench it back, or it is to be allowed to continue on its new course. Hamlet's wisdom baffles both alternatives. The Ghost, representing 'something from outside life trying to get into life', presents Hamlet with a simple task – 'All tasks are simple to the simple-minded.' The translation of this act into practical terms is 'a defilement' which it is 'difficult for a wise mind to justify'. But if Hamlet in a sense defeats both the principles which are presented to him, he is himself defeated by life. 'She destroys the man who wrenched her from her course, and the man who would neither wrench her back nor let her stay.'[2]

There is something in Masefield of Ulrici's theory that Hamlet could not take revenge unless he were able to metamorphose the barbaric act by coming to it with a voluntary inward motivation and equate it with Christian moral law. Masefield stressed the superiority of Hamlet's ethical principles to those of the Ghost, and the defilement that Hamlet is in danger of by an incautious obedience. This looks not only back to Ulrici but forward to what one might call the 'contamination theory' much in evidence in the mid twentieth century. This holds that Hamlet's chief perplexity is one of translation: of finding a way to convert the Ghost's injunction into action without being stained by the corruption of Denmark or becoming like the murderer whom he is to punish. Versions of this view can be found, for example, in Maynard Mack's well-known essay, 'The World of *Hamlet*' (1952),[3] H. F. D. Kitto's *Form and Meaning in Drama* (1956), Harry Levin's *The Question of 'Hamlet'* (1959), G. K. Hunter's 'The Heroism of Hamlet' (1963),[4] and Nigel Alexander's *Poison, Play, and Duel* (1967). Mack writes: 'The act required of him, though retributive justice, is one that necessarily involves the doer in the general guilt' (p. 103). Alexander writes: 'The certain proof supplied by the inner play does not solve the problem of *Hamlet*. The question remains, how does one deal with such a man without becoming like him?' (p. 125).

One of the most striking and important contributions during the first half of the twentieth century was George Wilson Knight's essay, 'The Embassy of Death' in

[1] Eliot, *Selected Essays*, 1932, pp. 141–6.

[2] Masefield's Introduction is reprinted in his *William Shakespeare* in the Home University Library, n.d. [1911].

[3] Reprinted in *Shakespeare: 'Hamlet': A Casebook*, ed. J. Jump, 1968, pp. 86–107.

[4] In '*Hamlet*', ed. J. R. Brown and B. Harris, 1963, pp. 90–109.

The Wheel of Fire (1930). Although few people have expressed agreement with it, and though the author later retreated and modified his position, the essay swiftly and silently infused itself into the consciousness of literary criticism.[1] Knight refused to accept Hamlet's jaundiced view of the Danish court. Denmark is a healthy and contented community with Claudius as its efficient and kindly administrator, sensibly not wishing to let memories of the past impede the promise of the future. By contrast, Hamlet is a figure of nihilism and death. He has been poisoned by his grief, and he has communed with the dead. He has been instructed never to let the past be forgotten. He is 'a sick soul...commanded to heal' and is in fact a poison in the veins of the community, 'an element of evil in the state of Denmark'. Knight strongly stressed Hamlet's apartness: 'inhuman – or superhuman...a creature of another world'. Neither side can understand the other. Claudius is a murderer and Hamlet of course has right on his side. But which of the two, he asked, 'is the embodiment of spiritual good, which of evil? The question of the relative morality of Hamlet and Claudius reflects the ultimate problem of this play.'

> A balanced judgement [he continued] is forced to pronounce ultimately in favour of life as contrasted with death, for optimism and the healthily second-rate, rather than the nihilism of the superman: for he is not, as the plot shows, safe; and he is not safe, primarily because he is right. (p. 40)

Prompt vengeance might have saved the day, but, in view of the disasters that Hamlet brings about, Knight's judgement was that 'Had Hamlet forgotten both the Ghost's commands [to remember the past and avenge the dead], it would have been well, since Claudius is a good king, and the Ghost but a minor spirit.' Claudius a good king, and the Ghost but a minor spirit – this is a deeply significant opposition for later criticism to digest. Having quoted Hamlet's words, 'The spirit that I have seen / May be the devil...', Knight added 'It was.' Or at least, 'The Ghost may or may not have been a "goblin damned"; it certainly was no "spirit of health".'

Knight's essay seems to me brilliant and wrong. I have treated it at some length because a mass of criticism of the fifty years following can in some ways be considered as footnotes and codicils to it. Moreover, in setting up an opposition of an alienated, inhuman prophet and a smoothly running, kindly society, and opting for the latter, the essay vividly shows the alteration of the play's tragic balance which is so striking a feature of contemporary criticism.[2] Although for a long time the orthodox interpretation of *Hamlet* as taught in schools and universities (in Britain at any rate) remained predominantly Bradleyan,[3] it becomes harder to find critics who to any extent 'believe in' Hamlet and his mission. Extreme forms of distaste for the hero are to be seen in Salvador de Madariaga's *On Hamlet* (1948) and L. C. Knights's *An*

[1] As late as 1981 we can find John Bayley repeating Knight's view that Claudius's advice to Hamlet to forget his father's death shows a mature understanding of 'how life must be lived' (*Shakespeare and Tragedy*, p. 179). See note to 1.2.102.

[2] See P. Edwards, 'Tragic balance in *Hamlet*', *Shakespeare Survey* 36 (1983), 43–52.

[3] Except in those advanced places which followed Lascelles Abercrombie and E. E. Stoll in denying that there was any problem of delay to be solved. See Abercrombie, *The Idea of Great Poetry*, 1925, and Stoll, *Art and Artifice in Shakespeare*, 1933 (using *Hamlet* material from 1919).

Approach to 'Hamlet' (1960). Madariaga stressed Hamlet's cruelty, egocentricity and aristocratic disdain. Knights stressed Hamlet's immaturity and his lack of 'a ready responsiveness to life'.

Wilson Knight's essay presented the identity and the authority of the Ghost as a major point of debate. What the Elizabethans were likely to think on this matter became a primary issue for scholarship. John Dover Wilson, whose pioneering and indispensable research into the text of *Hamlet* had been published in 1934, included in his *What Happens in 'Hamlet'* of 1935 an early study of Elizabethan attitudes to ghosts. His conclusion that there were three degrees of scepticism, with Catholics being less sceptical than Protestants, has proved too much of a simplification. Later research is reviewed, and the investigation carried further, in Eleanor Prosser's *Hamlet and Revenge* (1967). It is impossible to ignore, in considering *Hamlet*, the deep caution and scepticism with which Shakespeare's contemporaries, whether Catholic or Protestant, viewed ghosts and reports of ghosts. They might be hallucinations, or angels, or demons out to ensnare one's soul. That a ghost might be the soul of a dead person revisiting earth was a very remote possibility.[1] Hamlet's early affirmation of the Ghost's genuineness has come to look more questionable than his later doubts, and the confidence of generations of critics, and hence of schoolchildren, that Hamlet's profession of scepticism in 2.2, with his plan to test the Ghost, is mere procrastination now seems insecurely founded. Not many would go as far as Eleanor Prosser in holding that the Ghost *was* a demon. But one of the important achievements of modern scholarship is to have unsettled the Ghost and made it impossible to accept his credentials and authority as a matter of course and without question. The ambiguity of the Ghost is not just Hamlet's problem. Much is to be built on Nigel Alexander's perception that Shakespeare's guardedness about the Ghost is an essential feature of the play: 'the nature of the Ghost is intended to be an open question'.[2]

Associated with the issue of the origin of the Ghost is the question of the morality of what he enjoins on Hamlet, revenge for murder. As we have seen, this question has been asked for a long time, since Ulrici at least. Scholarship has concerned itself for many years with what would have been the Elizabethan answer to the question. Massive evidence has been assembled that private vengeance was abhorrent to Elizabethans as anti-Christian and anti-social – and also that the Elizabethans were a pretty vindictive lot. Once again, Eleanor Prosser's book can be cited for its review of the debate. And once again her own position is at the extreme edge of the spectrum, namely that the *donnée* of the play is the conviction that revenge was evil in the extreme. It is best not to be too keen on certainties in this matter. The Elizabethan revenge-play, and *Hamlet* in particular, is concerned with exploration, not preachment. It devotes itself to the whole issue of the legitimacy of violence and the responsibility of the individual in pursuing justice, finding in the revenge convention an extraordinarily rich source of conflicts to exhibit and illuminate the many faces of violence and redress. To prejudge the plays by saying that for the Elizabethans revenge was of course evil or was of course acceptable is to defeat them completely – as completely

[1] Prosser, *Hamlet and Revenge*, pp. 102–6.

[2] Alexander, *Poison, Play, and Duel*, pp. 32–3.

as does the superior view that the whole revenge convention is barbarous and silly. Some of the best pages of the mid century on *Hamlet* arose from a sharp reaction against simplistic conclusions about Elizabethan attitudes to revenge. In *The Business of Criticism*, 1959, Helen Gardner wrote excellently of the division of mind that must exist for every thinking person in every age who tries to achieve justice without outrage to conscience.

I conclude this 'personal graph' of criticism with a look at the very small group of twentieth-century critics who have seen *Hamlet* as a religious play. Middleton Murry (*Shakespeare,* 1936) believed that Hamlet's fear of damnation was an immensely important factor in the play, overlooked by us because we provide Shakespeare's tragic heroes 'with every modern convenience' including our indifference to an after-life. E. M. W. Tillyard (*Shakespeare's Problem Plays,* 1950) wrote: 'In *Hamlet* if anywhere in Shakespeare we notice the genealogy from the Miracle Plays with their setting of Heaven, Purgatory, and Hell... *Hamlet* is one of the most medieval as well as one of the most acutely modern of Shakespeare's plays' (p. 30). C. S. Lewis's British Academy Shakespeare Lecture of 1942, 'Hamlet: the prince or the poem?', was a curiously directed piece with a lot of shadow-boxing which seems quite unnecessary for the main argument. The particularity of Hamlet as a character was for him as unimportant as the particularity of revenge. Hamlet is 'not "a man who has to avenge his father" but "a man who has been given a task by a ghost"'. The appearance of the Ghost 'means a breaking down of the walls of the world'. Chaos supervenes: 'doubt, uncertainty, bewilderment to almost any degree is what the ghost creates'. Hamlet goes through a spiritual region, traversed by most of us. Hamlet's phrase, 'such fellows as I' (3.1.124) 'means *men*' – 'and the vast empty vision of them "crawling between earth and heaven" is what really counts and really carries the burden of the play'. 'Its true hero is man – haunted man – man with his mind on the frontier of two worlds, man unable either quite to reject or quite to admit the supernatural.'

The action of the play

THE PLATFORM

Hamlet opens with soldiers on guard at night in a scene full of perturbation and anxiety. It is nervousness about the apparition which predominates, of course, 'this thing', 'this dreaded sight', looking exactly like the late king in full armour. It is an ominous thing, and the sceptic Horatio, who is quickly converted, fears that it 'bodes some strange eruption to our state'. The state is already in turmoil, being hastily put on a war footing. Fortinbras of Norway is threatening to invade Denmark to recover lands which his father lost to the late King Hamlet a generation ago. Recollection of that old combat coming on top of the apparition focuses all attention on the dead king. The practice of calling the king by the name of his country enforces an identity between king and kingdom, the health of the one reflecting the health of the other, so that the old king's death seems to mark the end of an era. 'The king that's dead' is referred to as 'the majesty of buried Denmark'. Much later, the first words of the mad Ophelia are 'Where is the beauteous majesty of Denmark?' Even a routine cry like Bernardo's 'Long live the king!' in the third line of the play takes an additional meaning as we sense the apprehension of the watch for what may be the consequences for Denmark of the loss of their hero-king.

Hamlet is about Denmark as well as its prince. How Denmark fares as a society is in our minds all the time. But of course it's not just Hamlet and Denmark. Though Hamlet is at the centre of the play, he exists in his relationships, familial, social, sexual, political, divine; and even Hamlet, the most famous 'individual' in drama, is not so exclusively the centre that he diminishes the importance of what he is related to: family, society, God.

Since it is his threat to the kingdom which is the cause of the watch being set, young Fortinbras may be said to start the play off. In fact he encircles it, seeing that he enters at the very end to take over the kingdom without having to fight for it. Having so satisfactorily concluded his business, he will be able to give his 'landless resolutes' whatever they would like to have. Fortinbras succeeds where Hamlet fails, though Hamlet has been trying to right a great wrong and Fortinbras has been interested only in reversing the lawful outcome of his father's reckless challenge.

'I KNOW NOT SEEMS'

Prince Hamlet in black carries into the court (in 1.2) that memory of the dead king which Claudius and Gertrude are anxious to erase. His grief, he says, is real not assumed, unlike (he implies) the emotions being expressed around him. But the most determined candour could scarcely reveal in public what he pours out when he is alone: his feeling of total despair, of *taedium vitae*, of the weary meaninglessness of 'all the uses of this world'. He has no wish to continue living, but divine law forbids suicide. Why is all this? Because his father has suddenly died and his mother has speedily taken a new husband. Too slight a ground for despair? Hamlet's protestations are extreme. To call Claudius a satyr – a lecherous goat-like creature – does not make much sense to an audience who has just seen the new king efficiently managing his courtiers and the affairs of the nation. His mother's remarriage makes him call in question the constancy of all women. 'Hyperion to a satyr!' 'Frailty, thy name is woman!' Such passionate attachment to his father, such contempt for his uncle, such disgust with his mother, may seem pathological, what Eliot would call 'in excess of the facts'. Hamlet's indignation does indeed go deeper than the 'facts' but its source is not morbid.

The story of Cain and Abel is brought into the play during this scene (105) and appears again twice (3.3.38 and 5.1.65).[1] That first murder shattered the human family; it resulted from and betokened man's falling away from God. The identification of Claudius with Cain – which he himself makes – gives us the context in which we should put the 'unreasonable' bitterness of Hamlet, though as yet he knows nothing about any murder. In his book *Violence and the Sacred*, René Girard argued that

[1] See Rosalie L. Colie, *Shakespeare's Living Art*, 1974, p. 230, and Honor Matthews, *The Primal Curse: The Myth of Cain and Abel in the Theatre*, 1967.

cultural breakdown in early society, what he terms the 'sacrificial crisis', involves the failure to recognise acknowledged distinctions and differences. The erasure of difference shows itself in myth in the mortal rivalry of two brothers for what cannot be shared, a throne, a woman. Girard quotes the 'degree' speech in Shakespeare's *Troilus and Cressida* as an inspired perception of the chaos and violence which flow from the weakening of accepted distinctions. If, instead of the reading 'each thing meets in mere oppugnancy', he had followed the quarto text with 'each thing *melts* in mere oppugnancy', he would have shown how even more forcefully the passage conveys the rooted fear of the loss of category, of identity, of distinctiveness.

The obliteration of distinction, before Hamlet knows anything about fratricide or adultery, lies in Claudius taking his brother's place as king and husband and in Gertrude tranquilly accepting him as substitute. Their acts may offend against taste and ethics but the deeper offence is the undermining of an ideal of the person enshrined in antiquity and law. Hamlet's expressions, 'Hyperion to a satyr' and 'no more like my father / Than I to Hercules', show a mythographic ordering of the human differences. So in the closet scene Hamlet tries to force the distinction of the two men on to his mother by means of the two pictures. 'Have you eyes?' he shouts at her –

> See what a grace was seated on this brow;
> Hyperion's curls, the front of Jove himself,
> An eye like Mars, to threaten and command;
> A station like the herald Mercury... (3.4.55–8)

This matter of the blurring of distinctions in a man claiming to be his brother helps to explain Hamlet's passion against Claudius as a usurper –

> A slave that is not twentieth part the tithe
> Of your precedent lord, a vice of kings,
> A cutpurse of the empire and the rule... (3.4.97–9)

Denmark is an elective monarchy as Hamlet knows quite well (see 1.2.109, 5.2.65, 335).[1] But Shakespeare plays off this elective monarchy against his Elizabethan audience's deep emotional commitment to primogeniture and the right of a son to inherit. The Danish system condemns itself; a country which chooses its kings ends up with the rabble-cry of 'Choose we! Laertes shall be king!' (4.5.106). It has chosen for its king one who, did they but know, organised the vacancy by murder. For the audience, the system is a legalism which runs counter to their instinctive sense of rightness. There is a higher court than the court of Denmark, and in that court Hamlet is the dispossessed prince. Hamlet himself is both a Dane and an Elizabethan; whatever Danish law says, Claudius has usurped his brother, and violently appropriated a kingship he has no right to.

Gertrude's offence in confusing the two brothers is much deepened in the audience's eyes later in the first act when they learn that she committed adultery

[1] See the discussion by E. A. J. Honigmann in 'The Politics of *Hamlet*', in '*Hamlet*', ed. Brown and Harris, pp. 129–47.

with Claudius while her husband was alive. (There is no mistaking the plain sense of the Ghost's words; see Commentary at 1.5.46.) The willingness of this complaisant woman to sleep with either of two brothers is a forceful image of the failure of discrimination which is central to the tragedy of *Hamlet*.

In this second scene Hamlet is unaware of adultery or murder. But he has repudiated with contempt the appropriation of that vital distinction of fatherhood which Claudius grandly tries to add to his other appropriations. 'But now my cousin Hamlet, and my son...' Hamlet will not accept the relationship; it is 'more than kin'. He knows he is not Claudius's son, and the same knowledge tells him that Claudius is not Gertrude's husband, nor Denmark's king. It is this knowledge, as well as grief for a father's death and the shallowness of a mother's love, which makes the whole world an unweeded garden.

THE GHOST

Hamlet is galvanised into activity by the news of the appearance of a ghost that resembles his dead father. On the platform that night he sees it and is determined to speak to it whatever happens. It is explanation he wants; explanation and a course of action. 'Let me not burst in ignorance', he cries. 'What should we do?' Though it is specific explanation – why the Ghost has come – and a specific course of action – what the Ghost wants him to do – that he seeks, his words have a wider perspective. The Ghost may have some secret, some unimaginable truth to bring relief from those 'thoughts beyond the reaches of our souls', an explanation why things are as they are and a directive for meaningful action. To his demands in both their specific and their general senses he receives, or thinks he receives, a more than sufficient response.

The Ghost declares that he is his father's spirit, gives him the extraordinary tidings of murder and adultery, and asks him to take revenge. His injunctions are summed up in the three imperatives, 'Bear it not', 'Taint not thy mind', 'Leave her to heaven.' These interconnect. 'Bear it not' looks both backwards and forwards. The idea of retribution is implied by the Ghost's appeal to Hamlet's 'nature', that is, his filial piety. 'Bear it not' means that as a son he is not to acquiesce in and accept what has been done to his father. But it looks also to the future. The abuse of Denmark by the very continuation of this pair in sovereignty and in marriage is not to be endured: 'Bear it not.' The second imperative is very strange: 'howsomever thou pursues this act, / Taint not thy mind'. Whatever the exact meaning of 'taint' (see Commentary), the tone of the remark is that the Ghost does not consider this matter of revenge too difficult an act, and is anxious that Hamlet should not become too disturbed about it. No doubt for the Ghost the challenge is like that which he accepted all those years ago when he agreed to face old Fortinbras in a single combat: a matter of honour, determination, courage and skill. The final injunction, 'Leave her to heaven', must temper our feeling of the Ghost's personal vindictiveness. It is more important, however, in giving a religious context to the punishment of Claudius and Gertrude. Gertrude's earthly punishment is to be her conscience: 'those thorns that in her bosom lodge / To prick and sting her'. Whatever further punishment or exoneration is hers

1 Suggested Elizabethan staging of the Ghost scenes (1.4 and 1.5) by C. Walter Hodges. It is here supposed (as also in 1.1) that the Ghost enters each time by the same door, and makes the same circuit of the stage, until his final exit by a trap at 1.5.91

to receive belongs to an after-life. With Claudius it is different. By his words 'Leave *her* to heaven', the Ghost must imply that a higher justice requires the exemplary punishment of Claudius on earth, by the hand of an appointed human being. The Ghost's commands indicate not the pursuit of personal satisfaction but the existence of a world beyond the human world responsible for justice in the human world. Whether the Ghost has the authority to convey this the play never makes clear.

Awful though it is, Hamlet now has his explanation. What had seemed the degeneration of the world turns out to be a condition which is clearly and starkly the consequence of a double crime. He now also has his directive, a commission that is also a mission. His reaction to the Ghost is like a religious conversion. He wipes away all previous knowledge, all previous values, and baptises himself as a new man (1.5.95–104).

> And thy commandment all alone shall live
> Within the book and volume of my brain,
> Unmixed with baser matter.

The commandment is summed up by the Ghost as 'Remember!' 'Remember me', says the Ghost, and Hamlet repeats the word three times in his dedication. The Ghost is to be remembered 'whiles memory holds a seat / In this distracted globe', that is to say so long as this now-disordered world attributes any value to the past and its traditions, to the established standards of virtue and justice. (See the Commentary on this vital speech.) In this speech, to remember means more than to keep in mind; it means to maintain and to restore. In the section 'Of Redemption' in *Thus Spake Zarathustra*, Nietzsche deplored those who could not accept the 'It was' of time. He saw vengeance and punishment as an imprisonment of the will in concentrating on the past in an effort to undo what could not be undone. 'This, yea, this is very vengeance! – Will's abhorrence of time and its "It was".'[1] It is quite clear that Hamlet is not prepared to accept the 'It was' of time, and that he regards revenge as a task of creative remembrance, that is, the restoration of a society that has fallen to pieces. The act ends with

> The time is out of joint: O cursed spite,
> That ever I was born to set it right.

This is a terrible moment as, all exhilaration gone, he faces the burden of his responsibilities. But who has told him that it is his responsibility to put the world to rights? to restore the disjointed frame of things to its true shape? No one but himself. It is the entirely self-imposed burden of cleansing the world that he now groans under.

THE ANTIC DISPOSITION

'As a stranger give it welcome', says Hamlet to Horatio about the supernatural visitation.

> There are more things in heaven and earth, Horatio,
> Than are dreamt of in your philosophy.

[1] 'Des Willens Widerwille gegen die Zeit und ihr "Es war".'

He identifies himself with the world of the stranger, and shows his alienation from Denmark and its values by adopting the garb of madness. The 'antic disposition' (an essential element in the old Amleth story) puzzles and worries the man who is now his enemy and sworn victim; it also has symbolic significance in denoting that Hamlet, like Bunyan's Christian, having received his call, considers himself a pilgrim and a stranger in his own city of Vanity Fair. Madness is conduct which does not conform to society's standards. Very well, says Hamlet, I am a madman.[1]

Shakespeare carefully marks a considerable lapse of time between Acts 1 and 2 (see the Commentary, 2.1). The first event in Hamlet's mission that we hear about is his silent ritual of divorce from Ophelia. Ophelia's tragedy, like Hamlet's, is the tragedy of obedience to a father. Only she really goes mad. And then – always going one step further than the prince – she doesn't stop at thinking about ending her life. At this stage in the play, she has obeyed her father and refused to see Hamlet. She now tells Polonius of the very peculiar encounter she has had with him. Hamlet, in a set piece of antic theatre, went dishevelled to her room and in total silence carried out what we might interpret as a ceremony of questioning, denunciation and separation. By this, he cuts the closest tie that binds him to the court of Denmark, and takes his school-fellow Horatio as his only confidant.

What are the values of 'Denmark' as we are shown them? The court party, Claudius, Polonius, Laertes, are much given to expressing their beliefs in resonant platitudes. Claudius knows the proper response to death, Laertes to sex, Polonius to everything. With each person, we see the insufficiency of their moralising. What Claudius is hiding we learn in 1.5 (though it is not confirmed until 3.1.50), and he is hiding it even from his new wife, who in turn tried to hide her double-life from her husband. Laertes is suspected by both his sister and his father of an inclination towards the primrose path of dalliance. Polonius advocates reticence, truth and straightdealing, but is loquacious and devious. It is the ever-ready platitudes, betrayed both by their rhetoric and by the conduct of those who utter them, that Hamlet discards as mere 'saws of books' as he enters his new life. It is interesting that the heavy moralising of the court party accompanies a low view of human nature. Polonius and Laertes both expect Hamlet to be the insouciant seducer that is their stereotype of an aristocrat. (Hamlet, on the other hand, is an 'idealist', expecting mothers to be above sexual desire.) Polonius's proclivity for spying – which leads to his own violent death – is shown in the grotesque commission to Reynaldo to keep an eye on Laertes in Paris and then in his schemes to find out what's wrong with Hamlet. Claudius has much greater need than Polonius to find out what lies behind Hamlet's strange behaviour; his elaborate plot to use Rosencrantz and Guildenstern as decoys is quickly uncovered by Hamlet.

What Hamlet is really thinking about during the long scene 2.2 is impossible to say. Everything he says to Polonius, Rosencrantz and Guildenstern has its irony, and if his hearers do not know when he is being sane and serious, nor do we. When he tells Rosencrantz and Guildenstern that he is 'most dreadfully attended' (255) he is not really talking about his servants. He may have the Ghost in mind, but chiefly he must

[1] I am indebted here to Hiram Haydn, *The Counter-Renaissance*, 1950, p. 626.

mean his own thoughts. We are sure enough of him when he says he finds Denmark a prison. And with that extraordinary end to his joke about Polonius taking his leave – 'except my life, except my life, except my life' – we must feel the warning note that the *taedium vitae* which lifted from him when the Ghost spoke is descending again and that the ultimate dilemma of 'To be or not to be' is at hand.

What we should discount as an index of Hamlet's feelings is the famous speech 'What a piece of work is a man' (286–91). So often pointed to as a brilliant perception of the anguish of Renaissance man in general and of Hamlet in particular, it is a glorious blind, a flight of rhetoric by which a divided and distressed soul conceals the true nature of his distress and substitutes a formal and conventional state of *Weltschmerz*. At the end of it he punctures the rhetoric himself.

ROGUE AND PEASANT SLAVE

We are often reminded that Pyrrhus is, with Hamlet, Laertes and Fortinbras, another son avenging the slaying of his father (Achilles). But Hamlet swings into the rant of his second soliloquy not in any desire to emulate the cruel fury of Pyrrhus but out of shame that an actor's emotion for Pyrrhus's victim, Hecuba, should outdo his own emotion for Claudius's victim, his father. He has done nothing – it is true enough. But the effect of the eloquence of the old play and the actor's moving performance is to make him confuse doing with exhibition. His outburst is violent but essentially comic. His guilt runs away with him. Feeling that if he were a proper avenger he would exhibit a huge amount of passion he lets go a mammoth display of self-accusation and rage, culminating in a great stage-cry, 'O vengeance!'

With this, he becomes ashamed of his hysterical attitudinising and rebukes himself for unpacking his heart with words. He turns from rant to action. What has to be done? The idea of using the players to test the Ghost's veracity was in his mind before he fell 'a-cursing like a very drab' (see 2.2.493–5). Hamlet had approached the Ghost knowing it might be either a demon from hell or a spirit from heaven. Perhaps he accepted it as an 'honest ghost' with too little question. That he should test the Ghost's account before he proceeds to take the king's life is the most obvious precaution. He says all that needs to be said on this subject (551–5). The Ghost could be a spirit from hell taking advantage of his distress to lure him into an act that will damn his soul.

That Hamlet in deciding to use the test of a play is guilty of procrastination is scarcely tenable (see above, p. 39). Procrastination means putting off until tomorrow what you know ought to be done today. *Hamlet* is indeed a tragedy of delay, but procrastination is only one special form of delay. At least part of the reason for his delay so far must be Hamlet's fear that he is being deluded by the devil into imperilling the life of Claudius and the fate of his own soul.

'TO BE OR NOT TO BE'

Act 3 begins next day, the day that the court play is to be given. But even if we are aware of this lapse of time since Hamlet decided to use a play to test the king, it is a shock to us to find Hamlet speaking as he does, for the 'To be or not to be' soliloquy throws everything back into debate.

What *is* the question, 'to be or not to be'? All sorts of answers have been given. I can't doubt that Hamlet is asking whether one should go on living or whether one should take one's life. He is back in the depression of the first soliloquy, longing for the oblivion of death. But now the question whether life is worthwhile has much more knowledge and experience to take account of and brood over, and it assumes an entirely new significance. It is extraordinary that, at this moment in the play, the soliloquy should seem so indifferent to the immediate problem of killing the king. Implicitly the issue is there all the time, but never explicitly. The reason for that is that killing the king has become part of a much wider debate.

> To be or not to be, that is the question –
> Whether 'tis nobler in the mind to suffer
> The slings and arrows of outrageous fortune,
> Or to take arms against a sea of troubles,
> And by opposing end them. To die, to sleep –
> No more; and by a sleep to say we end
> The heart-ache and the thousand natural shocks
> That flesh is heir to – 'tis a consummation
> Devoutly to be wished.

The question is which of two courses is the nobler. The first alternative is 'to be', to go on living, and this is a matter of endurance, of contriving to accept the continuous punishing hostility of life. The second alternative is 'not to be', to take one's life, and this is described as ending a sea of troubles by taking arms against it. There is only the one opposition to be made against the sea of troubles (which is the definition of our life) and that is the constructive act of suicide. Suicide is the one way in which fighting against the ungovernable tide – that mythical symbol of hopeless endeavour – can succeed.

If we accept that Hamlet's alternative in these opening lines is the course of enduring or the course of evading life's onslaught, there is an important consequence. The life that has to be suffered or evaded is described as a continuous, permanent condition of misfortune, and must therefore include the state of the world even after vengeance has been taken and Claudius killed – supposing that to happen. The whips and scorns of time, the oppressor's wrong – there is no indication that these can ever disappear from the world, except by disappearing from the world oneself. By his stark alternative in these opening lines Hamlet implicitly rejects the possibility that any act of his could improve the condition of the world or the condition of its victims. Revenge is of no avail. Whether Hamlet kills the king or not, Denmark will continue to be a prison, a place of suffering ruled by fortune. The only nobleness which is available if one goes on living is not the cleansing of the world by some great holy deed, but endurance, suffering in the mind.

But, as the soliloquy proceeds, the one positive act available to man, suicide, has to be ruled out. The sleep of death becomes a nightmare, because of the dread of damnation. What began as a question which was more noble ends as a contest in cowardliness. What is one the more afraid of, the possibility of damnation or the certainty of suffering on earth?

2 Henry Irving as Hamlet and Ellen Terry as Ophelia in the 'nunnery' scene (3.1), as painted by Edward H. Bell, 1879

And so we do nothing, frightened to take the one route out of our misery. 'Thus conscience doth make cowards of us all.' 'Conscience' means what it normally means, what it means when Claudius uses it just before this (50) and when Hamlet uses it in the previous scene (2.2.558); that is to say, it has its religious meaning of an implanted sense of right and wrong. It is with this reflection that Hamlet moves away from suicide; it is with this 'regard' – this examination of the consequences of things and worrying about how they look in the eye of eternity – that *other* 'enterprises of great pitch and moment' lose the name of action. Hamlet must be thinking about killing Claudius. So, although only by inference and indirectly, Hamlet twice refers to his revenge in this soliloquy. On the first occasion we gather that he no longer has any faith that killing the king would be a cleansing act setting the world to rights; on the second, we gather that his resolution to exact revenge has been 'sicklied o'er' by respects of conscience. His conscience cannot convince him that the act is good; and, whether good or bad, it cannot change the world. We are condemned to unhappiness and to inactivity. Although this speech represents a trough of despair into which we don't see Hamlet fall again, the whole of the rest of the play is coloured by the extreme pessimism of this soliloquy.

It certainly affects his behaviour to Ophelia in the painful, cruel interview which now follows. All he says is backed by a loathing of the world, a loathing of himself, and a loathing of sex. It is hard for Ophelia that she should be in his way just at this moment, to trigger off an eruption of anger and disgust. At the same time, we realise that Hamlet sees his victim as life's victim. Her innocence cannot survive; she is unavoidably subject to the contagion of living; she will be corrupted by men as inevitably as, being a woman, she will corrupt them. When he says she should go to a nunnery, he means a nunnery. Only if she is locked up in perpetual virginity can she be saved. And there will be no more marriage. Hamlet begins to work at a new way of saving mankind – sexual abstinence.

Although I believe that *Hamlet* is primarily a religious play, and that Hamlet perpetually sees himself in a relationship with heaven and hell, yet it is noticeable that Hamlet voices very few really Christian sentiments – as contrasted with both Claudius and Ophelia. Only once, and then in his usual ironic manner, does he talk of praying (1.5.132). It is in this scene of cruelty to Ophelia, if anywhere, that behind the restless, unending teasing and taunting we might feel Hamlet's strong sense of his personal unworthiness and need of assistance. 'What should such fellows as I do crawling between earth and heaven?'

PLAY, PRAYER, MURDER

Hamlet is not content to let his 'mousetrap' play on the murder of Gonzago take its toll of Claudius's conscience without assistance. He forces its significance at Claudius as he later forces the poisoned cup at him (3.2.237–9). His insistent commentary gives Claudius the opportunity to cover his departure with righteous indignation against his nephew's impossible behaviour. At any rate, Hamlet has achieved his purpose. He is convinced of Claudius's guilt and he has made Claudius know that he knows. Hamlet does not lack courage. But what to do with this knowledge now? There is

3 Suggested Elizabethan staging of the play-within-the-play (3.2) by C. Walter Hodges

no way of avoiding the fact that at this critical juncture, with the Ghost's story confirmed, he chooses to do precisely what the Ghost forbade, take action against his mother.

First there is the difficult problem of how to take his extraordinary speech about drinking hot blood.

> 'Tis now the very witching time of night,
> When churchyards yawn, and hell itself breathes out
> Contagion to this world. Now could I drink hot blood,
> And do such bitter business as the day
> Would quake to look on. Soft, now to my mother.
> O heart, lose not thy nature... (3.2.349–54)

Some say that this speech is a sign that Hamlet has committed himself to hell; some say that he is rather awkwardly trying out the traditional role of the avenger of fiction. There is a grain of truth in both these theories, but neither can of itself explain the speech. We have just seen Hamlet, who has been at a peak of emotional intensity during and immediately after the play scene, in a keen and fierce verbal attack on Rosencrantz, Guildenstern and Polonius. That he should at this point in all seriousness bellow out like some Herod of the stage 'Now could I drink hot blood' is to me incredible. The rant of the 'rogue and peasant slave' soliloquy, induced by the emotion of the Pyrrhus speech, was understandable, but this seems quite out of keeping with character and situation. But that Hamlet should *fear* his declension into hellish activity, should *fear* himself slipping into the role of the stage-avenger, I could well imagine. The contagion of hell is what he wishes to avoid, and the *last* thing he wants to do is 'drink hot blood'. He says the words with a shiver of apprehension and disgust. Then, 'Soft, now to my mother.' As so often in this play, 'soft!' is a word of warning to oneself to turn away from some undesirable train of thought and attend to an immediate problem (see the note to 3.1.88). 'O heart, lose not thy nature.' He really does fear he may do something terrible.

Action is now hedged about with all sorts of warnings and limitations concerning the good it can do to the world or the harm it can do to him, But there is one task of primary urgency, whatever the Ghost said: to shame and reclaim his mother. On the way to see her, he comes across Claudius at prayer. He goes over to kill him, then pauses as he had paused over suicide, to reflect on the consequences. Again it is the after-life that is uppermost in his mind, but the fear about damnation now is that Claudius may *not* be damned. He wants Claudius damned, and he is not prepared to take the risk that if he kills him while he is praying he will go to heaven. He will wait for an opportunity that will make revenge more complete and damnation more certain.

> Then trip him that his heels may kick at heaven,
> And that his soul may be as damned and black
> As hell whereto it goes. (3.3.93–5)

Savagery of this order is familiar to students of Elizabethan revenge fiction.[1] Perhaps

[1] See Prosser, *Hamlet and Revenge*, pp. 261–75.

4 'Now might I do it pat' (3.3.73). One of a series of lithographs of the play published by Eugène Delacroix in 1844. Although Delacroix had seen *Hamlet* performed in Paris by the Smithson–Kemble company in 1827, this is purely imaginative, as the prayer scene was cut in performance

the contagion of hell *has* touched Hamlet. But, repellent though it is that Hamlet so passionately wants the eternal perdition of his victim, it is perhaps more striking that he should think that it is in his power to control the fate of Claudius's soul. It is surely a monstrously inflated conception of his authority that is governing him, distorting still further the scope of the Ghost's injunctions. In this scene the arrogance of the man who is trying to effect justice is strongly contrasted with the Christian humility of the man who has done murder.

Hamlet means what he says in the prayer scene. The procrastination theory held that once again Hamlet was finding some excuse for not acting. This cannot be right, for a minute or two later, thinking he has found Claudius in the ignominious and dishonourable position of eavesdropping behind the arras in Gertrude's chamber, he kills him – only to find that it is Polonius. The killing of Polonius is a major climax. In spite of whatever doubts and mental stress about the authority of the Ghost and the meaning of its message, about the need to do the deed or the good it would do, here deliberately and violently he keeps his word and carries out his revenge; and he kills the wrong man. This terrible irony is the direct result of his decisions since the end of the play scene, which imply his belief in his power to control the destinies in this life and in the after-life of both Gertrude and Claudius, his assumption of the role of Providence itself.

From the killing of Polonius the catastrophe of the play stems.[1] This false completion of Hamlet's revenge initiates the second cycle of revenge for a murdered father, that of Laertes for Polonius. *That* revenge is successful and ends in the death of Hamlet. By unwittingly killing Polonius, Hamlet brings about his own death.

THE CLOSET SCENE

Nothing in the play is more bizarre than that Hamlet, having committed the terrible error of killing Polonius, should be so consumed with the desire to purge and rescue his mother that he goes right on with his castigation even with the dead body of Polonius at his feet. No wonder the Ghost enters again to whet his 'almost blunted purpose'. Hamlet well knows that in this present heat ('time and passion') he should be obedient to his vow and apply himself to a grimmer task. But he does nothing. It is remarkable that he fears the presence of the Ghost will actually weaken his resolve to kill Claudius: that his response to this shape of his dead father will be pity not retribution. The Ghost could 'convert / My stern effects' and there would be 'tears perchance for blood' (3.4.126–29). This fear for the strength of his resolution should be compared with the heavy-heartedness at the prospect of carrying out the execution as he looks at Polonius's corpse: 'Thus bad begins and worse remains behind' (180).

There seems no deep compunction for Polonius's death, however, and no lessening of the sense of his privilege to ordain for others.

> For this same lord,
> I do repent; but heaven hath pleased it so,
> To punish me with this, and this with me,
> That I must be their scourge and minister. (3.4.173–6)

[1] Compare A. C. Bradley, *Shakespearean Tragedy*, 1904, p. 136.

Poor Polonius! Hamlet is at his worst in these scenes. His self-righteousness expands in his violent rebukes of his mother and his eagerness to order her sex-life. 'Forgive me this my virtue', he says, going on to explain that in these upside-down times 'virtue itself of vice must pardon beg'. Yet the force of his words, and what appears to be the first intimation that her husband was murdered, instil into her that sense of difference which he has fought to re-establish. At the beginning she asks in indignation and bewilderment, 'What have I done?' But later she says, 'O Hamlet, speak no more', and 'What shall I do?'

TO ENGLAND

From this point onwards there are two plays of *Hamlet*, that of the second quarto and that of the Folio. I have argued (pp. 14–19) that the Folio version with its omissions and additions has much to be said for it, knowing what its hero has become by the end of the closet scene in a way that the seemingly more tentative and exploratory version in the second quarto does not. The changes in the Folio substitute for a rather contradictory talkativeness in Hamlet about being sent to England with his revenge unaccomplished a silence as mysterious and suggestive as the silence that lies between Acts 1 and 2. They also add a central passage in 5.2 in which the problem of damnation which has occupied Hamlet throughout is given an answer.

There is a real want of resolution concerning his revenge in Hamlet's going away to England, though it is concealed in the exciting scenes in which he courageously and scornfully spars with Claudius, who is now absolutely determined to destroy the man who knows his secret. It may be that he is biding his time, or is baffled and mortified by his own inability to act, as the two main passages omitted from the Folio suggest, but we feel that there are deeper things restraining him, hinted at in what he says to Horatio when he comes back.

> Sir, in my heart there was a kind of fighting
> That would not let me sleep. (5.2.4–5)

While Hamlet is away, we see the effects of what he has so far achieved, in the madness of Ophelia and the furious return of Laertes. To avenge his father is for Laertes an inalienable duty, whatever may be its status in the eternal world.

> Conscience and grace to the profoundest pit!
> I dare damnation. To this point I stand,
> That both the worlds I give to negligence,
> Let come what comes, only I'll be revenged
> Most throughly for my father. (4.5.132–6)

For Hamlet it is quite the contrary. Revenge in itself is uninteresting and foreign. It is only the question of its place as a creative and restorative 'remembering' deed within the values of the eternal world that is important to him.

THE RETURN

The news of Hamlet's return astounds the king, and he hastens to employ Laertes in a scheme to destroy him finally. Act 5 opens with the two clowns digging a grave for Ophelia. The joke of the senior of these, the sexton, that of all men he who builds strongest is the gravedigger, is something to ponder on at the end of the play. The sexton is the only person in the play who is a match for Hamlet in the combat of words. He manages to avoid answering Hamlet's question, 'Whose grave's this?' Not until the funeral procession arrives does Hamlet learn that the grave is for Ophelia, and it does not appear from the play that he was aware of her madness. Many people feel that in Hamlet's reflections over the empty grave on the vanity of life and the inevitability of death there is a mature and sober wisdom. But the presentation of this wisdom is entirely ironic. His truths are based on a chasm of ignorance. He speaks his words over a grave which he does not know is intended for a woman whose madness and death he is responsible for.[1] The fact of the dead girl punctures his philosophy. For us, at any rate. He never speaks of his regret for the suffering he caused her even before Polonius's death. On the contrary, when Laertes leaps into the grave and expresses, too clamantly perhaps, an affection for Ophelia which he genuinely feels, Hamlet will not accept it, and chooses this moment to advance and declare himself, with a challenge to Laertes' sincerity. He claims 'I loved Ophelia' – with a love forty thousand brothers could not match. It is hard to know what right Hamlet has to say that when we think of how we have seen him treat her. The dispute over Ophelia's grave seems very important. Laertes is more than a foil to Hamlet; he is a main antagonist, diametrically opposed to him in every way of thought and action, who is scheming to kill him by a dreadful trick. But Shakespeare refuses to belittle him or let us despise him. And he refuses to sentimentalise his opponent or whitewash his failings. For those of us who to any extent 'believe in' Hamlet, Shakespeare makes things difficult in this scene. It is tragedy not sentimental drama that he is writing, and our division of mind about Hamlet is partly why the play is a tragedy.

In the all-important colloquy with Horatio at the beginning of the final scene, Hamlet tells him of the strong sense he has that his impulsive actions on board ship were guided by a divinity which takes over from us 'when our deep plots do pall' and redirects us. This is a critical juncture of the play, implying Hamlet's surrender of his grandiose belief in his power to ordain and control, and his release from the alternating belief in the meaningless and mindless drift of things. His recognition, vital though it is, is his own, and we do not necessarily have to share it.

The sense of heaven guiding him reinforces rather than diminishes his sense of personal responsibility for completing his mission. The discovery of the king's treachery in the commission to have him murdered in England has fortified Hamlet's determination. Yet it is with a demand for assurance that he puts the matter to Horatio.

> Does it not, think thee, stand me now upon –
> He that hath killed my king, and whored my mother,
> Popped in between th'election and my hopes,
> Thrown out his angle for my proper life,
> And with such cozenage – is't not perfect conscience
> To quit him with this arm? And is't not to be damned
> To let this canker of our nature come
> In further evil? (5.2.63–70)

[1] See the excellent comment by Dover Wilson, *What Happens in 'Hamlet'*, 1935; 3rd edn, 1951, p. 268.

5 The staging of the scene at Ophelia's grave (5.1), drawn by C. Walter Hodges. It is assumed (as argued in the Commentary at 5.1.225) that Hamlet does not leap into the grave after Laertes, but that Laertes scrambles out to attack him

It is difficult to see how we can take this speech except as the conclusion of a long and deep perplexity. But if it is a conclusion, that question mark – conveying so much more than indignation – makes it an appeal by this loneliest of heroes for support and agreement, which he pointedly does not get from the cautious Horatio, who simply says,

> It must be shortly known to him from England
> What is the issue of the business there.

Horatio won't accept the responsibility of answering, and only gives him the exasperating response that he hasn't much time.

Once again Hamlet has raised the question of conscience and damnation. Conscience is no longer an obstacle to action, but encourages it. As for damnation, Hamlet had felt the threat of it if he contemplated suicide, felt the threat of it if he were to kill at the behest of a devil–ghost; now he feels the threat of it if he should fail to remove from the world a cancer which is spreading. This new image for Claudius, a 'canker of our nature', is important. All the vituperation which Hamlet has previously thrown at Claudius seems mere rhetoric by this. Hamlet now sees himself undertaking a surgical operation to remove a cancer from human society. Whether the slings and arrows of outrageous fortune continue or not is immaterial. To neglect, ignore or encourage the evil is to imperil one's soul.

THE SILENCE OF THE GHOST

When in reply to Hamlet's unanswerable question Horatio tells him that if he is going to act he had better move quickly, because as soon as Claudius learns the fate of Rosencrantz and Guildenstern Hamlet won't have another hour to live, Hamlet exclaims 'The interim's mine.' But of course it isn't, because the plot against his life has already been primed and is about to go off. Hamlet has no time left to act upon his new conviction that it is a religious duty to strike down Claudius. He accepts the fake challenge of the fencing match in the awareness that something may be afoot, and he faces it without any exhilaration: 'Thou wouldst not think how ill all's here about my heart.' When he says 'If it be now, 'tis not to come... the readiness is all', we assume he has some kind of prevision of what actually happens, the coming together of his revenge and his own death. Laertes wounds him fatally before he is able to make his second attempt to kill the king. The first time, he killed the wrong man; the second time, he kills the king indeed, but not until he is within moments of his own death.

There is no doubt of the extent of Hamlet's failure. In trying to restore 'the beauteous majesty of Denmark' he has brought the country into an even worse state, in the hands of a foreigner. He is responsible, directly or indirectly, for the deaths of Polonius, Ophelia, Rosencrantz and Guildenstern. With more justification, he has killed Laertes and Claudius. But if his uncle is dead, so is his mother.

What does the Ghost think of it all? He has disappeared. There is no word of approval, or sorrow, or anger. He neither praises his dead son nor blames him. Nor, if he was a devil, does he come back to gloat over the devastation he has caused. The rest is silence indeed.[1]

In Kyd's *Spanish Tragedy*, the ghost of the dead Andrea and his escort from the infernal world of spirits, named Revenge, were on stage during the whole of the play. It was absolutely clear that the ultimate direction of things was entirely in the hands of the gods of the underworld. At the end of the play Andrea rejoiced in the fulfilment of his revenge and happily surveyed the carnage on the stage. 'Ay, these were spectacles to please my soul!' He helped to apportion eternal sentences, whose 'justice' makes our blood run cold.

In spite of the seeming crudity of *The Spanish Tragedy*, it is a subtle and sinister view of the relation of gods and men that the play conveys. Kyd's gods are dark gods. Men and women plot and scheme to fulfil their desires and satisfy their hatreds, they appeal to heaven for guidance, help and approval, but the dark gods are in charge of everything, and they use every morsel of human striving in order to achieve their predestined purposes. Hieronimo's heroic efforts to obtain justice, which drive him into madness and his wife to suicide, are nothing to the gods except as they may be used to fulfil their promise to Andrea.

Hamlet resists the grim certainties of Kyd's theology and the certainties of any other.[2] Hamlet's own belief towards the end of the play that a benign divinity works through our spontaneous impulses and even our mistakes is neither clearly endorsed by the play nor repudiated in ironic Kydean laughter. Hamlet is a tragic hero who at a time of complete despair hears a mysterious voice uttering a directive which he interprets as a mission to renovate the world by an act of purifying violence. But this voice is indeed a questionable voice. How far it is the voice of heaven, how its words are to be translated into human deeds, how far the will of man *can* change the course of the world – these are questions that torment the idealist as he continues to plague the decadent inhabitants, as he sees them, of the Danish court.[3]

His doubts, at one edge of his nature, are as extreme as his confidence at the other. His sense of his freedom to create his own priorities and decisions, and indeed his sense of being heaven's scourge and minister privileged to destroy at will, bring him to the disaster of killing Polonius, from which point all changes, and he becomes the hunted as well as the hunter. Eventually, in a new humility as his 'deep plots' pall, Hamlet becomes convinced that heaven is guiding him and that the removal of Claudius is a task that he is to perform at the peril of his immortal soul. He does indeed kill Claudius, but the cost is dreadful. What has he achieved, as he dies with Claudius?

[1] The absence of the Ghost at the end, in contrast with *The Spanish Tragedy*, is noted by H. Levin, *The Question of 'Hamlet'*, 1959, p. 98. A view of the reason for the Ghost's disappearance which is very different from mine is given in two adjoining articles in *Shakespeare Survey* 30 (1977), by Philip Brockbank (p. 107) and Barbara Everett (p. 118).

[2] The view that Shakespeare is making a positive comment on Kyd is developed in Edwards, 'Shakespeare and Kyd', in *Shakespeare, Man of the Theatre*, ed. K. Muir, J. L. Halio and D. J. Palmer, 1983.

[3] For the relation of this passage to Lucien Goldmann's *The Hidden God*, 1955, see Edwards, 'Tragic balance in *Hamlet*', pp. 45–6.

It is very hard for us in the twentieth century to sympathise with Hamlet and his mission. Hearing voices from a higher world belongs mainly in the realm of abnormal psychology. Revenge may be common but is hardly supportable. The idea of purifying violence belongs to terrorist groups. Gertrude's sexual behaviour and remarriage do not seem out of the ordinary. Yet if we feel that twentieth-century doubt hampers our understanding of the seventeenth-century *Hamlet*, we must remember that *Hamlet* was actually written in our own age of doubt and revaluation – only a little nearer its beginning. *Hamlet* takes for granted that the ethics of revenge are questionable, that ghosts are questionable, that the distinctions of society are questionable, and that the will of heaven is terribly obscure. The higher truth which Hamlet tries to make active in a fallen world belongs to a past which he sees slipping away from him. Shakespeare movingly presents the beauty of a past in which kingship, marriage and the order of society had or was believed to have a heavenly sanction. A brutal Cain-like murder destroys the order of the past. Hamlet struggles to restore the past, and as he does so we feel that the desirability is delicately and perilously balanced against the futility. Shakespeare was by no means eager to share Nietzsche's acquiescence in time's *es war*. This matter of balance is an essential part of our answer about the ending of the play. It is a precarious balance, and perhaps impossible to maintain.

The Elizabethans too doubted ghosts. Shakespeare used the concern of his time about voices and visions to suggest the treacherousness of communication with the transcendent world. We come in the end to accept the Ghost not as a devil but as a spirit who speaks truth yet who cannot with any sufficiency or adequacy provide the answer to Hamlet's cry, 'What should we do?' Everything depends on interpretation and translation. A terrible weight of responsibility is thrown on to the human judgement and will. Kierkegaard, in *Fear and Trembling*, spoke of Abraham hearing a voice from heaven and trusting it to the extent of being willing to kill his own son; and he wrote brilliantly of the knife-edge which divides an act of faith from a demoniacal impulse. In Shakespeare's age, William Tyndale also used Abraham as an example of where faith might go outside the boundaries of ethics, but he warned against 'holy works' which had their source in what he contemptuously called 'man's imaginations'.[1] These distinctions between acts of faith and the demoniacal, between holy works and works of man's imagination, seem fundamental to *Hamlet*. We know that Hamlet made a mess of what he was trying to do. The vital question is whether what he was trying to do was a holy work or a work of man's imagination. Shakespeare refuses to tell us.

Hamlet's attempt to make a higher truth operative in the world of Denmark, which is where all of us live, is a social and political disaster, and it pushes him into inhumanity and cruelty. But the unanswerable question, 'Is't not to be damned / To let this canker of our nature come / In further evil?', if it could be answered 'Yes!' would make us see the chance-medley of the play's ending in a light so different that it would abolish our merely moral judgement. Bradley's final remark on the play was that 'the apparent failure of Hamlet's life is not the ultimate truth concerning him'.[2]

[1] Edwards, 'Tragic balance in *Hamlet*', p. 51.

[2] *Shakespearean Tragedy*, p. 174.

But it might be. That is where the tragic balance lies. The play of *Hamlet* takes place within the possibility that there is a higher court of values than those which operate around us, within the possibility of having some imperfect communication with that court, within the possibility that an act of violence can purify, within the possibility that the words 'salvation' and 'damnation' have meaning. To say that these possibilities are certainties is to wreck the play as surely as to say they are impossibilities.

So the silence of the Ghost at the end of the play leaves the extent of Hamlet's victory or triumph an open question. To answer it needs a knowledge that Horatio didn't have, that Shakespeare didn't have, that we don't have. The mortal havoc is plain to our eyes on the stage; the rest is silence.

Hamlet and the actors

The stage history of *Hamlet* is richly documented. A great deal of information is available on scenery and settings, on costume, on stage-business, on how the great actors of the past handled individual scenes. In this section I shall concentrate on one aspect of stage history alone, and continue with the theme of the shape of this Protean play by looking at the tradition of cutting and its effect on the *Hamlet* that was presented to audiences until the end of the nineteenth century.

Our first evidence of the shape of the play on the stage is provided by the bad quarto of 1603. Here is *Hamlet*, within a year or two of its first production on Shakespeare's stage, in a severely truncated form, with the order of scenes changed, with new material written in to make up for scenes cut out, and stage-business introduced (like Hamlet's leap into the grave). This acting text, corruptly rendered in the quarto, was based on the version prepared by Shakespeare's company, and it has to be accepted that some of its cuts and changes may derive from the original promptbook (see above, p. 25). Whatever its underlying authority, the first quarto well illustrates the desire to speed up the action after the death of Polonius, a desire which will manifest itself for another two hundred years.

How far what one might call the promptbook tradition of the acting-text of *Hamlet* (shown however eccentrically in the bad quarto) was affected by the literary version available from 1604 in the good quarto and its reprints is impossible to say, but there is some evidence that the two traditions intertwined.

What John Downes said (in his *Roscius Anglicanus* of 1708) about the unbroken tradition in the acting of *Hamlet* from the time of Shakespeare to the end of the century cannot be accepted literally. But as Downes was 'Book keeper and prompter' at the Lincoln's Inn Fields Theatre from 1662 to 1706, his testimony must be attended to. He claimed that Sir William Davenant, the theatre's licensee, had seen Joseph Taylor act Hamlet in the old Blackfriars theatre; that Taylor had been instructed by Shakespeare himself; that Davenant had 'taught Mr Betterton in every particle of it'.[1]

[1] *The Shakspere Allusion-Book*, 1932, II, 433–6.

Now Taylor joined the King's men only after the death of Shakespeare; he replaced Burbage as chief actor when the latter died in 1619. Nevertheless, as the man who took over Burbage's roles, Taylor presumably took over in Hamlet a part that in text and general conduct was the one played by Burbage and familiar to his colleagues. To that extent Taylor's Hamlet goes back to Shakespeare's time, though it is far from certain that Shakespeare took a controlling hand in creating the final acting version of his *Hamlet* or in coaching Burbage in his part.

Our evidence for the Restoration shape of the play is what is known as the Players' Quarto of 1676 'as it is now acted at his Highness the Duke of York's Theatre'.[1] This is a reprint of the last pre-Civil War quarto of 1637 with such passages as are 'left out upon the Stage' enclosed within inverted commas. This is done, says the note to the reader, 'according to the original copy'. It is not at all clear how the printed text of 1637 was collated with the stage version. The line that now appears in the received text at 1.2.77, following the Folio reading, as

> 'Tis not alone my inky cloak, good mother

had appeared in the good quarto as

> Tis not alone my incky cloake coold mother

and is now transformed into

> 'Tis not alone this mourning cloke could smother

Could this possibly have been spoken by Betterton on the stage? What could anyone think it meant? Hazelton Spencer made a detailed study of the 1676 quarto[2] and concluded from the style of the numerous verbal refinements that Davenant was the person responsible for this adaptation. But he did not explain why such nonsense as the line quoted above was allowed to stand, nor why the smoothing and regularising of Shakespeare's diction extended to passages marked as having been 'left out upon the Stage'.

Spencer insisted that the 1676 quarto does not derive in any way from the Folio version of 1623. But one wonders if the 'original copy' used in the playhouse was so innocent of Folio influence. The way in which Davenant's cuts agree with the Folio cuts is uncanny if they were made independently. Here at least the tradition of playing in Shakespeare's day may be felt. The cuts which appear in the Folio text were made, I have argued (p. 19), just before and during the preparation of the fair copy when the play had still to receive its first stage performance. By whatever route these cuts were transmitted, their general pattern was preserved in the Restoration theatre, and hence in the Players' Quarto of 1676 which otherwise has a purely non-Folio provenance. These same cuts, probably made in 1601, endured in the theatre for nearly 300 years. The Folio *additions*, however, did not come through; if any of them were

[1] The very interesting Restoration promptbook of *Hamlet* for Smock Alley, Dublin, preserved in Edinburgh University Library, clearly shows an attempt to bring its Third Folio text into line with the cutting of the 1676 quarto. See G. Blakemore Evans (ed.), *Shakespearean Prompt-Books of the Seventeenth Century*, IV, 1966. A single leaf (from the First Folio) of an unrecorded seventeenth-century promptbook was sold at Sotheby's in July 1983.

[2] See *Shakespeare Improved*, 1927, pp. 174–87; and *PMLA* 38 (1923), 770–91.

spoken on the Restoration stage they were not inserted in the Players' Quarto, and were lost to the stage version of *Hamlet*. Even though later acting editions show knowledge of the Folio text, it would appear that, after Shakespeare's time, those key lines, 'Is't not to be damned / To let this canker of our nature come / In further evil?', were not heard again in the theatre until Booth's performance around 1870 – they are not often heard now.

The additional cuts which were made in the Davenant–Betterton *Hamlet* did not establish a definitive pattern for the acted play, but many of them became standard. (So did many rephrasings. Hamlet's words as he sees the kneeling Claudius should be 'Now might I do it pat, now he is a-praying', but they became 'Where is this murderer, he kneels and prays'. This version lasted until the whole scene was ditched in the mid eighteenth century by Garrick.) The Norwegian element is much reduced. The account of Fortinbras's 'revenge' in 1.1 is truncated, and the whole business of Claudius sending ambassadors to Norway (1.2 and 2.1) is omitted. In 1.3 a 'permanent' cut is established with the omission of Polonius's advice to Laertes, and another with the omission of his instructions to Reynaldo in 2.1. (By 'permanent' I mean until the initiation at the very end of the nineteenth century of theatrical versions based upon the full standard editions.)

A bad cut, not repeated, is that most of Hamlet's speech on being confronted by the Ghost disappears – 'Angels and ministers of grace defend us...' The 'rogue and peasant slave' soliloquy at the end of 2.2 is gutted. This was never popular, though it was later cut in different ways. The nature of Hamlet is quite changed by the abbreviation of this soliloquy. Like the revenger in some much simpler tragedy, Hamlet just blames himself for delay and then gets on with a plan of action. Claudius is also simplified by the omission of his guilty aside in 3.1, 'How smart a lash...' This remains a permanent cut. The advice to the players in 3.2 goes out (restored in later versions), while the dumb-show, always cut in later versions, stays in. There is a good deal of abbreviation in the latter part of the third act, including Hamlet's hope to damn Claudius's soul, and the beginning of the fourth. The scene with Fortinbras's army in 4.4 is omitted entirely, though at the end of the play Fortinbras's entry is retained in full.

Thomas Betterton had first played Hamlet in 1663 and he appeared for the last time in the part in 1709, when he was in his seventies. The main Hamlets of the early eighteenth century, up to the London debut of Garrick in the part in 1742, were Robert Wilks, who acted it from 1707 to his death in 1732, Lacy Ryan, who played the part for thirty-one years from 1719, and Henry Giffard, who took the role for seventeen years from 1730. To Robert Wilks goes the credit of establishing the standard Hamlet of the theatre; for his version of the Davenant–Betterton text held sway, with comparatively minor alteration, for well over a hundred years. His version 'as it is now acted by his Majesty's servants' was first published in 1718 and was reprinted many times up to 1761. It was prepared by John Hughs, who had helped Rowe with his edition of Shakespeare,[1] and derives both from Rowe's edition and from the old Players' Quarto. Some Folio readings are included, for example Hamlet's passionate

[1] See H. N. Paul, *MLN* 49 (1934), 438–43.

line, 'Why man, they did make love to this employment' (5.2.57), only to be marked with the tell-tale inverted commas to indicate it was not spoken on the stage!

The Davenant–Betterton thinning of the Fortinbras–Old Hamlet duel and its consequence in 1.1, and the omission of all the Norwegian material in 1.2 and 2.1, are accepted. In 1.4/5, most of Hamlet's lines on seeing the Ghost are restored, but the Ghost's self-praise, 'what a falling off was there', is cut by ten lines. The advice to the players is restored, but the dumb-show is cut.

The chief innovation of the Hughs–Wilks version is the removal of Fortinbras from the end of the play. Fortinbras and the ambassadors are announced. Hamlet dies, giving Fortinbras his voice in the election, as in the received text. But the play now ends with Horatio, annexing the last lines of Fortinbras.

> Now cracks the cordage of a noble heart: good night, sweet prince,
> And choirs of angels sing thee to thy rest.
> Bear Hamlet like a soldier to the stage,
> For he was likely...[etc.]

Fortinbras does not reappear in the play's ending until Forbes Robertson's production in 1897.

For many years, David Garrick acted a *Hamlet* based upon the Hughs–Wilks text, with one or two important changes. His acting version, put out in 1763 by George Colman, who thought that Garrick, then abroad because of ill health, would never return to the stage,[1] restores a good deal of the 'rogue and peasant slave' soliloquy, but astonishingly removes the whole of Hamlet's entry and speech in 3.3 with Claudius at prayer, 'Now might I do it pat.' The closet scene is further curtailed, with no mention of Hamlet going to England. In 5.2, Hamlet's relation to Horatio of what happened on shipboard is entirely cut. So no one knows of the fate of Rosencrantz and Guildenstern.

In 1772 Garrick was moved to do 'the most imprudent thing I ever did in my life'. 'I have played the devil this winter', he wrote to Morellet, 'I have dared to alter *Hamlet*, I have thrown away the gravediggers, and all the fifth act...' 'A bold deed,' he said to another French correspondent, 'but the event has answered my most sanguine expectation.'[2] Garrick brought Hamlet back after Ophelia's final 'mad' exit in 4.5. He and Laertes fight, and, as Claudius tries to stop them, Hamlet kills him. Gertrude rushes off, to an indeterminate fate. Hamlet 'runs upon Laertes's sword and falls'. He and Laertes exchange forgiveness, and the play ends. This collapsing of the fifth act has the very interesting consequence that in order to fill out the play a good deal of material found only in the 1604 quarto is brought back into the play. This includes lines in 1.1 which are omitted in the Folio text and Hamlet's soliloquy in 4.4, 'How all occasions do inform against me'. Probably this was the first time this soliloquy was performed and once Garrick's alteration ceased to be played it vanished again for more than a hundred years. Other restorations were Voltimand and Cornelius, and Polonius's advice to Laertes (in part).[3]

[1] See G. W. Stone, Jr, *PMLA* 49 (1934), 896.
[2] *Ibid.*, p. 893; see also Garrick's *Letters*, ed. D. M. Little and G. M. Kahrl, 1963, II, 841, 840.
[3] See G. W. Stone's helpful table comparing cuts, *PMLA* 49 (1934), 903.

6 'Do you not come your tardy son to chide?' (3.4.106). Redrawn by Du Guernier for the 1714 edition of Rowe's Shakespeare, appearing also in Pope's second edition (1728) from which this is taken. The earlier engraving showed Hamlet's overturned chair, but not the large double bed. For the portraits on the wall, see the Commentary at 3.4.53. This engraving and its predecessor have no specific theatrical authority

Garrick's version was well received in France – Voltaire approved – and it managed to hold its own on the English stage for some years. But new Hamlets went back to the earlier acting version of Garrick's, and that is basically what we find in the printed acting-text of 1779, with its frontispiece of 'Mr Henderson in the Character of Hamlet'. Garrick refused to publish his altered version; it was lost to view after his death, but is now in the Folger Shakespeare Library in Washington.

With the *Hamlet* of John Philip Kemble (who acted in it from 1783 to 1817), the play reached its leanest version. Well under 3,000 lines in length, the text reads very well; it *is* a play, fast-moving, exciting. But the audience could have found little depth or mystery in this disembowelled *Hamlet*. The 'rogue and peasant slave' soliloquy is devastated, so that Hamlet, quite unaffected by the Hecuba speech, moves straight on to plan the 'mousetrap'. Again the speech in which Hamlet refrains from killing the praying Claudius is absent. One strange innovation was to put into the prose of Hamlet's letter to Horatio the later verse account (from 5.2) of the exchange of the commission on board ship and the doom of Rosencrantz and Guildenstern. *Hamlet* in the theatre has become a series of famous scenes taken from a libretto that is never acted in full: meeting the Ghost, 'To be or not to be', the nunnery scene, the closet scene, Ophelia mad, the graveyard scene, and so on. It was in comparing Kemble's Hamlet with Kean's that Hazlitt – who so passionately loved the theatre – was led to say: 'We do not like to see our author's plays acted, and least of all, HAMLET. There is no play that suffers so much in being transferred to the stage.'[1] It is an important truth about *Hamlet* that it always has to be 'transferred to the stage'; it never was, as we have seen, a work that the theatre could accommodate without severe alteration. One can't really complain that the stage debases *Hamlet*: it has to. One can complain about degrees of debasement, however.

Kean's Hamlet made no important innovations in the text. Macready is supposed to have been the first to bring the curtain down on 'The rest is silence.'[2] The version of Charles Kean – he started acting Hamlet in 1838 – restored Polonius's precepts to Laertes and the whole of the 'rogue and peasant slave' soliloquy. The erosion of the latter part of the play continues; it had been going on since 1601. Claudius's prayer and Hamlet's 'Now might I do it pat' are out. Hamlet's letter to Horatio is cut entirely – so the king's puzzlement about Hamlet's return is shared by the audience. Neither Gertrude nor Claudius dies on stage. Gertrude is 'conveyed off...in a dying state', and Claudius 'is borne away...mortally wounded'.[3]

The Hamlet of the American actor, Edwin Booth, is very fully documented, with an entire book devoted to it by C. H. Shattuck (*The Hamlet of Edwin Booth*, 1969). Booth's version varied a good deal in the thirty-eight years he played the part, 1853–91. Though he 'only tinkered with the acting version which he had received from tradition', he had the courage to bring back the prayer scene, including 'Now might I do it pat', and the full version of Hamlet's account to Horatio of his adventures at sea in 5.2. Whether the New York audience realised it or not, they were being

[1] *The Characters of Shakespeare's Plays*, 1817, in *Complete Works*, ed. P. P. Howe, 1930–4, IV, 237.
[2] See Harold Child in Dover Wilson's edition, 1934, p. xc.
[3] There is a facsimile reprint of Kean's 1859 acting version in the Cornmarket series, 1971.

allowed to witness essential parts of the play that had scarcely ever been staged in an unmutilated form. Booth was perhaps the first actor since the days of Burbage and Taylor to speak the crucial lines, 'Is't not to be damned...' (5.2.68–70). Charles Clarke, who recorded Booth's 1870 performance in the greatest detail, thought that this narration of Hamlet to Horatio was 'of little interest save to the literary people' and believed that Booth included it only to give the stage-hands time to clear away the graveyard scene and prepare for the final court scene.[1] Be that as it may, Booth found that his 2,750-line version of 1870 was too long for his audience. Both 'Now might I do it pat' and the narration in 5.2 were dropped in the performances of later years.

Henry Irving's stage version for the Lyceum, which he published in 1879, was the conventional abbreviated version without Fortinbras, the ambassadors, the dumb-show, the prayer scene, 'How all occasions', the narration in 5.2 etc. Yet it lasted four hours, according to the introduction. An unfamiliar figure in the theatre, Reynaldo, made a brief appearance in 2.1. At the Lyceum in the next decade, Forbes Robertson was much more adventurous. Although to someone coming fresh from a knowledge of the full text his published version of 1897 would seem scandalously curtailed and bowdlerised, it was in fact boldly innovative. Some account of the duel between the Fortinbras and Hamlet of the older generation is included in 1.1. 'Now might I do it pat' is given – including the hope to have Claudius damned. At the end, after an absence of nearly two hundred years, Fortinbras appears to take over the Danish throne. The material is truncated but Fortinbras is there. Bernard Shaw had encouraged Forbes Robertson to resurrect Fortinbras, and he was delighted with the result.[2]

With the re-appearance of Fortinbras we are at the end of an acting tradition going back to Betterton. In 1881 William Poel had produced the first quarto version of 1603 at St George's Hall, and in 1899 at the Shakespeare Memorial Theatre in Stratford-upon-Avon F. R. Benson produced a complete *Hamlet* – the whole play as it appears in standard editions, in the composite good quarto plus First Folio version. It took six hours to play. The complete version continued to be staged from time to time. Martin Browne, who acted in it in 1936, says it was known as the 'Entirety'; it was a regular feature at the Old Vic for several years, and always sold out.[3]

The text of *Hamlet* in the twentieth-century theatre does not have a single story to tell. Pressures of very different kinds have pushed the play into all sorts of shapes. The film, modern dress, Elizabethan staging, Freudian interpretations, director's theatre, have all required a *Hamlet* with a particular emphasis, and the play has been tailored accordingly. The laudable wish to be faithful to Shakespeare's text has had some odd consequences. The 'Entirety' is a monster, an assemblage which was never seen on Shakespeare's stage and was never meant to be. A well-known director, asked in public if he would explain the policy he had adopted in what had seemed to the audience a bizarre cutting of the play, replied that he had wished to give *some*

[1] Shattuck, *Hamlet of Edwin Booth*, pp. 265–7.
[2] See W. A. Armstrong, *SQ* 15 (1964), 27–31.
[3] *Shakespeare Survey* 9 (1956), 19.

7 J. P. Kemble as Hamlet, by Sir Thomas Lawrence (Royal Academy, 1801). This was bought by W. A. Madocks, who intended it as an altar-piece in the church of his model town of Tremadoc in North Wales. But the bishop of the diocese refused to allow this, and it was eventually sold to George IV

8 'Go on, I'll follow thee' (1.4.86). Forbes Robertson as Hamlet in a 1913 film made by Hepworth Studios. Walton-on-Thames. The cast was the same as for Forbes Robertson's farewell performance at Drury Lane earlier in the year

representation of every speech in the full composite version and that this had necessitated scooping out the middle of the lengthier speeches.

One cannot help thinking that the panjandrums of 'director's theatre' have done greater damage to the integrity of *Hamlet* than the old actor-managers ever did. Perhaps more of the lines which Shakespeare wrote are included, but since the import of those lines is squeezed and contorted to fit the mould of the director's idea of the play, the gain is not worth having. The excitement of witnessing *Hamlet* in the theatre used to be in seeing how a great actor like Kean or Irving would handle the meeting with the Ghost or treat Ophelia in the nunnery scene. Good acting can always quicken one's understanding of individual moments of the text, whatever happens to the play as a whole. My personal experience of the 'director's theatre' of the last few decades is that the servile business of conforming to the director's idea of the play as a whole positively discourages great acting, and that the true interpretive value of Shakespeare on stage has sadly declined in productions that are all 'interpretation'.

9 The burial of Ophelia (5.1). Modern-dress production at the London Old Vic, 1938, produced by Tyrone Guthrie, with settings and costumes by Roger Furse. Alec Guinness as Hamlet

Names

The names in *Hamlet* are a motley collection. Hamlet and Gertrude derive from the original names in Saxo Grammaticus, and an attempt to provide further Danish names can be seen in Rosencrantz and Guildenstern, in Voltemand (Valdemar), and also in Yaughan and Yorick (both mentioned in Act 5), and Osric (though as Jenkins points out this latter is also a good Anglo-Saxon name).

Laertes and Ophelia are from Greek, Laertes being the name of Ulysses' father. Claudius is very Roman, like Marcellus and Cornelius. Horatio, Francisco, Barnardo are run-of-the-mill playhouse names. (Horatio was the name of the murdered son in *The Spanish Tragedy*.) Fortinbras, with its Frenchness ('Strong-arm'), is an odd name for a Norwegian king and his son. Polonius is even more perplexing; Polonia was a regular name for Poland.

The forms of the names, like almost everything to do with the play, are very unstable. Gertrude, the established spelling of the queen's name, comes from the Folio, and is almost certainly not the way Shakespeare wrote it, for it appears in the second quarto as Gertrard (and once as Gertrad). The spelling Rosencrantz was not established until the eighteenth century. It looks as though the second quarto spelling Rosencraus is this time not Shakespeare's but a continued misreading of 'Rosencrans';

the regular form in the Folio is Rosincrance. It has been thought best to retain the established forms of Gertrude and Rosencrantz in this edition. Barnardo is a different matter; this is the spelling of both quarto and Folio, and there is no reason to follow the editorial form Bernardo.

The most striking change in naming takes place outside the two main texts. Polonius becomes Corambis in the bad quarto, and his man becomes Montano. I have argued earlier (p. 25) that the change may well have been official; that is, the bad quarto may register a change made for performance by the Chamberlain's men at the Globe. If so, it is impossible now to say what led to the change. Perhaps there was the danger of some offence in the earlier name; perhaps someone thought it was odd to suggest that the Danish counsellor was a Pole. Whether the change was made by Shakespeare's company or not, it is interesting that the new name was certainly in Shakespeare's mind around the year 1603, for he included 'Corambus' in the rag-bag list of names of officers produced by Parolles in *All's Well That Ends Well* 4.3.161–5. But it looks as though Corambis was coined to suit the role of the Danish counsellor. Gollancz made the excellent suggestion that the name comes from 'crambe' or 'crambo', which, deriving from 'crambe repetita' (cabbage served up again), referred to silly verbal repetition. Apparently the form 'corambe' is occasionally found. (See Duthie, p. 223, and *OED* under 'crambe'.)

There are many minor variants in the spelling of names, and these are not usually taken account of in the collation. Reynaldo, for example, is the second quarto form; in the Folio he is Reynoldo. Elsinore appears regularly in the second quarto as Elsonoure, and in the Folio as Elsenour and Elsonower. Osric is called Osrick once in the quarto and on all other occasions Ostrick or Ostricke; in the Folio he is always Osricke.

NOTE ON THE TEXT

The basis of the modernised text given in this edition is fully discussed in the Introduction, pp. 8–32. The section concludes with a summary of the argument and an explanation of some features and principles of the present text (see pp. 30–2).

The collation confines itself almost entirely to recording the significant variations between Q2 and F, and to giving the source of all readings which do not derive from Q2 or F. In every case the reading of the present text is given first, followed by its source. Readings from the 'bad' Q1 are given when their agreement (or disagreement) with Q2 or F is of importance. The readings of seventeenth-century texts other than Q1, Q2, and F, and later editorial emendations not accepted in the present edition, are not normally recorded.

Hamlet
Prince of Denmark

LIST OF CHARACTERS

HAMLET, *Prince of Denmark*
CLAUDIUS, *King of Denmark, Hamlet's uncle*
GERTRUDE, *Queen of Denmark, Hamlet's mother*
GHOST *of Hamlet's father, the former King of Denmark*
POLONIUS, *counsellor to the king*
LAERTES, *his son*
OPHELIA, *his daughter*
REYNALDO, *his servant*
HORATIO, *Hamlet's friend and fellow-student*
MARCELLUS, BARNARDO, FRANCISCO } *officers of the watch*
VOLTEMAND, CORNELIUS } *ambassadors to Norway*
ROSENCRANTZ, GUILDENSTERN } *former schoolfellows of Hamlet*
FORTINBRAS, *Prince of Norway*
CAPTAIN *in the Norwegian army*
First PLAYER
Other PLAYERS
OSRIC, LORD, GENTLEMAN } *courtiers*
First CLOWN, *a gravedigger and sexton*
Second CLOWN, *his assistant*
SAILOR
MESSENGER
PRIEST
English AMBASSADOR
LORDS, ATTENDANTS, SAILORS, SOLDIERS, GUARDS

SCENE: *The Danish royal palace at Elsinore*

Notes

A list of 'The Persons Represented' (omitting the First Player) first appeared in the Players' Quarto of 1676.

GERTRUDE So spelt in F. Normally Gertrard in Q2. See Introduction, p. 70.

POLONIUS Concerning the change to Corambis or Corambus in stage performance, see Introduction, pp. 25 and 71.

OFFICERS OF THE WATCH Barnardo and Francisco are introduced as 'sentinels' (1.1.0 SD), and Francisco is called 'honest soldier' (1.1.16). But, although Hamlet seems on friendlier terms with Marcellus than Barnardo (1.2.165–7), Horatio calls them both 'gentlemen' (1.2.196).

PLAYERS A minimum of four players in all is required, or three if 'Lucianus' also speaks the prologue (3.2.133).

HAMLET
PRINCE OF DENMARK

1.1 *Enter* BARNARDO *and* FRANCISCO, *two sentinels*

BARNARDO Who's there?
FRANCISCO Nay answer me. Stand and unfold yourself.
BARNARDO Long live the king!
FRANCISCO Barnardo?
BARNARDO He. 5
FRANCISCO You come most carefully upon your hour.
BARNARDO 'Tis now struck twelve, get thee to bed Francisco.
FRANCISCO For this relief much thanks, 'tis bitter cold
And I am sick at heart.
BARNARDO Have you had quiet guard?
FRANCISCO Not a mouse stirring. 10
BARNARDO Well, good night.
If you do meet Horatio and Marcellus,
The rivals of my watch, bid them make haste.
FRANCISCO I think I hear them.

Enter HORATIO *and* MARCELLUS

Stand ho! Who is there?
HORATIO Friends to this ground.
MARCELLUS And liegemen to the Dane. 15
FRANCISCO Give you good night.
MARCELLUS Oh farewell honest soldier,
Who hath relieved you?

Act 1, Scene 1 1.1] *Actus Primus. Scœna Prima.* F; *no indication in* Q2 1 Who's] F; Whose Q2 14 SD] *Adams; follows* make haste *in* Q2, F 14 Stand ho] Q2; Stand F 14 Who is] Q2; who's F 16 soldier] F; souldiers Q2

Act 1, Scene 1
0 SD The sentinels enter from opposite sides of the stage. Barnardo is relieving Francisco. The action is to be seen taking place on the 'platform' (1.2.213; 1.2.251), a high terrace for mounting guns and keeping watch, in the Castle of Elsinore.
2 Nay answer me It is Francisco, the sentinel on duty, who should be giving the challenge, not the newcomer.
2 unfold yourself reveal who you are.
13 rivals partners.
15 ground territory, country.
15 liegemen sworn followers.
15 the Dane the Danish King: compare 1.2.44 and 5.1.225.

FRANCISCO Barnardo hath my place.
Give you good night. *Exit Francisco*
MARCELLUS Holla, Barnardo!
BARNARDO Say,
What, is Horatio there?
HORATIO A piece of him.
BARNARDO Welcome Horatio, welcome good Marcellus. 20
MARCELLUS What, has this thing appeared again tonight?
BARNARDO I have seen nothing.
MARCELLUS Horatio says 'tis but our fantasy,
And will not let belief take hold of him
Touching this dreaded sight, twice seen of us. 25
Therefore I have entreated him along
With us to watch the minutes of this night,
That if again this apparition come
He may approve our eyes, and speak to it.
HORATIO Tush, tush, 'twill not appear.
BARNARDO Sit down awhile, 30
And let us once again assail your ears,
That are so fortified against our story,
What we two nights have seen.
HORATIO Well, sit we down,
And let us hear Barnardo speak of this.
BARNARDO Last night of all, 35
When yond same star that's westward from the pole

17 hath my] Q2; ha's my F 18–19 Say...there] *as one line* Q2, F 21 MARCELLUS] F, Q1; *Hora.* Q2 33 two nights have seen] F; haue two nights seene Q2, Q1

18 Give i.e. God give.
18 SD *Exit Francisco* He takes no further part in the play.
18–19 Say,/What, They are calling to each other in the supposed darkness, and these are just exclamation-words. They must not be taken to indicate Barnardo's surprise, since he is expecting Horatio.
19 A piece of him He is so cold he is not wholly himself.
21 What...tonight? Both F and Q1 give this line to Marcellus; strong indication that it was so spoken on the stage. Q2 assigns it to Horatio. It seems more likely that Q2 is in error; Marcellus's next speech follows very naturally from this anxious enquiry.
21 thing creature – without implying contempt. In the second scene of *The Tempest*, 'a thing most brutish' refers to Caliban and 'a thing divine' to Ferdinand.
23 fantasy imagination.
25 dreaded awful, fearsome. Compare *Coriolanus* 3.3.98 'in the presence/Of dreaded justice'.
26 along to come along.
27 watch...night keep watch for the period of this night. Compare *Shrew* 5.2.150: 'to watch the night in storms, the day in cold'. For 'watch' in this sense, see 1.2.213 below.
29 approve our eyes confirm that we saw correctly.
33 What With what (following 'assail').
36 pole pole star.

Had made his course t'illume that part of heaven
Where now it burns, Marcellus and myself,
The bell then beating one –

Enter GHOST

MARCELLUS Peace, break thee off. Look where it comes again. 40
BARNARDO In the same figure, like the king that's dead.
MARCELLUS Thou art a scholar, speak to it Horatio.
BARNARDO Looks a not like the king? Mark it Horatio.
HORATIO Most like. It harrows me with fear and wonder.
BARNARDO It would be spoke to.
MARCELLUS Question it Horatio. 45
HORATIO What art thou that usurp'st this time of night,
Together with that fair and warlike form
In which the majesty of buried Denmark
Did sometimes march? By heaven I charge thee speak.
MARCELLUS It is offended.
BARNARDO See, it stalks away. 50
HORATIO Stay! Speak, speak, I charge thee speak!

Exit Ghost

MARCELLUS 'Tis gone and will not answer.
BARNARDO How now Horatio? you tremble and look pale.
Is not this something more than fantasy?
What think you on't? 55
HORATIO Before my God, I might not this believe
Without the sensible and true avouch
Of mine own eyes.

43 a] Q2; it F, Q1 44 harrows] F; horrowes Q2; horrors Q1 45 Question] F, Q1; Speake to Q2

37 **illume** illuminate. Shakespeare seems to have coined this word, and he does not use it elsewhere. Compare 'relume' (re-light) in *Othello* 5.2.13, for which, again, *OED* quotes no parallel.
39 **beating** striking ('tolling' Q1).
41 **figure** shape, form.
42 **scholar** Horatio is learned enough to know how to address a spirit.
43 **a** he. This representation of an informal slurred pronunciation (ə) of the pronoun, presumed to derive from Shakespeare's MS., is retained in this text, in spite of occasional difficulties for the modern reader (see note to 3.3.73). F normally sophisticates 'a' to 'he', but here reads 'it' – with a gain in consistency, since everyone refers to the apparition as 'it'.
44 **harrows** deeply disturbs (breaks up with a harrow).
46 **usurp'st** wrongfully takes over.
47 **Together with** The spirit is also appropriating the form of the old king.
48 **buried Denmark** the dead king of Denmark. This customary figure of speech (synecdoche) is very common in the play, emphasising the interdependence of king and kingdom.
49 **sometimes** formerly.
50 **stalks** moves with a stately stride. Compare 66 below. *OED* v^1 c notes that 'stalk' is often used in connection with ghosts.
57 **sensible** sensory.
57 **avouch** warrant. The word is not recorded elsewhere.

MARCELLUS Is it not like the king?
HORATIO As thou art to thyself.
Such was the very armour he had on 60
When he th'ambitious Norway combated;
So frowned he once, when in an angry parle
He smote the sledded Polacks on the ice.
'Tis strange.
MARCELLUS Thus twice before, and jump at this dead hour, 65
With martial stalk hath he gone by our watch.
HORATIO In what particular thought to work I know not,
But in the gross and scope of mine opinion
This bodes some strange eruption to our state.
MARCELLUS Good now sit down, and tell me he that knows, 70
Why this same strict and most observant watch
So nightly toils the subject of the land,
And why such daily cast of brazen cannon,
And foreign mart for implements of war,
Why such impress of shipwrights, whose sore task 75
Does not divide the Sunday from the week.
What might be toward, that this sweaty haste
Doth make the night joint-labourer with the day?
Who is't that can inform me?
HORATIO That can I –
At least the whisper goes so. Our last king, 80
Whose image even but now appeared to us,

61 he] Q2; *not in* F 61 th'] F; the Q2 63 sledded] F; sleaded Q2, Q1 63 Polacks] *Malone;* pollax Q2, Q1; Pollax F; Poleaxe F4 65 jump] Q2, Q1; iust F 68 mine] Q2; my F, Q1 73 why] F; with Q2 73 cast] F; cost Q2, Q1

61 Norway King of Norway.

62 parle parley. Properly a conference during a truce, but here seemingly used to mean an altercation leading to violence.

63 sledded Polacks Both Q1 and Q2 read 'sleaded pollax'; F reads 'sledded Pollax'. It is a celebrated question whether we are speaking of a poleaxe (often spelt 'pollax') or Polacks (= Poles). If the word is poleaxe, then the passage means that King Hamlet, during a heated exchange (with Norwegians?), struck his fighting axe on the ice. But it is then very dubious what 'sleaded' or 'sledded' can mean. It seems more likely that Horatio is talking of two encounters, one with Norwegians and one with Poles. In the second, in a confrontation, or after an angry exchange, he routed the Poles in their sledges.

65 jump precisely.

66 martial stalk See 50 above. The actor has to achieve a solemnity of movement that is both military and spectral.

67–8 In what particular...opinion i.e. I don't know in which particular area to concentrate my thoughts (in order to explain this) but, taking a wide view, so far as I can judge...

70 Good now Please you. Dowden compares *Winter's Tale* 5.1.19: 'Now, good now, / Say so but seldom.'

72 toils wearies with toil.

74 foreign mart bargaining abroad.

75 impress conscription.

77 toward in preparation, afoot.

Was as you know by Fortinbras of Norway,
Thereto pricked on by a most emulate pride,
Dared to the combat; in which our valiant Hamlet –
For so this side of our known world esteemed him – 85
Did slay this Fortinbras; who by a sealed compact,
Well ratified by law and heraldy,
Did forfeit (with his life) all those his lands
Which he stood seized of, to the conqueror;
Against the which a moiety competent 90
Was gagèd by our king, which had returned
To the inheritance of Fortinbras
Had he been vanquisher; as by the same comart
And carriage of the article design,
His fell to Hamlet. Now sir, young Fortinbras, 95
Of unimprovèd mettle hot and full,
Hath in the skirts of Norway here and there
Sharked up a list of landless resolutes
For food and diet to some enterprise
That hath a stomach in't; which is no other, 100

87 heraldy] Q2; Heraldrie F 88 those] F; these Q2 89 of] Q2; on F 91 returned] return'd F; returne Q2 93 comart] Q2; Cou'nant F 94 design] designe F; desseigne Q2; design'd F2 98 landless] Landlesse F; lawelesse Q2 lawlesse Q1

83 emulate pride A sense of self-esteem which made him strive to equal and outgo others. 'emulate' as adjective is not recorded elsewhere.

86 Did slay this Fortinbras This was thirty years before. See 5.1.121, 138.

86 sealed i.e. agreed, confirmed.

87 ratified by law and heraldy sanctioned by law and the code of chivalry. 'heraldy', a less familiar form than 'heraldry', appears in Q2 here and at 2.2.414.

89 stood seized of was the legal owner of (i.e. his personal estates were the forfeit, not his dominions as king).

90 moiety competent adequate portion.

91 gagèd pledged.

93–4 as by...article design as by the same compact and the intention of the agreement drawn up. The whole phrase is obscure and repetitive, and suggests hesitation on Shakespeare's part as he wrote. 'comart' (Q2) is a nonce-word having something to do with 'bargain' (compare 74). F's 'covenant' might be correct, but the extra length of this line suggests a difficulty in Shakespeare's MS. which it is useless to try to disentangle. 'article' is probably an item in an agreement, hence 'stipulation' or 'condition'. 'design' is usually emended to 'designed', which is no whit clearer than what is the definite reading of both texts. Possibly Shakespeare intended to delete all of 94.

96 unimprovèd mettle undisciplined spirit (?). Shakespeare scarcely uses the word 'improve': in *Julius Caesar* 2.1.159 it means 'put to good use'.

98 Sharked up Gathered together indiscriminately, like a shark swallowing its prey.

98 list an assemblage or band of soldiers. (Compare 'the army list', or 'on the active list'; to enlist is to join such a band.)

98 landless So F; Q2 shares with Q1 the reading 'lawless'. The idea here is not of an army of criminals but of disinherited gentry and younger sons who have nothing better to do – like the Bastard in *King John*. See Introduction, p. 41. If F has the true reading, then Q2 must here follow Q1 (see Introduction, pp. 10, 29).

99–100 For food...stomach in't The resolutes are prepared to enlist in return for their keep only, because they are attracted to an adventurous enterprise. 'diet' = 'diet-money', living expenses. The enterprise has 'stomach' in two senses: it provides the resolutes with their real nourishment, and it is bold and spirited.

As it doth well appear unto our state,
But to recover of us by strong hand
And terms compulsatory those foresaid lands
So by his father lost. And this, I take it,
Is the main motive of our preparations, 105
The source of this our watch, and the chief head
Of this post-haste and romage in the land.
[BARNARDO I think it be no other but e'en so.
Well may it sort that this portentous figure
Comes armèd through our watch so like the king 110
That was and is the question of these wars.
HORATIO A mote it is to trouble the mind's eye.
In the most high and palmy state of Rome,
A little ere the mightiest Julius fell,
The graves stood tenantless and the sheeted dead 115
Did squeak and gibber in the Roman streets;
As stars with trains of fire, and dews of blood,
Disasters in the sun; and the moist star,
Upon whose influence Neptune's empire stands,
Was sick almost to doomsday with eclipse. 120
And even the like precurse of feared events,
As harbingers preceding still the fates
And prologue to the omen coming on,
Have heaven and earth together demonstrated

101 As] Q2; And F 103 compulsatory] Q2; Compulsatiue F 107 romage] Romage F; Romeage Q2 *(uncorrected)*; Romadge Q2 *(corrected)* 108–25] Q2; *not in* F 115 tenantless] Q 1611; tennatlesse Q2 121 feared] *Ridley, conj. Collier*; feare Q2; fearce Q 1611

101 our state the Danish government.

103 compulsatory Pronounce 'compúlsat'ry': there is not much to choose between this reading (Q2) and F's 'compulsative'. Neither word is recorded in *OED* before this.

107 romage commotion and bustle, especially with relation to loading a ship's cargo (usually spelt 'rummage').

108–25 It is argued in the Introduction (p. 14) that this passage, found only in Q2, had been marked by Shakespeare for deletion.

109 sort be accordant with (Horatio's explanation).

111 question cause of dispute.

112 A mote...eye Like an irritant in the eye, it disturbs and perplexes the mind, which cannot see ahead clearly.

113–20 The portents preceding the death of Caesar had been extensively used by Shakespeare in the early acts of *Julius Caesar*.

113 palmy triumphant. No previous occurrence recorded in *OED*.

116 gibber utter inarticulate sounds (compare 'gibberish', and 'gibbering idiot'). The word is another form of 'jabber'.

117–18 As stars...sun Either the beginning or the end of this is missing, a further sign that the speech was never finished off.

118 Disasters Portents of disaster. (Etymologically, the word implies evil astral influence.)

118 the moist star the moon. She is 'the watery star' in *Winter's Tale* 1.2.1, and 'governess of floods' in *Midsummer Night's Dream* 2.1.103.

120 almost to doomsday almost as if it were the day of judgement.

121 precurse advance warning (that which runs ahead). *OED* has no other example of this word.

122 harbingers Officials who went ahead of the king to announce his approach.

123 omen Used here for the calamity itself.

Unto our climatures and countrymen.] 125

Enter GHOST

But soft, behold, lo where it comes again!
I'll cross it though it blast me. Stay, illusion.
It spreads his arms
If thou hast any sound or use of voice,
Speak to me.
If there be any good thing to be done 130
That may to thee do ease, and grace to me,
Speak to me.
If thou art privy to thy country's fate,
Which happily foreknowing may avoid,
Oh speak. 135
Or if thou hast uphoarded in thy life
Extorted treasure in the womb of earth,
For which they say you spirits oft walk in death, *The cock crows*
Speak of it. Stay and speak! Stop it Marcellus.

MARCELLUS Shall I strike at it with my partisan? 140

HORATIO Do if it will not stand.

BARNARDO 'Tis here.

HORATIO 'Tis here.

MARCELLUS 'Tis gone.

Exit Ghost

We do it wrong being so majestical

127 SD] Q2; *not in* F; *He spreads his arms* Q 1676   138 you] F; your Q2   138 SD] Q2; *not in* F   140 strike at] F; strike Q2   142 SD] F; *not in* Q2

125 climatures regions (an unusual variant of 'climates').

126 soft enough! See note on 3.1.88.

127 cross it cross its path.

127 SD *It spreads his arms* 'his' for 'its' is normal in Shakespeare (compare 5.2.90–1, 'put your bonnet to his right use'). It is tempting to follow the quarto of 1676, Rowe, and many succeeding editors in thinking 'It' (= the Ghost) is wrong, and that it is Horatio who spreads his arms, 'crossing' the Ghost in the double sense of barring its way and making the sign of the cross. While it is true that in Elizabethan writing 'he' might have been misread as 'yt', there is no reason to suppose that Q2 is wrong. This dumb gesture by the Ghost, preluding the speech he never makes, could be extremely effective.

128–38 'Horatio shows a scholar's knowledge in his enumeration of the causes that send ghosts back to earth' (Kittredge).

134 happily haply, perhaps.

136 uphoarded hoarded up.

137 Extorted Obtained by unfair means. Compare *2 Henry VI* 4.7.99: 'Are my chests filled up with extorted gold?'

140 partisan A long-handled weapon combining spear and axe.

143 being so majestical since it has such majesty (?). This is the accepted sense, and editors therefore normally put commas round the phrase. They thus make Marcellus give two separate reasons why they are wrong to offer violence; (1) the majesty of the Ghost; (2) its invulnerability. It may however be *they* who are being 'majestical'

To offer it the show of violence,
For it is as the air invulnerable, 145
And our vain blows malicious mockery.

BARNARDO It was about to speak when the cock crew.

HORATIO And then it started like a guilty thing
Upon a fearful summons. I have heard,
The cock, that is the trumpet to the morn, 150
Doth with his lofty and shrill-sounding throat
Awake the god of day; and at his warning,
Whether in sea or fire, in earth or air,
Th'extravagant and erring spirit hies
To his confine. And of the truth herein 155
This present object made probation.

MARCELLUS It faded on the crowing of the cock.
Some say that ever 'gainst that season comes
Wherein our Saviour's birth is celebrated,
This bird of dawning singeth all night long, 160
And then, they say, no spirit dare stir abroad,
The nights are wholesome, then no planets strike,
No fairy takes, nor witch hath power to charm,
So hallowed and so gracious is that time.

HORATIO So have I heard, and do in part believe it. 165
But look, the morn in russet mantle clad
Walks o'er the dew of yon high eastward hill.
Break we our watch up, and by my advice
Let us impart what we have seen tonight
Unto young Hamlet, for upon my life 170
This spirit, dumb to us, will speak to him.

150 morn] Q2; day F; morning Q1 **158** say] Q2; sayes F **160** This] Q2; The F, Q1 **161** dare stir] dare sturre Q2; can walke F; dare walke Q1 **163** takes] Q2; talkes F **164** that] Q2; the F **167** eastward] Q2; Easterne F

(= imperious) in offering violence: 'We do wrong to a ghost to be so overbearing as to offer it violence, because it is immaterial.'

146 malicious mockery a mockery of the malice we intend.

150 trumpet trumpeter.

152 the god of day Phoebus Apollo.

154 extravagant and erring wandering beyond bounds (the original meanings of these words).

155 confine (1) one's own special territory, (2) a place of confinement. Both meanings are present here. See also 2.2.236.

156 probation proof.

158 'gainst just before.

161 dare stir See Introduction, pp. 29–30.

162 strike i.e. affect with their malign influence.

163 takes attacks, lays hold (*OED v* 7).

164 gracious full of grace.

166 the morn In a few minutes of acting time we have moved from deepest midnight to the dawn.

166 russet The name of a coarse cloth worn by country people, and also its colour, a neutral reddish-brown. Cotgrave translates 'Rousset' as 'Russet, brown, ruddy, inclining to dark red'.

Do you consent we shall acquaint him with it,
As needful in our loves, fitting our duty?
MARCELLUS Let's do't I pray, and I this morning know
Where we shall find him most conveniently. 175
Exeunt

1.2 *Flourish. Enter* CLAUDIUS *King of Denmark*, GERTRUDE *the Queen*, HAMLET, POLONIUS, LAERTES, OPHELIA, [VOLTEMAND, CORNELIUS,] LORDS *attendant*

CLAUDIUS Though yet of Hamlet our dear brother's death
The memory be green, and that it us befitted
To bear our hearts in grief, and our whole kingdom
To be contracted in one brow of woe,
Yet so far hath discretion fought with nature 5
That we with wisest sorrow think on him,
Together with remembrance of ourselves.
Therefore our sometime sister, now our queen,
Th'imperial jointress to this warlike state,
Have we, as 'twere with a defeated joy, 10
With one auspicious and one dropping eye,

175 conveniently] F, Q1; conuenient Q2 Act 1, Scene 2 1.2] *Scena Secunda* F 0 SD] *Florish. Enter Claudius, King of Denmarke, Gertrad the Queene, Counsaile: as Polonius, and his Sonne Laertes, Hamlet, Cum Alijs.* Q2; *Enter Claudius King of Denmarke, Gertrude the Queene, Hamlet, Polonius, Laertes, and his Sister Ophelia, Lords Attendant.* F 8 sometime] Q2; sometimes F 9 to] Q2; of F 11 one...one] F; an...a Q2

Act 1, Scene 2.

0 SD This SD combines elements from both Q2 and F, on the principle explained in the Introduction (pp. 21–3, 32). F adds Ophelia, which seems right, though she has no speaking part. Q2's 'Counsaile: as' (? for 'Councillors') has by some been taken to indicate a formal meeting of the Danish council, which is highly implausible. A second omission in Q2 is the ambassadors. These are given a very awkward entry in F, half-way through Claudius's speech (25). Shakespeare must have meant them to be on stage from the start of the scene.

4 contracted...woe drawn together in a single mourning visage.

7 Together...ourselves Being also mindful of ourselves.

9 jointress A wife who shares property with her husband, and continues her rights in it after his death. It is not at all clear whether Claudius is referring to Gertrude's share of the crown with her former husband or with himself. If he means the former, it sounds as though he sees himself inheriting her. It is more likely that the whole phrase is in apposition to 'now our queen'; i.e. 'and to rule this state with me'. The word is in any case used metaphorically, not in a proper legal sense. See Clarkson and Warren, *The Law of Property in Shakespeare*, 1942, pp. 81–4.

11 With one auspicious and one dropping eye 'auspicious': looking happily to the future; 'dropping': cast down with grief, or possibly dropping tears. Steevens noted the similar sentence, in a semi-jocular context, in *Winter's Tale* 5.2.74–6, 'She had one eye declined for the loss of her husband, another elevated that the oracle was fulfilled.' Beatrice White found the genesis of this 'contradictory facial expression' in descriptions of the false and fickle goddess Fortune, and argued that the saying 'to cry with one eye and laugh with the other' became a standard phrase for hypocrisy and

With mirth in funeral and with dirge in marriage,
In equal scale weighing delight and dole,
Taken to wife; nor have we herein barred
Your better wisdoms, which have freely gone 15
With this affair along – for all, our thanks.
Now follows that you know: young Fortinbras,
Holding a weak supposal of our worth,
Or thinking by our late dear brother's death
Our state to be disjoint and out of frame, 20
Colleaguèd with this dream of his advantage,
He hath not failed to pester us with message
Importing the surrender of those lands
Lost by his father, with all bands of law,
To our most valiant brother. So much for him. 25
Now for ourself and for this time of meeting
Thus much the business is: we have here writ
To Norway, uncle of young Fortinbras,
Who, impotent and bed-rid, scarcely hears
Of this his nephew's purpose, to suppress 30
His further gait herein, in that the levies,
The lists, and full proportions, are all made
Out of his subject; and we here dispatch
You, good Cornelius, and you, Voltemand,
For bearers of this greeting to old Norway, 35
Giving to you no further personal power
To business with the king, more than the scope

17 follows] Q2; followes, F 17 know:] *Dowden, conj. Walker;* know Q2; F 21 this] Q2; the F 24 bands] Q2; bonds F 35 bearers] Q2; bearing F

inconstancy. 'To an Elizabethan...an indication of duplicity would have been at once apparent' (*Anglia* 77 (1959), 204–7).

The reading of F, adopted here, is less likely to be a sophistication than Q's is to be a misreading.

13 dole grief.

14 Taken to wife See note to 1.2.157.

15 Your better wisdoms Your excellent wisdoms, or, perhaps, the best fruits of your wisdoms.

17 that you know what you already know.

18 supposal supposition, conjecture.

20 Our state to be disjoint and out of frame In airily dismissing the idea of administrative disorder, Claudius uses an image which powerfully suggests the deeper displacement which in fact now afflicts the state. Indeed, Hamlet echoes his words, 'The time is out of joint' (1.5.189). Compare Macbeth's 'But let the frame of things disjoint' (3.2.16), and Lear's 'Wrenched my frame of nature from the fixed place' (1.4.268–9).

21 Colleaguèd...advantage Having as an ally only this illusion of a favourable opportunity.

24 bands agreements binding a person. F gives the alternative form 'bonds'.

29 impotent helpless, incapacitated.

31 gait i.e. proceedings.

32 lists See note to 1.1.98.

32 proportions given numbers of troops raised for specific purposes. Compare *Henry V* 1.2.304–5, 'Let our proportions for these wars/Be soon collected.'

33 his subject those who are subject to him. Compare the use of the collective singular in 1.1.72.

Of these dilated articles allow.
Farewell, and let your haste commend your duty.

CORNELIUS / VOLTEMAND In that and all things will we show our duty. 40

CLAUDIUS We doubt it nothing, heartily farewell.

Exeunt Voltemand and Cornelius

And now Laertes, what's the news with you?
You told us of some suit, what is't Laertes?
You cannot speak of reason to the Dane
And lose your voice. What wouldst thou beg Laertes, 45
That shall not be my offer, not thy asking?
The head is not more native to the heart,
The hand more instrumental to the mouth,
Than is the throne of Denmark to thy father.
What wouldst thou have Laertes?

LAERTES My dread lord, 50
Your leave and favour to return to France,
From whence though willingly I came to Denmark
To show my duty in your coronation,
Yet now I must confess, that duty done,
My thoughts and wishes bend again toward France, 55
And bow them to your gracious leave and pardon.

CLAUDIUS Have you your father's leave? What says Polonius?

POLONIUS He hath my lord wrung from me my slow leave
By laboursome petition, and at last
Upon his will I sealed my hard consent. 60
I do beseech you give him leave to go.

CLAUDIUS Take thy fair hour Laertes, time be thine,
And thy best graces spend it at thy will.
But now my cousin Hamlet, and my son –

38 dilated] F; delated Q2 40 CORNELIUS/VOLTEMAND] *Cor. Vo.* Q2; *Volt.* F 41 SD] F; *not in* Q2 50 My dread] Q2; Dread my F 55 toward] Q2; towards F 58 He hath] F; Hath Q2 58–60 wrung...consent] Q2; *not in* F

38 **dilated** amply expressed. Q2's 'delated' is only a spelling variant.

44 **the Dane** the Danish king.

45 **lose your voice** speak to no avail.

46 **not thy asking** rather than thy asking.

47 **native** naturally related.

51 **Your leave and favour** The favour of your permission.

56 **pardon** permission.

58–60 **wrung...consent** Two and a half lines are missing in F. Since Q1 indicates that they were spoken on stage, the omission must be the responsibility of the second scribe or the Folio compositor.

60 **Upon...consent** I gave my reluctant agreement to his strong wish. 'sealed' suggests official or legal approval (compare 1.1.86).

63 **thy best...will** Claudius hopes that in enjoying himself Laertes will be exercising his best qualities.

HAMLET (*Aside*) A little more than kin, and less than kind. 65
CLAUDIUS How is it that the clouds still hang on you?
HAMLET Not so my lord, I am too much i'th'sun.
GERTRUDE Good Hamlet cast thy nighted colour off,
And let thine eye look like a friend on Denmark.
Do not forever with thy vailèd lids 70
Seek for thy noble father in the dust.
Thou know'st 'tis common, all that lives must die,
Passing through nature to eternity.
HAMLET Ay madam, it is common.
GERTRUDE If it be,
Why seems it so particular with thee? 75
HAMLET Seems madam? nay it is, I know not seems.
'Tis not alone my inky cloak, good mother,
Nor customary suits of solemn black,
Nor windy suspiration of forced breath,
No, nor the fruitful river in the eye, 80
Nor the dejected haviour of the visage,
Together with all forms, moods, shapes of grief,
That can denote me truly. These indeed seem,
For they are actions that a man might play,
But I have that within which passes show – 85
These but the trappings and the suits of woe.
CLAUDIUS 'Tis sweet and commendable in your nature Hamlet,
To give these mourning duties to your father;
But you must know, your father lost a father,

65 *Aside*] *Theobald*[3]; *not in* Q2, F 67 Not so] F; Not so much Q2 67 i'th'sun] F; in the sonne Q2 68 nighted] Q2; nightly F 70 vailèd] Q2; veyled F 77 good] F; coold Q2 82 shapes] Q 1611; chapes Q2; shewes F 83 denote] F; deuote Q2 85 passes] Q2; passeth F

65 **A little...kind** To call me 'son' is more than our actual kinship warrants; and there is less than the natural feelings of such a relationship between us. In this riddling aside, there is a play on the two meanings of 'kind': (1) belonging to nature, (2) affectionate, benevolent.

67 **Not so...sun** So F. Modern editors reject Q2's first 'much' but keep Q2's expanded form 'in the sun'. The Q2 compositors regularly expand contractions and syncopes which seem genuinely Shakespearean. In this case, the contraction is not only necessary for the metre, but also helps the quibble (i'th'sun; o'th'son). How can he be in the clouds when he has so much 'son'?

68 **nighted colour** i.e. the darkness of both clothes and mood.

69 **Denmark** the king.

70 **vailèd lids** lowered eyes.

78 **customary** conventional.

79 **suspiration** sighing.

82 **moods** emotional states as outwardly displayed. Compare Sonnet 93, line 8.

82 **shapes** external appearances. See note to 1.4.43.

85 **passes** So Q2. F reads 'passeth'; the presence of the older -th form in what is by and large a modernising text is an argument for considering the F reading very carefully. 'passes show' is much easier to say. Either reading could be the original.

87 **commendable** The main accent falls on the first and not the second syllable.

That father lost, lost his, and the survivor bound 90
In filial obligation for some term
To do obsequious sorrow; but to persever
In obstinate condolement is a course
Of impious stubbornness, 'tis unmanly grief,
It shows a will most incorrect to heaven, 95
A heart unfortified, a mind impatient,
An understanding simple and unschooled.
For what we know must be, and is as common
As any the most vulgar thing to sense,
Why should we in our peevish opposition 100
Take it to heart? Fie, 'tis a fault to heaven,
A fault against the dead, a fault to nature,
To reason most absurd, whose common theme
Is death of fathers, and who still hath cried,
From the first corse till he that died today, 105
'This must be so.' We pray you throw to earth
This unprevailing woe, and think of us
As of a father, for let the world take note
You are the most immediate to our throne,
And with no less nobility of love 110
Than that which dearest father bears his son,
Do I impart toward you. For your intent
In going back to school in Wittenberg,
It is most retrograde to our desire,

96 a mind] F; or minde Q2 **112** toward] Q2; towards F **114** retrograde] F; retrogard Q2

92 Scan 'Tŏ dó ŏbséquióus sórrŏw; bút tŏ persévĕr'. 'obsequious' = relating to obsequies for the dead.

93 condolement grief.

95 incorrect to heaven improperly directed as regards heaven.

99 As...sense As the most ordinary thing that affects our senses.

101–2 fault wrongdoing, transgression (a stronger sense than in modern English).

102 a fault to nature Concerning G. W. Knight's extravagant praise of Claudius's good sense, Nigel Alexander wrote, 'The critic has forgotten what Claudius wants him to forget – that death is not always "natural"' (*Poison, Play, and Duel*, 1971, p. 51).

105 the first corse Unfortunately for Claudius, this was Abel, murdered by his brother Cain.

107 unprevailing that can gain nothing.

109 the most immediate to our throne i.e. the next in succession. The monarchy being elective, not hereditary, Claudius, the most important member of an electoral college, here gives his 'voice' to Hamlet as his heir. Compare Hamlet's own words at 5.2.335.

112 impart toward you convey (this gift of my vote) to you. This is admittedly an unusual intransitive usage of 'impart', but I think it agrees with Johnson's not very clear gloss: 'I believe *impart* is, *impart myself*, *communicate* whatever I can bestow.' Kittredge glossed the word as 'express myself'.

113 to school i.e. his studies.

113 Wittenberg The University of Wittenberg, founded in 1502. Famous in Elizabethan England as the university of Luther – and of Dr Faustus.

114 retrograde contrary.

And we beseech you bend you to remain 115
Here in the cheer and comfort of our eye,
Our chiefest courtier, cousin, and our son.

GERTRUDE Let not thy mother lose her prayers Hamlet.
I pray thee stay with us, go not to Wittenberg.

HAMLET I shall in all my best obey you madam. 120

CLAUDIUS Why, 'tis a loving and a fair reply.
Be as ourself in Denmark. Madam, come.
This gentle and unforced accord of Hamlet
Sits smiling to my heart, in grace whereof,
No jocund health that Denmark drinks today 125
But the great cannon to the clouds shall tell,
And the king's rouse the heaven shall bruit again,
Re-speaking earthly thunder. Come away.
Flourish. Exeunt all but Hamlet

HAMLET O that this too too solid flesh would melt,
Thaw and resolve itself into a dew, 130
Or that the Everlasting had not fixed
His canon 'gainst self-slaughter. O God, God,

119 pray thee] Q2; prythee F 127 heaven] Q2; Heauens F 128 SD] Q2; *Exeunt / Manet Hamlet.* F 129 solid] F; sallied Q2, Q1 132 self] F; seale Q2 132 O God, God] Q2; O God, O God F

115 bend you to incline yourself.

125 Denmark Once again, the king is meant.

127 rouse ceremonial drink, or toast. Compare 1.4.8–9.

127 bruit loudly proclaim (echoing the cannon).

129 solid So F. Q2 reads 'sallied'. Q1 has 'too much griev'd and sallied flesh'. Q2 makes considerable use of Q1 in this part of the play, and the coincidence of a very unusual spelling argues strongly that Q2 derives from Q1. Q1 is a 'reported' text. What did the reporter hear on stage to make him write 'griev'd and sallied flesh'? It is argued that 'sallied' means 'sullied'. The evidence is in 2.1.39, where Q2 has 'sallies' and F 'sulleyes', and *Love's Labour's Lost* 5.2.352, 'unsallied'. (An adducement by Bowers and Jenkins of 'sally' = 'sully' in Dekker's *Patient Grissil*, 1.1.12, is based on a misunderstanding of the line.) Even if 'sallied' means 'sullied', it is quite certain that 'griev'd and sallied' is a corruption. If 'griev'd' is wrong, 'sallied' may be wrong. I suspect that 'sullied' was the Q1 reporter's creative mishearing of 'solid' and that 'griev'd and sallied' was his reconstruction of the misheard phrase. That Q2 should repeat such a strange word is no more surprising than many other mysterious choices. What, for example, did the Q2 compositor mean at 5.2.95: 'it is very sully and hot'? (F: 'soultry'.)

The case for 'sullied' is tortuous, though it is the reading of most modern editions. The case for 'solid' is simple. It is the unequivocal reading of one of the two authoritative texts, and it suits the context much better. Hamlet's lament is that his flesh is too solid to melt away, and that he is forbidden by God to do away with himself. In the context of the speech, it would hardly be surprising if Shakespeare heard the word 'sullied' as he wrote 'solid' and that the reporter caught only the unexpressed part of the pun.

132 canon 'gainst self-slaughter There seems to be no biblical injunction specifically against suicide. In *Pilgrim's Progress*, Hopeful deters Christian from suicide by arguing that the sixth commandment, Thou shalt do no murder, applies *a fortiori* to murder of oneself. In the case of the suicide of Sir James Hales, which Shakespeare drew on later in the play (5.1.8–19), it was said that suicide was an offence against God 'in that it is a breach of his commandment, *Thou shalt not kill*, and to kill himself, by which act he kills in presumption his own soul, is a greater offence than to kill another' (Plowden's *Commentaries*, 1761, p. 261).

How weary, stale, flat and unprofitable
Seem to me all the uses of this world!
Fie on't, ah fie, 'tis an unweeded garden 135
That grows to seed, things rank and gross in nature
Possess it merely. That it should come to this!
But two months dead – nay not so much, not two –
So excellent a king, that was to this
Hyperion to a satyr, so loving to my mother 140
That he might not beteem the winds of heaven
Visit her face too roughly – heaven and earth,
Must I remember? why, she would hang on him
As if increase of appetite had grown
By what it fed on, and yet within a month – 145
Let me not think on't; frailty, thy name is woman –
A little month, or ere those shoes were old
With which she followed my poor father's body
Like Niobe, all tears, why she, even she –
O God, a beast that wants discourse of reason 150
Would have mourned longer – married with my uncle,
My father's brother, but no more like my father
Than I to Hercules – within a month,
Ere yet the salt of most unrighteous tears
Had left the flushing in her gallèd eyes, 155
She married. Oh most wicked speed, to post
With such dexterity to incestuous sheets.

133 weary] F; wary Q2 134 Seem] Q2; Seemes F 135 ah fie] Q2; Oh fie, fie F 137 to this] F; thus Q2 143 would] F; should Q2 149 she, even she] F; she Q2 150 God] Q2; Heauen F 151 my] Q2; mine F 155 in] Q2, Q1; of F

133 **flat** lifeless, spiritless. Compare 4.7.31.

134 **uses** customary doings.

137 **merely** absolutely.

140 **Hyperion** One of the Titans; frequently identified, as here, as the sun-god.

140 **satyr** Grotesque creature, half-human but with the legs of a goat, attendant on Dionysus, and synonymous with lechery.

141 **beteem** allow. (The context insists on this meaning, but it is a strained usage of a rare word; see *OED*.)

147 **or ere** even before. Both words mean 'before', so the phrase 'or ere', 'or e'er', 'or ever' (see 1.2.183) is just an intensification.

147 **those shoes were old** An extraordinarily homely touch among these references to Hyperion and Niobe. His mother had worn new shoes for her husband's funeral, and they were still as good as new for her marriage to Claudius.

149 **Niobe** The mythical mother whose fourteen children were slain by the gods because she boasted about them. She wept until she was turned to stone – and still the tears flowed.

150 **discourse of reason** faculty of reasoning.

155 **left...eyes** (1) gone from the redness of her sore eyes, (2) ceased flowing in her sore eyes. The meaning of 'flushing' is uncertain here, and it is therefore difficult to choose between 'flushing in' (Q2, Q1) and 'flushing of' (F).

157 **incestuous** Marriage to a brother's wife was explicitly forbidden by the Church. See the 'Table of Kindred and Affinity' in the Book of Common Prayer. Henry VIII had been given special dispensation by the Pope to marry his brother's

It is not, nor it cannot come to good.
But break, my heart, for I must hold my tongue.

Enter HORATIO, MARCELLUS *and* BARNARDO

HORATIO Hail to your lordship.
HAMLET I am glad to see you well. 160
Horatio – or I do forget myself.
HORATIO The same, my lord, and your poor servant ever.
HAMLET Sir, my good friend, I'll change that name with you.
And what make you from Wittenberg, Horatio?
Marcellus. 165
MARCELLUS My good lord.
HAMLET I am very glad to see you. (*To Barnardo*) Good even sir.
But what in faith make you from Wittenberg, Horatio?
HORATIO A truant disposition, good my lord.
HAMLET I would not hear your enemy say so, 170
Nor shall you do my ear that violence
To make it truster of your own report
Against yourself. I know you are no truant.
But what is your affair in Elsinore?
We'll teach you to drink deep ere you depart. 175
HORATIO My lord, I came to see your father's funeral.
HAMLET I pray thee do not mock me fellow student,
I think it was to see my mother's wedding.
HORATIO Indeed my lord, it followed hard upon.

170 hear] Q2*;* haue F 171 my] Q2*;* mine F 175 to drink deep] F*;* for to drinke Q2 177 pray thee] F*;* prethee Q2 *(corrected);* pre thee Q2 *(uncorrected)*, Q1 178 see] F*; not in* Q2

widow, Catherine of Aragon. His later inability to obtain from the Pope a dissolution of his marriage precipitated the English Reformation and the succession of Queen Elizabeth. W. F. Trench thought that Shakespeare and the audience of *Hamlet* would share the national view that such a marriage was sinful. See his *Shakespeare's 'Hamlet'*, 1913, pp. 55, 257–60.

159 break, my heart i.e. with unuttered grief. The heart was thought to be kept in place by ligaments or tendons (the heart-strings) which might snap under the pressure of great emotion.

160 I...well He has not yet recognised Horatio.

163 change exchange.

163 that name i.e. 'good friend'.

176 came...funeral How have Hamlet and Horatio contrived to avoid meeting each other in a small court during the last few weeks? Horatio's part is full of inconsistencies: he serves the role which the moment demands. Though he has been absent at Wittenberg, he is able to inform the Danish soldiers about what is happening in their own country in the first scene. Yet in 5.1.191 he has to be told who Laertes is! See note to 186 below.

177 pray thee Q2's 'pre thee' (corrected to 'prethee') is obviously copied from Q1's 'pre thee', and we must prefer F's form as more likely to be Shakespeare's, especially in view of F's shorter form at 119 above. The pronunciation of all forms is probably 'prithee'.

179 upon Used here adverbially, as elsewhere in Shakespeare, with another adverb, to denote a nearness in time. Clark and Wright compare *Measure for Measure* 4.6.14, 'And very near upon/The duke is entering', and Schmidt adds *Troilus and Cressida* 4.3.3, 'the hour prefixed... Comes fast upon'.

HAMLET Thrift, thrift, Horatio. The funeral baked meats 180
Did coldly furnish forth the marriage tables.
Would I had met my dearest foe in heaven
Or ever I had seen that day, Horatio.
My father, methinks I see my father –
HORATIO Where my lord?
HAMLET In my mind's eye, Horatio. 185
HORATIO I saw him once, a was a goodly king.
HAMLET A was a man, take him for all in all.
I shall not look upon his like again.
HORATIO My lord, I think I saw him yesternight.
HAMLET Saw? Who? 190
HORATIO My lord, the king your father.
HAMLET The king my father!
HORATIO Season your admiration for a while
With an attent ear, till I may deliver
Upon the witness of these gentlemen
This marvel to you.
HAMLET For God's love let me hear. 195
HORATIO Two nights together had these gentlemen,
Marcellus and Barnardo, on their watch
In the dead waste and middle of the night,
Been thus encountered. A figure like your father,
Armèd at point exactly, cap-a-pe, 200

183 Or ever I had] Q2; Ere I had euer F; Ere euer I had Q1 185 Where] Q2, Q1; Oh where F 186 a] Q2; he F 187 A] Q2; He F 190 Saw? Who?] F; saw, who? Q2 195 God's] Q2; Heauens F 198 waste] wast Q2, F; vast Q1; waist *Malone* 200 at point exactly,] at poynt, exactly Q2; at all points exactly, F; to poynt, exactly Q1

181 coldly The remains of the pies baked for the funeral were economically served cold for the wedding feast.

182 dearest closest. That the worst thing you can imagine is meeting your greatest enemy in heaven seems very strange. Kittredge suspected a proverbial saying. It is nevertheless characteristic of Hamlet to wish his opponents to go to hell (see 3.3.93–5 and 5.2.47); it is an aspect of his fierce conviction that moral discriminations ought to have a timeless value. See Introduction, p. 42.

183 or ever See note to 147.

186 I saw him once Greater knowledge of him is implied in 1.1.59–64, and in 211 below.

190 Saw? Who? All three texts give some kind of a pause between 'saw' and 'who'. The Davenant–Betterton quarto of 1676 treats the phrase as a single question, 'Saw who?'. But the Hughs–Wilks promptbook of 1718 has 'Saw! Who?' and this is found in J. P. Kemble's version of 1800. Charles Kean's version (1859) has 'Saw who?'. Both treated it as a single question, and so did Kean and Macready, according to Dyce (NV). Irving, however, restored 'Saw? – Who?' (see Winter, *Shakespeare on the Stage*, 1911, p. 357).

192 Season Make more temperate, restrain.

192 admiration wonder.

193 attent attentive.

198 waste Q2 and F read 'wast'; Q1 has 'vast' and in view of *The Tempest*'s 'vast of night' some editors (e.g. Dowden, Kittredge, Cambridge) adopt it. Malone reads 'waist'. The desolation of 'dead waste' is surely what is required here, though the latent pun 'waist' no doubt suggested 'middle'.

200 at point exactly, cap-a-pe properly and correctly, from head to foot.

Appears before them, and with solemn march
Goes slow and stately by them. Thrice he walked
By their oppressed and fear-surprisèd eyes
Within his truncheon's length, whilst they, distilled
Almost to jelly with the act of fear, 205
Stand dumb and speak not to him. This to me
In dreadful secrecy impart they did,
And I with them the third night kept the watch,
Where, as they had delivered, both in time,
Form of the thing, each word made true and good, 210
The apparition comes. I knew your father,
These hands are not more like.

HAMLET But where was this?

MARCELLUS My lord, upon the platform where we watched.

HAMLET Did you not speak to it?

HORATIO My lord, I did,
But answer made it none. Yet once methought 215
It lifted up it head and did address
Itself to motion like as it would speak;
But even then the morning cock crew loud,
And at the sound it shrunk in haste away
And vanished from our sight.

HAMLET 'Tis very strange. 220

HORATIO As I do live my honoured lord 'tis true,
And we did think it writ down in our duty
To let you know of it.

HAMLET Indeed, indeed sirs, but this troubles me.
Hold you the watch tonight?

MARCELLUS }
BARNARDO } We do, my lord. 225

204 distilled] distil'd Q2; bestil'd F **209** Where, as] Where as Q 1637; Whereas Q2, F **213** watched] watcht F; watch Q2 **224** Indeed, indeed] F, Q1; Indeede Q2 **225, 6, 7** MARCELLUS/BARNARDO] *Capell; All.* Q2, Q1; *Both.* F

204 distilled dissolved.

205 act action.

207 dreadful awe-struck (referring to their manner) rather than solemn (referring to the secrecy).

213 platform See note to 1.1.0 SD.

213 watched were on watch. Q2's 'watch' makes the meaning 'normally keep the watch'.

216 it head its head. The normal possessive form of 'it' was 'his' (see note to 1.1.127) but 'it' is occasionally used by Shakespeare, and less frequently 'its'.

216–17 address...speak started to move as though it were about to speak.

225 The speech heading in Q2 is '*All.*', and in F, '*Both.*' Capell's judgement that '*Both*' is correct, meaning Marcellus and Barnardo, is a proper one, since Horatio is not a member of the watch. (All the same, it is notable that Barnardo never turns up for duty. See 1.4.0 SD.)

HAMLET Armed say you?

MARCELLUS / BARNARDO Armed my lord.

HAMLET From top to toe?

MARCELLUS / BARNARDO My lord, from head to foot.

HAMLET Then saw you not his face?

HORATIO Oh yes my lord, he wore his beaver up.

HAMLET What, looked he frowningly? 230

HORATIO A countenance more in sorrow than in anger.

HAMLET Pale, or red?

HORATIO Nay very pale.

HAMLET And fixed his eyes upon you?

HORATIO Most constantly.

HAMLET I would I had been there.

HORATIO It would have much amazed you. 235

HAMLET Very like, very like. Stayed it long?

HORATIO While one with moderate haste might tell a hundred.

MARCELLUS / BARNARDO Longer, longer.

HORATIO Not when I saw 't.

HAMLET His beard was grizzled, no?

HORATIO It was as I have seen it in his life, 240
A sable silvered.

HAMLET I will watch tonight,
Perchance 'twill walk again.

HORATIO I warrant it will.

HAMLET If it assume my noble father's person,
I'll speak to it though hell itself should gape
And bid me hold my peace. I pray you all, 245

236 Very like, very like] F, Q1; Very like Q2 238 MARCELLUS/BARNARDO] *Capell; Both.* Q2; *All.* F; *Mar.* Q1 239 grizzled] grissl'd Q2; grisly F; grisleld Q1 241 I will] Q2, Q1; Ile F 242 walk] walke Q2, Q1; wake F 242 warrant] Q1; warn't Q2; warrant you F

229 beaver the movable visor.

235 amazed bewildered, thrown into confusion.

239 grizzled grey. There is something to be said for following F and reading 'grizzly', which means exactly the same thing. Q2's 'grissl'd' looks as though it may derive from Q1.

241 sable silvered black touched with white.

243 assume take on. Hamlet thinks of the apparition as a spirit appearing in the guise of his father, though a few lines later he speaks of 'my father's spirit' (254). Maynard Mack, in 'The world of *Hamlet*', *Yale Review* 41 (1952), noted the importance of the word 'assume' in this play where many people adopt characters not their own. Compare 1.4.72, 2.2.552–3, and 3.4.161.

244 hell...gape the mouth of hell should open wide.

245 bid...peace As Jenkins points out, it is the threat of damnation for having commerce with a devil that would bid him to be silent.

If you have hitherto concealed this sight,
Let it be tenable in your silence still,
And whatsomever else shall hap tonight,
Give it an understanding but no tongue.
I will requite your loves. So fare you well: 250
Upon the platform 'twixt eleven and twelve
I'll visit you.

ALL Our duty to your honour.

HAMLET Your loves, as mine to you. Farewell.

Exeunt all but Hamlet

My father's spirit, in arms! All is not well.
I doubt some foul play. Would the night were come. 255
Till then sit still my soul. Foul deeds will rise
Though all the earth o'erwhelm them to men's eyes. *Exit*

1.3 *Enter* LAERTES *and* OPHELIA *his sister*

LAERTES My necessaries are embarked, farewell.
And sister, as the winds give benefit
And convoy is assistant, do not sleep
But let me hear from you.

OPHELIA Do you doubt that?

LAERTES For Hamlet, and the trifling of his favour, 5
Hold it a fashion, and a toy in blood,
A violet in the youth of primy nature,
Forward, not permanent, sweet, not lasting,
The perfume and suppliance of a minute,
No more.

OPHELIA No more but so?

247 tenable] Q2; treble F 248 whatsomever] what someuer Q2; whatsoeuer F, Q1 250 fare] F; farre Q2 250 you] Q2; ye F 251 eleven] F; a leauen Q2 253 loves] Q2, Q1; loue F 253 SD] *Cambridge; Exeunt. (252)* Q2, F; *Exeunt. Manet Hamlet.* Q 1676 254 spirit, in arms!] spirit (in armes) Q2; Spirit in Armes? F 256 Foul] foule F; fonde Q2 Act 1, Scene 3 1.3] *Scena Tertia* F 0 SD *his sister*] Q2; *not in* F 1 embarked] imbark't F; inbarckt Q2; in barkt Q1 3 convoy is] F; conuay, in Q2 5 favour] Q2; fauours F 8 Forward] Q2; Froward F 9 perfume and] Q2; *not in* F

247 tenable something that can be held.

248 whatsomever A quite regular form, eventually ousted by 'whatsoever'.

255 doubt suspect.

Act 1, Scene 3

3 convoy is assistant conveyance is at hand.

6 a fashion just a way of behaving.

6 a toy in blood a whim of passion.

7 the youth...nature the spring-time of life ('primy' seems to be a Shakespearean coinage).

9 suppliance supply (i.e. the violet serves for a minute only).

LAERTES Think it no more. 10

For nature crescent does not grow alone
In thews and bulk, but as this temple waxes
The inward service of the mind and soul
Grows wide withal. Perhaps he loves you now,
And now no soil nor cautel doth besmirch 15
The virtue of his will; but you must fear,
His greatness weighed, his will is not his own,
For he himself is subject to his birth.
He may not, as unvalued persons do,
Carve for himself, for on his choice depends 20
The sanctity and health of this whole state,
And therefore must his choice be circumscribed
Unto the voice and yielding of that body
Whereof he is the head. Then if he says he loves you,
It fits your wisdom so far to believe it 25
As he in his peculiar sect and force
May give his saying deed, which is no further
Than the main voice of Denmark goes withal.
Then weigh what loss your honour may sustain

12 bulk] F; bulkes Q2 12 this] Q2; his F 16 will] Q2; feare F 18 For...birth] F; *not in* Q2 21 sanctity] F; safty Q2; sanity *Hanmer, conj. Theobald* 21 this whole] Q2; the weole F 26 peculiar sect and force] F; particular act and place Q2

11–14 For nature...withal Growing up is not a matter of physical size only: while the body grows, the inner life of mind and soul develops also. ('thews' = sinews.)

15 soil stain.

15 cautel deceitfulness.

17 His greatness weighed If you consider his greatness.

20 Carve for himself i.e. serve his own interests.

21 sanctity So F. Q2 reads 'safty' and most editions read 'safety'. Theobald conjectured 'sanity' (= soundness of condition), which Wilson and others accept. 'Safety' is altogether the feebler reading, and no scribe or compositor could have substituted 'sanctity' in its stead. I believe N. Alexander is alone among modern editors in accepting 'sanctity', glossing it 'holiness, sacred quality'. It seems to me, most powerfully, the correct reading. It fits admirably the rather fervent and excessive way in which Laertes speaks of everything. More than that, it illustrates how everyone in the play contributes, in his or her own marked manner of speaking, to the central meanings of the play. The health of the kingdom is a spiritual health, and it is indeed true, though Laertes cannot know it, that the present spiritual sickness of the kingdom arises from Gertrude's infidelity to the king.

23 voice and yielding vote and consent.

24 The line has thirteen syllables.

26 his peculiar sect and force the special circumstances of his class and power. So F. Q2 reads 'particular act and place', and it is hard to see how this eroded phrase has won almost universal acceptance. (J. Q. Adams, 1929, is a notable exception in following F). While 'act' can mean little in this context, 'sect' has the well-established meaning of a class or kind of person, as in *Measure for Measure* 2.2.5: 'All sects, all ages, smack of this vice.' 'force' refers to the limited freedom of Hamlet's social class as Laertes has just described it. Q2 gives a misreading of such unusual length that one may ascribe it to the decreasing legibility of Shakespeare's MS. between the transcription which lies behind F and the printing of Q2 in 1604. (See Introduction, pp. 27–9.)

28 main voice general assent.

If with too credent ear you list his songs, 30
Or lose your heart, or your chaste treasure open
To his unmastered importunity.
Fear it Ophelia, fear it my dear sister,
And keep you in the rear of your affection,
Out of the shot and danger of desire. 35
The chariest maid is prodigal enough
If she unmask her beauty to the moon.
Virtue itself scapes not calumnious strokes.
The canker galls the infants of the spring
Too oft before their buttons be disclosed, 40
And in the morn and liquid dew of youth
Contagious blastments are most imminent.
Be wary then, best safety lies in fear:
Youth to itself rebels, though none else near.

OPHELIA I shall th'effect of this good lesson keep 45
As watchman to my heart. But good my brother,
Do not as some ungracious pastors do,
Show me the steep and thorny way to heaven,
Whiles like a puffed and reckless libertine
Himself the primrose path of dalliance treads, 50
And recks not his own rede.

LAERTES Oh fear me not.

34 you in] Q2; within F 45 th'effect] F; the effect Q2 46 watchman] Q2; watchmen F 48 steep] steepe Q2 *(corrected)*, F; step Q2 *(uncorrected)* 49 Whiles] Q2; Whilst F 49 like] F; *not in* Q2 51 recks] Q1, *Pope*; reakes Q2; reaks F

30 credent believing.

30 list listen to.

31 your chaste treasure the treasure of your chastity. Compare with this florid language the words of the song Ophelia sings in her madness: 'Let in the maid, that out a maid/Never departed more' (4.5.54–5).

34 keep...affection A military metaphor; Ophelia is not to go so far forward as her affection might lead her.

35 shot range, shooting distance.

36–7 The chariest...moon The most cautious maid goes almost too far, if she does no more than reveal her beauty to the chaste moon.

36, 38, 39 Q2 marks these lines with inverted commas, the signs of 'sentences', or improving moral generalities – the 'saws of books' which Hamlet later disavows. Laertes no doubt learned the trick of coining these sententious observations from his father. The tables are turned on him when, after these preachments to Ophelia, he is forced to listen to a battery of moral sentences from his father.

39 canker insect pest feeding on plants. (For the more general, figurative use, see 5.2.69.)

40 buttons be disclosed i.e. buds open out.

42 blastments blightings. *OED* records no other usages of this word, except late ones deriving from this.

44 to itself rebels 'acts contrary to its better nature' (Kittredge).

48, 50 thorny way / primrose path The image of two contrasting roads was one of the commonest ways of distinguishing a life of virtue from one of vice. It was frequently pictured as 'the choice of Hercules', showing the hero making up his mind which path to follow. See E. Panofsky, *Hercules am Scheidewege*, 1930.

51 recks...rede pays no attention to his own counsel.

Enter POLONIUS

I stay too long – But here my father comes.
A double blessing is a double grace;
Occasion smiles upon a second leave.
POLONIUS Yet here Laertes? Aboard, aboard for shame! 55
The wind sits in the shoulder of your sail,
And you are stayed for. There, my blessing with thee,
And these few precepts in thy memory
Look thou character. Give thy thoughts no tongue,
Nor any unproportioned thought his act. 60
Be thou familiar, but by no means vulgar.
Those friends thou hast, and their adoption tried,
Grapple them unto thy soul with hoops of steel,
But do not dull thy palm with entertainment
Of each new-hatched, unfledged courage. Beware 65
Of entrance to a quarrel, but being in,
Bear't that th'opposèd may beware of thee.
Give every man thy ear, but few thy voice;

57 with thee] Q2, Q1; with you F 59 Look] Q2; See F 62 Those] Q2, Q1; The F 63 unto] Q2; to F 65 new-hatched] new hatcht Q2; vnhatch't F 65 courage] Q2, Q1; Comrade F 68 thy ear] Q2; thine eare F

54 Occasion...leave A second leave-taking is a fortunate occurrence. As with Ophelia's two paths (above) this is an emblem or moral picture; Occasion or Opportunity is shown as a goddess. See H. Green, *Shakespeare and the Emblem Writers*, 1870, pp. 261–5.

55 aboard for shame! 'for shame' attached to an imperative (or a word of injunction) creates an admonition. Compare 'Doff it for shame!' *King John* 3.1.128. Most editors put a comma after 'aboard' as though 'for shame' were a separate exclamation and reproof.

58 these few precepts In the previous scene, the present scene and the next, parents are busy advising and instructing children, and attempting to regulate their lives. The tables are turned in the second half of the play, when Hamlet admonishes his mother and the dutiful Laertes rebels against his king.

59 character inscribe. Accent on second syllable.

60 Nor...act Once again (see note to 1.3.21) a speech in an entirely separate context seems to refer directly to a central problem of the play – the proper relation between 'thought' and 'act'. Compare the rather different advice given to Laertes by Claudius at 4.7.117–18.

61 but...vulgar i.e. but don't be familiar with everybody.

62 and...tried whose worthiness to be adopted you have tested.

64 dull thy palm make your hand insensitive. The handshake is seen as a sensitive means of registering true friendship. 'Palm to palm is holy palmers' kiss', said Juliet.

65 courage So Q2 and Q1. F reads 'comrade', a much easier reading. Kittredge suggested 'com-rague', or fellow-rogue, and this, or 'comrogue' has won some support. *OED* (1b), giving the main meaning of 'courage' as heart, spirit, disposition, says it can be used of a person (as we use both 'heart' and 'spirit') and cites Hoby's translation of Castiglione's *The Courtier*, Book 4. Certain buildings erected by various great men are 'a great witness of the prowess of those divine courages'. If we consult the trilingual edition of 1588, we find (sig. Ll 3 recto) that the last three words are the equivalent of the Italian *quegli animi divini* and the French *ces esprits divins*. So the word means a man of spirit, and no doubt could be used in a derogatory way: a dashing fellow. The accent must fall on the second syllable.

67 Bear't that Manage it so that, so carry it that.

Take each man's censure, but reserve thy judgement.
Costly thy habit as thy purse can buy, 70
But not expressed in fancy: rich, not gaudy.
For the apparel oft proclaims the man,
And they in France of the best rank and station
Are of a most select and generous chief in that.
Neither a borrower nor a lender be, 75
For loan oft loses both itself and friend,
And borrowing dulls the edge of husbandry.
This above all, to thine own self be true,
And it must follow, as the night the day,
Thou canst not then be false to any man. 80
Farewell, my blessing season this in thee.

LAERTES Most humbly do I take my leave, my lord.
POLONIUS The time invites you. Go, your servants tend.
LAERTES Farewell Ophelia, and remember well
What I have said to you.
OPHELIA 'Tis in my memory locked, 85
And you yourself shall keep the key of it.
LAERTES Farewell. *Exit Laertes*
POLONIUS What is't Ophelia he hath said to you?
OPHELIA So please you, something touching the Lord Hamlet.
POLONIUS Marry, well bethought. 90
'Tis told me he hath very oft of late
Given private time to you, and you yourself

70 buy] Q2 *(corrected)*, F; by Q2 *(uncorrected)* 74 Are] F; Or Q2 74 generous] F; generous, Q2; generall Q1 74 chief] chiefe Q2, Q1; cheff F 75 be] F; boy Q2 76 loan] lone F; loue Q2 77 dulls the] F; dulleth Q2 83 invites] F; inuests Q2

69 censure judgement (not necessarily adverse).

70 habit apparel, clothes.

74 Are...that i.e. have an exquisite and noble gift in choosing the right clothes. The main problem in this much-discussed line is 'chief', which appears in F as 'cheff'. With some strain, we can take it as a noun meaning 'excellence'. But I think it possible that a somewhat unusual word appeared in Shakespeare's MS., which eventually turns up as 'cheff' in F, and which defeated the Q compositor so that, as so often, he had recourse to Q1 and borrowed 'chiefe' from it (having earlier in the line misread 'And' as 'Or'). It is tempting to think that Polonius had his own idea of what French *chef* meant.

77 husbandry thrift.

78 to...true There are higher aims in life than to be true to such a limited self as Polonius. Again, these words rise from their immediate context and radiate over the whole play. Such an injunction, of dubious value for Polonius and Laertes, touches the centre of Hamlet's predicament. 'To thine own self be true'! But to which self? He cannot reach the self to which he must be true.

81 season bring to due season, ripen.

83 invites A number of editors, from Theobald on, have felt that Q's 'invests' could be justified (= lays siege to). It is certainly an odd word to come up as a misreading, and it ought to be preferred on the principle of 'the more difficult reading', but F's 'invites' seems obviously correct.

83 tend attend.

90 Marry By the Virgin Mary.

90 well bethought he did well to think of that. Compare *Pericles* 5.1.44.

Have of your audience been most free and bounteous.
If it be so, as so 'tis put on me,
And that in way of caution, I must tell you 95
You do not understand yourself so clearly
As it behooves my daughter, and your honour.
What is between you? Give me up the truth.

OPHELIA He hath my lord of late made many tenders
Of his affection to me. 100

POLONIUS Affection? Puh! You speak like a green girl,
Unsifted in such perilous circumstance.
Do you believe his tenders as you call them?

OPHELIA I do not know my lord what I should think.

POLONIUS Marry I'll teach you. Think yourself a baby 105
That you have tane these tenders for true pay,
Which are not sterling. Tender yourself more dearly,
Or – not to crack the wind of the poor phrase,
Roaming it thus – you'll tender me a fool.

OPHELIA My lord, he hath importuned me with love 110
In honourable fashion.

POLONIUS Ay, fashion you may call it. Go to, go to.

OPHELIA And hath given countenance to his speech, my lord,
With almost all the holy vows of heaven.

POLONIUS Ay, springes to catch woodcocks. I do know, 115
When the blood burns, how prodigal the soul

97 behooves] Q2; behoues F 105 I'll] Ile F; I will Q2 106 these] Q2; his F 107 sterling] Q2; starling F 109 Roaming] F; Wrong Q2; Running *Dyce, conj. Collier* 113 my lord / With] / My Lord, with Q2, F 114 almost] Q2; *not in* F 115 springes] F; springs Q2

94 put on me given to me.

97 behooves becomes, befits.

102 Unsifted Inexperienced (literally, not strained through a sieve).

106 tane taken: the common shortened form of the past participle. Modern editions usually give the awkward and unhistorical spelling 'ta'en', which wrongly suggests a two-syllable pronunciation.

107 Tender yourself Look after yourself.

109 Roaming Polonius means he doesn't want to tire the phrase out by too much verbal roaming. The use of 'it' as the indefinite object of a more-or-less intransitive verb is fully exemplified in Franz, *Die Sprache Shakespeares*, 1939, p. 272. Most examples are of noun-verbs; e.g. 'my true lip / Hath virgined it e'er since' (*Coriolanus* 5.3.48), or 'I will queen it no inch farther' (*Winter's Tale* 4.4.449). But compare 'I come to wive it wealthily in Padua' (*Shrew* 1.2.73); 'And revel it as bravely as the best' (*Shrew* 4.3.54); 'Nor should that nation boast it so with us' (*1 Henry VI* 3.3.23); 'She sweeps it through the court with troops of ladies' (*2 Henry VI* 1.3.77). See further in *OED* It 9.

As for Q2's 'Wrong', *w* and *r* are easily mistaken in Elizabethan handwriting, or Shakespeare's 'romĩg' might have been read as 'rong' (compare Wilson, *MSH*, pp. 315–16).

109 tender me a fool present me as a fool. (Other interpretations include 'present yourself as a fool to me' and Dowden's ingenious idea, 'present me with an illegitimate baby'.) Polonius's concern here is for himself. He is thinking what a fool he will look at court if Ophelia is involved in a scandal.

110 importuned Accent on second syllable.

112 fashion See line 6 above.

115 springes snares.

116–17 how...Lends i.e. how prodigal (lavish) the soul is in lending.

Lends the tongue vows. These blazes daughter,
Giving more light than heat, extinct in both
Even in their promise as it is a-making,
You must not take for fire. From this time 120
Be something scanter of your maiden presence.
Set your entreatments at a higher rate
Than a command to parley. For Lord Hamlet,
Believe so much in him, that he is young
And with a larger tedder may he walk 125
Than may be given you. In few Ophelia,
Do not believe his vows, for they are brokers,
Not of that dye which their investments show,
But mere implorators of unholy suits,
Breathing like sanctified and pious bonds, 130
The better to beguile. This is for all:
I would not in plain terms from this time forth
Have you so slander any moment leisure
As to give words or talk with the Lord Hamlet.
Look to't I charge you. Come your ways. 135

OPHELIA I shall obey, my lord.

Exeunt

117 Lends] Q2, Q1; Giues F **120** From] Q2; For F **120** time] Q2; time Daughter F **121** something] Q2; somewhat F **123** parley] F; parle Q2 **125** tedder] Q 1676; tider Q2; tether F **128** that dye] that die Q2; the eye F **129** implorators] F; imploratotors Q2 **130** bonds] Q2, F; bawds *Pope*[2], *conj. Theobald* **131** beguile] F; beguide Q2

122–3 Set...parley 'When a besieger appears before the castle of your heart and summons you to a parley, do not immediately enter into negotiations (*entreatments*) for surrender' (Kittredge).

125 tedder A widely used alternative form of 'tether'. Probably the MS. had 'teder'.

126 In few In few words.

127 brokers negotiatiors, esp. go-betweens, pimps. Nigel Alexander suggests that in the 'complex series of images' which follows, three meanings of 'broker' are intertwined, 'a shady financier, a pander who promises marriage, and an old clothes man'.

128 investments vestments, robes. The brokers wear the garments of dignitaries.

129 mere no less than, out-and-out.

129 implorators solicitors. *OED* records no other occurrence of the word.

130 bonds agreements, contracts. Malone compared Sonnet 142, 'sealed false bonds of love'. Theobald's ludicrous emendation, 'bawds', has been widely followed, because of the difficulty of imagining anyone breathing like a bond. But 'Breathing' here means 'speaking'. The line as a whole means 'using the words of holy contracts of love'.

133 slander disgrace, misuse.

135 your ways This is an adverbial form, 'on your way'. See Franz, *Die Sprache Shakespeares*, p. 219.

[1.4] *Enter* HAMLET, HORATIO *and* MARCELLUS

HAMLET The air bites shrewdly, it is very cold.
HORATIO It is a nipping and an eager air.
HAMLET What hour now?
HORATIO I think it lacks of twelve.
MARCELLUS No, it is struck.
HORATIO Indeed? I heard it not. It then draws near the season 5
Wherein the spirit held his wont to walk.
A flourish of trumpets and two pieces goes off
What does this mean, my lord?
HAMLET The king doth wake tonight and takes his rouse,
Keeps wassail, and the swaggering up-spring reels,
And as he drains his draughts of Rhenish down, 10
The kettle-drum and trumpet thus bray out
The triumph of his pledge.
HORATIO Is it a custom?
HAMLET Ay marry is't,
But to my mind, though I am native here
And to the manner born, it is a custom 15
More honoured in the breach than the observance.
[This heavy-headed revel east and west

Act 1, Scene 4 1.4] Scene IV *Capell; no indication in* Q2, F 1 shrewdly] F; shroudly Q2 1 it is] Q2; is it F 2 is a] F; is Q2 5 Indeed?] *Capell;* Indeede; Q2; Indeed F, Q1 5 It then] Q2; then it F 6 SD] Q2; *not in* F 9 wassail] wassell Q2; wassels F 14 But] Q2; And F; Q1 17–38 This heavy-headed...scandal] Q2; *not in* F

Act 1, Scene 4

0 SD In this and the next scene we return to the 'platform' of the first scene.

1 **shrewdly** keenly, injuriously. Compare *Richard II* 3.2.59, 'To lift shrewd steel against our golden crown'. (The original meaning of 'shrewd' is 'malicious', 'ill-disposed'.)

2 **eager** sharp, biting. Compare 1.5.69.

3 **lacks of** i.e. is just short of.

6 **held his wont** had its custom.

6 SD *two pieces goes off* i.e. a salvo from two cannons is fired.

8 **wake** make a night-time celebration.

8–9 **takes his rouse, / Keeps wassail** More or less synonymous phrases for ceremonious carousal and wine-drinking.

9 **swaggering up-spring reels** The meaning is uncertain. 'up-spring' may be a German dance, in which case Jenkins's solution is best. He argues that 'reel' means to dance riotously, and that the subject of the verb is Claudius, who dances the up-spring.

10 **Rhenish** Rhine wine.

10–12 **And as...pledge** As the king had promised. See 1.2.124–8.

12 **triumph** Properly, a public celebration of an important event. Used ironically here.

12 **pledge** toast.

15 **to the manner born** i.e. accustomed to this way of behaving since birth.

16 **More honoured...observance** i.e. it shows more honour in a man to break the custom than to observe it.

17–38 It is argued in the Introduction (p. 14) that this passage, which is found in Q2 but not in F, was in fact discarded by Shakespeare during the composition of the play.

17 **east and west** everywhere (i.e. by other nations everywhere).

Makes us traduced and taxed of other nations.
They clepe us drunkards, and with swinish phrase
Soil our addition; and indeed it takes 20
From our achievements, though performed at height,
The pith and marrow of our attribute.
So, oft it chances in particular men,
That for some vicious mole of nature in them,
As in their birth, wherein they are not guilty, 25
Since nature cannot choose his origin,
By their o'ergrowth of some complexion,
Oft breaking down the pales and forts of reason,
Or by some habit that too much o'erleavens
The form of plausive manners – that these men, 30
Carrying I say the stamp of one defect,
Being nature's livery or fortune's star,
His virtues else be they as pure as grace,
As infinite as man may undergo,
Shall in the general censure take corruption 35
From that particular fault. The dram of eale
Doth all the noble substance of a doubt
To his own scandal.]

Enter GHOST

HORATIO Look my lord, it comes!

19 clepe] Q 1637; clip Q2 23 So, oft] *Theobald*[2]; So oft Q2 27 their] Q2; the *Pope*

18 traduced and taxed of slandered and censured by.

19 clepe call.

19–20 with swinish...addition pollute our proper title or description ('addition') by calling us pigs.

20–2 it takes...attribute our fondness for drink robs the best of our achievements of the very essence of the reputation due to us.

24 mole of nature natural mark.

26 his its.

27 their o'ergrowth of some complexion the excessive growth of some natural tendency. The allusion is to the doctrine of the four humours, blood, phlegm, choler and melancholy, whose proper balance was necessary for a stable temperament.

28 pales palisades.

29 habit (here) a bad habit.

29 too much o'erleavens Too much leaven in the dough will ruin the bread. So too great an admixture of 'some habit' will ruin the form of pleasing manners.

32 nature's livery a dress marking one's servitude to nature.

32 fortune's star a destiny falling to one by chance. For 'star' in this transferred sense (cause for effect), see *OED sv sb*[1] 3c which cites *Hamlet* 2.2.141, 'a prince out of thy star'.

34 undergo support.

36–8 dram of eale...scandal It is impossible to recover the correct reading of these lines. Nosworthy argued that the sentence is unfinished; that Shakespeare had lost faith in the speech, and 'gave up the struggle' (*Shakespeare's Occasional Plays*, p. 141). 'eale' is clearly a misreading; there have been many conjectures to replace it. It is obvious that the general significance is that a mere 'dram' of bad matter ruins an entire 'noble substance'.

HAMLET Angels and ministers of grace defend us!
Be thou a spirit of health, or goblin damned, 40
Bring with thee airs from heaven or blasts from hell,
Be thy intents wicked or charitable,
Thou com'st in such a questionable shape
That I will speak to thee. I'll call thee Hamlet,
King, father, royal Dane. Oh answer me. 45
Let me not burst in ignorance, but tell
Why thy canonised bones, hearsèd in death,
Have burst their cerements; why the sepulchre,
Wherein we saw thee quietly enurned,
Hath oped his ponderous and marble jaws 50
To cast thee up again. What may this mean,
That thou, dead corse, again in complete steel
Revisits thus the glimpses of the moon,
Making night hideous, and we fools of nature
So horridly to shake our disposition 55
With thoughts beyond the reaches of our souls?
Say, why is this? wherefore? What should we do?

Ghost beckons Hamlet

HORATIO It beckons you to go away with it,
As if it some impartment did desire
To you alone.

MARCELLUS Look with what courteous action 60

42 intents] Q2; euents F 45 Oh] ô Q2, Q1; Oh, oh, F 49 enurned] F; interr'd Q2, Q1 56 the reaches] Q2; thee; reaches F 57 SD] F; *Beckins* Q2

40 spirit of health an uncorrupted spirit, bringing 'airs from heaven' (41) and 'charitable' intents (42).

40 goblin damned a demon, bringing 'blasts from hell' and 'wicked' intents.

43 questionable shape 'shape' means the external dress or guise (see Glossary to Massinger, ed. Edwards and Gibson, vol. V). Whatever the ghost may be essentially, its external appearance is of a being who can be questioned.

47 canonised consecrated. Accent on second syllable.

47 hearsèd coffined. Accent on first syllable. The line as a whole gets a strong rhythmic effect from disputing the underlying iambic structure; viz. 'Whý thy̆ căńoňis'd bónes, heársěd iň deáth.'

48 cerements grave-clothes. Pronounced seer-ments.

49 enurned So F ('enurn'd'). Some modern editions prefer Q2's 'interr'd', which also appears in Q1. No one but Shakespeare could have created so strong a reading as 'enurned'. 'urn' was often used loosely by Shakespeare and others to mean a grave, but the word is here not literal but metaphorical: the sepulchre envelops and encloses the body as though it were a funerary urn. It has been suggested that Shakespeare wrote 'enurned' during revision. It is much more probable that it was the original word, and that the Q2 compositor, faced with a coinage that was not in his vocabulary, turned to the safety of Q1's familiar but weakened reading.

52 complete steel full armour ('cómplete').

53 glimpses pale gleams.

54 fools of nature natural creatures, too ignorant to understand what lies beyond.

55 horridly...disposition to upset ourselves so violently.

59 impartment communication.

It wafts you to a more removèd ground.
But do not go with it.

HORATIO No, by no means.

HAMLET It will not speak. Then I will follow it.

HORATIO Do not my lord.

HAMLET Why, what should be the fear?
I do not set my life at a pin's fee, 65
And for my soul, what can it do to that,
Being a thing immortal as itself?
It waves me forth again. I'll follow it.

HORATIO What if it tempt you toward the flood my lord,
Or to the dreadful summit of the cliff 70
That beetles o'er his base into the sea,
And there assume some other horrible form
Which might deprive your sovereignty of reason,
And draw you into madness? Think of it.
[The very place puts toys of desperation, 75
Without more motive, into every brain
That looks so many fathoms to the sea
And hears it roar beneath.]

HAMLET It wafts me still. Go on, I'll follow thee.

MARCELLUS You shall not go my lord.

HAMLET Hold off your hands. 80

HORATIO Be ruled, you shall not go.

HAMLET My fate cries out,
And makes each petty arture in this body

61 wafts] F; waues Q2, Q1 63 I will] Q2; will I F, Q1 70 summit] *Rowe*; somnet Q2; Sonnet F 70 cliff] F; cleefe Q2 71 beetles] F; bettles Q2 72 assume] Q2, Q1; assumes F 75–8 The very...beneath] Q2; *not in* F 79 wafts] F; waues Q2 80 off] F; of Q2 80 hands] Q2; hand F 82 arture] Q2; Artire F

61 wafts F's reading; it means the same as Q2's 'waves', which is probably derived from Q1. Compare *Timon* 1.1.70, 'Whom Fortune with her ivory hand wafts to her'. 'wafts' for Q2's 'waves' occurs again at 79, but both texts agree on 'waves' at 68.

65 fee payment; hence 'worth'.

69 flood sea.

71 beetles o'er overhangs like bushy eyebrows. As *OED* notes, Shakespeare coined the verb 'beetle' from a recollection of a passage in Sidney's *Arcadia*, Book 1, ch. 10, 'they past in a pleasant valley, (of either side of which high hils lifted up their beetle-brows, as if they would over looke the pleasantness of their under-prospect).'

73 deprive...reason take away the sovereignty (supremacy) of your reason.

74 draw you into madness By the end of the next scene, the Ghost has indeed drawn Hamlet into 'madness' of a very different kind (1.5.172). Both Horatio and the Ghost (1.5.85) are concerned for the 'sovereignty' of Hamlet's reason.

75–8 These four lines are found only in Q2, and not in F. It is argued in the Introduction (pp. 13–14) that these lines were marked for deletion by Shakespeare, as confusing Horatio's main point.

75 toys of desperation whims of desperate behaviour (i.e. suicidal impulse).

81 My fate cries out My destiny is calling. That is, his future lies in what the ghost has to tell him.

82 arture artery, thought to convey the vital spirits.

As hardy as the Nemean lion's nerve.
Still am I called. Unhand me gentlemen!
By heaven I'll make a ghost of him that lets me. 85
I say away! – Go on, I'll follow thee.

Exit Ghost and Hamlet

HORATIO He waxes desperate with imagination.
MARCELLUS Let's follow, 'tis not fit thus to obey him.
HORATIO Have after. To what issue will this come?
MARCELLUS Something is rotten in the state of Denmark. 90
HORATIO Heaven will direct it.
MARCELLUS Nay let's follow him.

Exeunt

[1.5] *Enter* GHOST *and* HAMLET

HAMLET Whither wilt thou lead me? Speak, I'll go no further.
GHOST Mark me.
HAMLET I will.
GHOST My hour is almost come
When I to sulph'rous and tormenting flames
Must render up myself.
HAMLET Alas poor ghost!
GHOST Pity me not, but lend thy serious hearing 5
To what I shall unfold.
HAMLET Speak, I am bound to hear.
GHOST So art thou to revenge, when thou shalt hear.
HAMLET What?
GHOST I am thy father's spirit,
Doomed for a certain term to walk the night, 10

87 imagination] F; imagion Q2 **Act 1, Scene 5** 1.5] Scene V *Capell; no indication in* Q2, F 1 Whither] Whether Q2; Where F; whither Q1

83 **Nemean lion** Hercules accomplished his first labour by strangling the invulnerable Nemean lion. Pronounced Né-me-an.

83 **nerve** sinew.

85 **lets** hinders.

87 **waxes...imagination** has become totally reckless because of what is in his mind. Horatio believes that Hamlet's dangerous behaviour arises from his *idea* of the Ghost, which has obliterated the reality that the Ghost is capable of tremendous harm. Hamlet himself talks of his 'imaginations' about the Ghost in 3.2.73–4. See also Introduction, p. 60.

89 **Have after** Let us go after him.

Act 1, Scene 5

6 **bound** all prepared. The word came to be used for proceeding in a certain direction, as in 'homeward bound'. The Ghost in his reply turns to the quite separate word 'bound' meaning 'obliged' or 'compelled'.

And for the day confined to fast in fires,
Till the foul crimes done in my days of nature
Are burnt and purged away. But that I am forbid
To tell the secrets of my prison house,
I could a tale unfold whose lightest word 15
Would harrow up thy soul, freeze thy young blood,
Make thy two eyes like stars start from their spheres,
Thy knotted and combinèd locks to part
And each particular hair to stand an end
Like quills upon the fretful porpentine. 20
But this eternal blazon must not be
To ears of flesh and blood. List, list, oh list!
If thou didst ever thy dear father love –

HAMLET O God!

GHOST Revenge his foul and most unnatural murder. 25

HAMLET Murder?

GHOST Murder most foul, as in the best it is,
But this most foul, strange, and unnatural.

HAMLET Haste me to know't, that I with wings as swift
As meditation or the thoughts of love 30
May sweep to my revenge.

GHOST I find thee apt,
And duller shouldst thou be than the fat weed
That rots itself in ease on Lethe wharf,

18 knotted Q2, Q1; knotty F 20 fretful] F, Q1; fearefull Q2 22 List, list] Q2; list *Hamlet* F 24 God] Q2; Heauen F 29 Haste me] Q2, Q1; Hast, hast me F 29 know't] Q2; know it F, Q1 29 that I with] Q2; That with F 33 rots] F; rootes Q2, Q1

11 fast in fires Fasting amidst the purifying flames is necessary for the Ghost because he never received the absolution of the last rites (76–7).

12 foul crimes See Hamlet's reference to his father in the prayer scene (3.3.81), 'with all his crimes broad blown'. In both places the ordinary sinfulness of humanity is meant; in both places the language is strong with revulsion against the poisoner who did not allow King Hamlet the absolution he would have sought at the time of death. For crimes = faults, see 2.1.43.

16 harrow up See note to 1.1.44.

17 Make...spheres i.e. make your eyes start from your head as though they were stars jerked out of their appointed spheres (so indicating a dislocation in nature).

19 an end Obsolete form of 'on end'.

20 fretful So F. Q2's 'fearefull' is a weaker reading which does not accord with the contemporary animal-lore. Compare Joseph Hall, 'The Satire should be like the Porcupine, / That shoots sharp quills out in each angry line' (*Virgidemiarum*, 1599, V, 3, 1–2).

20 porpentine porcupine. The name was spelled in many different ways: this is the normal Shakespearean form.

21 eternal blazon promulgation of what belongs to the eternal world.

31 apt quick in response.

32 fat heavy, torpid, sluggish.

33 rots So F. Both Q2 and Q1 read 'rootes', which is widely accepted by editors (Kittredge and Cyrus Hoy being notable exceptions). As with 'fearful' (20 above), the Q2 reading is less appropriate for the context. The notion of a weed tenaciously rooting itself in the ground so that it can't stir is wide of the Ghost's point. The image is of some heavy riverside weed growing in rank profusion and

Wouldst thou not stir in this. Now Hamlet, hear.
'Tis given out that, sleeping in my orchard, 35
A serpent stung me. So the whole ear of Denmark
Is by a forgèd process of my death
Rankly abused; but know, thou noble youth,
The serpent that did sting thy father's life
Now wears his crown.

HAMLET O my prophetic soul! 40
My uncle?

GHOST Ay, that incestuous, that adulterate beast,
With witchcraft of his wits, with traitorous gifts –
O wicked wit and gifts that have the power
So to seduce – won to his shameful lust 45
The will of my most seeming virtuous queen.
O Hamlet, what a falling off was there,
From me whose love was of that dignity
That it went hand in hand even with the vow
I made to her in marriage, and to decline 50
Upon a wretch whose natural gifts were poor
To those of mine.
But virtue as it never will be moved,
Though lewdness court it in a shape of heaven,

35 'Tis] Q2, Q1; It's F 35 my] Q2, Q1; mine F 40–1 O...uncle] *as one line* Q2, F 41 My] Q2, Q1; mine F 43 wits] Q2, F; wit *Pope* 43 with] Q2; hath F 45 to his] Q2; to to this F 47 what a] F; what Q2 52–3 To...moved] *as one line* Q2, F

festering in its own overgrowth; a 'lazy, stagnant life', says Kittredge. It is assumed therefore that the Q1 reporter was responsible for 'roots', and was again followed by Q2. It is notable that Q2 follows Q1 letter for letter from 'fat' to 'wharf', including the striking identity of '*Lethe* wharffe'.

33 **Lethe** A river in Hades. The spirits of the dead, waiting to cross, drank its waters and so became oblivious of their previous existence.

35 **orchard** garden.

37 **process** narrative.

40 **my prophetic soul** Implying not that Hamlet had already guessed the truth, but that the Ghost's revelation is in accord with Hamlet's general suspicions about Claudius and the recent goings-on.

43 **wits** Pope and many succeeding editors read 'wit', to balance the singular in the next line, and with the idea that 'wit' (= intellectual activity) is more appropriate. Shakespeare frequently uses 'wits' in the sense of 'activities of the mind'; e.g. *Shrew* 1.1.170, 'Bend thoughts and wits to achieve her.' The singular 'wit' in the following line is the assemblage of the activities of the mind into 'mind' itself.

43 **gifts** talents (see 'natural gifts', 51 below). Claudius uses his gifts treasonably, as he uses his wits to bewitch.

46 **The will** This is more than inclination or assent, since the word has strong sexual undertones. Gertrude was sexually responsive to Claudius's advances. This passage unmistakably indicates that the two had sexual relations before King Hamlet's death. (The indignity still burns in a very human way in the 'poor ghost' – witness 50–2 – though he wants no retribution – 85–8.) Hamlet certainly so understands the Ghost: he says Claudius 'whored my mother', 5.2.64. It is the fact that Gertrude had been sleeping with two brothers that gives special force to the otherwise somewhat academic charge of incest (42 above).

49 **even with the vow** with the very vow (*not* even as far as the vow).

53 **virtue as it** as virtue.

54 **shape** See note to 1.4.43.

So lust, though to a radiant angel linked, 55
Will sate itself in a celestial bed,
And prey on garbage.
But soft, methinks I scent the morning air;
Brief let me be. Sleeping within my orchard,
My custom always of the afternoon, 60
Upon my secure hour thy uncle stole,
With juice of cursèd hebenon in a vial,
And in the porches of my ears did pour
The leperous distilment, whose effect
Holds such an enmity with blood of man 65
That swift as quicksilver it courses through
The natural gates and alleys of the body,
And with a sudden vigour it doth posset
And curd, like eager droppings into milk,
The thin and wholesome blood. So did it mine, 70
And a most instant tetter barked about,
Most lazar-like, with vile and loathsome crust,
All my smooth body.
Thus was I, sleeping, by a brother's hand,
Of life, of crown, of queen, at once dispatched; 75
Cut off even in the blossoms of my sin,
Unhouseled, disappointed, unaneled;

55 lust] F; but Q2 55 angel] F; Angle Q2 56 sate] F; sort Q2 58 morning] Q2; Mornings F 59 my] Q2, Q1; mine F 60 of] Q2; in F, Q1 62 hebenon] Hebenon F; Hebona Q2, Q1 63 my] Q2, Q1; mine F 68 posset] F; possesse Q2 69 eager] Q2, Q1; Aygre F 71 barked] barckt Q2; bak'd F 75 of queen] Q2; and Queene F

56 sate itself become satiated; cease to find satisfaction.

61 Upon my secure hour (sécure) at a time when I felt free from all danger. ('secure' implied an absence of precaution, almost the opposite of its modern meaning.)

62 hebenon Both the true reading and the meaning are uncertain. Q2's 'Hebona' seems to derive from Q1. Marlowe has 'the juice of hebon' as a poison in *Jew of Malta* 3.4.101. *Hebenus* is Latin for ebony, but was applied to other trees, and the resin of the guaiacum tree has been suggested as the drug in question. Possibly there is confusion with henbane, which *is* a poison. See R. R. Simpson in *The Listener*, 17 April 1947.

63 the porches of my ears i.e. the ears as porches of the body. It was widely believed that drugs, therapeutic or toxic, could be administered via the ear. The auditory or eustachian tube which might allow a liquid in the ear to find its way to the pharynx and be swallowed, was known to the Greeks but not fully described until 1564, by Bartolommeo Eustachio. See *New England Journal of Medicine* 307 (1982), 259–61, 1531.

64 leperous causing leprosy.

64 distilment distillation (in a general sense; a liquid preparation).

68 posset curdle.

69 eager sour, acid. French *aigre*.

71 tetter skin disease.

71 barked about surrounded like bark.

72 lazar-like like a leper (from Lazarus, in Luke 16.20).

75 dispatched bereft by being put to death.

76 in the blossoms of my sin i.e. in a state of sinfulness. Compare the similar image in 3.3.81, 'his crimes broad blown, as flush as May'.

77 Unhouseled . . . unaneled Without the sacrament, not appointed or prepared for death, without extreme unction.

No reckoning made, but sent to my account
With all my imperfections on my head –
Oh horrible, oh horrible, most horrible! 80
If thou hast nature in thee bear it not;
Let not the royal bed of Denmark be
A couch for luxury and damnèd incest.
But howsomever thou pursues this act
Taint not thy mind, nor let thy soul contrive 85
Against thy mother aught. Leave her to heaven
And to those thorns that in her bosom lodge
To prick and sting her. Fare thee well at once.
The glow-worm shows the matin to be near,
And gins to pale his uneffectual fire. 90
Adieu, adieu, adieu. Remember me. *Exit*

HAMLET O all you host of heaven! O earth! what else?
And shall I couple hell? Oh fie! Hold, hold, my heart,
And you my sinews grow not instant old
But bear me stiffly up. Remember thee? 95
Ay thou poor ghost, whiles memory holds a seat
In this distracted globe. Remember thee?

84 howsomever] Q2; howsoeuer F **84** pursues] Q2; pursuest F **85** Taint] F; Tain't Q2 **91** Adieu, adieu, adieu] Q2; Adue, adue, *Hamlet* F **91** SD] F; *not in* Q2 **93** Hold, hold] Q2; hold F **95** stiffly] F; swiftly Q2 **96** whiles] Q2; while F

78 reckoning the settling of an account.

80 Dr Johnson accepted a suggestion that this ought to be Hamlet's line, and he has had a good deal of support. Garrick, as Hamlet, spoke the line, and so have other Hamlets. To break the speech here would indeed give emphasis to the great injunction of the Ghost, which immediately follows.

81 nature natural feelings. Here, filial affection especially. Compare 3.2.354.

83 luxury lust.

84 howsomever The older form of 'howsoever'.

84 thou pursues this -es rather than -est before a following th- (see Franz, *Die Sprache Shakespeares,* §152, p. 154).

85 Taint not thy mind Do not let your mind become affected or blemished. But does the Ghost mean this in a moral or in a physical sense? Does he fear that Hamlet may become corrupted in pursuing revenge, or that the burden of revenge may overtax his mind? Perhaps it is a moral rather than a mental breakdown which is uppermost in the Ghost's mind. Either way, the Ghost's prohibition is a tall order. How is Hamlet to carry out so formidable a task without mental and emotional damage? In *Philaster* 1.1.202, the sentence 'Sure he's somewhat tainted' refers to mental disturbance.

93 And shall I couple hell? The enormity of what he has heard makes Hamlet appeal first to heaven to witness, then turn to earth as the scene of these crimes, and finally to hell as their source.

95 bear me stiffly up keep me from collapsing.

97 this distracted globe It is the world that Hamlet is talking about, not his head. Editors suggest he should 'put his hand upon his head'. But the power and importance of this sentence is that it refers to a disordered world, and preludes Hamlet's conviction that he is called upon, not to right a personal wrong, but to repair a distracted world (189–90 below). The Ghost and his terrible news are to be remembered as long as memory continues to exist among mankind, so long as they value the past as a guide to future conduct, and remember order, morality, justice. Then, with his second 'Remember thee?', Hamlet turns to himself, to 'my memory'. For his part, he will erase all inessential and misleading memory, and preserve only what is truly valuable. It only dilutes the strength of this passage to find a triple pun here: world, head and theatre.

Yea, from the table of my memory
I'll wipe away all trivial fond records,
All saws of books, all forms, all pressures past, 100
That youth and observation copied there,
And thy commandment all alone shall live
Within the book and volume of my brain,
Unmixed with baser matter: yes, by heaven!
O most pernicious woman! 105
O villain, villain, smiling damnèd villain!
My tables – meet it is I set it down
That one may smile, and smile, and be a villain;
At least I'm sure it may be so in Denmark. [*Writing*]
So uncle, there you are. Now to my word: 110
It is 'Adieu, adieu, remember me.'
I have sworn't.

HORATIO (*Within*) My lord, my lord!
MARCELLUS (*Within*) Lord Hamlet!

Enter HORATIO *and* MARCELLUS

HORATIO Heavens secure him!
HAMLET So be it.
MARCELLUS Illo, ho, ho, my lord! 115

104 yes] Q2; yes, yes F, Q1 **107** My tables] Q2; My Tables, my Tables F **109** I'm] F; I am Q2 **109** SD] *Rowe; not in* Q2, F **113** SH HORATIO] *Hora.* Q2; *Hor. & Mar.* F **113** SD *Within*] F; *not in* Q2 **113** SD *Enter*...MARCELLUS] *Capell; after* sworn't Q2; *after* my lord! F **113** Heavens] Q2, Q1; Heauen F **114** SH HAMLET] *Ham.* Q2; *Mar.* F **115** SH MARCELLUS] *Mar.* Q2; *Hor.* F

98 table tablet, slate.

99 fond foolish.

99 records Things written down worthy to be remembered. Accent on second syllable.

100 saws common sayings or maxims.

100 forms set phrases, formulistic thoughts.

100 pressures imprints or impressions (continues the image of clichés and stereotyped thoughts).

101 observation dutiful attention. Hamlet is not talking of what he had noted from a personal and independent viewpoint – even a youthful one. 'observation' more often than not meant in Shakespeare's time a deferential, even obsequious, attention to one's superiors, and imitation of them or obedience to them. So Faulconbridge in *John* 1.1.207–8 says 'he is but a bastard to the time / That doth not smack of observation'. Jonson, in *Poetaster* 4.3.104–7 has 'Alas, sir, Horace! he is a mere sponge; nothing but humours and observation; he goes up and down sucking from every society, and when he comes home again, squeezes himself dry again.'

107 tables memorandum book (see 98 above)

108 smile...villain Compare Chaucer, 'The smiler with the knife under the cloak' (*Knight's Tale* 1999). Coleridge remarks that Hamlet, having vowed 'to make his memory a blank of all maxims and generalised truths', immediately notes down this 'generalised fact'. Hamlet's point, I take it, is that *this* truth is one he has discovered for himself; it's the first of the new entries. The general truth is immediately qualified by the certificate of personal experience: 'At least I am sure it may be so in Denmark.' The grim humour of this little piece of theatre, in a speech commencing in shock and horror, is extraordinary.

110 Now to my word Hamlet has not yet vowed to obey the Ghost's command. He now gives his word – very solemnly, perhaps kneeling as Wilson suggests, and rising with 'I have sworn't' (112) or 'So be it' (114).

HAMLET Hillo, ho, ho, boy! Come bird, come.
MARCELLUS How is't, my noble lord?
HORATIO What news my lord?
HAMLET Oh, wonderful!
HORATIO Good my lord, tell it.
HAMLET No, you will reveal it.
HORATIO Not I my lord, by heaven.
MARCELLUS Nor I my lord. 120
HAMLET How say you then, would heart of man once think it –
But you'll be secret?
HORATIO, MARCELLUS Ay, by heaven, my lord.
HAMLET There's ne'er a villain dwelling in all Denmark
But he's an arrant knave.
HORATIO There needs no ghost, my lord, come from the grave, 125
To tell us this.
HAMLET Why right, you are i'th'right,
And so without more circumstance at all
I hold it fit that we shake hands and part –
You as your business and desire shall point you,
For every man hath business and desire, 130
Such as it is, and for my own poor part,
Look you, I'll go pray.
HORATIO These are but wild and whirling words, my lord.
HAMLET I'm sorry they offend you, heartily,
Yes faith, heartily.
HORATIO There's no offence my lord. 135
HAMLET Yes by Saint Patrick but there is Horatio,
And much offence too. Touching this vision here,

116 Come bird,] F; come, and Q2 **119** you will] Q2; you'l F, Q1 **122** my lord] F; *not in* Q2 **123** ne'er] nere F; neuer Q2, Q1 **126** i'th'right] F; in the right Q2, Q1 **129** desire] Q2; desires F, Q1 **130** hath] Q2; ha's F **131** my] Q2, Q1; mine F **132** Look you, I'll] F; I will Q2 **133** whirling] whurling Q2; hurling F **134** I'm] F; I am Q2, Q1 **136** Horatio] Q2, Q1; my Lord F

116 Come bird Hamlet mocks the hallooing by pretending they are out hawking.

127 circumstance roundabout talk and formality.

132 Look you] So F; not in Q2. It is a characteristic turn of Hamlet's speech; e.g. 3.2.326, 329.

132 I'll go pray Hamlet has no 'business and desire' because his proper office has been taken from him by the usurper Claudius, and because his continued life as a student at Wittenberg has been refused him. So, he jokes, he'll have to say his prayers. But the audience knows that he has urgent 'business and desire', and for that, prayer might well be needful. Nowhere else in the play does Hamlet talk of praying.

136 Saint Patrick It is not clear why Hamlet should pick on this saint. Some say it is because he was the patron saint of Purgatory.

It is an honest ghost, that let me tell you.
For your desire to know what is between us,
O'ermaster't as you may. And now good friends, 140
As you are friends, scholars, and soldiers,
Give me one poor request.

HORATIO What is't my lord? we will.

HAMLET Never make known what you have seen tonight.

HORATIO }
MARCELLUS } My lord we will not.

HAMLET Nay but swear't.

HORATIO In faith 145
My lord not I.

MARCELLUS Nor I my lord in faith.

HAMLET Upon my sword.

MARCELLUS We have sworn my lord already.

HAMLET Indeed, upon my sword, indeed.

GHOST Swear. *Ghost cries under the stage*

HAMLET Ha, ha, boy, sayst thou so? art thou there truepenny? 150
Come on, you hear this fellow in the cellarage,
Consent to swear.

HORATIO Propose the oath my lord.

HAMLET Never to speak of this that you have seen,
Swear by my sword.

GHOST Swear. 155

HAMLET *Hic et ubique?* then we'll shift our ground.
Come hither gentlemen,
And lay your hands again upon my sword.
Never to speak of this that you have heard,
Swear by my sword. 160

GHOST Swear.

HAMLET Well said old mole, canst work i'th'earth so fast?

145–6 In faith...not I] *as one line* Q2, F **150** Ha, ha,] Q2; Ah ha F **151** Come on, you hear] Q2; Come on you here F **156** our] Q2; for F **159–60**] F; *lines transposed in* Q2 **161** Swear.] F; *Sweare by his sword.* Q2 **162** earth] Q2, Q1; ground F

138 honest honourable, genuine (i.e. the Ghost is what he appears to be).

146 not I...Nor I They here promise not to divulge what they have seen – they are not refusing to swear: 'We have sworn already', they say next (referring to 120).

147 Upon my sword The hilt forms a cross.

150 truepenny trusty fellow.

151 in the cellarage down below, in the cellars.

156 ***Hic et ubique*** Here and everywhere.

159–61 So F. Lines 159 and 160 are transposed in Q2, and the Ghost in 161 is made to say 'Swear by his sword.' The F version is borne out by Q1, and is certainly what was said upon the stage. Q2 seems to be a compositor's jumble, which breaks up the firm ritual of the scene.

A worthy pioneer. Once more remove, good friends.

HORATIO O day and night, but this is wondrous strange.

HAMLET And therefore as a stranger give it welcome. 165

There are more things in heaven and earth, Horatio,
Than are dreamt of in your philosophy.
But come –
Here as before, never so help you mercy,
How strange or odd some'er I bear myself, 170
As I perchance hereafter shall think meet
To put an antic disposition on –
That you at such times seeing me never shall,
With arms encumbered thus, or this head-shake,
Or by pronouncing of some doubtful phrase, 175
As 'Well, well, we know,' or 'We could and if we would,'
Or 'If we list to speak,' or 'There be and if they might,'
Or such ambiguous giving out, to note
That you know aught of me: this not to do,
So grace and mercy at your most need help you, 180
Swear.

GHOST Swear.

HAMLET Rest, rest, perturbèd spirit. So gentlemen,
With all my love I do commend me to you,

167 your] Q2, Q1; our F 167–8 Than...come] *as one line* Q2, F 170 some'er] so mere Q2; so ere F 173 times] Q2, Q1; time F 174 this] Q2; thus, F 176 Well, well] Q2, Q1; well F 177 they] Q2; there F 179 this not to do] F, Q1; this doe sweare Q2 181 Swear] F, Q1; *not in* Q2

163 pioneer soldier responsible for excavations and tunnelling.

165 as a stranger...welcome i.e. it has a special call on your hospitality. For the particular importance of this remark, see the Introduction, pp. 45–6.

167 your philosophy So Q2 and Q1. F's 'our' is probably a compositor's error. 'your' is less likely to blame Horatio for his scepticism than to indicate slight contempt for philosophy itself (meaning intellectual investigation, science). Compare 5.1.145, 'a score decayer of your whoreson dead body'.

170 How strange...myself Hamlet will ally himself with the 'stranger' by estranging himself from accepted norms of behaviour.

172 an antic disposition fantastic and foolish manner.

174 encumbered entangled. An unusual word in this context, but see Johnson's *Dictionary*.

176, 177 and if if.

177 list wished.

179–81 this not to do...Swear So F and Q1. This must be what was said on the stage before 1603. Q2 puts it quite differently (see collation). Shakespeare had got Hamlet into an impossible grammatical tangle. It looks as if the different readings of F and Q2 represent different views of a perplexed MS. (possibly containing interlined revision) showing Shakespeare trying to save a grammatical lost cause.

183 Perhaps at this point Horatio and Marcellus silently swear on the hilt of Hamlet's sword. Wilson, Spencer and Jenkins think they swear silently three separate times. There is no indication in the text when, if ever, the formal oath is taken. It seems best not to impose a decision by means of a stage direction.

184 I do commend me to you I entrust myself to you. This routine way of expressing devotion has here something of the force of the phrase's proper meaning.

And what so poor a man as Hamlet is 185
May do t'express his love and friending to you,
God willing shall not lack. Let us go in together,
And still your fingers on your lips I pray. –
The time is out of joint: O cursèd spite,
That ever I was born to set it right. – 190
Nay come, let's go together.

Exeunt

2.1 *Enter* POLONIUS *and* REYNALDO

POLONIUS Give him this money, and these notes, Reynaldo.
REYNALDO I will my lord.
POLONIUS You shall do marvellous wisely, good Reynaldo,
Before you visit him, to make inquire
Of his behaviour.
REYNALDO My lord, I did intend it. 5
POLONIUS Marry well said, very well said. Look you sir,
Inquire me first what Danskers are in Paris,
And how, and who, what means, and where they keep,
What company, at what expense; and finding
By this encompassment and drift of question 10
That they do know my son, come you more nearer
Than your particular demands will touch it.
Take you as 'twere some distant knowledge of him,
As thus, 'I know his father and his friends,

Act 2, Scene 1 2.1] *Actus Secundus* F; *no indication in* Q2 0 SD] F; *Enter old Polonius, with his man or two* Q2 1 this] Q2; his F 3 marvellous] Q 1611; meruiles Q2; maruels F 4 to make] Q2; you make F 4 inquire] Q2; inquiry F 14 As] Q2; And F

188 still always.

189–90 The time...set it right See Introduction, p. 45.

189 The time i.e. things generally, the state of the world.

189 cursèd spite the accursèd malice of life!

Act 2, Scene 1

1 Shakespeare gives several indications of a lapse of time between Acts 1 and 2. Laertes is settled in Paris, Ophelia has refused to see Hamlet or receive his letters (Scene 1). The king and queen have been alarmed by the transformation in Hamlet's behaviour and have sent for Rosencrantz and Guildenstern, who have reached Elsinore. The ambassadors have been to Norway and have returned (Scene 2).

0 SD *Enter*...REYNALDO So F. See collation for Q2's striking authorial direction.

3 marvellous marvellously, extremely.

7 Danskers Danes.

8 what means what means they have.

8 keep lodge, stay.

10 encompassment surrounding, i.e. comprehensiveness.

10 drift driving, directing.

11 come you you will come.

11 nearer i.e. to an understanding of Laertes' behaviour.

And in part him' – do you mark this Reynaldo? 15
REYNALDO Ay, very well, my lord.
POLONIUS 'And in part him, but' – you may say – 'not well,
But if't be he I mean, he's very wild,
Addicted so and so' – and there put on him
What forgeries you please; marry, none so rank 20
As may dishonour him, take heed of that,
But sir, such wanton, wild, and usual slips
As are companions noted and most known
To youth and liberty.
REYNALDO As gaming my lord?
POLONIUS Ay, or drinking, fencing, swearing, 25
Quarrelling, drabbing – you may go so far.
REYNALDO My lord, that would dishonour him.
POLONIUS Faith no, as you may season it in the charge.
You must not put another scandal on him,
That he is open to incontinency, 30
That's not my meaning. But breathe his faults so quaintly
That they may seem the taints of liberty,
The flash and outbreak of a fiery mind,
A savageness in unreclaimèd blood,
Of general assault.
REYNALDO But my good lord – 35
POLONIUS Wherefore should you do this?
REYNALDO Ay my lord,
I would know that.
POLONIUS Marry sir, here's my drift,
And I believe it is a fetch of warrant.
You laying these slight sullies on my son,

24 lord?] *Adams;* lord. Q2, F 28 Faith no] F*;* Fayth Q2 34–5 A savageness...assault] Q2*; as one line* F 36–7 Ay...that] *as one line* Q2, F 38 warrant] F*;* wit Q2 39 sullies] sulleyes F*;* sallies Q2

20 **forgeries** invented matters.

20 **rank** gross.

25 **fencing** i.e. spending time in fencing-schools. One of Sir Thomas Overbury's 'characters', *An Ordinary Fencer*, gives a scornful description of these places (1614).

26 **drabbing** going round with drabs, or loose women.

28 **season** modify.

30 **incontinency** sexual excess. Though it is possible that Polonius makes a distinction between an occasional visit to a prostitute ('drabbing') and notorious profligacy ('incontinency'), I rather think that the joke is against Polonius, who, though he prides himself on a knowledge of the world, supposes that young men like his son might associate with undesirable females without actual fornication, and so believes that 'drabbing' is not necessarily 'incontinency'.

31 **quaintly** artfully.

32 **taints of liberty** faults of free-living.

34 **savageness...blood** wildness in untamed vigour.

35 **Of general assault** Which assails everyone.

38 **fetch of warrant** approved stratagem.

39 **sullies** See collation and note to 1.2.129.

As 'twere a thing a little soiled i'th'working, 40
Mark you,
Your party in converse, him you would sound,
Having ever seen in the prenominate crimes
The youth you breathe of guilty, be assured
He closes with you in this consequence, 45
'Good sir', or so, or 'friend', or 'gentleman',
According to the phrase and the addition
Of man and country.

REYNALDO Very good my lord.

POLONIUS And then sir does a this – a does – what was I about to say? By the mass I was about to say something. Where did I leave? 50

REYNALDO At 'closes in the consequence', at 'friend, or so', and 'gentleman'.

POLONIUS At 'closes in the consequence' – ay marry,
He closes with you thus: 'I know the gentleman,
I saw him yesterday, or th'other day, 55
Or then, or then, with such or such, and as you say,
There was a gaming, there o'ertook in's rouse,
There falling out at tennis', or perchance,
'I saw him enter such a house of sale' –
Videlicet, a brothel – or so forth. See you now, 60
Your bait of falsehood takes this carp of truth,
And thus do we of wisdom and of reach,
With windlasses and with assays of bias,

40 i'th'] F; with Q2; wi'th' *P. Alexander* 41–2 Mark...sound] *as one line* Q2, F 47 and] F; or Q2 49–50 And then...leave] *as prose Malone*; say?/By...something,/ Where Q2; this?/He does...say?/I was F 49 a] Q2; he F *[twice]* 50 By the mass] Q2; *not in* F 51–2 at 'friend...'gentleman'] F; *not in* Q2 54 with you] F; *not in* Q2 55 th'other] Q2; t other F 56 such or such] Q2; such and such F 57 a] Q2; he F 57 there o'ertook] there o'retooke F; there, or tooke Q2 61 takes] F; take Q2 61 carp] carpe Q2; Cape F

40 i'th'working in the process of making it.

43 prenominate already named.

43 crimes faults. See note to 1.5.12.

44 breathe of speak about.

45 closes with you will fall in with you.

45 in this consequence in the following way.

47–8 the phrase...country So F. All editors since Rowe, except it seems Caldecott and Knight, have preferred Q2's 'the phrase or the addition', which must be a compositor's misreading. In the Polonian chiasmus, 'phrase' (= conventional expression) goes with 'country', and 'addition' (= title) goes with 'man'. The mode of address varies with the country's conventions of address, *and* the status of the man talking. There is no 'or' in it.

51–2 at 'friend'...'gentleman' So F; not in Q2. Presumably an accidental omission by the compositor.

57 a he.

57 o'ertook in's rouse overtaken (by drink) while carousing. That is, he got drunk.

60 Videlicet 'viz.', that is to say.

62 we of wisdom and of reach we who are wise and far-seeing.

63 windlasses circuitous movement (in hunting) Nothing to do with windlasses in ships.

63 assays of bias indirect attempts. The 'bias' in bowls is the weighting which makes the bowl take a curved course towards the jack.

By indirections find directions out.
So, by my former lecture and advice, 65
Shall you my son. You have me, have you not?

REYNALDO My lord, I have.

POLONIUS God buy ye, fare ye well.

REYNALDO Good my lord.

POLONIUS Observe his inclination in yourself.

REYNALDO I shall my lord. 70

POLONIUS And let him ply his music.

REYNALDO Well my lord.

POLONIUS Farewell.

Exit Reynaldo

Enter OPHELIA

How now Ophelia, what's the matter?

OPHELIA Oh my lord, my lord, I have been so affrighted.

POLONIUS With what, i'th'name of God?

OPHELIA My lord, as I was sewing in my closet, 75
Lord Hamlet with his doublet all unbraced,
No hat upon his head, his stockings fouled,
Ungartered, and down-gyvèd to his ankle,
Pale as his shirt, his knees knocking each other,
And with a look so piteous in purport 80
As if he had been loosèd out of hell
To speak of horrors – he comes before me.

POLONIUS Mad for thy love?

OPHELIA My lord I do not know,
But truly I do fear it.

POLONIUS What said he?

OPHELIA He took me by the wrist, and held me hard; 85
Then goes he to the length of all his arm,

67 ye] Q2; you F *[twice]* 67 fare] F; far Q2 72 SD] Q2 *at 71*; *Exit.* F *at 71* 73 Oh my lord, my lord] Q2; Alas my Lord F 74 i'th'] Q2; in the F 74 God] Q2; Heauen F 75 closet] Q2; Chamber F

64 directions the way things are going.

67 God buy ye One of the many ways of writing the shortened 'God be with ye' = goodbye.

69 in yourself personally.

75 closet private room.

76 doublet the Elizabethan jacket.

76 unbraced unfastened.

78 down-gyvèd fallen down and resembling fetters.

80 in purport in what it expressed.

83 Mad for thy love? Totally beside himself, for love of thee? This idea of 'the ecstasy of love' (100 below), a distraction making the lover oblivious of customary forms, merges easily in the Elizabethan mind with actual insanity. Compare *All's Well* 5.3.260–1, 'he was mad for her, and talked of Satan and Limbo and of furies'. (Compare US slang 'mad about someone'.)

And with his other hand thus o'er his brow
He falls to such perusal of my face
As a would draw it. Long stayed he so;
At last, a little shaking of mine arm, 90
And thrice his head thus waving up and down,
He raised a sigh so piteous and profound
As it did seem to shatter all his bulk,
And end his being. That done, he lets me go,
And with his head over his shoulder turned 95
He seemed to find his way without his eyes,
For out-a-doors he went without their helps
And to the last bended their light on me.

POLONIUS Come, go with me, I will go seek the king.
This is the very ecstasy of love, 100
Whose violent property fordoes itself,
And leads the will to desperate undertakings
As oft as any passion under heaven
That does afflict our natures. I am sorry.
What, have you given him any hard words of late? 105

OPHELIA No my good lord; but as you did command,
I did repel his letters, and denied
His access to me.

POLONIUS That hath made him mad.
I am sorry that with better heed and judgement
I had not quoted him. I feared he did but trifle, 110
And meant to wrack thee, but beshrew my jealousy.
By heaven, it is as proper to our age
To cast beyond ourselves in our opinions
As it is common for the younger sort

89 a] Q2; he F **93** As] Q2; That F **95** shoulder] Q2, Q1; shoulders F **97** helps] Q2; helpe F, Q1 **99** Come, go] Q2; Goe F **103** passion] F; passions Q2 **109** heed] Q2; speed F **110** quoted] F; coted Q2 **110** feared] fear'd Q2; feare F **112** By heaven] Q2; It seemes F

93–4 shatter...being Ophelia discerns rightly. This sigh is Hamlet's expulsion of his past life.

99, 115 Come, go with me...Come, go we to the king But Polonius goes alone to the king (2.2.40). In Q1, however, Ophelia does accompany him. These phrases are clear signs of a possible alternative ordering of the scenes in Shakespeare's mind. See Introduction, pp. 25–7.

100 ecstasy madness.

101 Whose...itself Which has violence enough to cause self-destruction.

110 quoted noted, observed. Q2's 'coted, a frequent Shakespearean spelling, indicates the contemporary pronunciation.

111 wrack ruin, by seducing.

111 beshrew my jealousy shame upon my suspiciousness.

112 as proper to as characteristic of.

113 cast calculate, compute. The old read too much into things, while the young are too heedless of possible implications.

To lack discretion. Come, go we to the king. 115
This must be known, which being kept close, might move
More grief to hide than hate to utter love.
Come.

Exeunt

2.2 *Flourish. Enter* KING *and* QUEEN, ROSENCRANTZ *and* GUILDENSTERN, *with others*

CLAUDIUS Welcome dear Rosencrantz and Guildenstern!
Moreover that we much did long to see you,
The need we have to use you did provoke
Our hasty sending. Something have you heard
Of Hamlet's transformation – so call it, 5
Sith nor th'exterior nor the inward man
Resembles that it was. What it should be,
More than his father's death, that thus hath put him
So much from th'understanding of himself,
I cannot dream of. I entreat you both, 10
That being of so young days brought up with him,
And sith so neighboured to his youth and haviour,
That you vouchsafe your rest here in our court
Some little time, so by your companies
To draw him on to pleasures, and to gather 15
So much as from occasion you may glean,
Whether aught to us unknown afflicts him thus,

118 Come] Q2; *not in* F Act 2, Scene 2 2.2] *Scena Secunda* F 0.1 SD *Flourish*] Q2; *not in* F 0.2 SD *with others*] *Cum alijs* F; *not in* Q2 5 so call] Q2; so I call F 6 Sith] Q2; Since F 6 nor...nor] Q2; not...nor F 10 dream] Q2; deeme F 12 sith] Q2; since F 12 haviour] Q2; humour F 16 occasion] Q2; Occasions F 17 Whether...thus] Q2; *not in* F

116 close secret.

116–17 might move...love i.e. might cause more sorrow by concealment than unpleasantness by making the love known.

Act 2, Scene 2

2.2 After this, there are no further indications of act or scene division in either quarto or Folio.

0 SD *with others* This is F's addition ('*Cum alijs*') to Q2, showing the theatre's usual concern that royalty should be attended.

1 Rosencrantz and Guildenstern For the forms of these names in F and Q2, see Introduction, pp. 70–1.

2 Moreover that In addition to the fact that.

6 Sith Since.

11 of from.

12 sith This probably has the causative sense used in 6 above. It is *because* they are 'so neighboured' to him that they have been invited. Some editors give an adverbial sense, = 'afterward'. F gives 'since' here and at 6.

12 youth and haviour youthful way of behaving.

16 occasion opportunity.

That opened lies within our remedy.

GERTRUDE Good gentlemen, he hath much talked of you,
And sure I am, two men there is not living 20
To whom he more adheres. If it will please you
To show us so much gentry and good will
As to expend your time with us a while,
For the supply and profit of our hope,
Your visitation shall receive such thanks 25
As fits a king's remembrance.

ROSENCRANTZ Both your majesties
Might by the sovereign power you have of us
Put your dread pleasures more into command
Than to entreaty.

GUILDENSTERN But we both obey,
And here give up ourselves in the full bent 30
To lay our service freely at your feet
To be commanded.

CLAUDIUS Thanks Rosencrantz, and gentle Guildenstern.

GERTRUDE Thanks Guildenstern, and gentle Rosencrantz.
And I beseech you instantly to visit 35
My too much changèd son. Go some of you
And bring these gentlemen where Hamlet is.

GUILDENSTERN Heavens make our presence and our practices
Pleasant and helpful to him.

GERTRUDE Ay, amen.

Exeunt Rosencrantz and Guildenstern [*and some Attendants*]

Enter POLONIUS

POLONIUS Th'ambassadors from Norway, my good lord, 40
Are joyfully returned.

20 is] Q2; are F **29** But we] Q2; We F **31** service] Q2; Seruices F **36** you] Q2; ye F **37** these] Q2; the F **39** Ay] I Q2; *not in* F **39** SD *Exeunt...Guildenstern*] Q2; *Exit* F (*after* to him) **39** SD *and some Attendants*] *Malone, following Capell; not in* Q2, F

18 opened being revealed.

20 there is So Q2. Corrected in F to 'there are', but the use of 'there is' and 'here is' with a plural subject is frequent in Shakespeare. See Franz, *Die Sprache Shakespeares*, §672, pp. 565–6.

22 gentry courtesy.

24 supply aid.

24 profit advancement.

24 our hope what we hope for.

26 remembrance notice or recognition of services rendered. Compare 3.1.93.

27 of over.

28 dread pleasures This extension of the very common 'my dread lord' etc. is not found elsewhere in Shakespeare, and illustrates the comic obsequiousness of the speakers.

30 bent extent. From bending a bow. Compare 'to the top of my bent', 3.2.346.

38 practices doings, activities. But as the word was very frequently used to mean a stratagem, or underhand scheme (e.g. 4.7.76), it has ironic overtones here.

CLAUDIUS Thou still hast been the father of good news.
POLONIUS Have I my lord? Assure you, my good liege,
I hold my duty, as I hold my soul,
Both to my God and to my gracious king; 45
And I do think, or else this brain of mine
Hunts not the trail of policy so sure
As it hath used to do, that I have found
The very cause of Hamlet's lunacy.
CLAUDIUS Oh speak of that, that do I long to hear. 50
POLONIUS Give first admittance to th'ambassadors;
My news shall be the fruit to that great feast.
CLAUDIUS Thyself do grace to them and bring them in.
[*Exit Polonius*]
He tells me, my dear Gertrude, he hath found
The head and source of all your son's distemper. 55
GERTRUDE I doubt it is no other but the main:
His father's death, and our o'erhasty marriage.
CLAUDIUS Well, we shall sift him.

Enter POLONIUS, VOLTEMAND *and* CORNELIUS

Welcome my good friends.
Say Voltemand, what from our brother Norway?
VOLTEMAND Most fair return of greetings and desires. 60
Upon our first, he sent out to suppress
His nephew's levies, which to him appeared
To be a preparation 'gainst the Polack;
But better looked into, he truly found
It was against your highness; whereat grieved 65
That so his sickness, age and impotence

43 Assure you] F; I assure Q2, Q1 45 and] Q2; one F 48 it hath] Q2; I haue F; it had Q1 52 fruit] Q2; Newes F 53 SD] *Rowe; not in* Q2, F 54 my dear Gertrude] my deere *Gertrard* Q2; my sweet Queene, that F 57 o'erhasty] F; hastie Q2 58 SD] F; *Enter Embassadors* Q2

44 hold maintain. He means he maintains his duty to his God and king as firmly as he guards his soul.

47 policy statecraft.

49 lunacy Claudius more delicately called it a 'transformation' (5 above).

54 my dear Gertrude Q2 consistently spells the name 'Gertrard'; see Introduction, pp. 70–1. At this point, F reads 'my sweet Queene, that'; a very interesting example of the playhouse scribe's freedom in the interest of maintaining the decorum of royalty on stage. He quite misunderstood the intimacy of this little private exchange while Polonius is fetching the ambassadors.

56 doubt suspect.

56 the main the main matter.

58 sift him examine carefully what he (Polonius) has to say.

61 Upon our first As soon as we made representations to him.

66 impotence helplessness.

Was falsely borne in hand, sends out arrests
On Fortinbras, which he in brief obeys,
Receives rebuke from Norway, and in fine
Makes vow before his uncle never more 70
To give th'assay of arms against your majesty.
Whereon old Norway, overcome with joy,
Gives him three thousand crowns in annual fee,
And his commission to employ those soldiers,
So levied as before, against the Polack; 75
With an entreaty, herein further shown,
That it might please you to give quiet pass
Through your dominions for this enterprise,
On such regards of safety and allowance
As therein are set down.

[*Gives a document*]

CLAUDIUS It likes us well, 80
And at our more considered time we'll read,
Answer, and think upon this business.
Meantime, we thank you for your well-took labour.
Go to your rest; at night we'll feast together.
Most welcome home.

Exeunt Ambassadors

POLONIUS This business is well ended. 85
My liege, and madam, to expostulate
What majesty should be, what duty is,
Why day is day, night night, and time is time,
Were nothing but to waste night, day, and time.
Therefore, since brevity is the soul of wit 90
And tediousness the limbs and outward flourishes,
I will be brief. Your noble son is mad.

73 three thousand] F, Q1; threescore thousand Q2 76 shown] shewne F; shone Q2 78 this] Q2; his F 80 SD] *gives a paper / Malone (76); not in* Q2, F 85 well] Q2; very well F 90 since] F; *not in* Q2

67 borne in hand imposed on, abused with false pretences.

69 in fine in conclusion.

71 give th'assay make the trial.

73 three thousand So F and Q1. Q2 reads 'threescore thousand', which bedevils the metre. Probably Q2 failed to observe the intended deletion of 'score'. See Introduction, p. 10.

73 fee payment.

79 regards considerations.

79 allowance permission.

80 likes pleases.

81 more considered time time more suitable for consideration.

82 Answer, and think Either this is the wrong way round, or Claudius means by 'think' that he will reflect upon what this affair implies for the future.

86 expostulate argue about, discuss.

90 wit intellectual keenness.

91 tediousness prolixity, long-windedness.

91 flourishes embellishments.

Mad call I it, for to define true madness,
What is't but to be nothing else but mad?
But let that go.

GERTRUDE More matter with less art. 95

POLONIUS Madam, I swear I use no art at all.
That he is mad, 'tis true; 'tis true 'tis pity,
And pity 'tis 'tis true – a foolish figure,
But farewell it, for I will use no art.
Mad let us grant him then, and now remains 100
That we find out the cause of this effect,
Or rather say, the cause of this defect,
For this effect defective comes by cause.
Thus it remains, and the remainder thus.
Perpend. 105
I have a daughter – have while she is mine –
Who in her duty and obedience, mark,
Hath given me this. Now gather and surmise.

Reads the letter

'To the celestial, and my soul's idol, the most beautified Ophelia,' –
That's an ill phrase, a vile phrase, 'beautified' is a vile phrase – but 110
you shall hear. Thus:
'In her excellent white bosom, these, *et cetera*.'

GERTRUDE Came this from Hamlet to her?

POLONIUS Good madam stay awhile, I will be faithful.
'Doubt thou the stars are fire, 115
Doubt that the sun doth move,

97 he is] F; hee's Q2 98 'tis 'tis] Q2; it is F 106 while] Q2, Q1; whil'st F 108 SD] *Kittredge; The Letter* F; *Letter* Q2 (*115*) 111 Thus] Q2; these F 112 *et cetera.*] *&c.* Q2; *not in* F

94 **What is't...but mad?** What Polonius means to say is that it would be madness to try to define madness. Unfortunately, his little joke miscarries, because he finds himself defining madness as being nothing else but mad. This unintended circularity embarrasses him, and he hurriedly dismisses his rhetoric – 'But let that go.'

98 **figure** rhetorical device (as in figure of speech).

103 **For this...cause** For this manifestation, which is a defect (madness), does have a cause.

105 **Perpend** Ponder, consider.

108 **gather and surmise** make your deductions.

109–22 Hamlet's letter to Ophelia is a great puzzle; it is so affected, juvenile and graceless. We should be glad to take it as part of Hamlet's recent heartless treatment of Ophelia but it is very firmly said that Ophelia, in obedience to her father, has refused to receive his letters (2.1.109; 2.2.144). If this is one of Hamlet's real love-letters, why did Shakespeare make him write like Don Armado in *Love's Labour's Lost*?

109 **beautified** The word was quite widely used; by Shakespeare himself in *Two Gentlemen of Verona* 4.1.53. Greene's contemptuous use of it in his attack on Shakespeare in 1592 may have rankled ('an upstart crow, beautified with our feathers').

112 **In...*et cetera*** This is a continuation of the florid address of the letter. It is directed to her heart. Compare the insincere Proteus in *Two Gentlemen of Verona* 3.1.250–2: 'Thy letters...shall be delivered/Even in the milk-white bosom of thy love.' 'these, *et cetera*' is a formal abbreviation (for 'these present greetings' or whatever).

Doubt truth to be a liar,
But never doubt I love.
'O dear Ophelia, I am ill at these numbers, I have not art to reckon
my groans; but that I love thee best, O most best, believe it. Adieu. 120
'Thine evermore, most dear lady, whilst this machine is
to him, Hamlet.'
This in obedience hath my daughter shown me,
And, more above, hath his solicitings,
As they fell out, by time, by means, and place, 125
All given to mine ear.

CLAUDIUS But how hath she
Received his love?

POLONIUS What do you think of me?

CLAUDIUS As of a man faithful and honourable.

POLONIUS I would fain prove so. But what might you think,
When I had seen this hot love on the wing – 130
As I perceived it, I must tell you that,
Before my daughter told me – what might you,
Or my dear majesty your queen here, think,
If I had played the desk, or table-book,
Or given my heart a winking, mute and dumb, 135
Or looked upon this love with idle sight –
What might you think? No, I went round to work,
And my young mistress thus I did bespeak:
'Lord Hamlet is a prince out of thy star.
This must not be.' And then I prescripts gave her, 140
That she should lock herself from his resort,

123 This] F; *Pol.* This Q2 **123** shown] Q2; shew'd F **124** above] F; about Q2 **124** solicitings] Q2; soliciting F **126–7** But...love] *as one line* Q2, F **135** winking] F; working Q2 **140** prescripts] Q2; Precepts F **141** his] F; her Q2

117 Doubt truth 'doubt' changes meaning here to 'suspect', but each of the first three lines means the same, 'you may challenge the unchallengeable, but...'

119 ill at these numbers no good at making verses.

119 reckon enumerate in metrical form, or 'numbers'.

121 this machine his body.

124 more above furthermore, moreover.

124–6 hath his...mine ear She has given Polonius information about all his overtures to her, in their order of occurrence, with details of the time, the means of communication and the place.

129 fain gladly. Always used by Shakespeare in the construction 'would fain'.

134 played...or table-book i.e. taken note and said nothing.

135 given...winking closed the eyes of his heart; i.e. connived at the affair.

137 round (= roundly) without prevarication.

138 bespeak speak to.

139 out of thy star outside your destiny. See note to 1.4.32.

140 prescripts orders.

141 his resort his visiting.

Admit no messengers, receive no tokens.
Which done, she took the fruits of my advice,
And he, repulsed – a short tale to make –
Fell into a sadness, then into a fast, 145
Thence to a watch, thence into a weakness,
Thence to a lightness, and by this declension
Into the madness wherein now he raves,
And all we mourn for.

CLAUDIUS Do you think 'tis this?

GERTRUDE It may be, very like. 150

POLONIUS Hath there been such a time, I'ld fain know that,
That I have positively said, 'tis so,
When it proved otherwise?

CLAUDIUS Not that I know.

POLONIUS Take this from this, if this be otherwise.
If circumstances lead me, I will find 155
Where truth is hid, though it were hid indeed
Within the centre.

CLAUDIUS How may we try it further?

POLONIUS You know sometimes he walks four hours together
Here in the lobby.

GERTRUDE So he does indeed.

POLONIUS At such a time I'll loose my daughter to him. 160

144 repulsed] F; repell'd Q2   146 watch] F; wath Q2   147 a] F; *not in* Q2   148 wherein] Q2; whereon F   149 mourn] Q2; waile F   149 'tis] F; *not in* Q2   150 like] Q2; likely F   151 I'ld] I'de F; I would Q2   159 does] Q2; ha's F

143 took the fruits received the benefit; reaped the harvest. The absurdity of Polonius's self-satisfaction is made clear in the ensuing lines: the only fruit of his advice was Hamlet's madness.

144 repulsed So F. Q2 reads 'repell'd'. F is the stronger and rarer reading, more likely to be reduced in transcription or composition to 'repelled' than vice versa. Ophelia 'repels' Hamlet's letters (2.1.107), but Hamlet himself is 'repulsed'.

146 watch wakefulness.

147 lightness lightheadedness. The word is not otherwise recorded in this sense, but editors point to *Othello* 4.1.269, 'Is he not light of brain?'

147 declension decline.

149 mourn So Q2. F reads 'wail', a strong reading which could be the true one; the word did not have its present exclusive meaning of loud crying, but signified 'lament' in any form. Compare *Macbeth* 3.1.121.

154 Take this from this Theobald thought Polonius pointed to his head and shoulders. Dowden suggested he meant taking his wand of office from his hand.

157 centre (of the earth).

157 try test.

159 lobby ante-room, vestibule. It is on an upper floor of the palace (4.3.34).

Dover Wilson believed that Hamlet began to enter at this point and overheard the plot (*What Happens in 'Hamlet'*, p. 106). Beerbohm Tree had already tried this out on the stage (Sprague, *Shakespeare and the Actors*, pp. 146–7). Hamlet's foreknowledge of the eavesdropping would put a totally different complexion on his behaviour in the nunnery scene; but there is no authority whatever for the early entry, and the theory should be strongly resisted. See also note to 3.1.126.

160 loose An unpleasant word to use, more suitable to animals than a daughter.

Be you and I behind an arras then.
Mark the encounter: if he love her not,
And be not from his reason fallen thereon,
Let me be no assistant for a state,
But keep a farm and carters.

CLAUDIUS We will try it. 165

Enter HAMLET *reading on a book*

GERTRUDE But look where sadly the poor wretch comes reading.

POLONIUS Away, I do beseech you both, away.
I'll board him presently.

Exeunt Claudius and Gertrude [*and Attendants*]

Oh give me leave.
How does my good Lord Hamlet?

HAMLET Well, God-a-mercy. 170

POLONIUS Do you know me, my lord?

HAMLET Excellent well, y'are a fishmonger.

POLONIUS Not I my lord.

HAMLET Then I would you were so honest a man.

POLONIUS Honest my lord? 175

HAMLET Ay sir. To be honest, as this world goes, is to be one man picked out of ten thousand.

POLONIUS That's very true my lord.

HAMLET For if the sun breed maggots in a dead dog, being a good kissing carrion – Have you a daughter? 180

165 But] Q2; And F **165** SD *reading on a book*] F; *not in* Q2 **168** SD *Exeunt...Gertrude*] *Exit King & Queen* F; *at 167 in* Q2 **168** SD *and Attendants*] *Malone; and Train/Capell; not in* Q2, F **172** Excellent well] Q2; Excellent, excellent well F **172** y'are] F, Q1; you are Q2 **177** ten] tenne Q2, Q1; two F **179** good] Q2, F; god *Warburton*

161 arras tapestry or hangings covering a wall.

165 At this point in Q1, the plan to use Ophelia as decoy is put into immediate effect (Ophelia has entered with Polonius). Gertrude exits, Claudius and Polonius withdraw, Hamlet enters with 'To be or not to be'. After the confrontation, Polonius remains on stage, and the fishmonger scene follows. See Introduction, pp. 25–7.

172 fishmonger When Hamlet calls Polonius a fishmonger, he means fishmonger and not something else. It is the zany inappropriateness of supposing this dignified and self-important councillor an unsavoury low-class seller of fish that makes the joke. Since Malone's time it has been commonly thought that Hamlet uses the term to mean wencher, bawd or fleshmonger. It seems true that fishmongers were thought of as a disreputable class (see Wilson's note) but it is important not to let secondary meanings and connotations – which are far from certainly established – invade and overwhelm primary meanings and diminish the main point of a passage. Compare the very similar case of 'nunnery', in the next scene.

179–80 a good kissing carrion The sun breeds maggots in a dead dog because it's a good bit of flesh to kiss – and talking of kissing and breeding, 'have you a daughter?' Hamlet has in mind the sun/son pun of 1.2. He feeds his victim with his victim's own fears: you can't keep me away any more than you can forbid the sun. If the sun can make a dead dog breed, a son can make your daughter breed.

POLONIUS I have my lord.

HAMLET Let her not walk i'th'sun. Conception is a blessing, but as your daughter may conceive – Friend, look to't.

POLONIUS (*Aside*) How say you by that? Still harping on my daughter. Yet he knew me not at first, a said I was a fishmonger – a is far gone, far gone. And truly, in my youth I suffered much extremity for love, very near this. I'll speak to him again. – What do you read my lord? 185

HAMLET Words, words, words.

POLONIUS What is the matter, my lord? 190

HAMLET Between who?

POLONIUS I mean the matter that you read, my lord.

HAMLET Slanders sir, for the satirical rogue says here that old men have grey beards, that their faces are wrinkled, their eyes purging thick amber and plumtree gum, and that they have a plentiful lack of wit, together with most weak hams. All which sir, though I most powerfully and potently believe, yet I hold it not honesty to have it thus set down. For yourself sir shall grow old as I am, if like a crab you could go backward. 195

POLONIUS (*Aside*) Though this be madness, yet there is method in't. – Will you walk out of the air, my lord? 200

HAMLET Into my grave?

POLONIUS Indeed that's out of the air. (*Aside*) How pregnant sometimes his replies are! a happiness that often madness hits on, which reason and sanity could not so prosperously be delivered of. I will leave 205

182 but as] Q2; but not as F 184 SD *Aside*] *Malone; not in* Q2, F 185 a said] Q2; he said F 185 a is] Q2; he is F 185–6 far gone, far gone] F; farre gone Q2 192 matter that you] Q2; matter you F, Q1 192 read] Q2; meane F 193 rogue] Q2; slaue F 195 amber and] Amber, & Q2; Amber, or F 195 lack] Q2; locke F 196 most weak] Q2; weake F 198 yourself] Q2, Q1; you yourselfe F 198 shall grow] Q2; should be F; shalbe Q1 202 grave?] F; graue. Q2 203 that's out of the] Q2; that is out o' th' F 205 sanity] F; sanctity Q2

184 harping on To harp on one string was a proverbial phrase for sticking to a single subject.

185 a is This is presumably what stood in Shakespeare's MS. to represent the slurred pronunciation of 'he is'; something like 'uz'? Compare 3.3.73.

190 matter subject-matter (but Hamlet pretends to understand it as the subject of contention or dispute).

194 purging discharging.

195 amber and plumtree gum Whereas the latter is a very familiar resin, 'amber' was used very vaguely and could mean half-a-dozen substances, from the Baltic fossil-resin to ambergris. Here it presumably means liquidamber, a tree resin. See *OED* Amber *sb*[1] 7, with quotation from 1569, 'The gumme called Amber, groweth out of a tree'.

195 wit understanding.

197 honesty i.e. honourable.

201 out of the air The open air, presumably; but this scene is supposed to be taking place in the lobby. Compare 3.2.339 and note.

203 pregnant quick-witted (*OED sv a*[2] 3).

204 happiness successful aptness (*OED* 3).

205–8 Q2 omits eleven words, reading 'I will leave him and my daughter. My Lord, I will take my leave of you.' It is interesting that this omission has to do with what seems to have been a vexed area of the plot – the organisation of the meeting between Hamlet and Ophelia, which is to be spied

him, and suddenly contrive the means of meeting between him and my daughter. – My honourable lord, I will most humbly take my leave of you.

HAMLET You cannot sir take from me anything that I will more willingly part withal; except my life, except my life, except my life. 210

POLONIUS Fare you well my lord.

HAMLET These tedious old fools!

Enter GUILDENSTERN *and* ROSENCRANTZ

POLONIUS You go to seek the Lord Hamlet, there he is.

ROSENCRANTZ God save you sir.

[*Exit Polonius*]

GUILDENSTERN My honoured lord! 215

ROSENCRANTZ My most dear lord!

HAMLET My excellent good friends! How dost thou Guildenstern? Ah, Rosencrantz. Good lads, how do you both?

ROSENCRANTZ As the indifferent children of the earth.

GUILDENSTERN Happy in that we are not over-happy; on Fortune's cap we are not the very button. 220

HAMLET Nor the soles of her shoe?

ROSENCRANTZ Neither, my lord.

HAMLET Then you live about her waist, or in the middle of her favours?

GUILDENSTERN Faith, her privates we. 225

HAMLET In the secret parts of Fortune? Oh most true, she is a strumpet. What news?

ROSENCRANTZ None my lord, but that the world's grown honest.

HAMLET Then is doomsday near – but your news is not true. Let me

206 and suddenly...between him] F; *not in* Q2 **207** honourable lord] F; Lord Q2 **207** most humbly] F; *not in* Q2 **209** sir] F; *not in* Q2 **209** will] F; will not Q2 **210** except my life, except my life, except my life] Q2; except my life, my life F **212** SD] Q2 *at 210*, F *at 213 with names interchanged* **213** the] Q2; my F **214** SD] *Capell; not in* Q2, F **215** My] Q2; Mine F **217** excellent] F; extent Q2 **217** Ah,] A Q2; Oh, F **218** you] Q2; ye F **220** over] F; euer Q2 **221** cap] F; lap Q2 **227** What news] Q2; What's the newes F **228** but that the] F; but the Q2 **229–56** Let me...attended] F; *not in* Q2

on (see Introduction, p. 26). It may be that some indication for rewriting has been misunderstood by the Q2 compositor. Jenkins's note on this passage, concentrating on the spread-out typography in F, does not mention the Q2 omission. It seems highly likely that the imperfections of both Q2 and F at this point are related.

206 suddenly immediately.

219 indifferent i.e. in-between, at neither extreme.

221–2 very button...her shoe i.e. neither on the top nor trodden down.

224 favours Fortune's favours are compared with the sexual favours of a woman. (The word is not much used in this sense now, but was important in less free-spoken ages. See *OED* favour *sb* 2d.)

225 her privates we 'we are *very* intimate with her'.

229–56 This whole passage is not found in Q2 (see collation). It is much more likely that this is a cut than that F provides a later addition. By the time Q2 was printed in 1604, the position of Anne of Denmark as King James's consort might have made the printer cautious about setting up material naming Denmark as one of the worst prisons in the world.

question more in particular. What have you, my good friends, deserved at the hands of Fortune, that she sends you to prison hither? 230

GUILDENSTERN Prison, my lord?

HAMLET Denmark's a prison.

ROSENCRANTZ Then is the world one. 235

HAMLET A goodly one, in which there are many confines, wards, and dungeons; Denmark being one o'th'worst.

ROSENCRANTZ We think not so my lord.

HAMLET Why then 'tis none to you, for there is nothing either good or bad but thinking makes it so. To me it is a prison. 240

ROSENCRANTZ Why then your ambition makes it one; 'tis too narrow for your mind.

HAMLET O God, I could be bounded in a nutshell, and count myself a king of infinite space, were it not that I have bad dreams.

GUILDENSTERN Which dreams indeed are ambition, for the very substance of the ambitious is merely the shadow of a dream. 245

HAMLET A dream itself is but a shadow.

ROSENCRANTZ Truly, and I hold ambition of so airy and light a quality that it is but a shadow's shadow.

HAMLET Then are our beggars bodies, and our monarchs and outstretched heroes the beggars' shadows. Shall we to th'court? for by my fay I cannot reason. 250

BOTH We'll wait upon you.

HAMLET No such matter. I will not sort you with the rest of my servants; for to speak to you like an honest man, I am most 255

236 **confines, wards** Terms for places of confinement.

239–40 **nothing...makes it so** While this phrase voices an uncertainty about absolutes which reverberates throughout the play, Jenkins makes clear that at this point Hamlet is not directly maintaining 'that there are no ethical absolutes'. The relativism is about happiness: whether a place is good or bad to be in depends on one's mental attitude.

245, 248 Rosencrantz and Guildenstern make strenuous attempts to keep the conversation on the subject of ambition.

246 **substance of the ambitious** material which ambitious people live on.

250–1 Hamlet seems to mean that if the substance of the ambitious is a shadow, only the lowest in society will have real bodies – monarchs and great men are all ambitious, and are therefore shadows. But why are monarchs etc. 'the beggars' shadows'? ('outstretched' indicates those who have aspired or reached out, also applicable to a long shadow.)

252 **fay** faith.

252 **I cannot reason** Hamlet is wearing his antic disposition very lightly in this first encounter with Rosencrantz and Guildenstern. His teasing, ironic stance is little removed from an acceptable banter between friends. But the cloak of feigned madness is never far away.

254 **sort you** class you.

255–6 **I am...attended** I have such a rotten lot of servants. But the phrase has private meanings for Hamlet. He must mean the pressure of his own thoughts; Hudson points to the 'bad dreams' (NV). J. Q. Adams thinks Hamlet is already aware of Claudius's surveillance. D. R. C. Marsh, noting that the modern colloquial use of 'dreadfully' is not established as early as this by OED, suggests that the phrase must bring the Ghost to mind (*SQ* 33 (1982), 181–2).

dreadfully attended. But in the beaten way of friendship, what make you at Elsinore?

ROSENCRANTZ To visit you my lord, no other occasion.

HAMLET Beggar that I am, I am even poor in thanks, but I thank you – and sure, dear friends, my thanks are too dear a halfpenny. 260 Were you not sent for? Is it your own inclining? Is it a free visitation? Come, deal justly with me. Come, come. Nay, speak.

GUILDENSTERN What should we say my lord?

HAMLET Why, anything but to the purpose. You were sent for – and there is a kind of confession in your looks which your modesties 265 have not craft enough to colour. I know the good king and queen have sent for you.

ROSENCRANTZ To what end my lord?

HAMLET That you must teach me. But let me conjure you, by the rights of our fellowship, by the consonancy of our youth, by the obligation 270 of our ever-preserved love, and by what more dear a better proposer can charge you withal, be even and direct with me, whether you were sent for or no.

ROSENCRANTZ (*To Guildenstern*) What say you?

HAMLET (*Aside*) Nay then I have an eye of you. – If you love me, hold 275 not off.

GUILDENSTERN My lord, we were sent for.

HAMLET I will tell you why. So shall my anticipation prevent your discovery, and your secrecy to the king and queen moult no feather. I have of late, but wherefore I know not, lost all my mirth, forgone 280

259 even] F; euer Q2 **262** Come, deal] F; come, come, deale Q2 **264** Why] F; *not in* Q2 **265** kind of] Q2; kinde F **272** can] Q2; could F **274** SD *To Guildenstern*] *Theobald*[2]; *not in* Q2, F **275** SD *Aside*] *Steevens*[3]; *not in* Q2, F **279** and your] Q2; of your F

256 beaten...friendship He means he has neglected the ordinary politeness of greeting. He thus makes an offhand introduction of his own cross-examination.

259 Beggar that I am A beggar, in the terms of the preceding conversation, as he is not ambitious; but a beggar in his own eyes as a dispossessed prince in prison.

260 too dear a halfpenny (i.e. at a halfpenny) not worth anything; certainly not like a king's remembrance (see 26 above).

265 modesties sense of shame.

269 conjure solemnly entreat.

270 consonancy accord, agreement. He means the harmony between them in their younger days (see 11 above).

272 even straightforward, 'on the level'.

275 of you on you.

278–9 my anticipation...discovery my being beforehand save you from disclosing your commission.

280–90 This famous speech, so often quoted as an example of the world-weariness not only of Hamlet but of a whole age, is part of Hamlet's campaign to mislead Rosencrantz and Guildenstern and keep them off the true scent. Its plausibility is not meant to deceive the audience who, having been permitted to share Hamlet's deepest feelings, and to know the cause of them, can distinguish a parade of fashionable melancholy from the real thing. See Introduction, p. 47.

all custom of exercises; and indeed it goes so heavily with my disposition that this goodly frame, the earth, seems to me a sterile promontory; this most excellent canopy the air, look you, this brave o'erhanging firmament, this majestical roof fretted with golden fire – why, it appeareth no other thing to me but a foul and pestilent 285 congregation of vapours. What a piece of work is a man! How noble in reason, how infinite in faculties, in form and moving how express and admirable, in action how like an angel, in apprehension how like a god! The beauty of the world, the paragon of animals – and yet to me, what is this quintessence of dust? Man delights not 290 me – no, nor woman neither, though by your smiling you seem to say so.

ROSENCRANTZ My lord, there was no such stuff in my thoughts.

HAMLET Why did ye laugh then, when I said man delights not me?

ROSENCRANTZ To think, my lord, if you delight not in man, what 295 lenten entertainment the players shall receive from you. We coted them on the way, and hither are they coming to offer you service.

HAMLET He that plays the king shall be welcome, his majesty shall have tribute of me; the adventurous knight shall use his foil and target, the lover shall not sigh gratis, the humorous man shall end his part 300 in peace, the clown shall make those laugh whose lungs are tickle

281 exercises] Q2; exercise F 281 heavily] Q2; heauenly F 284 firmament] Q2; *not in* F 285 appeareth] Q2; appeares F 285 no other thing] F; nothing Q2 285 but] Q2; than F 286 What a] F; What Q2 287 faculties] Q2; faculty F 287 moving how] F; moouing, how Q2 288 admirable, in] admirable? in F; admirable in Q2 288 angel, in] Angel? in F; Angell in Q2 291 no, nor] F; nor Q2 291 woman] F; women Q2 294 ye] Q2; you F 294 then] Q2, Q1; *not in* F 299 of] F; on Q2 301–2 the clown...sere] F; *not in* Q2 301 tickle] *Clark and Wright, conj. Staunton;* tickled F

281 custom of exercises i.e. pursuing the activities of a gentleman, as fencing, riding, hawking, dancing. F reads 'custom of exercise', a very different matter, meaning 'exercise' as we would use it – what you do to keep your body fit.

282–3 sterile promontory 'a barren rocky point jutting out into the sea of eternity' (Kittredge).

284 fretted interlaced, patterned (as in a decorated ceiling).

286 What a piece of work Jenkins defends the reading of Q2, 'What piece of work', pointing out that the indefinite article could be omitted in an exclamation, e.g. 'What night is this', *Julius Caesar* 1.3.42. But compare 5.2.323, 'What a wounded name'.

287–9 in form...god Punctuation follows F; the punctuation in Q2 gives a quite different meaning. Wilson was a strong advocate of Q2's punctuation.

287 express It is not clear what this means. The gloss 'well fitted to its purpose' has been suggested. I think it has something to do with 'clearly stamped', or 'expressive'.

289 paragon pattern of excellence.

296 lenten i.e. austere.

296 entertainment reception.

296–7 coted them passed them by.

298–9 his majesty...tribute of me as we pay money and offer adulation to real kings, so the Player King will get payment and praise. But there are no real kings in Elsinore at the moment; the implication is that Hamlet is prepared to honour one pseudo-king with as much seriousness as another.

299 foil and target sword and shield.

300 gratis for nothing.

300 humorous man Man with a humour in the Elizabethan sense, the eccentric.

301–2 tickle o'th'sere easily triggered (the 'sere' is a catch affecting the trigger-mechanism of a gun; 'tickle' means lightly set – and, of course, 'ticklish').

o'th'sere, and the lady shall say her mind freely – or the blank verse shall halt for't. What players are they?

ROSENCRANTZ Even those you were wont to take such delight in, the tragedians of the city. 305

HAMLET How chances it they travel? their residence, both in reputation and profit, was better both ways.

ROSENCRANTZ I think their inhibition comes by the means of the late innovation.

HAMLET Do they hold the same estimation they did when I was in the city? Are they so followed? 310

ROSENCRANTZ No indeed are they not.

HAMLET How comes it? Do they grow rusty?

ROSENCRANTZ Nay, their endeavour keeps in the wonted pace, but there is sir an eyrie of children, little eyases, that cry out on the top of question and are most tyrannically clapped for't. These are 315

302 blank] F; black Q2 **304** such delight] Q2; delight F, Q1 **306** travel] trauaile Q2, F **311** are they] Q2; they are F **313–33** HAMLET How...load too] F; *not in* Q2

302–3 the lady...halt for't The many ingenious explanations of this sentence seem to miss the obvious point – if the lady can't say all she has to say – which will be the part that is written down for her – then clearly there will be some holes in the blank verse.

303 halt limp.

305 tragedians Properly, tragic actors; here, actors generally.

306–7 their residence...ways they did better in reputation and profit when they stayed at home.

308–9 their inhibition...innovation i.e. they are forbidden to play in the city because of the recent political disturbance. Although it is certain that this conversation is more about English than Danish theatrical conditions, it may be a mistake to try to locate this too precisely in the England of *c.* 1601. 'the late innovation' is sometimes taken to refer to the fashion for the children's companies, shortly to be discussed. But that can hardly be: Hamlet shows no interest, and the subject is introduced quite independently four lines later. 'Inhibition' implies a closing of the theatres in the capital (which was a constant threat to the players' livelihood in England). 'Innovation' at this time usually meant a political upheaval (*OED* 1b, 2b) but it could mean a major change of any sort. If it is a Danish 'innovation', we must suppose that the upheavals of the king's death, the succession and the preparations for war with Fortinbras are meant. If it is an English 'innovation', then it is impossible to guess what is meant. Some have thought that the reference is to Essex's rebellion of February 1601.

313–33 This whole passage on the child-actors and the 'war of the theatres' is missing from Q2. Although it is quite possible that by 1604 this excursus on the theatre troubles of 1600–1 seemed too out-of-date and uninteresting to print, it is also quite possible that the passage had in some way become detached from the main MS. This bravura on contemporary theatre problems is unique in Shakespeare. Perhaps he inserted it in the heat of the moment to replace a much briefer remark about fashion in the theatre, which would carry us from Rosencrantz at 312 to Hamlet at 334. This passage was available to the transcriber in the playhouse but the insertion was either overlooked by or not available to the Q2 compositors. See further in the Introduction, pp. 4–5, 19.

315 eyrie...eyases nest of children, little unfledged hawks. This is a reference to the revival of the boys' acting companies about 1600 (Paul's and the Chapel). Their new organisation, more professional and commercial, made them, for a brief time, formidable rivals to the adult companies (see E. K. Chambers, *Elizabethan Stage*, 1923, I, 378–80).

315–16 cry...question 'question' frequently means 'dispute' or 'controversy'. Perhaps this means that the boys enthusiastically carry on the theatre war in their treble voices.

316 tyrannically inordinately, outrageously.

now the fashion, and so be-rattle the common stages (so they call them) that many wearing rapiers are afraid of goose-quills, and dare scarce come thither.

HAMLET What, are they children? Who maintains 'em? How are they escoted? Will they pursue the quality no longer than they can sing? Will they not say afterwards, if they should grow themselves to common players – as it is most like if their means are no better, their writers do them wrong to make them exclaim against their own succession? 320 325

ROSENCRANTZ Faith, there has been much to do on both sides, and the nation holds it no sin to tar them to controversy. There was for a while no money bid for argument unless the poet and the player went to cuffs in the question.

HAMLET Is't possible? 330

GUILDENSTERN Oh there has been much throwing about of brains.

HAMLET Do the boys carry it away?

ROSENCRANTZ Ay that they do my lord, Hercules and his load too.

HAMLET It is not very strange, for my uncle is king of Denmark, and those that would make mouths at him while my father lived give twenty, forty, fifty, a hundred ducats apiece for his picture in little. 'Sblood, there is something in this more than natural, if philosophy could find it out. 335

A flourish

GUILDENSTERN There are the players.

317 be-rattle] F2; be-ratled F 323 most like] *Pope*; like most F 334 very strange] Q2; strange F 334 my] Q2, Q1; mine F 335 mouths] Q2; mows F 336 fifty] Q2; *not in* F 336 a] Q2; an F 337 'Sblood] Q2; *not in* F 338 SD *A flourish*] Q2; *Flourish for the Players* F

317 **be-rattle** rattle, shake.

317 **common stages** The usual term for the public theatres.

318 **many...rapiers** the men-about-town, the gallants.

318 **afraid of goose-quills** The satire of the children's dramatists has so discredited the public theatres that fashionable gallants don't like being seen there (Dowden's suggestion).

321 **escoted** maintained financially. (From the French *escotter*; very rare in English.)

321 **quality** profession.

323 **common players** professional actors.

323 **if their means...better** if they do not acquire a better means of supporting themselves. Compare the 'public means' of Sonnet 111.

325 **succession** that which they will succeed to.

327 **tar** incite, provoke. (Editors often preserve the old spelling 'tarre'.)

328 **no money...argument** i.e. no company wanted to hear about a new play.

329 **cuffs** blows, punches.

332 **Do the boys carry it away?** Jonson claimed they did in *Poetaster* (acted by a boys' company). See Introduction, p. 4.

333 **Hercules and his load** The emblem of the Globe Theatre is supposed to have been Hercules carrying the celestial globe on his shoulders.

335 **mouths** grimaces. So Q2. F reads 'mows', which means the same thing, but in view of 4.4.50 'mouths' looks like Shakespeare's word.

336 **ducats** coins of gold or silver, used in many European countries. The value might be two or three to the English pound.

337–8 **more than natural...find it out** i.e. there is something abnormal about it as scientific investigation would show.

HAMLET Gentlemen, you are welcome to Elsinore. Your hands, come then. Th'appurtenance of welcome is fashion and ceremony. Let me comply with you in this garb, lest my extent to the players, which I tell you must show fairly outwards, should more appear like entertainment than yours. You are welcome – but my uncle-father and aunt-mother are deceived. 340 345

GUILDENSTERN In what my dear lord?

HAMLET I am but mad north-north-west. When the wind is southerly, I know a hawk from a handsaw.

Enter POLONIUS

POLONIUS Well be with you gentlemen.

HAMLET Hark you Guildenstern, and you too – at each ear a hearer. That great baby you see there is not yet out of his swaddling clouts. 350

ROSENCRANTZ Happily he's the second time come to them, for they say an old man is twice a child.

HAMLET I will prophesy: he comes to tell me of the players, mark it. – You say right sir, a Monday morning, 'twas then indeed. 355

POLONIUS My lord, I have news to tell you.

HAMLET My lord, I have news to tell you. When Roscius was an actor in Rome –

POLONIUS The actors are come hither my lord.

HAMLET Buzz, buzz! 360

POLONIUS Upon my honour.

HAMLET Then came each actor on his ass –

POLONIUS The best actors in the world, either for tragedy, comedy, history, pastoral, pastoral-comical, historical-pastoral, tragical-

340–1 come then. Th'] come then, th' Q2; come: The F 342 this garb] Q2; the Garbe F 342 lest my] F; let me Q2 343 outwards] Q2; outward F 351 swaddling] swadling Q2, Q1; swathing F 352 he's] F; he is Q2 355 a] Q2; for a F 357 was] Q2; *not in* F 361 my] Q2; mine F 362 came] Q2; can F 364–5 tragical-...pastoral] F; *not in* Q2

342 comply with you pay you the usual courtesies. Compare 5.2.170, 'comply with his dug'.

342 garb manner of doing things.

342 my extent what I extend, how I behave.

344 entertainment welcome.

347 but mad north-north-west He means (1) that he is only a little away from the true north of sanity, and (2) that he is not mad at all points of the compass, i.e. at all times.

348 a hawk from a handsaw Those who are determined to rub the fine edge off the wit of Hamlet's 'madness' have supposed that these two terms must belong to the same family, so 'handsaw' has been thought to be 'hernshaw', a kind of heron, and 'hawk' has been thought to be the plasterer's tool so named. But it is the utter dissimilarity of a hawk and a saw which makes Hamlet's point, i.e. 'I am mad only at certain times, at other times I can discriminate as well as a madman.' Even as he pretends confidentially to impart the secret that he is not mad, he confirms that he is raving.

352 Happily Perhaps.

357 Roscius A great Roman comic actor (d. 62 BC).

360 Buzz, buzz! A 'buzz' is a rumour. Hamlet is making a stock response to a story which is not believed.

historical, tragical-comical-historical-pastoral, scene individable or 365
poem unlimited. Seneca cannot be too heavy, nor Plautus too light.
For the law of writ and the liberty, these are the only men.

HAMLET O Jephtha judge of Israel, what a treasure hadst thou!

POLONIUS What a treasure had he my lord?

HAMLET Why – 370

'One fair daughter and no more,
The which he lovèd passing well.'

POLONIUS Still on my daughter.

HAMLET Am I not i'th'right, old Jephtha?

POLONIUS If you call me Jephtha my lord, I have a daughter that I 375
love passing well.

HAMLET Nay, that follows not.

POLONIUS What follows then my lord?

HAMLET Why –

'As by lot God wot,' 380

And then you know –

'It came to pass, as most like it was,' –

the first row of the pious chanson will show you more, for look where
my abridgement comes.

365 individable] indeuidible Q2; indiuible F 371–2 more, / The] F; *not divided in* Q2 383 pious chanson] Q2; *Pons Chanson* F 384 abridgement comes] Q2, Q1; Abridgements come F

365 tragical-comical-historical-pastoral Shakespeare illustrates the inadequacy of categorising the modern drama of his day by the old genres. It has been pointed out that his own *Cymbeline* might require this last super-category.

365–6 scene...unlimited The traditional interpretation is that this contrasts plays which observe the unities of time, place and action with those that don't. But Jenkins interestingly suggests that 'individable' and 'unlimited' are the terms to use when there can be no further refinement or subdivision in this absurd progress of categorisation.

366 Seneca...Plautus These Roman dramatists, one tragic and one comic, were the classical dramatists who were best known to the Elizabethans, and who most influenced their drama.

367 the law of writ and the liberty Obscure: possibly Polonius means plays which obey prescribed rules ('writ' = authoritative guidance), and those which are free from such rules. (Wilson thought that the two acting areas of London were in question, that where the Sheriff's writ ran within the City, and the liberty outside.)

368–72 Jephtha...passing well Jephtha vowed to sacrifice the first living thing he met if he returned successfully from war. It turned out to be his own daughter and he sacrificed her after she had gone into the mountains to 'bewail her virginity' – so she died and 'knew no man' (Judges 11.30–40). The ballad Hamlet quotes is known in an early-seventeenth-century version: 'Had one faire daughter and no moe,/Whom he beloved passing well,/And as by lot God wot,/It came to passe, most like it was...' (The single surviving copy of this print, in the Manchester Central Library, differs in its readings from the reprints quoted by Jenkins and others.)

383 first row...chanson A 'row' is properly a line, but, as this does not make much sense, some editors suggest, without much authority, 'stanza' – i.e. 'you'll have to read the first stanza of this pious ballad if you want more...' Q1 says 'the first verse of the godly Ballet'.

384 abridgement that which shortens my recitation. It is frequently suggested, because of the use of the word in *A Midsummer Night's Dream* 5.1.39, in a context suggesting the meaning 'entertainment', that Hamlet is here punning on two senses, 'abbreviation', and 'entertainment'. But this secondary meaning is not well attested.

Enter the PLAYERS

Y'are welcome masters, welcome all. I am glad to see thee well. 385
Welcome good friends. Oh, my old friend! why, thy face is valanced
since I saw thee last; com'st thou to beard me in Denmark? What,
my young lady and mistress – byrlady, your ladyship is nearer to
heaven than when I saw you last by the altitude of a chopine. Pray
God your voice like a piece of uncurrent gold be not cracked within 390
the ring. Masters, you are all welcome. We'll e'en to't like French
falconers, fly at anything we see: we'll have a speech straight. Come
give us a taste of your quality: come, a passionate speech.

I PLAYER What speech, my good lord?

HAMLET I heard thee speak me a speech once, but it was never acted, 395
or if it was, not above once, for the play I remember pleased not
the million: 'twas caviary to the general. But it was, as I received
it, and others whose judgements in such matters cried in the top
of mine, an excellent play, well digested in the scenes, set down with
as much modesty as cunning. I remember one said there were no 400
sallets in the lines to make the matter savoury, nor no matter in
the phrase that might indict the author of affectation, but called it

384 SD] Q2; *Enter foure or fiue Players* F **385** Y'are] F; You are Q2 **386** my old] F, Q1; old Q2 **386** why] Q2; *not in* F **386** valanced] valanct Q2; valiant F **388** byrlady] Byrlady F; by lady Q2 **388** nearer to] Q2; neerer F **391–2** French falconers] F; friendly Fankners Q2 **394** my good lord] Q2; my Lord F **398** judgements] Q2; iudgement F **400** were] Q2; was F **402** affectation] F; affection Q2

384 SD So Q2. F's 'four or five players' is a characteristic example of the book-keeper's preliminary efforts to put limits on the permissiveness of Shakespeare's MS. See Introduction, p. 22.

385–91 Compare the entry of the players in *Shrew*, Induction, 1.79, where also the lord of the house welcomes them, and speaks warmly of his recollection of one of them playing a certain part years ago (and requests them to assist his plans by means of their play).

386 valanced fringed, curtained round.

387 beard challenge, defy.

388 my young lady A boy actor who takes female roles; presumably the Player Queen of 3.2.

388 byrlady by our Lady. Pronounced berlády. See note to 3.2.118.

389 chopine Additional base to a lady's shoe to increase height.

390–1 cracked...ring 'There was a ring on the coin, within which the sovereign's head was placed; if the crack extended from the edge beyond this ring, the coin was rendered unfit for currency' (Douce, in NV). But there is also a bawdy quibble on losing virginity here; see Partridge, *Shakespeare's Bawdy* (1947, revised 1955), under 'crack/crackt'. Hamlet means 'I hope you haven't lost your virginity as a player of female parts, and ceased to be acceptable (current), by the breaking of your voice.'

393 quality professional skill.

397 caviary A common early form of 'caviare'. Pronounced caviáry.

397 the general people in general, the multitude.

398–9 cried...mine An unusual phrase. It must mean 'counted more than mine'.

399 digested arranged, disposed.

400 modesty moderation, restraint (*OED* 1).

400 cunning skill.

401 sallets salads. Generally thought to mean 'spicy bits' – indecencies.

402 affectation So F. Q2 reads 'affection', which some claim means 'affectation', but the argument is not strong, and the word is likely to be a misreading.

an honest method, as wholesome as sweet and by very much more handsome than fine. One speech in't I chiefly loved, 'twas Aeneas' tale to Dido, and thereabout of it especially where he speaks of Priam's slaughter. If it live in your memory, begin at this line, let me see, let me see – 405

'The rugged Pyrrhus, like th'Hyrcanian beast' –

'Tis not so, it begins with Pyrrhus –

'The rugged Pyrrhus, he whose sable arms, 410
Black as his purpose, did the night resemble
When he lay couchèd in the ominous horse,
Hath now this dread and black complexion smeared
With heraldy more dismal. Head to foot
Now is he total gules, horridly tricked 415
With blood of fathers, mothers, daughters, sons,
Baked and impasted with the parching streets,
That lend a tyrannous and a damnèd light
To their lord's murder. Roasted in wrath and fire,
And thus o'er-sizèd with coagulate gore, 420
With eyes like carbuncles, the hellish Pyrrhus
Old grandsire Priam seeks –'

So, proceed you.

POLONIUS 'Fore God my lord, well spoken, with good accent and good discretion. 425

403–4 as wholesome...fine] Q2; *not in* F 404 speech] Q2; cheefe Speech F 404 in't] Q2; in it F 405 tale] F; talke Q2 405 where] F; when Q2 408 th'Hyrcanean] F; Th'ircanian Q2 409 'Tis] Q2; It is F 412 the] F; th' Q2 414 heraldy] Q2; Heraldry F 415 total] Q2; to take F 418 a damnèd] Q2; damned F 419 lord's murder] Lords murther Q2; vilde Murthers F 420 o'er-sized] o're-sized F; ore-cised Q2 423 So, proceed you] Q2; *not in* F

403 **method** The disposition of material in a literary work.

404 **fine** showy, over-elaborate.

404–6 **Aeneas' tale...slaughter** See Virgil's *Aeneid* II, 506–58. Priam's death is the subject of an extended passage in *Dido, Queen of Carthage* by Marlowe and Nashe, and it is certain that Shakespeare had this earlier treatment in mind when creating the speech which now follows.

408 **rugged** rough and fierce. Applied to an animal, it could mean shaggy, which is perhaps why Hamlet makes a false start on the Hyrcanian beast.

408 **Pyrrhus** Pyrrhus, or Neoptolemus, the son of Achilles, was summoned to the Trojan war to avenge his father. With Hamlet, Fortinbras and Laertes, he makes a fourth son avenging a father. He was renowned for his savagery and barbarity.

408 **Hyrcanian beast** Tiger from Hyrcania, near the Caspian sea. Virgil spoke of them in *Aeneid* IV, 368.

412 **couchèd** concealed.

414 **heraldy** See note to 1.1.87.

414 **dismal** sinister.

415 **gules** The heraldic name for red.

415 **tricked** decorated.

417 **Baked...streets** The blood is dried into a paste on Pyrrhus by the heat of the burning street.

418 **tyrannous** ferocious.

420 **o'er-sizèd** To oversize is to cover over with size, the sticky wash used as a preparative by painters.

421 **carbuncles** large and supposedly luminous precious stones.

I PLAYER 'Anon he finds him,
Striking too short at Greeks; his antique sword,
Rebellious to his arm, lies where it falls,
Repugnant to command. Unequal matched,
Pyrrhus at Priam drives, in rage strikes wide, 430
But with the whiff and wind of his fell sword
Th'unnervèd father falls. Then senseless Ilium,
Seeming to feel this blow, with flaming top
Stoops to his base, and with a hideous crash
Takes prisoner Pyrrhus' ear; for lo, his sword, 435
Which was declining on the milky head
Of reverend Priam, seemed i'th'air to stick.
So, as a painted tyrant, Pyrrhus stood,
And like a neutral to his will and matter,
Did nothing. 440
But as we often see against some storm,
A silence in the heavens, the rack stand still,
The bold winds speechless, and the orb below
As hush as death, anon the dreadful thunder
Doth rend the region; so after Pyrrhus' pause, 445
A rousèd vengeance sets him new a-work,
And never did the Cyclops' hammers fall
On Mars's armour, forged for proof eterne,
With less remorse than Pyrrhus' bleeding sword
Now falls on Priam. 450
Out, out, thou strumpet Fortune! All you gods,
In general synod take away her power,
Break all the spokes and fellies from her wheel,

427 antique] *Pope;* anticke Q2, F 429 matched] matcht Q2; match F 432 Then...Ilium] F; *not in* Q2 433 this] Q2; his F 439 And] F; *not in* Q2 439–40 matter,/ Did] Q2; *not divided in* F 448 Mars's] *Marses* Q2; Mars his F 448 armour] Q2; Armours F 453 fellies] F4; follies Q2; Fallies F

426 **Anon** Presently.

429 **Repugnant to** Resisting.

431–2 **But with the whiff...falls** This sadly comic episode is at the expense of Marlowe and Nashe, who, in writing of the same scene in *Dido, Queen of Carthage* (2.1.253–4), said, 'Which he disdaining whisked his sword about,/And with the wound thereof the King fell down.'

432 **senseless** insensible.

432 **Ilium** Troy. Used here, Kittredge points out, for the citadel and not the whole city.

436 **milky** i.e. white-haired.

438 **painted tyrant** tyrant in a painting.

439 **like a neutral...matter** 'As a neutral stands idle between two parties, so Pyrrhus paused midway between his purpose and its fulfilment' (Kittredge).

441 **against** before.

442 **rack** cloud-formation.

443 **orb** globe, hence earth.

445 **region** sky.

447 **Cyclops** The one-eyed giants worked in Vulcan's smithy.

448 **proof eterne** everlasting resistance.

449 **remorse** pity.

453 **fellies** wooden pieces forming the rim of a wheel.

And bowl the round nave down the hill of heaven
As low as to the fiends.' 455

POLONIUS This is too long.

HAMLET It shall to th' barber's with your beard. Prithee say on. He's for a jig or a tale of bawdry, or he sleeps. Say on, come to Hecuba.

I PLAYER 'But who – ah woe! – had seen the mobled queen –' 460

HAMLET The mobled queen?

POLONIUS That's good, 'mobled queen' is good.

I PLAYER 'Run barefoot up and down, threat'ning the flames
With bisson rheum, a clout upon that head
Where late the diadem stood, and, for a robe, 465
About her lank and all o'er-teemèd loins
A blanket, in th'alarm of fear caught up –
Who this had seen, with tongue in venom steeped
'Gainst Fortune's state would treason have pronounced.
But if the gods themselves did see her then, 470
When she saw Pyrrhus make malicious sport
In mincing with his sword her husband's limbs,
The instant burst of clamour that she made,
Unless things mortal move them not at all,
Would have made milch the burning eyes of heaven, 475
And passion in the gods.

POLONIUS Look where he has not turned his colour, and has tears in's eyes. Prithee no more.

HAMLET 'Tis well, I'll have thee speak out the rest of this soon. – Good my lord, will you see the players well bestowed? Do you hear, let 480

457 to th'] to'th F; to the Q2 460 ah woe] a woe Q2; O who F, Q1 460, 461 mobled] Q2, Q1; inobled F 462 'mobled...good] F (Inobled): *not in* Q2 463 flames] Q2; flame F 464 bisson rheum] Bisson Rheume F; *Bison* rehume Q2 464 upon] Q2; about F 467 th'alarm] th'Alarum F; the alarme Q2 472 husband's] F; husband Q2 478 Prithee] Q2; Pray you F 479 of this] Q2; *not in* F 480 you hear] Q2; ye heare F

454 **nave** hub of the wheel.

458 **jig** The afterpiece, with song and dance, which often concluded theatre performances.

460 **mobled** muffled. It is made clear that this is a rare word. It appears as 'mobble' in 1655, indicating the pronunciation.

464 **bisson** Means blind, or near-blind. Her tears ('rheum') are blinding her.

464 **clout** cloth.

466 **all o'er-teemèd loins** loins which had borne too many children. The count of Hecuba's children varied greatly – seventeen, nineteen or more. In *Dido, Queen of Carthage* (2.1.234), Priam says he is 'father of fifty sons' – but they were not supposed to be all Hecuba's. See *Aeneid* II, 501–5.

469 **state** government.

475 **milch** Properly, exuding milk. The stars would weep milky tears (because of the Milky Way?).

476 **passion** violent sorrow.

477 **Look where** See if. 'where' is a common contracted form of 'whether'. The forms given by editors ('whe'r', 'whe'er' etc.) are orthographic inventions (compare 'ta'en'; see 1.3.106).

them be well used, for they are the abstract and brief chronicles of the time. After your death you were better have a bad epitaph than their ill report while you live.

POLONIUS My lord, I will use them according to their desert.

HAMLET God's bodkin man, much better. Use every man after his desert, and who shall scape whipping? Use them after your own honour and dignity; the less they deserve, the more merit is in your bounty. Take them in. 485

POLONIUS Come sirs. *Exit Polonius*

HAMLET Follow him friends, we'll hear a play tomorrow. – Dost thou hear me old friend, can you play *The Murder of Gonzago*? 490

I PLAYER Ay my lord.

HAMLET We'll ha't tomorrow night. You could for a need study a speech of some dozen or sixteen lines, which I would set down and insert in't, could you not? 495

I PLAYER Ay my lord.

HAMLET Very well. Follow that lord, and look you mock him not.

Exeunt Players

My good friends, I'll leave you till night. You are welcome to Elsinore.

ROSENCRANTZ Good my lord. 500

Exeunt Rosencrantz and Guildenstern

HAMLET Ay so, God bye to you. Now I am alone.
O what a rogue and peasant slave am I!
Is it not monstrous that this player here,
But in a fiction, in a dream of passion,
Could force his soul so to his own conceit 505

481 abstract] Q2; Abstracts F 483 live] Q2; liued F 485 bodkin] Q2; bodykins F 485 much better] Q2; better F 486 shall] Q2; should F 489 SD] F; *not in* Q2; *Exit Polonius with all the Players except the First / Dyce (490)* 493 a need] F; neede Q2 494 dozen...lines] F; dosen lines, or sixteene lines Q2 495 you] Q2; ye F 497 SD] *This edn; Exeunt Pol. and Players.* Q2 *(after* Elsinore, *499); not in* F 498 till] F; tell Q2 500 SD] *Capell; Exeunt.* Q2; *Exeunt./Manet Hamlet.* F 501 God bye to you] Q2 (buy); God buy 'ye F 505 own] Q2; whole F

481 **abstract** epitome, summing-up, distillation. Compare *Richard III* 4.4.28, 'Brief abstract and record of tedious days'.

485 **God's bodkin** Euphemism for the sacrilegious 'God's bodykins', which is the reading of F – a surprising survivor of the post-1606 removal of profanities (see Introduction, p. 30).

489 SD *Exit Polonius* So F. Q2 gives a general exeunt for Polonius and the players at 535. This seems a clear case of the book-keeper beginning to visualize the staging as he transcribed Shakespeare's MS. Polonius cannot be kept back, hanging about awkwardly for the actors. As they begin to follow him off-stage, Hamlet detains the First player. See Introduction, p. 22.

494 **dozen or sixteen lines** The identification of these in the play as acted is a famous but insoluble problem. For Shakespeare's hesitation over this phrase, see Introduction, p. 10.

497 **mock him not** Strange words from the crown prince to a common player about the chief councillor of the state! Perhaps Hamlet is embarrassed at the thought that his own rudeness to Polonius might be taken as a pattern by others.

505 **conceit** imaginings.

That from her working all his visage wanned,
Tears in his eyes, distraction in's aspect,
A broken voice, and his whole function suiting
With forms to his conceit? And all for nothing?
For Hecuba! 510
What's Hecuba to him, or he to Hecuba,
That he should weep for her? What would he do,
Had he the motive and the cue for passion
That I have? He would drown the stage with tears,
And cleave the general ear with horrid speech, 515
Make mad the guilty and appal the free,
Confound the ignorant, and amaze indeed
The very faculties of eyes and ears. Yet I,
A dull and muddy-mettled rascal, peak
Like John-a-dreams, unpregnant of my cause, 520
And can say nothing – no, not for a king,
Upon whose property and most dear life
A damned defeat was made. Am I a coward?
Who calls me villain, breaks my pate across,
Plucks off my beard and blows it in my face, 525
Tweaks me by th'nose, gives me the lie i'th'throat
As deep as to the lungs? Who does me this?

506 his] F; the Q2 506 wanned] wand Q2; warm'd F 507 in's] F; in his Q2 511 he to Hecuba] F; he to her Q2 513 the cue] F; that Q2 516 appal] *Rowe*; appale Q2; apale F 518 faculties] Q2; faculty F 526 th'nose] F; the nose Q2

506 from her working by reason of her (the soul's) activity.

506 wanned grew pale.

508–9 his whole function...conceit all his bodily powers producing the expressions proper to his imaginings. Coleridge unfairly spoke of a 'factitious and artificial display of feeling by the player' (*Shakespeare Criticism* 2nd edn, 1960, II, 152). The player, by imagining himself in the situation, in 'a dream of passion', becomes so affected that he weeps. He doesn't pretend to cry; he pretends until he cries.

516 free those who are free of crime. Compare 3.2.219.

517 Confound Astonish and confuse.

517 amaze A much stronger word then than now; 'paralyse'. See 1.2.235.

518 Yet I Hypermetrical; some editors give it a separate line.

519 muddy-mettled muddy-spirited.

519 peak A word of uncertain meaning. Because of Shakespeare's own 'dwindle, peak, and pine' in *Macbeth*, it is usually taken to mean 'go into a decline', 'droop'. But the dominant meaning seems to be 'sneak or slink about', or 'to make a mean figure', as Johnson puts it in his *Dictionary*.

520 John-a-dreams Apparently a nickname for a dreamy person.

520 unpregnant of my cause 'pregnant' means quick, prompt, ready, apt – so to be 'unpregnant' of something means *not* reacting quickly to it. Compare *Measure for Measure* 4.4.20, 'makes me unpregnant/And dull to all proceedings'. 'pregnant' is not used by Shakespeare to mean 'with child'.

522 property i.e. the kingdom (rather than his material possessions). It is just possible that it means what belonged to Hamlet senior exclusively as a person, his identity as king.

523 defeat destruction.

526 gives me the lie accuses me of lying.

526–7 i'th'throat...lungs i.e. deep-rooted and not superficial or casual lies.

Ha, 'swounds, I should take it, for it cannot be
But I am pigeon-livered, and lack gall
To make oppression bitter, or ere this 530
I should ha' fatted all the region kites
With this slave's offal. Bloody, bawdy villain!
Remorseless, treacherous, lecherous, kindless villain!
Oh, vengeance!
Why, what an ass am I! This is most brave, 535
That I, the son of the dear murderèd,
Prompted to my revenge by heaven and hell,
Must like a whore unpack my heart with words,
And fall a-cursing like a very drab,
A scullion! 540
Fie upon't, foh! About, my brains. Hum, I have heard
That guilty creatures sitting at a play
Have by the very cunning of the scene
Been struck so to the soul, that presently
They have proclaimed their malefactions; 545

528 'swounds] Q2; Why F **531** ha'] a Q2; haue F **532** Bloody, bawdy villain] Q2; bloody: a Bawdy villaine F **534** Oh, vengeance!] F; *not in* Q2 **535** Why] Q2; Who F **535** This] Q2; I sure, this F **536** the dear murderèd] the Deere murthered F; a deere murthered Q2; my deare father Q1; a deere father murthered Q 1611 **540** scullion] F; stallyon Q2 **541** brains] braines Q2 *(corrected)*; braues Q2 *(uncorrected)*; Braine F **541** Hum] Q2; *not in* F

529 pigeon-livered The liver is seen as the seat of courage. Compare 'lily-livered' and 'milk-livered' in *King Lear*. The pigeon has no gall.

530 To make oppression bitter i.e. to make Claudius's oppression bitter to himself.

531 region kites hawks, or birds of prey, circling in the sky.

533 Remorseless Pitiless.

533 kindless without natural feeling.

534 Oh, vengeance! This cry, the great climax of the rant with which Hamlet emulates the Player, exhausts his futile self-recrimination, and he turns, in proper disgust, from a display of verbal histrionics to more practical things. Q2 omits the phrase altogether, and many editors unfortunately follow suit. This short line and the silence after it are the pivot of the speech.

536 the son...murderèd the son of the loved victim. So F. Q2 reads 'a dear murdered', strong confirmation that Shakespeare did *not* write (what almost every edition gives) 'the son of a dear father murdered'. 'Father' stems from the very weak Q1 reading, 'the son of my dear father', and was inserted into the received text in the 1611 quarto. 'Father' is tautological, and actually dissipates Hamlet's stress on his filial duty.

537 by heaven and hell Hamlet means that the whole supernatural world of good and evil lies behind his revenge, not that both heaven and hell are urging him at the same time. His revenge is instigated by heaven in its war against the workings of hell, visible in Claudius's achievements. The terrible alternative, that he may have become one of hell's victims, he goes on to consider in 551–8.

538 unload unpack, relieve.

540 A scullion! 'a domestic servant of the lowest rank...a person of the lowest order, esp. as an abusive epithet' (*OED*). Q2 reads 'stallyon', and a number of recent editions give 'stallion', supposing that Hamlet means it in the cant sense of 'male whore'. This sense is not at all well established for Shakespeare's time, and 'scullion' is obviously the correct reading. Hamlet is looking for foul-mouthed, low-living people and (in his patrician way) finds them in 'drab', here a slatternly kitchen wench of low morals, and her companion, a 'scullion'.

541 About go about it!

543 cunning skill.

543 scene dramatic presentation.

For murder, though it have no tongue, will speak
With most miraculous organ. I'll have these players
Play something like the murder of my father
Before mine uncle. I'll observe his looks,
I'll tent him to the quick. If a do blench, 550
I know my course. The spirit that I have seen
May be a devil – and the devil hath power
T'assume a pleasing shape. Yea, and perhaps,
Out of my weakness and my melancholy,
As he is very potent with such spirits, 555
Abuses me to damn me. I'll have grounds
More relative than this. The play's the thing
Wherein I'll catch the conscience of the king. *Exit*

[3.1] *Enter* KING, QUEEN, POLONIUS, OPHELIA, ROSENCRANTZ, GUILDENSTERN, LORDS

CLAUDIUS And can you by no drift of circumstance
Get from him why he puts on this confusion,
Grating so harshly all his days of quiet
With turbulent and dangerous lunacy?
ROSENCRANTZ He does confess he feels himself distracted, 5
But from what cause a will by no means speak.
GUILDENSTERN Nor do we find him forward to be sounded,

550 a do] Q2; he but F 552 a devil] Q 1611; a deale Q2; the Diuell F **Act 3, Scene 1** 3.1] Act III. Scene I. Q 1676 1 And] F; An Q2 1 circumstance] F; conference Q2 6 a] Q2; he F

550 tent probe.

550 to the quick i.e. to where it hurts.

550 blench flinch and turn aside.

553 assume Compare 1.2.243 and 1.4.72.

555 very potent with such spirits It was a commonplace of ghost-lore that melancholics were specially prone to visitation by demons. See Prosser, *Hamlet and Revenge*, p. 110.

556 to damn me It is the fate of Hamlet's immortal soul that is at stake in his decision whether the ghost was genuine or not. See Introduction, pp. 47, 58.

556–7 grounds...relative reasons for acting which are nearer at hand, more tangible.

Act 3, Scene 1

1 drift of circumstance steering of roundabout enquiry. Compare Polonius's 'encompassment and drift of question', 2.1.10. For 'circumstance' (which means circuitous talk, as in 1.5.127), Q2 reads 'conference', a much weaker word, presumably the compositor's misreading, jarring with 'confusion' at the end of the next line.

2 puts on As the scene opens, Claudius is in the middle of a discussion with Rosencrantz and Guildenstern. He has already learned that the madness is 'put on' (Guildenstern speaks of 'crafty madness' in 8). At the beginning of 2.1, the question was what was wrong with Hamlet. Now the question is why is he assuming the guise of madness.

3 Grating The physical action of roughening by scraping and rasping.

7 forward disposed, inclined.

But with a crafty madness keeps aloof
When we would bring him on to some confession
Of his true state.

GERTRUDE Did he receive you well? 10

ROSENCRANTZ Most like a gentleman.

GUILDENSTERN But with much forcing of his disposition.

ROSENCRANTZ Niggard of question, but of our demands
Most free in his reply.

GERTRUDE Did you assay him
To any pastime? 15

ROSENCRANTZ Madam, it so fell out that certain players
We o'er-raught on the way; of these we told him,
And there did seem in him a kind of joy
To hear of it. They are about the court,
And as I think, they have already order 20
This night to play before him.

POLONIUS 'Tis most true,
And he beseeched me to entreat your majesties
To hear and see the matter.

CLAUDIUS With all my heart, and it doth much content me
To hear him so inclined. 25
Good gentlemen, give him a further edge,
And drive his purpose on to these delights.

ROSENCRANTZ We shall my lord.

Exeunt Rosencrantz and Guildenstern

CLAUDIUS Sweet Gertrude, leave us too,
For we have closely sent for Hamlet hither,

14–15 Did...pastime] *as one line* Q2, F 19 are about] F; are heere about Q2 24 heart, and] F; hart,/ And Q2 27 on to] F; into Q2 28 SD] Q2; *Exeunt* F 28 too] F; two Q2

8 crafty madness This clearly does not mean, as some commentators suggest, the cunning of madness, but an affecting of madness, for in the next line Guildenstern talks of 'his true state'. Hamlet talks to Gertrude of being 'mad in craft' at 3.4.189.

13–14 Niggard...reply Rosencrantz is anxious to cover up the cross-examination which led to the disclosure that they were being employed by Claudius. Unfortunately, this leads him into contradicting Guildenstern about Hamlet's readiness to answer questions.

14–15 assay...To i.e. try him with the suggestion of.

17 o'er-raught (over-reached) came up to and passed, overhauled.

21 This night This conversation is taking place on the day after the events of the previous scene. See 2.2.493.

26 edge keenness (of appetite).

27 on to So F. Q2 reads 'into', but the sense of 'drive...on' is 'urge on', as contrasted with 'drive me into a toil' at 3.2.314, where the image is of penning in a hunted animal.

29 closely secretly, applying to Claudius's purpose. He has sent for Hamlet, concealing his true purpose. But when Hamlet arrives he shows no knowledge of having been 'sent for'. See Introduction, pp. 25–7.

That he, as 'twere by accident, may here 30
Affront Ophelia. Her father and myself,
Lawful espials,
Will so bestow ourselves, that seeing unseen,
We may of their encounter frankly judge,
And gather by him, as he is behaved, 35
If't be th'affliction of his love or no
That thus he suffers for.

GERTRUDE I shall obey you.
And for your part Ophelia, I do wish
That your good beauties be the happy cause
Of Hamlet's wildness. So shall I hope your virtues 40
Will bring him to his wonted way again,
To both your honours.

OPHELIA Madam, I wish it may.

[*Exit Gertrude with Lords*]

POLONIUS Ophelia walk you here. – Gracious, so please you,
We will bestow ourselves. – Read on this book,
That show of such an exercise may colour 45
Your loneliness. – We are oft to blame in this:
'Tis too much proved, that with devotion's visage,
And pious action, we do sugar o'er
The devil himself.

CLAUDIUS (*Aside*) Oh, 'tis too true.
How smart a lash that speech doth give my conscience! 50

30 here] Q2; there F 32 Lawful espials] F; *not in* Q2 33 Will] F; Wee'le Q2 42 SD] *Exit Queen / Theobald*[2]; *not in* Q2, F 43 please you] Q2; please ye F 46 loneliness] F; lowlines Q2 48 sugar] Q2; surge F 49 too] Q2; *not in* F

31 **Affront** Come face-to-face with.

32 **Lawful espials** This extra-metrical phrase occurs only in F, where it appears in a parenthesis at the end of 31. Almost certainly an insertion by Shakespeare which escaped the Q2 compositors, as did many of his intended deletions. See Introduction, p. 10. An 'espial' is a spy, and the purpose of the insertion would seem to be not to stress the lawfulness of the action of Claudius and Polonius but to stress that it *is* spying, and that Claudius feels the need to justify it.

33, 44 **bestow ourselves** station or position ourselves.

34 **frankly** freely, without obstacle.

38–42 Gertrude's simple and open concern for Hamlet's health and happiness, evident in all her remarks in this scene, stands out strongly in the unpleasant atmosphere of distrust and intrigue.

43 **Gracious** i.e. your grace (to the king) – not a usual form of address.

44 **this book** This is obviously a prayer-book (see 47, 89).

45 **colour** provide a pretext for.

46 **loneliness** being alone.

47 **devotion's visage** a face expressing devoutness.

50 **How smart...conscience** It is at this point, not earlier and not later, that Shakespeare wants to assure the audience of Claudius's guilt and the credibility of the Ghost. We are not asked to share Hamlet's concern as he tests that credibility. Shakespeare seems careful in the line to echo Hamlet's 'catch the conscience of the king' at the end of the last scene.

The harlot's cheek, beautied with plastering art,
Is not more ugly to the thing that helps it
Than is my deed to my most painted word.
O heavy burden!

POLONIUS I hear him coming. Let's withdraw, my lord. 55

Exeunt Claudius and Polonius

Enter HAMLET

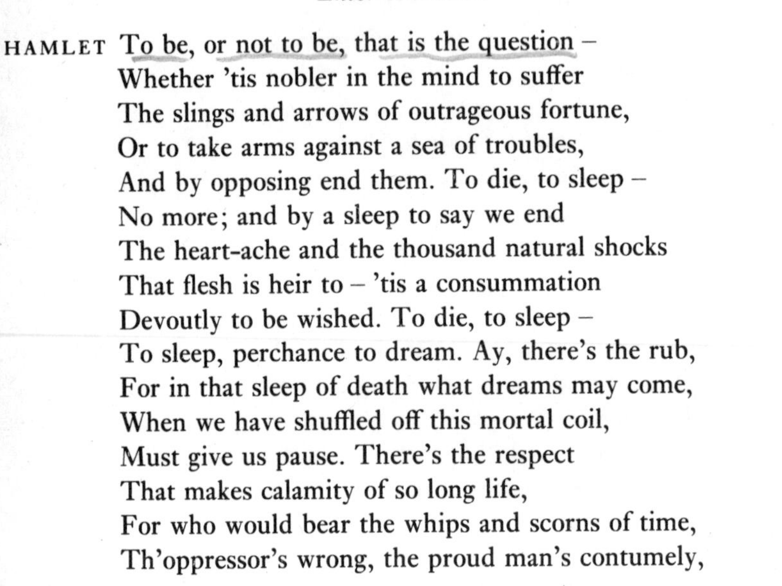

HAMLET To be, or not to be, that is the question –
Whether 'tis nobler in the mind to suffer
The slings and arrows of outrageous fortune,
Or to take arms against a sea of troubles,
And by opposing end them. To die, to sleep – 60
No more; and by a sleep to say we end
The heart-ache and the thousand natural shocks
That flesh is heir to – 'tis a consummation
Devoutly to be wished. To die, to sleep –
To sleep, perchance to dream. Ay, there's the rub, 65
For in that sleep of death what dreams may come,
When we have shuffled off this mortal coil,
Must give us pause. There's the respect
That makes calamity of so long life,
For who would bear the whips and scorns of time, 70
Th'oppressor's wrong, the proud man's contumely,

55 Let's] F; *not in* Q2 55 SD *Exeunt...Polonius*] *Capell; not in* Q2; *Exeunt.* F 55 SD *Enter* HAMLET] F; *after 54 in* Q2 71 proud] Q2; poore F

52 to the thing that helps it as compared with the cosmetic adornment.

56 To be or not to be Concerning the placing of this soliloquy and the nunnery scene which follows, see the Introduction, pp. 25–7. For a discussion of the soliloquy itself, see pp. 47–50.

56 that is the question But there are many opinions on what the question really is. I assume that Hamlet is debating whether to take his own life or not.

57 in the mind to suffer The stoical endurance which is Hamlet's first alternative is a matter of mental effort and strain.

58 slings missiles (by metonymy: that-which-throws standing for that-which-is-thrown; Latin *funda* could similarly mean either sling or sling-shot). A sling may be a hand-sling, a ballista or even a cannon.

60 by opposing end them The alternative to patient endurance is to use the only weapon which can overcome a sea of troubles – suicide. Such a death is the sleep by which we 'say we end' the woes of life (61). Hamlet no longer talks of setting right a world that is out of joint.

63 consummation completion.

65 rub impediment (from the game of bowls).

67 shuffled...coil got rid of the turmoil of living. 'shuffled off' is difficult. 'shuffled' is used twice more in the play, 3.3.61 and 4.7.136, in a derogatory sense deriving from cards, to mean 'manipulate with intent to deceive'. 'shuffle off' is found in *Twelfth Night* 3.3.16, and means 'get rid of in an unfair or fraudulent way'. There must be some slight sense of malpractice here: evasion, slipping out of things.

68 respect consideration.

69 of so long life so long-lived.

70 time the times; compare 1.5.189.

The pangs of disprized love, the law's delay,
The insolence of office, and the spurns
That patient merit of th'unworthy takes,
When he himself might his quietus make 75
With a bare bodkin? Who would fardels bear,
To grunt and sweat under a weary life,
But that the dread of something after death,
The undiscovered country from whose bourn
No traveller returns, puzzles the will, 80
And makes us rather bear those ills we have
Then fly to others that we know not of?
Thus conscience does make cowards of us all,
And thus the native hue of resolution
Is sicklied o'er with the pale cast of thought, 85
And enterprises of great pitch and moment
With this regard their currents turn awry

72 disprized] dispriz'd F; despiz'd Q2 76 fardels] Q2; these Fardles F 83 of us all] F; *not in* Q2 85 sicklied] F; sickled Q2 86 pitch] Q2; pith F 87 awry] Q2; away F

72 **disprized** unvalued. So F; Q2 gives us the weaker and less interesting 'despiz'd'.

74 **of th'unworthy takes** receives from unworthy people.

75 **quietus** discharge or acquittance (from the law phrase *quietus est*); frequently used in connection with death, probably because of the original Latin sense of repose and peace.

76 **a bare bodkin** a mere dagger. ('bodkin' was the name for sharp pointed instruments with various different uses; probably Hamlet is not being very specific.)

76 **fardels** burdens.

79 **bourn** boundary.

80 **No traveller returns** Although it is possible that Shakespeare simply overlooked the application of this to the Ghost, it is much more likely that he intended Hamlet's concern about the authenticity of the Ghost in the previous scene (2.2.551–6) to be deepening in his present mood of intense pessimism. But Hamlet could not be made to deny the *existence* of the Ghost. The after-life, he suggests, is one of those far-off countries of which only doubtful and untrustworthy reports exist; it is not one of those explored countries from which reputable travellers have actually returned to give us their eye-witness accounts.

80 **puzzles the will** i.e. brings it to a halt in confusion. 'puzzle' was a stronger word than it is now.

83 **conscience** Conscience here means conscience, the inner knowledge of right and wrong, as it does in 50 above and 2.2.568 above. Many commentators claim it means 'introspection', but Hamlet is talking about one's implanted sense of good and evil, which knows the canon of the Everlasting ''gainst self-slaughter' (1.2.132). There are those who like Laertes can 'dare damnation' or like Macbeth 'jump the life to come'. But Hamlet is not among those, and he calls himself a coward for having a conscience, and feeling 'dread of something after death'.

83–8 It is in these lines that, for the first time in the soliloquy, Hamlet turns, if indirectly, to the question of killing Claudius, and, as in the second soliloquy, he upbraids himself for being tardy. Thinking too much about the rights and wrongs of suicide stultifies the impulse to do away with oneself: thinking too much about rights and wrongs stultifies *all* action including the one he's supposed to be engaged in.

84 **native hue** natural colour or complexion.

85 **sicklied o'er** unhealthily covered.

85 **cast** tinge, tint. Though Hamlet has in mind the pallor of a sick man, the nearness of 'o'er' and 'cast' suggests also the pallor of clouds staining the face of the sun, as in Sonnet 33.

85 **thought** contemplation. Often glossed 'melancholy', which is not what Hamlet is talking about. Thinking causes the sickness of inaction.

86 **pitch** height, scope. So Q2; F's 'pith' is a possible reading.

87 **With this regard** On this account.

And lose the name of action. Soft you now,
The fair Ophelia. – Nymph, in thy orisons
Be all my sins remembered.

OPHELIA Good my lord, 90
How does your honour for this many a day?

HAMLET I humbly thank you, well, well, well.

OPHELIA My lord, I have remembrances of yours
That I have longèd long to re-deliver.
I pray you now receive them.

HAMLET No, not I, 95
I never gave you aught.

OPHELIA My honoured lord, you know right well you did,
And with them words of so sweet breath composed
As made the things more rich. Their perfume lost,
Take these again, for to the noble mind 100
Rich gifts wax poor when givers prove unkind.
There my lord.

HAMLET Ha, ha, are you honest?

OPHELIA My lord?

HAMLET Are you fair? 105

OPHELIA What means your lordship?

HAMLET That if you be honest and fair, your honesty should admit no discourse to your beauty.

OPHELIA Could beauty, my lord, have better commerce than with honesty? 110

92 well, well, well] F; well Q2 95 No, not I] Q2; No, no F 97 you know] Q2; I know F 99 the] F; these Q2 99 Their] Q2; then F 99 lost] Q2; left F 107 your honesty] F; you Q2 109 with] Q2; your F

88 soft you As usual, 'soft' as a verb in the imperative means 'restrain yourself, leave off, be cautious'. Compare 1.1.126, 1.5.58, 3.2.353, 4.2.3, 4.4.8, 4.7.153, 5.1.184.

89 Nymph This is a curious way to address Ophelia, and it is probably correct to suggest that Hamlet is ironic in his stilted formality with both this word and 'orisons' for prayers. If so, then he cannot be genuinely humble in asking her to remember his sins. Rather, it is sarcasm – 'Don't forget all those sins of mine which have forced you to reject me.'

91 for this many a day It is often pointed out that Ophelia had met Hamlet yesterday. But that was an eerily silent interview. In any case, Ophelia is no doubt extremely nervous in the very embarrassing position she is in, knowing Claudius and Polonius are watching and listening, and is hardly in command of herself.

93 remembrances keepsakes, gifts.

98 of so sweet breath composed 'breath' can here mean 'utterance' or 'language'; Ophelia may refer to words either spoken or written.

99 Their perfume lost The sweetness of both the words and the gifts has disappeared, because of the unkindness of the giver.

103 honest chaste. But this sudden and violent change of topic is caused by Ophelia's palpable lack of honesty in the more general sense, in not mentioning her own part in the breach between them.

107–8 your honesty...your beauty your virtue should not allow your beauty to converse with it. (An alternative gloss is 'your virtue ought to keep away those who want to chat with your beauty'; if that is correct, then Ophelia misunderstands him.)

HAMLET Ay truly, for the power of beauty will sooner transform honesty from what it is to a bawd, than the force of honesty can translate beauty into his likeness. This was sometime a paradox, but now the time gives it proof. I did love you once.

OPHELIA Indeed my lord you made me believe so. 115

HAMLET You should not have believed me, for virtue cannot so inoculate our old stock but we shall relish of it. I loved you not.

OPHELIA I was the more deceived.

HAMLET Get thee to a nunnery – why wouldst thou be a breeder of sinners? I am myself indifferent honest, but yet I could accuse me 120 of such things, that it were better my mother had not borne me. I am very proud, revengeful, ambitious, with more offences at my beck than I have thoughts to put them in, imagination to give them shape, or time to act them in. What should such fellows as I do crawling between earth and heaven? We are arrant knaves all, 125 believe none of us. Go thy ways to a nunnery. Where's your father?

OPHELIA At home my lord.

HAMLET Let the doors be shut upon him, that he may play the fool nowhere but in's own house. Farewell.

OPHELIA Oh help him you sweet heavens! 130

HAMLET If thou dost marry, I'll give thee this plague for thy dowry:

117 inoculate] innocculate F; euocutat Q2 119 thee to a] F; thee a Q2 125 earth and heaven] Q2; Heauen and Earth F 125 all] F; *not in* Q2 129 nowhere] Q2; no way F

117 inoculate our old stock The image is from grafting fruit trees or bushes. We cannot so engraft a new stem of virtue onto the old sinful trunk as to eradicate all trace of our previous nature.

117 relish have a touch or tinge.

119 Get thee to a nunnery Much of the power and meaning of this scene is lost if we accept the suggestion of J. Q. Adams and Dover Wilson that 'nunnery' is here used in its slang sense of 'brothel'. Hamlet is accusing men and women, including himself and Ophelia, of unremitting moral frailty, which they show most in their sexual relations. Only in a convent will Ophelia be able to resist the inclinations of her own nature, and by desisting from sex and propagation she will the sooner put an end to sinful mankind. As with Lear and Timon, Hamlet's disgust with mankind makes him think it were better if generation ceased.

120 indifferent honest moderately virtuous.

122 proud, revengeful, ambitious Hamlet is all these things: he considers himself better than other people, he wants revenge for his father, he desires the throne. These desires and feelings may be sinful or they may in their circumstances be justified and honourable. Hamlet speaks of his sinfulness with a mocking, teasing exaggeration, as he spoke of his world-weariness to Rosencrantz and Guildenstern. We mustn't take him at his word, or suppose that Shakespeare here definitively says that revenge is sinful. Yet here, as in the world-weary speech in 2.2, there lies beneath the rodomontade a nugget of truth. There is a self-loathing here which is more constructive than in 'O what a rogue and peasant slave', a perception of his own unworthiness which is a good deal more sanctifying than most of Hamlet's moods.

126 Where's your father? Some commentators think that Hamlet knew all the time he was being watched; some think he guessed it early in the interview; some think he learns it here. It is my view that Hamlet never knows about the watchers. We do not need his awareness of the spies to explain what he says. Stage-tradition varies a good deal on this, but it was common practice in the eighteenth century for Hamlet to catch sight of the eavesdroppers during the scene (Sprague, *Shakespeare and the Actors*, pp. 152–4).

be thou as chaste as ice, as pure as snow, thou shalt not escape calumny. Get thee to a nunnery, go. Farewell. Or if thou wilt needs marry, marry a fool, for wise men know well enough what monsters you make of them. To a nunnery go, and quickly too. Farewell. 135

OPHELIA O heavenly powers, restore him!

HAMLET I have heard of your paintings too, well enough. God hath given you one face and you make yourselves another. You jig, you amble, and you lisp, you nickname God's creatures, and make your wantonness your ignorance. Go to, I'll no more on't, it hath made 140 me mad. I say we will have no mo marriages. Those that are married already, all but one shall live, the rest shall keep as they are. To a nunnery, go. *Exit*

OPHELIA Oh what a noble mind is here o'erthrown!
The courtier's, soldier's, scholar's, eye, tongue, sword, 145
Th'expectancy and rose of the fair state,
The glass of fashion and the mould of form,
Th'observed of all observers, quite, quite down,

133 go] F; *not in* Q2 136 O] F; *not in* Q2 137 paintings] Q2, Q1; pratlings F 137 too] F; *not in* Q2 137 hath] Q2; has F 138 face] Q2; pace F 138 yourselves] your selfes Q2; your selfe F 138–9 you amble] F; & amble Q2 139 lisp] F; list Q2 139 you nickname] Q2; and nickname F 140 your ignorance] F; ignorance Q2 141 mo] Q2; more F 141 marriages] F; marriage Q2 143 SD] Q2; *Exit Hamlet* F 146 expectancy] expectansie F; expectation Q2

132–3 thou shalt not escape calumny Hamlet is the chief calumniator of Ophelia, and one hopes he includes himself. There is a flicker of an admission here of what Hamlet knows perfectly well – that Ophelia, however weak in character, is not 'frail' morally, and that it is sheer misrepresentation to claim she is. But Hamlet cancels out this admission quickly and thoroughly as he steps up his 'madness'.

134 monsters i.e. horned cuckolds.

138 jig This may refer more to singing than dancing. Compare *Love's Labour's Lost* 3.1.11–12, 'to jig off a tune at the tongue's end'.

139 amble walk affectedly.

139–40 make your wantonness your ignorance pretend your licence is just simplicity and innocence.

140–1 it hath made me mad Hamlet is sufficiently in control of himself to maintain the teasing mystification of his role. An actor might well decide to make lunatic grimaces here.

141 mo more.

142 all but one shall live 'live' here means 'remain' or 'continue', as in Sonnet 5: 'flowers distilled...Leese but their show, their substance still lives sweet.' There are to be no more marriages. All married couples, bar one, may stay married, but all single people are to stay single ('the rest shall keep as they are'). Hamlet intends to dissolve the marriage of his mother with Claudius violently, with the king's death; so that 'all but one shall live' takes a sharp ambiguity. But his mind is more on sexual misdemeanour than revenge at this moment.

145 The courtier's...sword Some editors understandably wish to interchange 'soldier's' and 'scholar's' to give the scholar the tongue and the soldier the sword. However, as my student Bernadette Connolly points out, this misalignment does throw light on the fact that Hamlet's sword is his intellect and that he fights with his tongue.

147 glass...form 'glass' is the mirror which gives an ideal image and so provides an example (compare 3.2.18). The word 'mould' is a strong indication that by 'fashion' Shakespeare means shaping or fashioning something, rather than good manners (*OED* 1 and 2), hence 'glass of fashion' = image teaching how to fashion oneself. 'form' is here probably 'behaviour', 'conduct'. People shaped themselves and their behaviour after his pattern.

148 Th'observed of all observers Looked up to respectfully by all who turn to others for guidance. 'Observe' is a difficult word: see note to 1.5.101. Although it is possible that this could mean

And I of ladies most deject and wretched,
That sucked the honey of his music vows, 150
Now see that noble and most sovereign reason,
Like sweet bells jangled, out of time and harsh;
That unmatched form and feature of blown youth
Blasted with ecstasy. Oh woe is me
T'have seen what I have seen, see what I see. 155

Enter KING *and* POLONIUS

CLAUDIUS Love? His affections do not that way tend;
Nor what he spake, though it lacked form a little,
Was not like madness. There's something in his soul
O'er which his melancholy sits on brood,
And I do doubt the hatch and the disclose 160
Will be some danger; which for to prevent,
I have in quick determination
Thus set it down: he shall with speed to England
For the demand of our neglected tribute.
Haply the seas, and countries different, 165
With variable objects, shall expel
This something-settled matter in his heart,
Whereon his brains still beating puts him thus
From fashion of himself. What think you on't?

POLONIUS It shall do well. But yet do I believe 170
The origin and commencement of his grief
Sprung from neglected love. How now Ophelia?
You need not tell us what Lord Hamlet said,
We heard it all. My lord, do as you please,
But if you hold it fit, after the play, 175

149 And] Q2; Haue F **150** music] Musicke F; musickt Q2 **151** that] F; what Q2 **152** time] Q2; tune F **153** feature] F; stature Q2 **161** for to] Q2; to F **168–71** ...thus / ...on't? / ...believe / ...grief] F; ...beating / ...himselfe. / ...on't? / ...well. / ...greefe, Q2 **171** his] Q2; this F

'one who is watched attentively by all who note men carefully', the context of the previous line strongly suggests the older meaning of 'observe'.

153 blown youth youth in full bloom.

154 ecstasy madness.

154–5 woe is me...what I see Ophelia speaks verse, ending with a rhymed couplet, to show the measure of her sanity against the disordered prose of Hamlet's 'madness'.

155 At the end of this line some copies of Q2 print '*Exit*'. It is interesting that Q1 makes Ophelia leave at this point. There must have been something in Shakespeare's MS. to make the press-corrector insert or cancel this SD. Probably a first thought.

156 affections emotions.

159 sits on brood Like a bird sitting on eggs – see 'hatch' in the next line.

164 tribute The Danegeld, by which the Anglo-Saxons bought off the Vikings.

169 fashion of himself his own proper way of behaving.

Let his queen mother all alone entreat him
To show his grief. Let her be round with him,
And I'll be placed, so please you, in the ear
Of all their conference. If she find him not,
To England send him; or confine him where 180
Your wisdom best shall think.

CLAUDIUS It shall be so.
Madness in great ones must not unwatched go.

Exeunt

[3.2] *Enter* HAMLET *and two or three of the* PLAYERS

HAMLET Speak the speech I pray you as I pronounced it to you, trippingly on the tongue; but if you mouth it as many of our players do, I had as lief the town-crier spoke my lines. Nor do not saw the air too much with your hand thus, but use all gently; for in the very torrent, tempest, and, as I may say, whirlwind of your passion, 5 you must acquire and beget a temperance that may give it smoothness. Oh, it offends me to the soul to hear a robustious periwig-pated fellow tear a passion to totters, to very rags, to split the ears of the groundlings, who for the most part are capable of

177 grief] Q2; Greefes F 182 unwatched] F; vnmatcht Q2 Act 3, Scene 2 3.2] Scene II *Capell* 0 SD *two or three*] F; *three* Q2 1 pronounced] pronounc'd F; pronoun'd Q2 2 our] Q2; your F 3 lief] liue Q2, F 3 spoke] Q2; had spoke F 4 with] Q2; *not in* F 5 whirlwind] Q2; the Whirle-winde F 5 your passion] Q2; Passion F 7 hear] Q2; see F 8 periwig] Pery-wig F; perwig Q2 8 totters] Q2, Q1; tatters F 8 split] F; spleet Q2

177 round direct and outspoken.

178–9 I'll be placed...conference This little scheme leads to Polonius's death, Laertes' revenge, and the final slaughter, including the deaths of Hamlet and Claudius.

179 find him not fails to discover his secret. Compare *Lear* 4.6.103, 'There I found 'em, there I smelt 'em out.'

Act 3, Scene 2

0 SD ***two or three*** So F. Q2 gives 'three'; for Shakespeare's MS. to be so specific against a MS. with theatre-influence is remarkable, especially as there is no need for three players. Probably a compositor's omission.

1 The time is the evening of the same day. Even if, notionally, several hours have passed since the end of the last scene, the swift re-entry of Hamlet, totally sane and utterly intent on the acting of his play, must leave an impression of insensitivity when we think of the distress he left Ophelia in. His attack on her was considered and deliberate; as soon as she re-enters he starts up again (97).

It is notable that both to the players here and to Horatio at 59–65 Hamlet is much concerned about the temperance, self-control and moderation which is so much wanting in his own behaviour.

3 I had as lief It would be as agreeable to me that.

6 acquire and beget If the actors obtain this balance and control in themselves, they will be able to produce it in their speeches.

7 robustious rough and rude.

8 periwig-pated wearing a wig.

8 totters So Q2 (and Q1); an alternative form of 'tatters', which F gives. Compare *1 Henry IV* 4.2.34, 'fifty tottered prodigals'.

9 groundlings Those who stood in the open yard directly in front of the stage, the cheapest part of the theatre.

9 are capable of have a capacity for, can understand.

nothing but inexplicable dumb-shows and noise. I would have such a fellow whipped for o'erdoing Termagant – it out-Herods Herod. Pray you avoid it. 10

I PLAYER I warrant your honour.

HAMLET Be not too tame neither, but let your own discretion be your tutor. Suit the action to the word, the word to the action, with this special observance, that you o'erstep not the modesty of nature. For anything so o'erdone is from the purpose of playing, whose end both at the first and now, was and is, to hold as 'twere the mirror up to nature; to show virtue her own feature, scorn her own image, and the very age and body of the time his form and pressure. Now this overdone, or come tardy off, though it makes the unskilful laugh, cannot but make the judicious grieve, the censure of the which one must in your allowance o'erweigh a whole theatre of others. Oh, there be players that I have seen play, and heard others praise and that highly, not to speak it profanely, that neither having 15 20 25

10 would] Q2; could F 16 o'erstep] ore-steppe Q2; ore-stop F 17 o'erdone] ore-doone Q2; ouer-done F 19 own feature] F; feature Q2 21 makes] Q2; make F 22–3 the which] F; which Q2 25 praise] F; praysd Q2

10 inexplicable Shakespeare does not use this word elsewhere. The context suggests 'meaningless'.

11 Termagant An imaginary deity supposed to be worshipped by Mohammedans (sometimes spelt Tervagant); but no medieval English play with him as a character is known. Ritson (NV) quoted Bale (1550), 'grinning upon her like termagants in a play', but there the word may be used in its general sense of 'violent person' as in *1 Henry IV* 5.4.114, 'that hot termagant Scot'. Marston, in 'A Cynicke Satyre' (1598), has 'let western Termagant / Shake heaven's vault' (referring to Jove).

11 Herod Familiar as a ranting tyrant in the medieval biblical cycles.

15 Suit...action 'action' is used here in two different senses, both belonging to the theatre. First, it means acting – in its fullest sense of an actor's management of himself on the stage, and not just gesture (see Glossary to Massinger, *Plays and Poems*, and *OED* 6). In the second phrase, it means the action of the play. 'word' also has two meanings; first, the language of the play, and, in the second phrase, the actor's speech. Hamlet instructs the Player to let his acting be governed by what he is given to speak, and to let his speech be governed by what he is given to act.

As with his advice on temperance, Hamlet finds it easier to order things in the theatre than in his own life. He has the greatest difficulty in acting in accordance with the 'word' he has been given (1.5.110), and in suiting his words to what he has to act (e.g. 2.2.535–40).

16 modesty restraints, limitations, measure. Compare 2.2.400.

17 from away from.

18 mirror As in 'the glass of fashion' (3.1.147), this is a mirror which sets standards; here by revealing things not as they seem, but as they really are.

19 scorn i.e. that which is to be scorned.

20 the very...pressure i.e. gives an impression of the shape of our times in the clearest detail. 'form and pressure' imply as at 1.5.100 a shape stamped from a mould. Many commentators think that 'very age' and 'body of the time' are separate and parallel phrases, but the run of the sentence clearly puts 'age and body' together. I take the phrase to be a hendiadys for 'aged body'; i.e. the stage will provide an image of this ageing world as faithful as a statue or an effigy of an old person 'wrinkled deep in time'.

21 come tardy off done inadequately or imperfectly.

21 unskilful ignorant and undiscerning.

22 censure judgement.

22–3 of the which one of one of whom.

23 your allowance i.e. what you will permit or sanction, hence 'your scale of values'. Kittredge's gloss seems strained: 'winning approval of your acting'.

th'accent of Christians, nor the gait of Christian, pagan, nor man, have so strutted and bellowed that I have thought some of nature's journeymen had made men, and not made them well, they imitated humanity so abominably.

I PLAYER I hope we have reformed that indifferently with us, sir. 30

HAMLET Oh reform it altogether. And let those that play your clowns speak no more than is set down for them, for there be of them that will themselves laugh, to set on some quantity of barren spectators to laugh too, though in the meantime some necessary question of the play be then to be considered. That's villainous, and shows 35 a most pitiful ambition in the fool that uses it. Go make you ready.

Exeunt Players

Enter POLONIUS, ROSENCRANTZ *and* GUILDENSTERN

How now my lord, will the king hear this piece of work?

POLONIUS And the queen too, and that presently.

HAMLET Bid the players make haste.

Exit Polonius

Will you two help to hasten them? 40

ROSENCRANTZ Ay my lord.

Exeunt Rosencrantz and Guildenstern

HAMLET What ho, Horatio!

Enter HORATIO

HORATIO Here sweet lord, at your service.

HAMLET Horatio, thou art e'en as just a man
As e'er my conversation coped withal. 45

HORATIO Oh my dear lord.

HAMLET Nay, do not think I flatter,
For what advancement may I hope from thee,
That no revenue hast but thy good spirits

26 th'accent] Q2; the accent F **26** nor man] Q2; or Norman F **30** sir] F; *not in* Q2 **36** SD *Exeunt Players*] F2; *Exit Players* F; *not in* Q2 **36.1** SD] F; *after 37 in* Q2 **39** SD] F; *not in* Q2 **41** ROSENCRANTZ Ay] *Ros.* I Q2; *Both.* We will F **41** SD] *Exeunt they two* Q2; *Exeunt* F **42** ho] hoa F; howe Q2 **44** SH HAMLET] *Ham.* F; *not in* Q2

27–8 nature's journeymen These bad actors must have been made not by God, but by some of Nature's hired men, little better than apprentices. (Hence Hamlet's 'not to speak it profanely'.)

29 abominably Spelt in Q2 and F 'abhominably', indicating what, from a false etymology, they thought the word meant: 'away from the nature of man'.

30 indifferently reasonably well.

34 necessary question i.e. essential part of the plot.

38 presently immediately.

44 e'en Emphatic, like modern 'absolutely'.

44 just Not 'judicious' but 'honourable', 'upright'.

45 my conversation coped withal my encounters with people have brought me in touch with.

48 That nó revénue hást but thý good spirits.

48 spirits inner qualities.

To feed and clothe thee? Why should the poor be flattered?
No, let the candied tongue lick absurd pomp 50
And crook the pregnant hinges of the knee
Where thrift may follow fawning. Dost thou hear?
Since my dear soul was mistress of her choice,
And could of men distinguish her election,
Sh'ath sealed thee for herself, for thou hast been 55
As one in suffering all that suffers nothing,
A man that Fortune's buffets and rewards
Hast tane with equal thanks. And blest are those
Whose blood and judgement are so well commeddled
That they are not a pipe for Fortune's finger 60
To sound what stop she please. Give me that man
That is not passion's slave, and I will wear him
In my heart's core, ay in my heart of heart,
As I do thee. Something too much of this.
There is a play tonight before the king: 65
One scene of it comes near the circumstance
Which I have told thee of my father's death.
I prithee when thou seest that act afoot,
Even with the very comment of thy soul
Observe my uncle. If his occulted guilt 70
Do not itself unkennel in one speech,

50 lick] Q2; like F 52 fawning] fauning Q2; faining F 53 her] Q2; my F 54 distinguish her election,] Q2; distinguish, her election F 55 Sh'ath] S'hath Q2; Hath F 58 Hast] Q2; Hath F 59 comeddled] comedled Q2; co-mingled F 69 thy] Q2; my F 70 my] Q2; mine F

50–1 The courtier kissing his patron's hands and bowing is pictured, in beast-fable fashion, as a fawning dog licking and crouching – though the dog is nowhere specifically mentioned. Compare *1 Henry IV* 1.3.251–2.

50 candied sugared.

50 absurd Accent on first syllable. Hilda Hulme (*Explorations in Shakespeare's Language*, 1962, pp. 160–2) gives etymological arguments for the meaning 'tasteless' which, she suggests, suits the image. I find this strained; pomp is absurd because it is ridiculous in its vanity and self-love. Compare 1.2.103.

51 pregnant 'quick, ready, prompt' (Johnson).

52 thrift ('thriving') profit, prosperity.

54–5 And could...herself And could be discriminating in her choice amongst men, she hath marked you out. I follow Q2. F's meaning is different: 'and could discriminate amongst men, her choice hath marked you out'.

The source of these lines seems to be Jonson's *The Case is Altered* (1597–8?), 1.6.31–2, 'one whom my election hath designed,/As the true proper object of my soul'.

55 sealed...herself Literally, put a legal seal on you as her property; hence, 'solemnly attested that you are hers'.

59 blood and judgement passion and reason.

59 commeddled mixed together. 'meddle' is common, but 'commeddle' is rare, and F changes to 'commingled'.

66 circumstance circumstances, details.

69–70 Even with...uncle i.e. use your most intense powers of observation in watching my uncle. 'comment' stands for the power to comment.

70 occulted hidden.

71 unkennel The word was used of dislodging or driving a fox from his hole or lair.

It is a damnèd ghost that we have seen,
And my imaginations are as foul
As Vulcan's stithy. Give him heedful note,
For I mine eyes will rivet to his face, 75
And after we will both our judgements join
In censure of his seeming.

HORATIO Well my lord.
If a steal aught the whilst this play is playing
And scape detecting, I will pay the theft.

Sound a flourish

HAMLET They are coming to the play. I must be idle. 80
Get you a place.

Danish march (trumpets and kettle-drums). Enter KING, QUEEN, POLONIUS, OPHELIA, ROSENCRANTZ, GUILDENSTERN *and other* LORDS *attendant, with his* GUARD *carrying torches*

CLAUDIUS How fares our cousin Hamlet?

HAMLET Excellent i'faith, of the chameleon's dish: I eat the air, promise-crammed. You cannot feed capons so.

74 stithy] Q2; Stythe F 74 heedful] Q2; needfull F 77 In] Q2; To F 78 a] Q2; he F 79 detecting] F; detected Q2 79 SD *Sound a flourish*] F *(concludes* SD *which follows); not in* Q2 81 SD] *This edn; Enter Trumpets and Kettle Drummes, King, Queene, Polonius, Ophelia.* Q2; *Enter King, Queene, Polonius, Ophelia, Rosincrance, Guildensterne, and other Lords attendant, with his Guard carrying Torches. Danish March. Sound a Flourish.* F

72 a damnèd ghost...seen the ghost which we have seen came from hell (and was an impostor and a liar).

73 my imaginations what my mind has suggested to me (about the Ghost). To have given credence to the Ghost, and built on its tale, shows a disease of his mind. See the note to 1.4.87. The power of the imagination to delude people about the supernatural was much discussed. See Introduction, p. 60. Reginald Scot, in his *Discovery of Witchcraft* (1584), spoke of a woman who was cured of her belief that she was bewitched as being 'ashamed of her imaginations, which she perceiveth to have grown through melancholy' (Bk 3, ch. 10).

74 Vulcan's stithy Vulcan's forge – generally regarded as a hellish sort of place.

77 in censure of his seeming in weighing up his appearance. They will have to infer from his outward expression what he is actually feeling.

77 Well Expresses Horatio's concurrence and approval.

78 If a steal aught i.e. if he conceals anything.

80 idle Not 'unoccupied', but 'idle-headed' = crazy.

81 SD See collation. F's rich version of this grand entry shows how the theatre worked on the bare essentials given by Shakespeare (as recorded in Q2). I have conflated the two by suggesting that F's 'Danish March' was, in fact, played by Q2's 'Trumpets and Kettle Drummes'. I have also separated F's 'Sound a flourish' from the main body of the SD. Both Q2 and F are obviously wrong in placing the solemn entry *before* Hamlet says 'They are coming to the play.' It is the warning flourish that alerts Hamlet.

82 fares Hamlet chooses to understand this in its alternative sense of being fed.

82 cousin Any close relation. *OED* notes that the term was often used by a sovereign to another sovereign, or to one of his nobles. Compare 1.2.117, 'our cousin and our son'. Hamlet and Claudius now come together for the first time since the second scene of the play.

83 the chameleon's dish The chameleon was supposed to live on air.

84 capons castrated cocks, fattened for the table.

CLAUDIUS I have nothing with this answer Hamlet, these words are not mine. 85

HAMLET No, nor mine now. – My lord, you played once i'th'university, you say.

POLONIUS That did I my lord, and was accounted a good actor.

HAMLET And what did you enact? 90

POLONIUS I did enact Julius Caesar. I was killed i'th'Capitol. Brutus killed me.

HAMLET It was a brute part of him to kill so capital a calf there. – Be the players ready?

ROSENCRANTZ Ay my lord, they stay upon your patience. 95

GERTRUDE Come hither my dear Hamlet, sit by me.

HAMLET No good mother, here's metal more attractive.

POLONIUS Oh ho, do you mark that?

HAMLET Lady, shall I lie in your lap?

OPHELIA No my lord. 100

HAMLET I mean, my head upon your lap?

OPHELIA Ay my lord.

HAMLET Do you think I meant country matters?

OPHELIA I think nothing my lord.

HAMLET That's a fair thought to lie between maids' legs. 105

OPHELIA What is, my lord?

HAMLET Nothing.

OPHELIA You are merry my lord.

HAMLET Who, I?

OPHELIA Ay my lord. 110

HAMLET O God, your only jig-maker. What should a man do but be merry? for look you how cheerfully my mother looks, and my father died within's two hours.

87 mine now. – My lord,] *Johnson (substantially)*; mine now my Lord. Q2; mine. Now my Lord, F 89 did I] Q2; I did F 90 And what] F; What Q2 96 dear] Q2; good F 101–2 HAMLET I mean...lord] F; *not in* Q2

85 have nothing with gain nothing from.

85–6 are not mine do not belong to my question.

91–2 I did enact...killed me For this as an allusion to Shakespeare's own *Julius Caesar*, see Introduction, pp. 5–6.

93 part action (compare *2 Henry IV* 4.5.63) – but also, continuing the theatre-language, 'part to play'.

93 calf Commonly used for a dolt or stupid person.

97 metal more attractive a substance more magnetic. But 'mettle' (the spelling in both Q2 and F) means also 'disposition', 'spirit'.

103 country matters the sort of thing that goes on among rustics in the country; coarse or indecent things. The sexual pun in 'country' is found also in the fifteenth-century *Castle of Perseverance*, when Humanum Genus says to Luxuria: 'Lechery... Few men will forsake thee / In any country that I know.' (See M. Collins, *N & Q* April 1981, p. 131.)

107 Nothing 'thing' was commonly used to refer to the sexual organ of either men or women. Compare *King Lear* 1.5.53 and *Othello* 3.3.302.

111 your only jig-maker i.e. 'there's no one like me for providing farcical entertainments'.

OPHELIA Nay, 'tis twice two months my lord.

HAMLET So long? Nay then let the devil wear black, for I'll have a suit of sables. O heavens! die two months ago, and not forgotten yet? Then there's hope a great man's memory may outlive his life half a year, but byrlady a must build churches then, or else shall a suffer not thinking on, with the hobby-horse, whose epitaph is, 'For O, for O, the hobby-horse is forgot.' 115 120

Hoboys play. The dumb-show enters

Enter a KING *and a* QUEEN, *very lovingly, the Queen embracing him. She*

115 devil] Diuel F; deule Q2 118 byrlady] F; ber lady Q2 118 a must] Q2; he must F 118 shall a] Q2; shall he F 120.1 SD *Hoboys...enters*] F; *The Trumpets sounds. Dumbe show followes* Q2 120.2 SD *a* QUEEN] Q2; *Queene* F 120.2 SD *very lovingly*] F; *not in* Q2 120.2 SD *embracing him.*] F; *embracing him, and he her,* Q2 120.2–3 SD *She...him*] F; *not in* Q2

114 twice two months Compare 1.2.138 – it was then less than two months since the former king's death: a further indication of the gap in time between Acts 1 and 2.

115–16 let the devil...sables 'sables' means the fur of a northern animal, the sable, which is brown. But 'sable' is also the heraldic word for 'black'. So this is a typical riddling remark of Hamlet's. Since his father has been dead so long, the devil can have his mourning garments and he will start wearing rich furs – but, by the pun, he will actually continue mourning.

118 byrlady Compare 2.2.388. This is F's spelling. Q2's 'ber Lady' may represent Shakespeare's spelling and pronunciation.

119 not thinking on being forgotten.

119–20 hobby-horse...forgot The hobby-horse was one of the additional characters in the morris-dance in the traditional English summer festivities, and has survived until modern times in Padstow and Minehead in the West Country. A man wore a huge hooped skirt in the likeness of a horse. The phrase 'the hobby horse is forgot' is very common (see *OED*); compare *Love's Labour's Lost* 3.1.29. It has been suggested that because of its lewdness, the hobby-horse had been suppressed through Puritan pressure, but A. Brissenden (*RES* XXX (1979), 1–11) shows it was as lively as ever in the early seventeenth century. He points out that 'hobby-horse' nearly always has a sexual connotation (see *Othello* 4.1.154; *Winter's Tale* 1.2.276). Brissenden describes how the horse used to sink to the ground as though dead, then come to energetic life again. This feature is singled out by C. Hole in *Dictionary of British Folk Customs*, 1976: 'He chases the girls, and sometimes corners one of them against a wall and covers her with his huge tarpaulin skirt ...Every now and then, the Oss dies a magical death...The Mayers, and most of the onlookers, sing: "O, where is St George? O where is he, O?" The Oss sinks to the ground as though he were dying...And then, suddenly, the music changes once more, the Oss leaps up high in the air, and off he goes again, as full of life as ever.'

So the hobby-horse does not die to be forgotten, but comes back with a vengeance, like Hamlet's father.

120 SD The versions of the dumb-show in Q2 and F differ in three ways. (1) Q2 accidentally omits what is almost certainly part of the original SD (chiefly 'She kneels...unto him' 2–3); (2) F firms up for stage presentation, altering the music, identifying characters ('Fellow', 'King', 'Mutes'), and inserting exits; (3) F substitutes more familiar and descriptive words like 'loath and unwilling' for 'harsh'.

What is printed here is an eclectic version, accepting some changes from F, but preserving Q2's language.

There are three problems about the dumb-show. (1) It is most unusual for a dumb-show to mime the action of the entire play to follow; (2) Did Hamlet know the dumb-show was going to be presented? (3) Why does Claudius not react? As regards (1), the show clearly puzzles Ophelia, and is therefore probably meant to seem rather peculiar. As regards (2), although Hamlet's ensuing remarks *can* be interpreted as showing anger against the players, they do not in the least demand that interpretation, and it is safer to assume that the sponsor of the play knew what was going to take place. (3) Claudius's silence has been explained on the grounds that he was not watching, or that the Ghost's story of a poisoning through the ear was a fabrication. But an impassive, or nearly impassive, Claudius is theatrically very effective, providing an enigma for Hamlet and Horatio, as well as the audience.

120.1 *Hoboys* Oboes.

kneels and makes show of protestation unto him. He takes her up, and declines his head upon her neck. He lies him down upon a bank of flowers. She, seeing him asleep, leaves him. Anon comes in another man, takes off his crown, kisses it, pours poison in the sleeper's ears, and leaves him. The Queen returns, finds the King dead, and makes passionate action. The poisoner, with some two or three mutes, comes in again, seeming to condole with her. The dead body is carried away. The poisoner woos the Queen with gifts. She seems harsh awhile, but in the end accepts his love. *Exeunt*

OPHELIA What means this my lord?
HAMLET Marry this is miching mallecho, it means mischief.
OPHELIA Belike this show imports the argument of the play?

Enter PROLOGUE

HAMLET We shall know by this fellow; the players cannot keep counsel, they'll tell all. 125
OPHELIA Will a tell us what this show meant?
HAMLET Ay, or any show that you'll show him. Be not you ashamed to show, he'll not shame to tell you what it means.
OPHELIA You are naught, you are naught. I'll mark the play.

PROLOGUE For us and for our tragedy, 130
Here stooping to your clemency,
We beg your hearing patiently.

HAMLET Is this a prologue, or the posy of a ring?
OPHELIA 'Tis brief my lord.
HAMLET As woman's love. 135

120.4 SD *He lies*] Q2; *Layes* F **120.5** SD *comes*] F; *come* Q2 **120.5** SD *another man*] Q2; *a Fellow* F **120.6** SD *pours*] Q2; *and powres* F **120.6** SD *the sleeper's*] Q2; *the Kings* F **120.6** SD *leaves him*] Q2; *Exits* F **120.7** SD *and makes*] F; *makes* Q2 **120.8** SD *two or three mutes*] F; *three or foure* Q2 **120.8** SD *comes*] F; *come* Q2 **120.8** SD *seeming*] F; *seeme* Q2 **120.8** *condole*] Q2; *lament* F **120.10** SD *harsh*] Q2; *loath and unwilling* F **120.10** SD *his love*] F; *loue* Q2 **120.10** SD *Exeunt*] F; *not in* Q2 **122** is] F; *not in* Q2 **122** miching] Miching F; munching Q2; myching Q1 **122** mallecho] *Malone; Mallico* Q2; *Malicho* F; Mallico Q1 **122** it] Q2; that F **123** play?] F; play. Q2 **123** SD] Q2; *after 129 in* F **124** this fellow] Q2; these Fellowes F **124** counsel] F; *not in* Q2 **126** a] Q2; they F **127** you'll] F; you will Q2 **133** posy] posie Q2; Poesie F **135** SD] *P. Alexander; Enter King and Queene* Q2; *Enter King and his Queene* F

120.3 ***protestation*** solemn vow.

120.10 ***harsh*** i.e. she is disdainful, cross.

122 miching mallecho Another insoluble problem. 'miching' is F's word; Q2 has 'munching'. 'miching' is a good English word meaning 'skulking'; 'mallecho' (Q2, *Mallico*; F, *Malicho*) may be for Spanish *malhecho*, a misdeed.

123 Belike...play? 'Perhaps this dumb-show explains what the play is about?'

125 they'll tell all It would seem unnecessary to point out that this is a joke, but some have taken it as a sign of Hamlet's anxiety lest his scheme should be sabotaged.

129 naught wicked.

133 posy inscribed motto or rhyme; a shortened version of 'poesie', which is how the word is spelt in F and Q1.

135 SD **KING...QUEEN** According to Hamlet in 220–5, it is a Duke called Gonzago and his wife Baptista. F makes an effort to call the Queen-Duchess

Enter the PLAYER KING *and* QUEEN

PLAYER KING Full thirty times hath Phoebus' cart gone round
Neptune's salt wash and Tellus' orbèd ground,
And thirty dozen moons with borrowed sheen
About the world have times twelve thirties been,
Since love our hearts, and Hymen did our hands, 140
Unite commutual in most sacred bands.

PLAYER QUEEN So many journeys may the sun and moon
Make us again count o'er ere love be done.
But woe is me, you are so sick of late,
So far from cheer and from your former state, 145
That I distrust you. Yet though I distrust,
Discomfort you my lord it nothing must.
For women's fear and love hold quantity,
In neither aught, or in extremity.
Now what my love is, proof hath made you know; 150
And as my love is sized, my fear is so.
[Where love is great, the littlest doubts are fear;
Where little fears grow great, great love grows there.]

PLAYER KING Faith, I must leave thee love, and shortly too:
My operant powers their functions leave to do; 155
And thou shalt live in this fair world behind,
Honoured, beloved; and haply one as kind
For husband shalt thou –

PLAYER QUEEN Oh confound the rest!
Such love must needs be treason in my breast.

137 orbèd ground] F; orb'd the ground Q2 **142, 158, 197** SH PLAYER QUEEN] *Steevens*[2]; *Quee.* Q2; *Bap.* F **145** your] F; our Q2 **145** former] Q2; forme F **147** *Following this line* Q2 *inserts* For women feare too much, euen as they loue, **148** For] F; And Q2 **148** hold] Q2; holds F **149** In] F; Eyther none, in Q2 **150** love] F; Lord Q2 **152–3**] Q2; *not in* F **155** their] Q2; my F

'*Bap.*' or '*Bapt.*' in speech headings – no doubt to distinguish her from Gertrude – but does nothing to alter 'King'. Interestingly, Q1 calls them Duke and Duchess throughout.

136 Phoebus' cart The chariot of the sun.

136–39 The emphasis on thirty years of marriage has been compared with the emphasis on Hamlet's age as thirty at 5.1.122–38.

137 Tellus' orbèd ground The sphere of the earth, the globe.

138 borrowed sheen reflected light.

140 Hymen God of marriage.

146 distrust you i.e. distrust the state of your health.

148 Fear and love go together in a woman. Either they are both non-existent, or they are both present in full. For Shakespeare's hesitations here see Introduction, p. 11.

150 proof experience, trial.

151 sized in size.

152–3 These two lines are omitted in F. Probably the Q2 compositor failed to note a mark for deletion. See Introduction, pp. 10–11.

155 leave to do cease to perform.

In second husband let me be accurst: 160
None wed the second but who killed the first.

HAMLET That's wormwood, wormwood.

PLAYER QUEEN The instances that second marriage move
Are base respects of thrift, but none of love.
A second time I kill my husband dead 165
When second husband kisses me in bed.

PLAYER KING I do believe you think what now you speak,
But what we do determine oft we break.
Purpose is but the slave to memory,
Of violent birth but poor validity, 170
Which now like fruit unripe sticks on the tree,
But fall unshaken when they mellow be.
Most necessary 'tis that we forget
To pay ourselves what to ourselves is debt.
What to ourselves in passion we propose, 175
The passion ending, doth the purpose lose.
The violence of either grief or joy
Their own enactures with themselves destroy.
Where joy most revels, grief doth most lament;
Grief joys, joy grieves, on slender accident. 180
This world is not for aye, nor 'tis not strange
That even our loves should with our fortunes change,
For 'tis a question left us yet to prove,
Whether love lead fortune, or else fortune love.

162 That's wormwood, wormwood] *Wilson;* That's wormwood Q2 *(margin);* Wormwood, Wormwood F **163** SH PLAYER QUEEN] *Steevens*[2]*; not in* Q2*; Bapt.* F **167** you think] Q2*;* you. Think F **171** like] F*;* the Q2 **177** either] Q2*;* other F **180** joys] F*;* ioy Q2 **180** grieves] F*;* griefes Q2

161 None wed...first Hamlet has no reason to believe that Gertrude had any hand in killing Claudius, but his words at 3.4.30 indicate that he assumed she was an accessory before the fact, and that her involvement was tantamount to murder.

162 Wormwood *Artemisia absinthium,* a bitter herb.

163 instances motives.

164 thrift profit, advancement.

169 slave to memory Purpose has no autonomous existence, but is completely dependent on memory – and on passion (176). These are words for Hamlet. See 1.5.96–7 and the note on 179–80 below.

170 Of violent birth Very strong at the beginning.

170 validity health and strength.

173 Most necessary 'tis A moment of sarcasm. A resolution to do something is a debt which we owe to ourselves – and of course we don't pay *those*!

177–8 The violence...destroy Repeats the preceding couplet. Violent grief and joy, when they cease, destroy the 'enactures' or actions which are associated with them.

179–80 Where joy...accident Those who have most capacity for joy have most capacity for grief, and the one changes into the other on the slightest occasion. The whole of this speech makes gnomic comments on Hamlet's own predicament. It is a fine irony that the play designed to catch the king's conscience should also probe his own problems.

181 for aye for ever.

The great man down, you mark his favourite flies; 185
The poor advanced makes friends of enemies,
And hitherto doth love on fortune tend;
For who not needs shall never lack a friend,
And who in want a hollow friend doth try
Directly seasons him his enemy. 190
But orderly to end where I begun,
Our wills and fates do so contrary run
That our devices still are overthrown;
Our thoughts are ours, their ends none of our own.
So think thou wilt no second husband wed, 195
But die thy thoughts when thy first lord is dead.

PLAYER QUEEN Nor earth to me give food, nor heaven light,
Sport and repose lock from me day and night,
[To desperation turn my trust and hope,
An anchor's cheer in prison be my scope,] 200
Each opposite that blanks the face of joy
Meet what I would have well, and it destroy;
Both here and hence pursue me lasting strife,
If once a widow, ever I be wife.

HAMLET If she should break it now! 205

PLAYER KING 'Tis deeply sworn. Sweet, leave me here awhile;
My spirits grow dull, and fain I would beguile
The tedious day with sleep.

Sleeps

PLAYER QUEEN Sleep rock thy brain,
And never come mischance between us twain. *Exit*

HAMLET Madam, how like you this play? 210

185 favourite] Q2; fauourites F **197** to me give] Q2; to giue me F **199–200**] Q2; *not in* F **200** An] *Theobald;* And Q2 **204** once a] F; once I be a Q2 **204** wife] F; a wife Q2 **208** SD] F *(after* brain*); not in* Q2 **209** SD] F; *Exeunt* Q2

187 hitherto to this extent.

187 tend attend, wait.

189 try make trial of.

190 seasons As in 1.3.81, 'to season' means 'to cause change by the passage of time', usually 'to ripen', but here simply 'changes (him into)'.

193 devices schemes, plans.

199–200 F omits these two lines. Again, probably Shakespeare's own deletion, not noted by the Q2 compositor, making the Player Queen's adjuration less flabby and more vehement.

200 anchor's cheer the fare of an anchorite or religious hermit.

200 scope limit.

201 opposite opposing force.

201 blanks blanches, makes pale. Not used elsewhere by Shakespeare.

204 If once...wife So F. Q2's expanded version again seems to reveal a confused MS. with a number of imperfectly deleted false starts.

207 spirits vital spirits.

GERTRUDE The lady doth protest too much methinks.
HAMLET Oh but she'll keep her word.
CLAUDIUS Have you heard the argument? Is there no offence in't?
HAMLET No, no, they do but jest, poison in jest, no offence i'th'world.
CLAUDIUS What do you call the play? 215
HAMLET The Mousetrap. Marry how? Tropically. This play is the image of a murder done in Vienna. Gonzago is the duke's name, his wife Baptista. You shall see anon. 'Tis a knavish piece of work, but what o' that? Your majesty, and we that have free souls, it touches us not. Let the galled jade winch, our withers are unwrung. 220

Enter LUCIANUS

This is one Lucianus, nephew to the king.
OPHELIA You are as good as a chorus my lord.
HAMLET I could interpret between you and your love if I could see the puppets dallying.
OPHELIA You are keen my lord, you are keen. 225
HAMLET It would cost you a groaning to take off mine edge.
OPHELIA Still better and worse.
HAMLET So you mistake your husbands. Begin, murderer. Pox, leave

211 doth protest] Q2; protests F **219** o' that] F; of that Q2 **220** SD] F; *after 221 in* Q2 **222** as good as a] Q2, Q1; a good F **226** mine] Q2; my F **228** your] Q2; *not in* F **228** Pox] F; *not in* Q2

211 doth protest makes protestation or promises. F's 'protests', followed by Q1, is a clear case of the original scribe's tendency to 'improve' his copy.

214 poison...i'th'world Hamlet pretends to think Claudius is asking if there is any 'offence' = 'crime' in the play, and he assures him it is only a mock-crime. This is the first verbal mention of poison. Later (263) Hamlet talks of Claudius reacting to 'talk of the poisoning', but he is probably referring to the moment when he lets the cat entirely out of the bag (237–9).

216 Tropically As a trope, a figure of speech. Q1's 'trapically' shows the Joycean pun.

219 free innocent. See 2.2.516.

220 Let...winch 'galled jade' is a poor horse with saddle-sores. 'winch' = 'wince'. It was a common saying that it was the galled horse that would soonest wince (Tilley H700).

220 withers The high part of a horse's back, between the shoulder-blades.

220 unwrung not pressed tight, pinched or chafed. See *OED* wring *v* 4.

221 nephew to the king In identifying Lucianus thus, Hamlet brings together past and future: Claudius's killing of his brother, and his own projected killing of his uncle.

223–4 I could...dallying I could act as a chorus in explaining what goes on between you and your lover if I could see the dalliance or flirting in the form of a puppet show. Many commentators, surely correctly, suspect some indecent secondary meaning in 'puppets'. The explanation may well lie in Q1's 'poopies'. It has been shown by H. Hulme that 'poop' meant the female genitals (*Explorations in Shakespeare's Language*, p. 114; see also Massinger, *Parliament of Love* 4.5.73). That the word could mean 'rump' (from 'poop' = stern of a ship) is clear from *OED*, and the obscene use is probably only an extension of that meaning, probably to the genital organs of either sex, as I think is intended by Hamlet.

225 keen sharp and bitter.

226 groaning i.e. of childbirth.

227 Still better and worse Ophelia refers to Hamlet's continual 'bettering' of her meaning, i.e. 'Always a "better" meaning with a more offensive slant'.

228 mistake i.e. mis-take: 'with such false vows (for better or for worse) you take your husbands'.

thy damnable faces and begin. Come, the croaking raven doth bellow for revenge. 230

LUCIANUS Thoughts black, hands apt, drugs fit, and time agreeing,
Confederate season, else no creature seeing.
Thou mixture rank, of midnight weeds collected,
With Hecat's ban thrice blasted, thrice infected,
Thy natural magic and dire property 235
On wholesome life usurp immediately.
Pours the poison in his ears

HAMLET A poisons him i'th'garden for's estate. His name's Gonzago. The story is extant, and written in very choice Italian. You shall see anon how the murderer gets the love of Gonzago's wife.
OPHELIA The king rises. 240
HAMLET What, frighted with false fire?
GERTRUDE How fares my lord?
POLONIUS Give o'er the play.
CLAUDIUS Give me some light. Away!
LORDS Lights, lights, lights! 245
Exeunt all but Hamlet and Horatio

HAMLET Why, let the strucken deer go weep,
The hart ungallèd play,
For some must watch while some must sleep,
Thus runs the world away.

232 Confederate] F; Considerat Q2 234 infected] F; inuected Q2 236 usurp] F; vsurps Q2 236 SD] F; *not in* Q2 237 A] Q2; He F 237 for's] F; for his Q2 238 written] Q2; writ F 238 very choice] Q2; choyce F 241 HAMLET...fire] F; *not in* Q2 245 SH LORDS] *This edn; Pol.* Q2; *All* F 245 SD] Q2; *Exeunt / Manet Hamlet & Horatio* F 249 Thus] Q2, Q1; So F

229–30 the croaking...revenge Simpson noted in 1874 that this was a 'satirical condensation' of two lines from *The True Tragedy of Richard III* (printed 1594): 'The screeking raven sits croaking for revenge, / Whole herds of beasts come bellowing for revenge' (Malone Society Reprint, 1892–3).

231 apt ready.

232 Confederate season i.e. this moment of time is his ally, and his only witness.

233 of midnight weeds collected put together from weeds gathered at midnight. 'collected' refers to the mixing of the weeds, the concoction, and not the picking. Compare 4.7.143.

234 Hecat Hecate, goddess of witchcraft.

234 ban curse.

235 dire property baleful quality.

236 usurp So F. Q2 reads 'usurps', but it is quite clear from the syntax that Lucianus is invoking the poison to work.

237 estate position (as king). Compare 3.3.5.

241 false fire gunfire with blank charge.

245 LORDS Q2 gives this to Polonius; F to '*All*.' Probably the theatre-scribe saw Polonius leading a general cry. The royal guard came in bearing torches (81 SD above); Claudius orders these torchbearers to light him to his own quarters.

246–9 Why, let...world away This song or ballad has not been identified.

247 ungalled uninjured.

248 watch keep awake.

Would not this, sir, and a forest of feathers, if the rest of my fortunes 250
turn Turk with me, with two provincial roses on my razed shoes,
get me a fellowship in a cry of players, sir?

HORATIO Half a share.

HAMLET A whole one I.

For thou dost know, O Damon dear, 255
This realm dismantled was
Of Jove himself, and now reigns here
A very, very – pajock.

HORATIO You might have rhymed.

HAMLET O good Horatio, I'll take the ghost's word for a thousand 260
pound. Didst perceive?

HORATIO Very well my lord.

HAMLET Upon the talk of the poisoning?

HORATIO I did very well note him.

Enter ROSENCRANTZ *and* GUILDENSTERN

HAMLET Ah ha! – Come, some music! Come, the recorders! 265
For if the king like not the comedy,

251 two] F; *not in* Q2 251 razed] raz'd Q2; rac'd F 252 sir] F; *not in* Q2 264 SD] F; *after 268 in* Q2 265 Ah ha!] Ah ha, Q2; Oh, ha? F

250 this The success of the performance?

250 forest of feathers The plumes which were a derided feature of the gallant's outfit were a notable feature of theatre costume. Dekker talks of a gallant who is furious at finding the forty-shilling 'felt and feather', which he has bought for his mistress as a new creation, being worn on the stage (*Gull's Hornbook*, end of ch. 6).

251 turn Turk with me To 'turn Turk' is to renounce one's religion, apostasise or become a renegade. 'with' has here the sense of 'against' (as we still use it in 'fight' or 'compete' *with* someone). So the phrase means 'renege on me', or 'renounce and desert me'.

251 provincial roses Roses orginating either from Provins in northern France or from Provence. (Jenkins in a long note strongly defends the latter origin.) Hamlet is speaking of rosettes and not the real flowers.

251 razed shoes Shoes which were 'razed', 'rased' or 'raced' were ornamented by cuts or slits in the leather.

252 fellowship partnership; the technical term was a 'share'.

252 cry pack (of hounds).

256 dismantled stripped, divested; i.e. the realm lost Jove himself as king.

258 pajock There seems no doubt that Shakespeare wrote 'paiock' and it is surely straining things too far to say he meant 'peacock', which is the reading of many editions. T. McGrath, in 1871 (cited in NV), cleverly suggested that 'pajock' is the 'patchock' used by Spenser in *A View of the Present State of Ireland* (ed. Renwick, p. 64) in a context suggesting a despicable person: 'as very patchocks as the wild Irish'. This is supported by *OED* sv Patchcock. It is usually said that Hamlet was about to finish with 'ass', but it seems to me he couldn't think of a word that would complete the rhyme.

263 Upon the talk of the poisoning Does this refer to Lucianus's words (231–6) or to Hamlet's outburst (237–9)? Or (much less likely) to 'poison in jest' (214)?

264 SD So placed by F. Q2 places it later, after 268. It is obvious that F is correct. Hamlet pointedly ignores Rosencrantz and Guildenstern by calling for music and singing a little song.

266–7 For if...perdy It has been suggested that this is an echo of the lines in *The Spanish Tragedy* (4.1.197–8), also referring to a revenger's playlet, 'And if the world like not this tragedy, / Hard is the hap of old Hieronimo'. ('Perdy' = by God.)

Why then – belike he likes it not, perdy.
Come, some music!

GUILDENSTERN Good my lord, vouchsafe me a word with you.

HAMLET Sir, a whole history. 270

GUILDENSTERN The king, sir –

HAMLET Ay sir, what of him?

GUILDENSTERN Is in his retirement marvellous distempered.

HAMLET With drink sir?

GUILDENSTERN No my lord, rather with choler. 275

HAMLET Your wisdom should show itself more richer to signify this to his doctor, for, for me to put him to his purgation would perhaps plunge him into far more choler.

GUILDENSTERN Good my lord, put your discourse into some frame, and start not so wildly from my affair. 280

HAMLET I am tame sir, pronounce.

GUILDENSTERN The queen your mother, in most great affliction of spirit, hath sent me to you.

HAMLET You are welcome.

GUILDENSTERN Nay good my lord, this courtesy is not of the right 285 breed. If it shall please you to make me a wholesome answer, I will do your mother's commandment. If not, your pardon and my return shall be the end of my business.

HAMLET Sir, I cannot.

ROSENCRANTZ What, my lord? 290

HAMLET Make you a wholesome answer; my wit's diseased. But, sir, such answer as I can make, you shall command, or rather, as you say, my mother. Therefore no more, but to the matter. My mother, you say.

ROSENCRANTZ Then thus she says. Your behaviour hath struck her 295 into amazement and admiration.

275 rather with] F; with Q2 **277** his doctor] F; the Doctor Q2 **278** far more] F; more Q2 **280** start] F; stare Q2 **288** my business] F; busines Q2 **290** SH ROSENCRANTZ] *Ros.* Q2; *Guild.* F **291** answer] Q2; answers F **292–3** as you say] Q2; you say F

273 distempered out of humour. But the word was also used as a euphemism for being drunk, as Hamlet's bland enquiry indicates. (For other examples, see the glossary in Dover Wilson, and also in Massinger's *Plays and Poems*.)

275 choler anger. But Hamlet chooses to understand 'bile'.

276 signify announce.

277–8 for me...more choler the way in which I would cure him of his distemper would make him much angrier.

279 frame ordered structure.

280 start make a sudden, surprised, movement.

281 tame subdued; i.e. a manageable horse that will not 'start'.

286 wholesome healthy, i.e. sane.

287 pardon permission (to leave).

292 command have at your service.

296 amazement See notes to 1.2.235 and 2.2.517.

296 admiration wonder.

HAMLET O wonderful son that can so stonish a mother! But is there no sequel at the heels of this mother's admiration? Impart.

ROSENCRANTZ She desires to speak with you in her closet ere you go to bed. 300

HAMLET We shall obey, were she ten times our mother. Have you any further trade with us?

ROSENCRANTZ My lord, you once did love me.

HAMLET And do still, by these pickers and stealers.

ROSENCRANTZ Good my lord, what is your cause of distemper? You 305 do surely bar the door upon your own liberty if you deny your griefs to your friend.

HAMLET Sir, I lack advancement.

ROSENCRANTZ How can that be, when you have the voice of the king himself for your succession in Denmark? 310

HAMLET Ay sir, but while the grass grows – the proverb is something musty.

Enter the PLAYERS *with recorders*

Oh, the recorders. Let me see one. To withdraw with you – Why do you go about to recover the wind of me, as if you would drive me into a toil? 315

GUILDENSTERN O my lord, if my duty be too bold, my love is too unmannerly.

HAMLET I do not well understand that. Will you play upon this pipe?

297 stonish] Q2; astonish F **298** Impart] Q2; *not in* F **304** And] Q2; So I F **306** surely] Q2; freely F **306** upon] Q2; of F **311** sir] Q2; *not in* F **312** SD] Q2 *(after 310)*; *Enter one with a Recorder* F **313** recorders] Q2; Recorder F **313** Let me see one] Q2; Let me see F

301 were she...mother In sane conversation, this would go with a *refusal* to obey.

304 pickers and stealers hands. From the Catechism in the Book of Common Prayer: 'To keep my hands from picking and stealing'.

306 liberty Rosencrantz means Hamlet would be more free in his mind, less burdened, if he would communicate his problems. But (as so often in this play) the bad people use unfortunate figures of speech. Rosencrantz must have at the back of his mind the possibility of Hamlet's being imprisoned.

308 I lack advancement Hamlet brazenly offers the explanation which Rosencrantz and Guildenstern had previously suggested and which he had denied (2.2.241–4).

311 while the grass grows – While waiting for the grass to grow, the horse starves. As Hamlet indicates, this is an old proverb (Tilley G423).

312 SD F's modification of this direction and the subsequent dialogue clearly indicate the theatre's concern not to bring on characters who were not strictly necessary (see Introduction, p. 22).

313 To withdraw with you Hamlet moves Rosencrantz and Guildenstern aside with him.

314 recover gain. The hunstsman will try to move to the windward of his prey, and so get the animal, scenting him, to run away from him and towards the trap.

316–17 if my duty...unmannerly If Hamlet finds this respectful attention bold, he is accusing love of being ill-mannered, because the duty is a matter of love. Hamlet understands the remark perfectly well. What he does not 'well understand' is the profession of love, which he thinks false.

GUILDENSTERN My lord, I cannot.

HAMLET I pray you. 320

GUILDENSTERN Believe me I cannot.

HAMLET I do beseech you.

GUILDENSTERN I know no touch of it my lord.

HAMLET 'Tis as easy as lying. Govern these ventages with your fingers and thumb, give it breath with your mouth, and it will discourse 325 most eloquent music. Look you, these are the stops.

GUILDENSTERN But these cannot I command to any utterance of harmony. I have not the skill.

HAMLET Why look you now how unworthy a thing you make of me. You would play upon me, you would seem to know my stops, you 330 would pluck out the heart of my mystery, you would sound me from my lowest note to the top of my compass – and there is much music, excellent voice, in this little organ, yet cannot you make it speak. 'Sblood, do you think I am easier to be played on than a pipe? Call me what instrument you will, though you can fret me, you cannot 335 play upon me.

Enter POLONIUS

God bless you sir.

POLONIUS My lord, the queen would speak with you, and presently.

HAMLET Do you see yonder cloud that's almost in shape of a camel?

POLONIUS By th'mass, and 'tis like a camel indeed. 340

HAMLET Methinks it is like a weasel.

324 'Tis] F; It is Q2 **324** fingers] Q2; finger F **325** thumb] thumbe F; the vmber Q2 **326** eloquent] Q2; excellent F **332** the top of] F; *not in* Q2 **333** speak] Q2; *not in* F **334** 'Sblood] Q2; Why F **334** think I] Q2, Q1; thinke, that I F **335** can fret me] F; fret me not Q2 **339** yonder] Q2, Q1; that F **339** in shape of] Q2; in shape like F **340** mass] masse Q2; Misse F **340** 'tis] Q2; it's F

324 ventages vents, i.e. holes.

331 mystery the skills of a particular craft. i.e. you would learn the innermost secret of my working, as a musician would learn the secret of playing the recorder.

333 this little organ the recorder.

335 fret 'frets' are the raised bars for fingering on a lute, providing a pun with 'irritate'. Q2's 'fret me not' seems to reflect some confusion in Shakespeare's MS.

338 presently immediately.

339 see yonder cloud Such is the freedom of the Elizabethan stage! This scene is supposed to be taking place indoors at night. Booth used to make Polonius look out of a window.

339–44 Hamlet's teasing of Polonius, playing the madman to make him humour him, and at the same time showing up his timid sycophancy, inevitably recalls the intensely serious use Shakespeare was to make in *Antony and Cleopatra* (4.14) of the changing shape of clouds: 'Sometime we see a cloud that's dragonish...That which is now a horse, even with a thought/The rack dislimns, and makes it indistinct/As water is in water.' In the later play, the evanescence of the cloud is used as an image of changes in one's identity, and the transience of things. But underlying Hamlet's mockery is his sense not of transience but of indeterminacy. 'There is nothing good or bad but thinking makes it so.' A cloud is whatever you think it to be, and, like the authenticity of the Ghost, one's view of it changes all the time.

POLONIUS It is backed like a weasel.
HAMLET Or like a whale?
POLONIUS Very like a whale.
HAMLET Then I will come to my mother by and by. – They fool me 345
to the top of my bent. – I will come by and by.
POLONIUS I will say so. *Exit*
HAMLET By and by is easily said. – Leave me, friends.
Exeunt all but Hamlet
'Tis now the very witching time of night,
When churchyards yawn, and hell itself breathes out 350
Contagion to this world. Now could I drink hot blood,
And do such bitter business as the day
Would quake to look on. Soft, now to my mother.
O heart, lose not thy nature; let not ever
The soul of Nero enter this firm bosom. 355
Let me be cruel, not unnatural:
I will speak daggers to her but use none.
My tongue and soul in this be hypocrites,
How in my words somever she be shent,
To give them seals never my soul consent. *Exit* 360

343 whale?] F; Whale. Q2 345 SH HAMLET] F; *as catchword only in* Q2 345 I will] Q2; will I F 347–8 POLONIUS...friends.] F; Leaue me friends. / I will, say so. By and by is easily said, Q2 350 breathes] breaths F; breakes Q2 352 bitter business as the day] F; busines as the bitter day Q2 357 daggers] F; dagger Q2 360 SD] Q2; *not in* F

345 **by and by** presently, quite soon.

345–6 **They fool me...bent** They tax to the uttermost my capacity to play the madman. Hamlet feels the strain of keeping up his 'madness' with Polonius at this particular juncture, as Edgar did in keeping up the role of mad Tom in *King Lear* 4.1.51, 'I cannot daub it further.' For 'bent', see note to 2.2.30.

349 **witching time** bewitching time, time of sorcery and enchantment. The reference is to the witches' sabbath, when their ceremonies conjured up the devil in physical form.

351 **Now could I drink hot blood** Witches were supposed to open the graves of newly buried children whom their charms had killed, boil the bodies and drink the liquid. Drinking of blood was one of the most frequent charges against witches. See R. Scot, *Discovery of Witchcraft*, 1584; ed. Nicholson, 1886, pp. 33, 41 etc.

This remark of Hamlet's, as baffling as any in the play, is discussed in the Introduction, p. 52. Hamlet does not mean he would *like* to drink hot blood; he is afraid that the power of hell may tempt him to some damnable practice.

353 **Soft** That's enough! (see 3.1.88 note).

354 **nature** natural feelings (as regards his mother). Compare 1.5.81.

355 **Nero** He contrived the murder of his mother.

358 **My tongue...hypocrites** A curious way to put it. Hypocrisy is a divorce between what is said and what is really felt or done; it is the person who owns both tongue and soul who is the hypocrite.

359 **shent** castigated, punished (by rebuke or reproach).

360 **seals** i.e. by deeds.

[3.3] *Enter* CLAUDIUS, ROSENCRANTZ *and* GUILDENSTERN

CLAUDIUS I like him not, nor stands it safe with us
To let his madness range. Therefore prepare you:
I your commission will forthwith dispatch,
And he to England shall along with you.
The terms of our estate may not endure 5
Hazard so near us as doth hourly grow
Out of his brows.

GUILDENSTERN We will ourselves provide.
Most holy and religious fear it is
To keep those many many bodies safe
That live and feed upon your majesty. 10

ROSENCRANTZ The single and peculiar life is bound
With all the strength and armour of the mind
To keep itself from noyance; but much more
That spirit upon whose weal depends and rests
The lives of many. The cess of majesty 15
Dies not alone, but like a gulf doth draw
What's near it with it. It is a massy wheel
Fixed on the summit of the highest mount,
To whose huge spokes ten thousand lesser things
Are mortised and adjoined, which when it falls, 20
Each small annexment, petty consequence,
Attends the boisterous ruin. Never alone
Did the king sigh, but with a general groan.

Act 3, Scene 3 3.3] *Capell* 6 near us] Q 1676; neer's Q2; dangerous F 7 brows] browes Q2; Lunacies F 14 weal] Q2; spirit F 15 cess] cesse Q2; cease F 17 It is] F; or it is Q2 18 summit] *Rowe*; somnet Q2; Somnet F 19 huge] F; hough Q2 22 ruin] F; raine Q2 23 but with] F; but Q2

Act 3, Scene 3

1 **I like him not** i.e. I do not like the way he is behaving.

1 **us** i.e. the person of the king.

3 **dispatch** make ready.

4 **along** go along. Compare 1.1.26.

5 **The terms of our estate** The conditions of my position as king.

7 **Out of his brows** So Q2; see collation. This curious expression seems to have been too much for the playhouse scribe. 'brows' means 'effrontery' (which derives from Latin *frons* = brow). Though 'effrontery' is not recorded in the language of Shakespeare's day in *OED*, 'effronted' (= bare-faced, shameless) does exist.

7 **ourselves provide** make provision for ourselves (to travel to England).

11 **The single and peculiar life** The life that belongs to the individual only.

13 **noyance** harm.

14 **weal** well-being.

15 **cess** cessation. So Q2. F gives the now more familiar 'cease'. We find 'cesse' (= cease) as a verb in *All's Well* 5.3.73.

16 **gulf** whirlpool (*OED* 3).

17 **massy** massive.

21 **annexment** This word seems to be Rosencrantz's gift to the English language.

21 **consequence** attachment. Again a curious word.

CLAUDIUS Arm you I pray you to this speedy voyage,
For we will fetters put about this fear 25
Which now goes too free-footed.

ROSENCRANTZ We will haste us.

Exeunt Rosencrantz and Guildenstern

Enter POLONIUS

POLONIUS My lord, he's going to his mother's closet.
Behind the arras I'll convey myself
To hear the process. I'll warrant she'll tax him home,
And as you said, and wisely was it said, 30
'Tis meet that some more audience than a mother,
Since nature makes them partial, should o'erhear
The speech of vantage. Fare you well my liege,
I'll call upon you ere you go to bed
And tell you what I know.

CLAUDIUS Thanks, dear my lord. 35

Exit Polonius

Oh my offence is rank, it smells to heaven;
It hath the primal eldest curse upon't,
A brother's murder. Pray can I not,
Though inclination be as sharp as will.
My stronger guilt defeats my strong intent, 40
And like a man to double business bound,
I stand in pause where I shall first begin,
And both neglect. What if this cursèd hand
Were thicker than itself with brother's blood,
Is there not rain enough in the sweet heavens 45
To wash it white as snow? Whereto serves mercy

24 voyage] F; viage Q2 25 about] Q2; vpon F 26 SH ROSENCRANTZ] *Ros.* Q2; *Both.* F 26 SD *Exeunt...Guildenstern*] *Hanmer; Exeunt Gent.* Q2, F 33 Fare] F; farre Q2 35 SD] *Capell; Exit.* Q2; *not in* F

24 **Arm you** Prepare yourselves.

28 **convey myself** secretly move myself.

29 **the process** what goes on.

29 **tax him home** censure him severely.

31 **meet** suitable.

32 **Since...partial** Polonius does not trust Gertrude to report accurately on her interview with her son. He is spying on her as well as on Hamlet. His transfer of responsibility for the scheme, in 'as you said' (30), is a matter of prudence as well as deference (see 3.1.175–9). 'nature' is 'natural feelings'.

33 **of vantage** from a good position.

37 **primal eldest** i.e. going back to Cain's murder of Abel.

39 **Though inclination...will** Though my desire to pray is as great as my determination.

41 **bound** Probably this means 'directed towards' (as in 'bound for England', 4.6.9) rather than 'obliged' or 'sworn'.

46–7 **Whereto...offence?** What is mercy for, except to meet crime face to face?

But to confront the visage of offence?
And what's in prayer but this two-fold force,
To be forestallèd ere we come to fall,
Or pardoned being down? Then I'll look up, 50
My fault is past. But oh, what form of prayer
Can serve my turn? 'Forgive me my foul murder'?
That cannot be, since I am still possessed
Of those effects for which I did the murder,
My crown, mine own ambition, and my queen. 55
May one be pardoned and retain th'offence?
In the corrupted currents of this world
Offence's gilded hand may shove by justice,
And oft 'tis seen the wicked prize itself
Buys out the law. But 'tis not so above; 60
There is no shuffling, there the action lies
In his true nature, and we ourselves compelled
Even to the teeth and forehead of our faults
To give in evidence. What then? What rests?
Try what repentance can. What can it not? 65
Yet what can it when one cannot repent?
Oh wretched state! Oh bosom black as death!
Oh limèd soul that struggling to be free
Art more engaged! Help, angels! – Make assay:
Bow stubborn knees, and heart with strings of steel 70
Be soft as sinews of the new-born babe.
All may be well.

[*He kneels*]

50 pardoned] pardon'd F; pardon Q2 **58 shove]** F; showe Q2 **72 SD** *He kneels*] Q1; *not in* Q2, F

54 effects things acquired or achieved.

55 mine own ambition i.e. those things I was ambitious for.

56 th'offence i.e. the fruits of the offence.

58–60 Offence's gilded hand...law Compare *King Lear* 4.6.165–6. 'Plate sin with gold, / And the strong lance of justice hurtless breaks.'

58 shove by thrust aside.

61 shuffling trickery, sharp practice, deception. See 3.1.67 note.

61 the action lies A legal phrase, meaning that a case is admitted to exist. But of course it also means that every deed lies exposed to God's scrutiny.

63–4 Even to...evidence To give evidence even about the worst of our sins. We are witnesses for the prosecution of ourselves. 'teeth' is for savagery and 'forehead' for effrontery (compare 'brows' above, 7).

64 rests remains.

68 limèd The image is of a bird caught by the smearing of a very sticky substance, called birdlime, on twigs and branches.

69 Make assay I think it is more likely that Claudius is addressing himself than the angels. After his appeal, 'Help, angels!' there is a silence, and then in a quieter tone he turns to himself, knowing that it is he who must make the effort.

Enter HAMLET

HAMLET Now might I do it pat, now a is a-praying,
And now I'll do't – and so a goes to heaven,
And so am I revenged. That would be scanned. 75
A villain kills my father, and for that,
I his sole son do this same villain send
To heaven.
Why, this is hire and salary, not revenge.
A took my father grossly, full of bread, 80
With all his crimes broad blown, as flush as May,
And how his audit stands who knows save heaven?
But in our circumstance and course of thought
'Tis heavy with him. And am I then revenged
To take him in the purging of his soul, 85
When he is fit and seasoned for his passage?
No.
Up sword, and know thou a more horrid hent,
When he is drunk asleep, or in his rage,
Or in th'incestuous pleasure of his bed, 90
At game a-swearing, or about some act
That has no relish of salvation in't –
Then trip him that his heels may kick at heaven,

73 do it pat] F; do it, but Q2 73 a is a-praying] Q2; he is praying F 74 a] Q2; he F 75 revenged] reueng'd F; reuendge Q2 76 A] Q2; He F 77 sole] Q2; foule F 79 Why] Q2; Oh F 79 hire and salary] F; base and silly Q2 81 flush] Q2; fresh F 89 drunk asleep] F; drunke, a sleep Q2 91 At game a-swearing] At game a swearing Q2; at game swaring Q1; at gaming, swearing F

73 **a is** Represents a slurred pronunciation of 'he is'; compare 2.2.185. We would write 'he's', but perhaps the pronunciation was nearer 'uz'.

75 **would be scanned** needs to be examined.

79 **hire and salary** So F. Q2's 'base and silly' seems to be not so much a misreading as a conjecture, from the context, of what two almost illegible words *might* be. Compare 'particular act and force' at 1.3.26.

80 **grossly** i.e. without consideration or decency.

80 **full of bread** Malone noted that this was a biblical echo, quoting Ezekiel 16.49: 'the iniquity of thy sister Sodom, pride, fulness of bread, and abundance of idleness'.

81 **broad blown** in full blossom.

81 **flush** vigorous.

83 **circumstance...thought** 'circumstance', as at 1.5.127 and 3.1.1, has the sense of circuitous or circling discourse. The construction here is the familiar Shakespearean use of two nouns for an adjective and a noun, i.e. 'circumstantial course of thought' = our course of thought which is necessarily indirect.

88 **hent** grasp (a rare word). He puts his sword up in its scabbard, promising to lay hold of it at a 'more horrid' opportunity.

89 **drunk asleep** i.e. in a drunken sleep.

91 **At game a-swearing** Gambling, and cursing the dice or cards as he plays. Although 'at game' is not elsewhere used by Shakespeare, there can be little doubt about the correctness of Q2 (followed here) which is supported by Q1, as against F's paraphrase, 'At gaming, swearing'.

92 **relish** touch, trace.

93–5 **trip him...it goes** This ambition to bring Claudius to eternal damnation – a speech, said Dr Johnson, 'too terrible to be read or to be uttered' – is discussed in the Introduction, pp. 52–4.

And that his soul may be as damned and black
As hell whereto it goes. My mother stays. 95
This physic but prolongs thy sickly days. *Exit*

CLAUDIUS My words fly up, my thoughts remain below.
Words without thoughts never to heaven go. *Exit*

[3.4] *Enter* GERTRUDE *and* POLONIUS

POLONIUS A will come straight. Look you lay home to him.
Tell him his pranks have been too broad to bear with,
And that your grace hath screened and stood between
Much heat and him. I'll silence me e'en here.
Pray you be round with him. 5

HAMLET (*Within*) Mother, mother, mother!

GERTRUDE I'll warrant you, fear me not. Withdraw, I hear him coming.
[*Polonius hides himself behind the arras*]

Enter HAMLET

HAMLET Now mother, what's the matter?

GERTRUDE Hamlet, thou hast thy father much offended.

HAMLET Mother, you have my father much offended. 10

GERTRUDE Come, come, you answer with an idle tongue.

Act 3, Scene 4 3.4] Capell 1 A] Q2; He F 4 e'en] e'ene F; euen Q2 5 with him] F; *not in* Q2 6 HAMLET...mother!] F; *not in* Q2; Mother, mother Q1 7 warrant] F; wait Q2 7 SD *Polonius...arras*] *Rowe; not in* Q2, F

96 This physic Hamlet sees his decision as a medicine temporarily preserving Claudius's life. Some commentators think the physic is Claudius's prayer.

Act 3, Scene 4

3.4 This is generally known as the 'closet scene' (see 3.2.299), a closet being a private apartment. Du Guernier's 1714 illustration, however, clearly shows a bed (see illus. 6). In 1927 in Prague the scene was staged with a bed, with Gertrude in a nightdress. In 1935, Dover Wilson called it 'the bedroom scene', and a bed on stage became almost obligatory. See A. C. Sprague and J. C. Trewin, *Shakespeare's Plays Today*, 1970, p. 19, and J. L. Styan, *The Shakespeare Revolution*, 1977, p. 162 and note.

1 lay home to him charge him to the full.

3 screened acted as a fire-screen – as the sentence goes on to illustrate.

4 I'll silence me Dowden thought this ironical, since it is Polonius's shout (24) that causes his death. Early editors were puzzled by 'silence' and preferred Hanmer's emendation 'sconce'. But Q1 has the best reading of all, the gruesomely apt sentence, 'I'le shrowd myself behind the arras.' Is it conceivable that this is the one place where an authoritative change, occurring to Shakespeare when the play was in production, is preserved only in the corrupt first quarto?

5 round See 3.1.177.

6 Mother, mother, mother! This cry of Hamlet's, omitted no doubt accidentally by Q2, was thought by Jenkins to be a spurious addition which 'degrades the play' (*Studies in Bibliography* 13 (1960), 35). It is surely very much in character, and not the kind of insertion the playhouse scribe would make.

HAMLET Go, go, you question with a wicked tongue.
GERTRUDE Why, how now Hamlet?
HAMLET What's the matter now?
GERTRUDE Have you forgot me?
HAMLET No by the rood, not so.
You are the queen, your husband's brother's wife, 15
And, would it were not so, you are my mother.
GERTRUDE Nay, then I'll set those to you that can speak.
HAMLET Come, come and sit you down, you shall not budge.
You go not till I set you up a glass
Where you may see the inmost part of you. 20
GERTRUDE What wilt thou do? thou wilt not murder me?
Help, help, ho!
POLONIUS (*Behind*) What ho! Help, help, help!
HAMLET (*Draws*) How now, a rat? Dead for a ducat, dead.
Kills Polonius
POLONIUS (*Behind*) Oh, I am slain!
GERTRUDE Oh me, what hast thou done? 25
HAMLET Nay I know not, is it the king?
GERTRUDE Oh what a rash and bloody deed is this!
HAMLET A bloody deed? Almost as bad, good mother,
As kill a king and marry with his brother.
GERTRUDE As kill a king?
HAMLET Ay lady, 'twas my word. 30
[*Lifts up the arras and reveals the body of Polonius*]
Thou wretched, rash, intruding fool, farewell.
I took thee for thy better. Take thy fortune.
Thou find'st to be too busy is some danger. –

12 a wicked] Q2; an idle F 16 And, would it] And would it Q2; But would you F 20 inmost] F; most Q2 22 Help, help, ho!] F; Helpe how. Q2 23, 25 SD *Behind*] *Capell; not in* Q2, F 23 Help, help, help!] F; helpe. Q2 24 SD *Draws*] *Malone (after* rat*); not in* Q2, F 24 SD *Kills Polonius*] F; *not in* Q2 30 'twas] F; it was Q2 30 SD] *following Capell (26) and Cambridge; not in* Q2, F 32 better] Q2; Betters F

14 **forgot me** forgotten who I am.

14 **the rood** the cross of Christ.

17 **can speak** Is this the understatement 'will have something to say to you'?

18 **Come, come** This is much more than the 'now then!' of Gertrude's 'Come, come' (12). I punctuate to indicate that Hamlet is forcing her to sit down.

18 **budge** move away (to fetch the others).

19 **glass** Once again, this is the mirror which reveals the truth and sets standards. See notes to 3.2.20 and 3.1.153.

24 **Dead for a ducat** Possibly, as Kittredge suggests, a wager, i.e. 'I'll bet a ducat I kill it.'

30 **As kill a king?...word** It is extraordinary that neither of them takes up this all-important matter again. Gertrude does not press for an explanation; Hamlet does not question further the queen's involvement. It is clear that this silence was thought to be a fault in the theatre. In Q1, Hamlet reiterates the fact that his father was murdered ('damnably murdred'), and the queen says 'I never knew of this most horride murder.'

Leave wringing of your hands. Peace! Sit you down
And let me wring your heart, for so I shall 35
If it be made of penetrable stuff,
If damnèd custom have not brazed it so,
That it be proof and bulwark against sense.

GERTRUDE What have I done, that thou dar'st wag thy tongue
In noise so rude against me?

HAMLET Such an act 40
That blurs the grace and blush of modesty,
Calls virtue hypocrite, takes off the rose
From the fair forehead of an innocent love
And sets a blister there, makes marriage vows
As false as dicers' oaths. Oh such a deed 45
As from the body of contraction plucks
The very soul, and sweet religion makes
A rhapsody of words. Heaven's face doth glow;
Yea, this solidity and compound mass,
With tristful visage as against the doom, 50
Is thought-sick at the act.

GERTRUDE Ay me, what act,
That roars so loud and thunders in the index?

38 be] Q2; is F 44 sets] Q2; makes F 48 doth] F; dooes Q2 49 Yea] F; Ore Q2 50 tristful] F; heated Q2 52 That] F; *Ham.* That Q2

37 **brazed** made brazen, hardened like brass.

38 **proof** armour.

38 **sense** feeling.

40 **Such an act** In the speech which follows, Hamlet quite certainly implies the breaking of marriage vows (see note to 1.5.46). But when Gertrude directly asks him 'what act?' (51), he does not directly answer 'adultery', but charges her with inconstancy, immoderate sexual desire, and a lack of any sense of value, in exchanging King Hamlet for Claudius. He does not pursue the charge of adultery, but nothing he says shows him forgetting it. Gertrude's collapse in 88–91 – which Hamlet scarcely notices – shows contrition for a worse sin than a hasty second marriage. She must recognise her son's unstated accusation.

42 **rose** A figurative rose, symbol of true love.

44 **sets a blister there** Assumed to mean the branding of a harlot on the forehead, with the backing of Laertes' speech at 4.5.119–20, 'brands the harlot / Even here, between the chaste unsmirched brow'. But I think Shakespeare in the latter place is speaking figuratively, and in both places is thinking of the forehead as the place which declares innocence or boldness (compare 3.3.7). Compare the proverbial 'honest as the skin between his brows' (*Much Ado* 3.5.12). The 'blister' I take to indicate disease. It was not the custom in Elizabethan times to brand prostitutes in the face, though this dire punishment was threatened by Henry VIII in 1513 and by the Commonwealth in 1650.

46 **contraction** pledging, making vows or contracts.

48 **rhapsody** a medley, a miscellaneous or confused collection.

48–51 **Heaven's face...at the act** i.e. the skies are red with shame, and the huge earth itself, with a countenance as sad as if it were doomsday, is distressed in mind by your act.

I follow F. Q2 misunderstands and garbles the passage. The compositor, substituting 'O'er' ('Ore') for 'Yea', thought the visage belonged to the glowing sun, and, unable to read or to understand 'tristful', supplied 'heated'. Possibly the MS. had become defective here; compare note to 1.3.26.

52 **index** table of contents (prefixed to a book).

HAMLET Look here upon this picture, and on this,
The counterfeit presentment of two brothers.
See what a grace was seated on this brow; 55
Hyperion's curls, the front of Jove himself,
An eye like Mars, to threaten and command;
A station like the herald Mercury,
New-lighted on a heaven-kissing hill;
A combination and a form indeed, 60
Where every god did seem to set his seal
To give the world assurance of a man.
This was your husband. Look you now what follows.
Here is your husband, like a mildewed ear
Blasting his wholesome brother. Have you eyes? 65
Could you on this fair mountain leave to feed
And batten on this moor? Ha! have you eyes?
You cannot call it love, for at your age
The heyday in the blood is tame, it's humble,
And waits upon the judgement; and what judgement 70
Would step from this to this? [Sense sure you have,
Else could you not have motion, but sure that sense
Is apoplexed, for madness would not err,
Nor sense to ecstasy was ne'er so thralled,
But it reserved some quantity of choice 75

53 SH HAMLET] *Ham.* F; *not in* Q2 57 and] Q2; or F 59 heaven-kissing] F; heaue, a kissing Q2 65 brother] Q2; breath F 71–6 Sense...difference] Q2; *not in* F

53 **this picture, and...this** There have been several ways of producing this in the theatre. The illustration in early editions (see illus. 6) suggests that in the Restoration portraits were hung on the wall. But the practice of using miniatures goes back a long way. Sometimes Hamlet drew miniatures of both kings from his pocket. A favourite practice is for Hamlet to have a locket of his father as a pendant, and to seize a similar locket, of Claudius, which hangs round Gertrude's neck.

54 **counterfeit presentment** i.e. portraits, representations in art.

56 **Hyperion** See 1.2.140.

56 **front** forehead.

58 **station** stance, way of standing.

59 **New-lighted** Newly alighted.

60 **combination** i.e. of divine qualities.

61 **set his seal** place his confirming mark.

64 **ear** of corn.

65 **Blasting** Blighting.

67 **batten** feed and grow fat. (Not an easy thing to do on moorland. The 'fair mountain' is faintly biblical: Wilson suggests an undertone of 'blackamoor' in 'moor'.)

69 **heyday** excitement.

69 **blood** passions, sexual desire.

71–6, 78–81 F makes two major excisions in the remainder of this speech. See Introduction, pp. 12–13, where it is argued that the cuts were Shakespeare's deletions, not observed by the Q2 compositors.

71–6 **Sense...difference** The difficulty of extracting meaning from this passage must support the theory that Shakespeare himself was dissatisfied with it. 'Sense' initially means 'feelings', but in the next two lines means 'reason'. The general idea seems to be that something worse than madness has happened to Gertrude's 'sense' because even if she was mad she could not prefer Claudius to her former husband.

74 **thralled** in thrall, enslaved.

To serve in such a difference.] What devil was't
That thus hath cozened you at hoodman-blind?
[Eyes without feeling, feeling without sight,
Ears without hands or eyes, smelling sans all,
Or but a sickly part of one true sense 80
Could not so mope.]
O shame, where is thy blush? Rebellious hell,
If thou canst mutine in a matron's bones,
To flaming youth let virtue be as wax
And melt in her own fire. Proclaim no shame 85
When the compulsive ardour gives the charge,
Since frost itself as actively doth burn,
And reason panders will.

GERTRUDE O Hamlet, speak no more.
Thou turn'st my eyes into my very soul,
And there I see such black and grainèd spots 90
As will not leave their tinct.

HAMLET Nay, but to live
In the rank sweat of an enseamèd bed,
Stewed in corruption, honeying and making love
Over the nasty sty.

77 hoodman] F; hodman Q2 78–81 Eyes...mope] Q2; *not in* F 86 ardour] ardure Q2, F 88 And] Q2; As F 88 panders] F; pardons Q2 89 turn'st my] Q2; turn'st mine F 89 eyes...soul] F; very eyes into my soule Q2 90 grainèd] F; greeued Q2 91 will not] F; will Q2 91 their] F; there their Q2 92 enseamèd] F; inseemed Q2

76 **serve...difference** i.e. to assist in differentiating between the two men.

77 **cozened...hoodman-blind** deceived you in a game of blindman's buff. (The devil substituted Claudius for King Hamlet when the blindfold Gertrude chose him.)

81 **mope** move around aimlessly, in a daze or trance. Compare *The Tempest* 5.1.240, 'Even in a dream were we divided from them, / And were brought moping hither.'

82 **Rebellious hell** i.e. The devil encourages our worser nature to rebel against our better judgement.

83 **mutine** incite mutiny (*OED v* 2).

84–5 **To flaming youth...fire** The argument runs that it is no good insisting on virtue as a rigid and unbending guide of conduct in the young, when age gives such a bad example. Virtue, in these circumstances, becomes a soft wax melting in the fire of youthful ardour.

86 **gives the charge** signals the attack.

88 **reason panders will** reason assists the passions to obtain their ends.

90 **grainèd** engrained, deep-dyed.

91 **leave their tinct** surrender their colour.

92 **enseamèd** The word has to do with 'grease'. Its commonest context in Shakespeare's time was scouring or purging animals, especially hawks and horses, of (it was thought) superfluous internal grease or fat. But 'enseam' could also mean not to *remove* but to *apply* grease, especially to cloth. The least disgusting meaning here would therefore be 'greasy'. It is more than likely, however, that what is uppermost in Hamlet's mind is the idea of evacuated foulness. The echo 'semen' is surely present. The bed is greasy with offensive semen. Beaumont and Fletcher probably had this passage in mind when writing 'dead-drunk...his lechery enseamed upon him' in *Four Plays* ('Triumph of Death', scene vi).

93 **Stewed** In this word, Shakespeare combines the heat, sweat and greasiness with the odium of the brothels, widely known as 'the stews'.

93 **honeying...sty** i.e. covering over foulness with sweet words and endearments. 'making love' has its usual pre-1950 sense of courtship, love-talk.

GERTRUDE Oh speak to me no more.
These words like daggers enter in my ears. 95
No more sweet Hamlet.

HAMLET A murderer and a villain,
A slave that is not twentieth part the tithe
Of your precedent lord, a vice of kings,
A cutpurse of the empire and the rule,
That from a shelf the precious diadem stole 100
And put it in his pocket.

GERTRUDE No more!

Enter GHOST

HAMLET A king of shreds and patches –
Save me and hover o'er me with your wings,
You heavenly guards! – What would your gracious figure?

GERTRUDE Alas he's mad! 105

HAMLET Do you not come your tardy son to chide,
That lapsed in time and passion lets go by
Th'important acting of your dread command? Oh say!

GHOST Do not forget. This visitation
Is but to whet thy almost blunted purpose. 110
But look, amazement on thy mother sits.
Oh step between her and her fighting soul:
Conceit in weakest bodies strongest works.
Speak to her, Hamlet.

HAMLET How is it with you lady?

GERTRUDE Alas, how is't with you, 115
That you do bend your eye on vacancy,

95 my] Q2; mine F **97** tithe] tythe F; kyth Q2 **104** your] Q2; you F **116** do] Q2; *not in* F

97 tithe tenth part.
98 vice clown or trickster of the old drama.
101 SD Q1 gives '*Enter the ghost in his night gowne*.'
102 shreds and patches i.e. the patchwork costume of the stage-clown.
107 lapsed Schmidt compares *Twelfth Night* 3.3.36, the only other occasion Shakespeare uses the word, 'If I be lapsed in this place, / I shall pay dear', and his gloss is 'surprised, taken in the act'. His paraphrase here is 'surprised by you in a time and passion fit for the execution of your command'. This is much more suitable than Johnson's 'having suffered time to slip and passion to cool'. The Ghost intervenes when Hamlet's passion is anything but cool. At a time when he has confirmed the Ghost's words and is all worked up, he is misusing his passion in doing what the Ghost has specifically forbidden – punishing his mother – and neglecting the revenge he was ordered to carry out.
108 important Neither 'momentous' nor 'urgent'; compare *All's Well* 3.7.21, 'his important blood will not deny'. We have no adjective which has the same sense of demanding or insisting. 'The acting – so urged on me and required of me – of your dread command.'
110 blunted purpose Compare Sonnet 95: 'the hardest knife, ill-used, doth lose his edge'. The Ghost is accusing Hamlet not of forgetting his revenge, but of misusing the energies which should be directed towards revenge.
111 amazement utter bewilderment. Compare 3.2.296.
113 Conceit Imagination.

And with th'incorporal air do hold discourse?
Forth at your eyes your spirits wildly peep,
And, as the sleeping soldiers in th'alarm,
Your bedded hair, like life in excrements, 120
Start up and stand an end. O gentle son,
Upon the heat and flame of thy distemper
Sprinkle cool patience. Whereon do you look?

HAMLET On him, on him! Look you how pale he glares.
His form and cause conjoined, preaching to stones, 125
Would make them capable. – Do not look upon me,
Lest with this piteous action you convert
My stern effects. Then what I have to do
Will want true colour: tears perchance for blood.

GERTRUDE To whom do you speak this? 130

HAMLET Do you see nothing there?

GERTRUDE Nothing at all, yet all that is I see.

HAMLET Nor did you nothing hear?

GERTRUDE No, nothing but ourselves.

HAMLET Why, look you there – look how it steals away – 135
My father in his habit as he lived –
Look where he goes, even now out at the portal.
Exit Ghost

GERTRUDE This is the very coinage of your brain.
This bodiless creation ecstasy
Is very cunning in.

117 th'incorporal] Q2; their corporall F 130 whom] Q2; who F 137 SD] Q2; *Exit* F 139–40 This...in] *as one line* Q2, F

118 spirits wildly peep 'In moments of excitement the *spirits* or "vital forces" were thought to come, as it were, to the surface, and to cause various symptoms of agitation' (Kittredge).

119 as the sleeping...alarm like soldiers startled out of sleep by a call to arms.

120 hair (considered plural).

120 like life in excrements 'excrement' can be either what is voided from, or what, like hair and nails, grows out of the body. Probably 'as though there were independent life in such outgrowths'.

121 an end A common form of 'on end'.

124 how pale he glares He is gazing fixedly with a ghastly expression. 'glares' is not necessarily an angry stare. 'pale' is several times used by Shakespeare in connection with a dying or lack-lustre look of the eyes. Schmidt (who is unusual in seeing that this phrase needs explanation) compares *Troilus* 5.3.81, 'Look how thou diest, look how thy eye turns pale.' See also 'their pale-dead eyes' (of horses) in *Henry V* 4.2.48.

126 capable receptive, susceptible.

127 piteous action behaviour which excites pity.

128 effects deeds (seen as issuing from anger and indignation). At their first meeting, the Ghost warned Hamlet not to pity him (1.5.5), presumably taking the same view that pity is not a state of mind likely to generate violent action.

129 true colour The 'effects' of pity would be colourless tears instead of blood. (The Ghost's reappearance seems to be weakening Hamlet's resolve instead of strengthening it.)

136 in his habit as he lived in the clothes he wore when alive.

138 very mere.

139 ecstasy madness.

140 cunning skilful.

HAMLET Ecstasy? 140
My pulse as yours doth temperately keep time,
And makes as healthful music. It is not madness
That I have uttered. Bring me to the test,
And I the matter will reword, which madness
Would gambol from. Mother, for love of grace, 145
Lay not that flattering unction to your soul,
That not your trespass but my madness speaks;
It will but skin and film the ulcerous place,
Whiles rank corruption, mining all within,
Infects unseen. Confess yourself to heaven, 150
Repent what's past, avoid what is to come,
And do not spread the compost on the weeds
To make them ranker. Forgive me this my virtue,
For in the fatness of these pursy times
Virtue itself of vice must pardon beg, 155
Yea, curb and woo for leave to do him good.

GERTRUDE Oh Hamlet, thou hast cleft my heart in twain.

HAMLET Oh throw away the worser part of it
And live the purer with the other half.
Good night – but go not to my uncle's bed; 160
Assume a virtue if you have it not.
[That monster custom, who all sense doth eat,

140 Ecstasy?] F; *not in* Q2 **144** And I] F; And Q2 **146** that] Q2; a F **149** Whiles] Q2; Whil'st F **152** on] Q2; or F **153** ranker] Q2; ranke F **154** these] Q2; this F **156** woo] wooe Q2; woe F **159** live] F; leaue Q2 **160** my] Q2; mine F **162–6** That monster...put on] Q2; *not in* F

145 gambol from spring away from.

146 unction healing oil or ointment.

148 skin and film serve as a skin and film over.

149 mining undermining.

152 spread...weeds She is not to use the good words of Hamlet as an encouragement to her vice, by supposing them to proceed only from his madness.

153–6 Forgive me...good It is perhaps a little disgusting that in the nearest thing to an apology to Gertrude for his abusive behaviour which Hamlet achieves, he stresses even further his self-righteousness – saying, in effect, 'I am sorry I have to apologise for speaking like this: virtue ought not to cringe before vice, but it is necessary because vice is so dominant these days.'

154 fatness grossness, ill condition (see note to 1.5.32 and 5.2.264).

154 pursy This is the same word as 'pursive' and it meant both short of breath and flatulent; it could be conveniently applied to a person who was grossly out of condition, panting, belching and breaking wind. Compare *Timon of Athens* 5.4.12, 'pursy insolence shall break his wind'. Cotgrave's *Dictionarie* (1611) defines 'Poussif' as '*Pursie, short-winded; also broken-winded*'. As *OED* indicates, the word had connotations of corpulence, probably from 'purse'. The words 'fatness' and 'pursy' move towards each other in meaning, suggesting in sum an overweight, pampered person in poor physical condition.

156 curb bow, make obeisance (Fr. *courber*).

162–6, 168–71 These passages are not present in the Folio, and again the assumption of this edition is that they were marked for deletion by Shakespeare during composition. See Introduction, pp. 10–13.

162–6 That monster...put on Custom is a monster who destroys sensitivity, and thus leads to devilish habits; but also angel, in that he can make us accustomed to good actions. 'aptly' = readily.

Of habits devil, is angel yet in this,
That to the use of actions fair and good
He likewise gives a frock or livery 165
That aptly is put on.] Refrain tonight,
And that shall lend a kind of easiness
To the next abstinence, [the next more easy,
For use almost can change the stamp of nature,
And either...the devil, or throw him out, 170
With wondrous potency.] Once more good night,
And when you are desirous to be blessed,
I'll blessing beg of you. For this same lord,
I do repent; but heaven hath pleased it so,
To punish me with this, and this with me, 175
That I must be their scourge and minister.
I will bestow him, and will answer well
The death I gave him. So again, good night.
I must be cruel only to be kind;
Thus bad begins, and worse remains behind. 180
One word more good lady.

GERTRUDE What shall I do?

HAMLET Not this by no means that I bid you do:
Let the bloat king tempt you again to bed,
Pinch wanton on your cheek, call you his mouse,
And let him for a pair of reechy kisses, 185
Or paddling in your neck with his damned fingers,
Make you to ravel all this matter out,

166 Refrain tonight] F; to refraine night Q2 **168–71** the next...potency] Q2; *not in* F **180** Thus] F; This Q2 **181** One...lady] Q2; *not in* F **183** bloat] blowt Q2; blunt F **187** ravel] F; rouell Q2

170 either...the devil A verb is missing. Many editions supply 'master' from the 1611 quarto. It may well be that this omission is not the compositor's fault; that Shakespeare had not found the word he wanted before he gave up the passage.

172–3 when you are...beg of you when you are contrite enough to ask God's blessing, I'll seek your blessing (i.e. resume my duty as your son).

174–6 heaven...minister it is the will of heaven, in making me the agent of their chastisement, that I myself should be punished by being the cause of Polonius's death, and that Polonius should be punished in his death at my hands. (See Introduction, pp. 54–5.) 'Scourge and minister' is a single concept (scourging officer), split by the familiar Shakespearean hendiadys. Compare 'Who made thee then a bloody minister?' asked of Clarence in *Richard III* 1.4.220, concerning the death of Plantagenet, after Clarence has said that private men must not carry out the vengeance which is the responsibility of God.

177 answer well i.e. give good reasons for.

179–80 I must be cruel...behind The remarkable change of tone in this couplet led one editor to suggest they were spoken aside. They do indeed have a meditative quality, and, in this recognition of the heaviness of his task, they resemble the couplet at the end of Act 2 – 'The time is out of joint...' His own cruelty repels him; he sees the death of Polonius as the bad beginning of a vengeance that will yet be 'worse'.

183 bloat bloated, swollen (with drink).

184 wanton wantonly, lasciviously.

185 reechy soiled and nauseating.

187 ravel...out unravel.

That I essentially am not in madness,
But mad in craft. 'Twere good you let him know,
For who that's but a queen, fair, sober, wise, 190
Would from a paddock, from a bat, a gib,
Such dear concernings hide? Who would do so?
No, in despite of sense and secrecy,
Unpeg the basket on the house's top,
Let the birds fly, and like the famous ape, 195
To try conclusions, in the basket creep
And break your own neck down.

GERTRUDE Be thou assured, if words be made of breath,
And breath of life, I have no life to breathe
What thou hast said to me. 200

HAMLET I must to England, you know that?

GERTRUDE Alack,
I had forgot. 'Tis so concluded on.

HAMLET [There's letters sealed, and my two schoolfellows,
Whom I will trust as I will adders fanged,
They bear the mandate. They must sweep my way 205
And marshal me to knavery. Let it work,
For 'tis the sport to have the engineer
Hoist with his own petar, an't shall go hard
But I will delve one yard below their mines

189 mad] Q2; made F **201–2** Alack / I...on.] *Capell*; Alack...forgot. / Tis...on. Q2; Alacke...on. F **203–11** There's letters...meet] Q2; *not in* F

189 in craft by design.

189–92 'Twere good...concernings hide Sarcastic. A respectable queen, as you consider yourself to be, has of course no reason to keep a secret from her loathsome husband.

191 paddock frog or toad.

191 gib tom-cat (an abbreviation of 'Gilbert'; the 'g' is hard).

193 secrecy discretion.

194–7 Unpeg...neck down Oddly enough, there is no record of this fable. It more or less explains itself, however. An ape takes a birdcage onto a roof; he opens the door and the birds fly out. In order to imitate them, he gets into the basket, jumps out and, instead of flying, falls to the ground. It does not seem a very appropriate way of telling the queen that she will get hurt if she releases the news of Hamlet's sanity.

196 To try conclusions To test results.

197 down An intensifier – 'utterly' or 'completely'.

198–200 In the 'bad' quarto of 1603, the queen promises also to assist Hamlet in his revenge.

203–11 There's letters...meet These nine lines are not found in F. It is argued in the Introduction (pp. 14–19) that their removal is part of a revision by Shakespeare of the later part of the play. (1) Hamlet's plan to postpone his revenge, it is suggested, seemed too definite; (2) Hamlet has had no way of learning of the king's plan to send Rosencrantz and Guildenstern with him to England; (3) the determination to kill Rosencrantz and Guildenstern does not accord with 5.2.6–11.

205 sweep my way clear a path for me.

207 engineer one who constructs or designs military machines or contrivances, especially for use in sieges. Q2 gives it the normal spelling for the time, 'enginer'.

208 Hoist i.e. blown up.

208 petar bomb. Also 'petard'.

208 an't and it.

And blow them at the moon. Oh 'tis most sweet 210
When in one line two crafts directly meet.]
This man shall set me packing.
I'll lug the guts into the neighbour room.
Mother, good night. Indeed, this counsellor
Is now most still, most secret, and most grave, 215
Who was in life a foolish prating knave.
Come sir, to draw toward an end with you.
Good night mother.
Exit Hamlet tugging in Polonius; [*Gertrude remains*]

[4.1] *Enter* CLAUDIUS *with* ROSENCRANTZ *and* GUILDENSTERN

CLAUDIUS There's matter in these sighs, these profound heaves.
You must translate, 'tis fit we understand them.
Where is your son?
GERTRUDE [Bestow this place on us a little while.]
[*Exeunt Rosencrantz and Guildenstern*]
Ah mine own lord, what have I seen tonight! 5
CLAUDIUS What, Gertrude? How does Hamlet?
GERTRUDE Mad as the sea and wind, when both contend
Which is the mightier. In his lawless fit,
Behind the arras hearing something stir,
Whips out his rapier, cries 'A rat, a rat!', 10
And in this brainish apprehension kills
The unseen good old man.
CLAUDIUS Oh heavy deed!

216 foolish] F; most foolish Q2 **218** SD *Exit...Polonius*] F; *Exit* Q2 **218** SD *Gertrude remains*] *following Wilson; not in* Q2, F **Act 4, Scene 1** 4.1] Q 1676 **0** SD] *Wilson (substantially); Eenter King, and Queene, with Rosencraus and Guyldensterne* Q2; *Enter King* F **1** matter] Q2; matters F **4** Bestow...while] Q2; *not in* F **4** SD] Q 1676; *not in* Q2, F **5** mine own] Q2; my good F **7** sea] Q2; Seas F **10** Whips...cries] Q2; He whips his Rapier out, and cries F **11** this] Q2; his F

211 in one line The image is of the mine and the countermine.

212 This man...packing This death will make them send me off immediately.

217 draw...with you conclude our discourse.

Act 4, Scene 1

0 SD The 1676 quarto, and Rowe, begin a new act at this point and everyone agrees with Johnson that the division is 'not very happy'. There should be no division of any kind, and I follow Dover Wilson in seeing the action as continuous. Gertrude remains on stage, and Claudius enters to her. Q2 gives a re-entry for the queen. The Folio makes clear the continuity of the action. F also cuts out the awkward entry of Rosencrantz and Guildenstern and their immediate dismissal by the queen. I preserve the traditional act and scene numbering to avoid confusion in references, although a number of editors, including J. Q. Adams, have manfully gone against the tide and continued Act 3.

11 brainish headstrong, obsessive.

It had been so with us had we been there.
His liberty is full of threats to all,
To you yourself, to us, to everyone. 15
Alas, how shall this bloody deed be answered?
It will be laid to us, whose providence
Should have kept short, restrained, and out of haunt,
This mad young man. But so much was our love,
We would not understand what was most fit, 20
But like the owner of a foul disease,
To keep it from divulging, let it feed
Even on the pith of life. Where is he gone?

GERTRUDE To draw apart the body he hath killed,
O'er whom his very madness, like some ore 25
Among a mineral of metals base,
Shows itself pure; a weeps for what is done.

CLAUDIUS Oh Gertrude, come away!
The sun no sooner shall the mountains touch
But we will ship him hence, and this vile deed 30
We must with all our majesty and skill
Both countenance and excuse. Ho, Guildenstern!

Enter Rosencrantz and Guildenstern

Friends both, go join you with some further aid.
Hamlet in madness hath Polonius slain,
And from his mother's closet hath he dragged him. 35
Go seek him out, speak fair, and bring the body
Into the chapel. I pray you haste in this.

Exeunt Rosencrantz and Guildenstern

Come Gertrude, we'll call up our wisest friends
And let them know both what we mean to do
And what's untimely done. 40
[Whose whisper o'er the world's diameter,

22 let] Q2; let's F 27 a] Q2; He F 35 mother's closet] Q2; Mother Clossets F 35 dragged] drag'd F; dreg'd Q2 37 SD] *Rowe; Exit Gent.* F; *not in* Q2 39 And] Q2; To F 41–4 Whose whisper...air] Q2; *not in* F

16 **answered** accounted for.

17 **providence** forethought and provision.

18 **kept short** restricted.

18 **out of haunt** away from public resort.

22 **divulging** being generally known.

25–7 **his very madness...pure** What Gertrude is trying to say is that even in his madness there was a streak of pure feeling; but the simile is confused.

26 **a mineral** the contents of a mine.

32 **countenance** accept. 'majesty' will 'countenance' and 'skill' will 'excuse'.

40 The last half of the line is lost. See next note. Capell's ingenious suggestion 'so haply slander' is supplied in most editions.

41–4 This passage is not found in F. Its sententious vein relates it to the cuts in 1.1 and 1.4. The view that this is one of the passages marked by Shakespeare for deletion in his MS. is supported by

As level as the cannon to his blank,
Transports his poisoned shot, may miss our name
And hit the woundless air.] Oh come away,
My soul is full of discord and dismay. 45

Exeunt

[4.2] *Enter* HAMLET

HAMLET Safely stowed.
GENTLEMEN (*Within*) Hamlet! Lord Hamlet!
HAMLET But soft, what noise? Who calls on Hamlet? Oh here they come.

Enter ROSENCRANTZ *and* GUILDENSTERN

ROSENCRANTZ What have you done my lord with the dead body? 5
HAMLET Compounded it with dust whereto 'tis kin.
ROSENCRANTZ Tell us where 'tis, that we may take it thence and bear it to the chapel.
HAMLET Do not believe it.
ROSENCRANTZ Believe what? 10
HAMLET That I can keep your counsel and not mine own. Besides, to be demanded of a sponge, what replication should be made by the son of a king?
ROSENCRANTZ Take you me for a sponge my lord?
HAMLET Ay sir, that soaks up the king's countenance, his rewards, his 15 authorities. But such officers do the king best service in the end: he keeps them like an ape in the corner of his jaw, first mouthed

Act 4, Scene 2 4.2] *Pope* 0 SD] F; *Enter Hamlet, Rosencraus, and others* Q2 2 GENTLEMEN...Lord Hamlet] F; *not in* Q2 3 But soft] Q2; *not in* F 6 Compounded] F; Compound Q2 17 ape] F; apple Q2

Wilson's suggestion (*MSH*, p. 30) that the upper arm of Shakespeare's deletion mark (a large square bracket in the margin) has scored through the last half of 40. See Introduction, pp. 11–12.

42 level directly aimed.

42 blank target.

44 woundless invulnerable.

Act 4, Scene 2

3 soft be cautious. See 3.1.88.

6 Compounded Mixed. Compare Sonnet 71, 'When I...compounded am with clay'. All Hamlet has done is put the body in a dusty place.

11 keep...mine own To keep counsel is to maintain silence about one's judgements and intentions. Hamlet's riddling remark hints that he knows the secrets of Rosencrantz and Guildenstern but is not revealing his own.

11–12 to be demanded of if one is interrogated by.

12 replication formal response.

15 countenance favour.

17 like an ape as an ape does. Q1 reads 'as an Ape doth nuttes'. Q2's 'apple' is a misreading based on a misunderstanding.

to be last swallowed. When he needs what you have gleaned, it is but squeezing you, and, sponge, you shall be dry again.

ROSENCRANTZ I understand you not my lord. 20

HAMLET I am glad of it, a knavish speech sleeps in a foolish ear.

ROSENCRANTZ My lord, you must tell us where the body is, and go with us to the king.

HAMLET The body is with the king, but the king is not with the body. The king is a thing – 25

GUILDENSTERN A thing my lord?

HAMLET Of nothing. Bring me to him. Hide fox, and all after!

Exeunt

[4.3] *Enter* CLAUDIUS, *and two or three*

CLAUDIUS I have sent to seek him, and to find the body.
How dangerous is it that this man goes loose,
Yet must not we put the strong law on him;
He's loved of the distracted multitude,
Who like not in their judgement, but their eyes; 5
And where 'tis so, th'offender's scourge is weighed,
But never the offence. To bear all smooth and even,
This sudden sending him away must seem
Deliberate pause. Diseases desperate grown

27 Hide...after] F; *not in* Q2 Act 4, Scene 3 4.3] *Pope* 0 SD] *Enter King, and two or three* Q2; *Enter King* F 7 never] Q2; neerer F

21 a knavish...ear you are too much of a fool to understand my insults.

24 The body...with the body As J. Johnson and N. Alexander have argued (see the latter's *Poison, Play and Duel*, p. 177) this is a riddling reference to the much-debated theory of the king's two bodies, natural and politic, made famous in Kantorowicz's book (*The King's Two Bodies*, 1957). Claudius has a body, but the kingship of Denmark is not inherent in *that* body. Hamlet does not believe in kingship as an abstraction, as did those like Plowden, who stressed the importance of the Body Politic. He believes fiercely in kings as rightful kings, true royal persons. This king is 'a thing of nothing'.

27 Hide fox...after Q2 omits. Hamlet runs out followed by the others. The reference is presumably to a children's game of chase or hide-and-seek.

Act 4, Scene 3

0 SD *two or three* So Q2; F makes Claudius enter alone. This is surely part of the book-keeper's economy drive. Compare notes to 3.2.312 SD, 4.5.1 etc. Unfortunately this totally changes Claudius's considered and calculated remarks to his councillors into a self-communing. This speech is part of the 'countenance and excuse' mentioned in 4.1.32.

4 distracted disordered, confused.

5 their eyes i.e. by appearances.

6–7 th'offender's scourge...offence more attention is paid to the criminal's sufferings than to his crime.

9 pause consideration, reflection (Schmidt, comparing *Lucrece* 277: 'Sad pause and deep regards beseems the sage').

9–10 Diseases...relieved Proverbial; Tilley D357.

By desperate appliance are relieved, 10
Or not at all.

Enter ROSENCRANTZ

How now, what hath befallen?

ROSENCRANTZ Where the dead body is bestowed, my lord,
We cannot get from him.

CLAUDIUS But where is he?

ROSENCRANTZ Without, my lord, guarded, to know your pleasure.

CLAUDIUS Bring him before us.

ROSENCRANTZ Ho! bring in my lord. 15

Enter HAMLET *and* GUILDENSTERN

CLAUDIUS Now Hamlet, where's Polonius?

HAMLET At supper.

CLAUDIUS At supper? Where?

HAMLET Not where he eats, but where a is eaten. A certain convocation of politic worms are e'en at him. Your worm is your only emperor 20 for diet: we fat all creatures else to fat us, and we fat ourselves for maggots. Your fat king and your lean beggar is but variable service, two dishes, but to one table; that's the end.

CLAUDIUS Alas, alas.

HAMLET A man may fish with the worm that hath eat of a king, and 25 eat of the fish that hath fed of that worm.

CLAUDIUS What dost thou mean by this?

HAMLET Nothing but to show you how a king may go a progress through the guts of a beggar.

CLAUDIUS Where is Polonius? 30

HAMLET In heaven, send thither to see. If your messenger find him not

11 SD] F; *Enter Rosencraus and all the rest* Q2 15 Ho! bring] How, bring Q2; Hoa, *Guildensterne*? Bring F 15 my] F; the Q2 15 SD] F; *They enter* Q2 19 a is] Q2; he is F 20 politic] Q2; *not in* F 21 ourselves] Q2; our selfe F 23 two] Q2; to F 24–6 CLAUDIUS Alas...that worm] Q2; *not in* F 27 SH CLAUDIUS] *King.* F; *King. King.* Q2

11 SD *Enter* ROSENCRANTZ Q2's addition '*and all the rest*' must have struck the playhouse scribe as contradicting '*They enter*' at 15. As usual, he reduced the crowd, and he made Rosencrantz call for Guildenstern at 15. I accept F's view that Guildenstern remains guarding Hamlet.

19 **where a is eaten** Compare 3.3.73. Presumably Shakespeare intended the syncope which nowadays we would write as 'he's'.

19–21 **convocation...diet** Hamlet is punning on the Diet (or assembly) of Worms (the city on the Rhine). The most famous meeting of the Diet was that called by the emperor, Charles V, in 1521, before which Luther appeared to justify his doctrines.

20 **politic worms** 'such worms as might breed in a politician's corpse' (Dowden). As the worm insinuates itself into the privacy of the body, it resembles Polonius's politic espionage.

22 **variable** interchangeable, i.e. they may be different dishes, but they are both served to the one table.

28 **progress** journey of state by the sovereign through his dominions.

there, seek him i'th'other place yourself. But if indeed you find him
not within this month, you shall nose him as you go up the stairs
into the lobby.

CLAUDIUS Go seek him there. 35

HAMLET A will stay till you come.

[*Exeunt Attendants*]

CLAUDIUS Hamlet, this deed, for thine especial safety,
Which we do tender, as we dearly grieve
For that which thou hast done, must send thee hence
With fiery quickness. Therefore prepare thyself. 40
The bark is ready and the wind at help,
Th'associates tend, and everything is bent
For England.

HAMLET For England?

CLAUDIUS Ay Hamlet.

HAMLET Good.

CLAUDIUS So is it if thou knew'st our purposes.

HAMLET I see a cherub that sees them. But come, for England! Farewell 45
dear mother.

CLAUDIUS Thy loving father, Hamlet.

HAMLET My mother. Father and mother is man and wife, man and wife
is one flesh, and so, my mother. Come, for England. *Exit*

CLAUDIUS Follow him at foot, tempt him with speed aboard. 50
Delay it not, I'll have him hence tonight.
Away, for everything is sealed and done
That else leans on th'affair. Pray you make haste.

[*Exeunt Rosencrantz and Guildenstern*]

And England, if my love thou hold'st at aught,
As my great power thereof may give thee sense, 55
Since yet thy cicatrice looks raw and red

32 if indeed] Q2; indeed, if F 33 within this month] Q2; this moneth F 36 A will] Q2; He will F 36 you] Q2; ye F 36 SD] *Capell; not in* Q2, F 37 for thine] Q2; of thine, for thine F 40 With...quickness] F; *not in* Q2 42 is] Q2; at F 45 them] Q2; him F 49 and so] F; so Q2 50 foot, tempt] *Rowe*; foote, / Tempt Q2, F 53 SD] *Theobald*[2]; *not in* Q2, F

34 **the lobby** A main corridor or ante-room. Compare 'here in the lobby' in 2.2.159.

38 **tender** have regard for.

42 **tend** attend.

42 **bent** in a state of readiness.

45 **I see a cherub...them** A mischievous 'antic' speech in which Hamlet both hints his own knowledge and warns Claudius that heaven is watching him.

50 **at foot** close at heel.

53 **leans on** appertains to.

54 **England** the king of England.

54 **at aught** at any value.

55 **thereof...sense** may give you a feeling of the importance of valuing my love.

56 **cicatrice** scar.

After the Danish sword, and thy free awe
Pays homage to us – thou mayst not coldly set
Our sovereign process, which imports at full,
By letters congruing to that effect, 60
The present death of Hamlet. Do it England,
For like the hectic in my blood he rages,
And thou must cure me. Till I know 'tis done,
Howe'er my haps, my joys were ne'er begun. *Exit*

[4.4] *Enter* FORTINBRAS *with his army over the stage*

FORTINBRAS Go captain, from me greet the Danish king.
Tell him that by his licence, Fortinbras
Craves the conveyance of a promised march
Over his kingdom. You know the rendezvous.
If that his majesty would aught with us, 5
We shall express our duty in his eye,
And let him know so.

CAPTAIN I will do't, my lord.

FORTINBRAS Go softly on.

[*Exit Fortinbras, with the army*]

[*Enter* HAMLET, ROSENCRANTZ, *etc.*

HAMLET Good sir, whose powers are these?
CAPTAIN They are of Norway sir. 10
HAMLET How purposed sir I pray you?
CAPTAIN Against some part of Poland.

60 congruing] Q2; coniuring F 64 were ne'er begun] F; will nere begin Q2 Act 4, Scene 4 4.4] *Pope* 0 SD] Q2; *Enter Fortinbras with an Armie* F 3 Craves] Q2, Q1; Claimes F 8 softly] Q2; safely F 8 SD] *Theobald*[2]; *not in* Q2; *Exit* F 8.1 SD–66 Enter HAMLET...worth. *Exit*] Q2; *not in* F

57 free uncompelled.

58 coldly set regard with indifference.

59 process writ.

60 congruing agreeing. So Q2. 'congrue' is a word unique to Shakespeare, occurring only here and in the bad quarto of *Henry V*. The F scribe was understandably shy of it.

61 present immediate.

62 hectic chronic fever.

64 haps fortunes.

Act 4, Scene 4

3 conveyance grant. See 2.2.76–80. Fortinbras asks for the formal execution of a previous promise. Many editors think he is asking for an escort.

6 duty humble respect.

6 in his eye in his presence.

8 softly circumspectly (being careful not to give offence). Compare Bacon's essay on Dissimulation, 'like the going softly, by one that cannot well see'.

8 SD–66 *Enter* HAMLET... The whole of the remainder of this scene is omitted in the Folio. This is the most extensive of the 'cuts'. See Introduction, pp. 16–19.

9 powers forces, troops.

HAMLET Who commands them sir?
CAPTAIN The nephew to old Norway, Fortinbras.
HAMLET Goes it against the main of Poland sir, 15
Or for some frontier?
CAPTAIN Truly to speak, and with no addition,
We go to gain a little patch of ground
That hath in it no profit but the name.
To pay five ducats, five, I would not farm it, 20
Nor will it yield to Norway or the Pole
A ranker rate, should it be sold in fee.
HAMLET Why then the Polack never will defend it.
CAPTAIN Yes, it is already garrisoned.
HAMLET Two thousand souls and twenty thousand ducats 25
Will not debate the question of this straw.
This is th'impostume of much wealth and peace,
That inward breaks, and shows no cause without
Why the man dies. I humbly thank you sir.
CAPTAIN God buy you sir. [*Exit*]
ROSENCRANTZ Will't please you go my lord? 30
HAMLET I'll be with you straight; go a little before.
[*Exeunt all but Hamlet*]
How all occasions do inform against me,
And spur my dull revenge! What is a man
If his chief good and market of his time
Be but to sleep and feed? A beast, no more. 35
Sure he that made us with such large discourse,
Looking before and after, gave us not
That capability and god-like reason
To fust in us unused. Now whether it be
Bestial oblivion, or some craven scruple 40
Of thinking too precisely on th'event –
A thought which quartered hath but one part wisdom
And ever three parts coward – I do not know
Why yet I live to say this thing's to do,

30 SD *Exit*] *Dyce; Exit Captain* / *Capell; not in* Q2   31 SD] *Dyce, following Rowe; not in* Q2

15 **main** whole.
17 **addition** exaggeration.
22 **ranker** more abundant.
22 **in fee** i.e. outright, without restrictions.
26 **Will not debate the question** Are not enough to fight out the dispute.
27 **impostume** abscess.
34 **market** profit.
36 **discourse** faculty of reasoning.
39 **fust** grow mouldy.
40 **oblivion** forgetfulness.
40 **craven** cowardly.
41 **precisely** scrupulously, pedantically.
41 **event** result, consequence.

Sith I have cause, and will, and strength, and means 45
To do't. Examples gross as earth exhort me.
Witness this army of such mass and charge,
Led by a delicate and tender prince,
Whose spirit with divine ambition puffed
Makes mouths at the invisible event, 50
Exposing what is mortal and unsure
To all that fortune, death and danger dare,
Even for an egg-shell. Rightly to be great
Is not to stir without great argument,
But greatly to find quarrel in a straw 55
When honour's at the stake. How stand I then,
That have a father killed, a mother stained,
Excitements of my reason and my blood,
And let all sleep, while to my shame I see
The imminent death of twenty thousand men, 60
That for a fantasy and trick of fame
Go to their graves like beds, fight for a plot
Whereon the numbers cannot try the cause,
Which is not tomb enough and continent
To hide the slain. Oh from this time forth, 65
My thoughts be bloody or be nothing worth. *Exit*]

45 **Sith** Since.

46 **gross** palpable, obvious.

47 **mass and charge** size and expense.

49 **puffed** inflated.

50 **Makes mouths at** Makes faces at, despises (compare 2.2.335).

52 **dare** Means little more here than 'can do'.

54 **not to stir** This should be understood as a double negative – 'not not to stir', that is, 'not a matter of refusing to stir'. Many commentators think that Hamlet is saying that it is *not* rightly to be great to stir without great argument, with the exception that when honour's at the stake, a straw is sufficient motive. This seems quite wrong. True greatness, Hamlet argues, has nothing to do with the size of the dispute, but everything to do with a willingness to act when honour is involved.

56 **at the stake** in hazard. The image is gaming, not burning, nor (as one commentator suggests) bear-baiting!

60 **twenty thousand men** In 25 above it was 20,000 ducats and only 2,000 men.

61 **trick** illusion, deceit (see 4.5.5 below). Fortinbras is enticed by a dream, and thousands must die for it. Hamlet's common sense about the absurdity of Fortinbras's venture shows the pointlessness of his envy. In the Hecuba soliloquy, Hamlet worked through his futile envy of the Player; in this soliloquy the contradiction remains unresolved.

63–5 **Whereon...slain** i.e. the plot of ground is not big enough to hold those who are to fight for it, or to bury those who are killed.

[4.5] *Enter* HORATIO, GERTRUDE *and a* GENTLEMAN

GERTRUDE I will not speak with her.
GENTLEMAN She is importunate, indeed distract;
Her mood will needs be pitied.
GERTRUDE What would she have?
GENTLEMAN She speaks much of her father, says she hears
There's tricks i'th'world, and hems, and beats her heart, 5
Spurns enviously at straws, speaks things in doubt
That carry but half sense. Her speech is nothing,
Yet the unshapèd use of it doth move
The hearers to collection. They yawn at it,
And botch the words up fit to their own thoughts, 10
Which, as her winks and nods and gestures yield them,
Indeed would make one think there might be thought,
Though nothing sure, yet much unhappily.
HORATIO 'Twere good she were spoken with, for she may strew
Dangerous conjectures in ill-breeding minds. 15
GERTRUDE Let her come in.
[*Exit Gentleman*]
(*Aside*) To my sick soul, as sin's true nature is,
Each toy seems prologue to some great amiss.
So full of artless jealousy is guilt,
It spills itself in fearing to be spilt. 20

Enter OPHELIA *distracted*

Act 4, Scene 5 4.5] *Pope* 0 SD] Q2; *Enter Queene and Horatio* F 2, 4 SH GENTLEMAN] *Gent.* Q2; *Hor.* F 9 yawn] Q2; ayme F 12 might] Q2; would F 14 SH HORATIO] *Hora.* Q2; *Qu.* F 16 GERTRUDE Let her come in.] *Hanmer (substantially)*: Q2 *prints* Let her come in. *as the conclusion of Horatio's speech.* F *conflates the speeches of Horatio and Gertrude* 16 SD] *Hanmer; not in* Q2, F 17 SD *Aside*] *Capell; not in* Q2, F 20 SD] F; *Enter Ophelia* Q2 *(at 16)*

Act 4, Scene 5

1–15 In order to save on characters, F gives the Gentleman's speeches to Horatio, and Horatio's to Gertrude. This greatly coarsens the way Ophelia's madness is introduced.

3 **Her mood...pitied** Her state of mind must necessarily cause pity.

5 **hems** makes the noise 'H'm'.

6 **Spurns...straws** 'takes offence angrily at trifles' (Kittredge).

6 **in doubt** of uncertain meaning.

9 **to collection** to infer a meaning.

9 **yawn** gape with surprise. Compare *Coriolanus* 3.2.11, 'to yawn, be still, and wonder'.

10 **botch...thoughts** patch the words up into patterns conforming to their own ideas. Compare the 'dangerous conjectures' feared by Horatio in 15 below.

13 **unhappily** clumsily.

15 **ill-breeding** intent on making mischief.

18 **toy** trifle.

19 **artless** unskilled, hence blundering, foolish.

19 **jealousy** suspicion.

20 **It spills...spilt** i.e. fear of detection leads to the very exposure one is trying to avert. 'spill' means 'destroy', but here has an obvious double sense with 'reveal'.

20 SD Q1 gives the famous direction: '*Enter Ofelia playing on a Lute, and her haire downe singing.*'

OPHELIA Where is the beauteous majesty of Denmark?
GERTRUDE How now Ophelia?
OPHELIA *She sings*

How should I your true love know
From another one?
By his cockle hat and staff 25
And his sandal shoon.

GERTRUDE Alas sweet lady, what imports this song?
OPHELIA Say you? Nay, pray you mark.

He is dead and gone lady, *Song*
He is dead and gone; 30
At his head a grass-green turf,
At his heels a stone.

Oho!
GERTRUDE Nay but Ophelia –
OPHELIA Pray you mark. 35

White his shrowd as the mountain snow – *Song*

Enter CLAUDIUS

GERTRUDE Alas, look here my lord.
OPHELIA Larded all with sweet flowers,
Which bewept to the grave did not go
With true-love showers. 40
CLAUDIUS How do you, pretty lady?
OPHELIA Well good dild you. They say the owl was a baker's daughter.

23 SD *She sings*] Q2; *not in* F **23–4** How...one] *as one line* Q2, F **25–6** By...shoon] *as one line* Q2, F **26** sandal] F; Sendall Q2 **29** SD *Song*] Q2; *not in* F **29–30** He...gone] *as one line* Q2, F **31–2** At...stone] *as one line* Q2, F **33** Oho!] O ho. Q2; *not in* F **36** SD *Song*] Q2 *(at 38)*; *not in* F **38** Larded all] Q2; *Larded* F, Q1 **39** grave] F; ground Q2 **41** you] Q2; ye F **42** good dild] Q2; God dil'd F

23–6 Obviously a recollection of the famous Walsingham ballad, which brings together a lonely pilgrim and a deserted lover. See the version attributed to Sir Walter Ralegh in *Poems*, ed. Latham, 1951, pp. 22–3. For the music, see Sternfeld, pp. 59–62.

25 cockle hat The pilgrim's emblem was a scallop shell, originally a sign that he had been to the shrine of St James of Compostella in Spain.

26 shoon shoes.

28 Say you?...mark i.e. 'Is that your question? Just pay attention.' Then she proceeds with the ballad, the dead father taking the place of the absent lover.

38 Larded all Decorated. F omits the extrametrical 'all'.

39 did not go It seems very likely that Ophelia inserts the 'not' into the original song, to suit the fate of Polonius.

42 good dild you God yield, or reward you. The phrase means only 'thank you'.

42 owl...baker's daughter This was recognised in the eighteenth century as a reference to a folktale in which a baker's daughter was parsimonious with the dough when a beggar asked her for bread. The beggar was Jesus, and he turned her into an owl. K. M. Briggs gives two English versions (*Dictionary of British Folk Tales*, 1970, I, 124, 443). It is indexed as A 1958.0.1 in Stith Thompson, *Motif Index of Folk Literature*, rev. edn 1955, I, 258. The tale is in Ophelia's mind as a story of transformation.

Lord, we know what we are, but know not what we may be. God be at your table.

CLAUDIUS Conceit upon her father. 45

OPHELIA Pray let's have no words of this, but when they ask you what it means, say you this –

Tomorrow is Saint Valentine's day, *Song*
All in the morning betime,
And I a maid at your window, 50
To be your Valentine.

Then up he rose and donned his clothes
And dupped the chamber door;
Let in the maid that out a maid
Never departed more. 55

CLAUDIUS Pretty Ophelia!

OPHELIA Indeed la! Without an oath I'll make an end on't.

By Gis and by Saint Charity,
Alack and fie for shame,
Young men will do't if they come to't – 60
By Cock, they are to blame.

Quoth she, 'Before you tumbled me,
You promised me to wed.'

46 Pray] Q2; Pray you F 48 SD *Song*] Q2; *not in* F 48–9 Tomorrow...betime] Q2; *as one line* F 50–1 And...Valentine] Q2; *as one line* F 52 clothes] F; close Q2 52–3 Then...door] *as one line* Q2, F 54–5 Let...more] *as one line* Q2, F 57 Indeed la!] Indeed la? F; Indeede Q2 62–3 Quoth...wed] F; *as one line* Q2

43–4 God be at your table – and bless you in *your* transformation.

45 Conceit upon her father Fanciful thoughts connected with her father.

46–7 ask you...say you this There is constant reference to a hidden meaning in Ophelia's utterances, introduced first by the Gentleman's speech, 4–13. Ophelia's 'explanations' go from one of her sadnesses to the other – from Hamlet to Polonius and back again.

48 Tomorrow is Saint Valentine's day The words of this are not known elsewhere. For Chappell's rendering of the tune traditionally given in the theatre, see the NV, and Sternfeld, pp. 62–4.

53 dupped 'dup' = do up = undo.

54–5 Let in...departed more A number of critics (including Madariaga) have supposed that Hamlet and Ophelia had had sexual relations, and some of them (including Allardyce Nicoll) thought that Ophelia was actually pregnant (and for that reason drowned herself). For most of us, Ophelia's words are intensely moving because they show her deranged mind wandering over the sexual relations which she has *not* had.

57 Indeed la! Scornful assent to Claudius's 'Pretty Ophelia!' 'la' intensifies an asseveration, as in *Coriolanus* 1.3.67. Q2 omits 'la'. F's punctuation, 'la?', indicates either a question or an exclamation.

57 Without an oath N. Alexander points to Ophelia's substitution of 'Gis' and 'Cock' for Jesus and God.

61 Cock A common 'mincing' of God. See Stow's *Survey of London*, 'Yea by cock, nay by cock, for greater oaths were spared' (Everyman edn, p. 195). Used here with an obvious double meaning.

62 tumbled had sexual intercourse with. Compare 'lie tumbling in the hay' (*Winter's Tale* 4.3.12) and 'to tumble on the bed of Ptolemy' (*Antony and Cleopatra* 1.4.17).

He answers –

So would I ha' done, by yonder sun, 65
And thou hadst not come to my bed.

CLAUDIUS How long hath she been thus?

OPHELIA I hope all will be well. We must be patient, but I cannot choose but weep to think they would lay him i'th' cold ground. My brother shall know of it, and so I thank you for your good counsel. 70 Come, my coach. Good night ladies, good night sweet ladies, good night, good night. *Exit*

CLAUDIUS Follow her close, give her good watch I pray you.
[*Exit Horatio*]

Oh this is the poison of deep grief, it springs
All from her father's death, [and now behold –] 75
Oh Gertrude, Gertrude,
When sorrows come, they come not single spies,
But in battalions. First, her father slain;
Next, your son gone, and he most violent author
Of his own just remove; the people muddied, 80
Thick and unwholesome in their thoughts and whispers
For good Polonius' death – and we have done but greenly
In hugger-mugger to inter him; poor Ophelia
Divided from herself and her fair judgement,
Without the which we are pictures, or mere beasts; 85
Last, and as much containing as all these,
Her brother is in secret come from France,
Feeds on his wonder, keeps himself in clouds,

64 He answers] Q2; *not in* F 65 ha'] F; a Q2 67 thus] Q2; this F 69 would] Q2; should F 71–2 Good...good...good...good] God...god...god...god Q2 72 SD] F; *not in* Q2 73 SD] *Theobald*[2]; *not in* Q2, F 74–6 springs / All...behold – / Oh...Gertrude,] *Steevens*[3]; *two lines of prose* Q2; springs / All...*Gertrude,* F 75 and now behold] Q2; *not in* F 78 battalions] battalians Q2; Battaliaes F 81 their] F; *not in* Q2 88 Feeds on] Q2; Keepes on F 88 his] F; this Q2

66 And If.

74–6 Oh this...Gertrude, Gertrude Q2 prints all of this as two lines of prose, which suggests a confused MS. F omits 'and now behold', creating two lines of regular verse. It seems very likely that 'and now behold' was a false start, that 'Oh, Gertrude, Gertrude' was substituted, and that once again the Q2 compositor has failed to register Shakespeare's deletion-marks.

80 muddied stirred up like muddy water.

82 greenly foolishly, as though from inexperience.

83 In hugger-mugger With secrecy. Shakespeare does not use this phrase elsewhere. He must have had at the back of his mind a passage from North's translation of Plutarch's Life of Brutus (the source of *Julius Caesar*) which had become associated with Polonius because of 3.2.91–2. Plutarch said that Antony, fearing that people might be further incensed, was anxious that Caesar's body 'should be honourably buried, and not in hugger-mugger'.

86 as much containing...these i.e. as serious as all the others together.

88 Feeds...clouds i.e. instead of finding out what has actually happened, he keeps himself in the

And wants not buzzers to infect his ear
With pestilent speeches of his father's death, 90
Wherein necessity, of matter beggared,
Will nothing stick our person to arraign
In ear and ear. O my dear Gertrude, this,
Like to a murdering piece, in many places
Gives me superfluous death. 95

A noise within

GERTRUDE Alack, what noise is this?

CLAUDIUS Attend! Where are my Swissers? Let them guard the door.

Enter a MESSENGER

What is the matter?

MESSENGER Save yourself my lord.
The ocean, overpeering of his list,
Eats not the flats with more impitious haste 100
Than young Laertes in a riotous head
O'erbears your officers. The rabble call him lord,
And, as the world were now but to begin,
Antiquity forgot, custom not known,
The ratifiers and props of every word, 105
They cry 'Choose we! Laertes shall be king.'
Caps, hands and tongues applaud it to the clouds,
'Laertes shall be king, Laertes king!'

GERTRUDE How cheerfully on the false trail they cry!

92 person] Q2; persons F **96** GERTRUDE...this?] F; *not in* Q2 **97** Attend] Q2; *not in* F **97** are] F; is Q2 **97** Swissers] Q2; *Switzers* F **97** SD] *after 95 in* Q2, F **106** They] F; The Q2

clouds of suspicion, and finds food for anger in his own uncertainty, or in what he guesses ('wonder'). This use of the noun 'wonder' is unusual in Shakespeare, though the verb is used to indicate doubt, as well as surprise and admiration.

89 buzzers rumour-mongers.

91–2 necessity...nothing stick i.e. having no evidence, they are obliged to invent and have no scruples in doing so.

93 ear and ear i.e. whispering to person after person.

94 murdering piece The name of a small cannon which was used to fire charges of small shot against infantry.

95 superfluous death i.e. kills him over and over again.

97 Swissers Swiss guards. F calls them 'Switzers'.

99 overpeering of his list rising above (literally, looking over) its boundary.

100 impitious Some think this a form of 'impetuous' but it is more likely a Shakespearean coinage = 'pitiless'.

105 ratifiers...word Tradition ('Antiquity') and custom should ratify and support everything we say.

106 'Choose we!...' The emphasis is on 'we'. The 'distracted multitude', who were supposed to 'love' Hamlet (4.3.4), have given their allegiance to Laertes, and are demanding to take over the prerogative of the electoral body which made Claudius king.

Oh this is counter, you false Danish dogs! 110

A noise within

CLAUDIUS The doors are broke.

Enter LAERTES *with others*

LAERTES Where is this king? – Sirs, stand you all without.
ALL No, let's come in.
LAERTES I pray you give me leave.
ALL We will, we will. 115
LAERTES I thank you. Keep the door.

[*Exeunt followers*]

O thou vile king,
Give me my father.
GERTRUDE Calmly, good Laertes.
LAERTES That drop of blood that's calm proclaims me bastard,
Cries cuckold to my father, brands the harlot
Even here, between the chaste unsmirchèd brow 120
Of my true mother.
CLAUDIUS What is the cause, Laertes,
That thy rebellion looks so giant-like? –
Let him go, Gertrude, do not fear our person.
There's such divinity doth hedge a king
That treason can but peep to what it would, 125
Acts little of his will. – Tell me Laertes,
Why thou art thus incensed. – Let him go Gertrude. –
Speak man.
LAERTES Where is my father?
CLAUDIUS Dead.
GERTRUDE But not by him.

110 SD *A noise within*] Q2 *(after* cry *109); Noise within* F 111 SD *Enter...others*] *placed by Capell; after* dogs *(110) in* Q2; *Enter Laertes* F *(after* 'Noise within') 112 this king? – Sirs] this King? sirs Q2; the King, sirs? F 116 SD] *Kittredge (substantially); not in* Q2, F; *Exeunt / Theobald*[2] 118 that's calm] Q2; that calmes F 128 Where is] Q2; Where's F

110 counter...dogs 'Hounds run *counter*, when they trace the trail backwards' (Johnson).

111 SD F omits '*with others*' in conformity with its consistent policy in reducing the number of extras who would need to be costumed etc. Laertes' followers are kept firmly outside the door.

119–20 brands the harlot...brow See note to 3.4.44. Laertes, like Hamlet previously, does not imply that harlots were so branded. The forehead is the symbolic showplace of chastity and unchastity. See *Comedy of Errors* 2.2.136, 'tear the stained skin off my harlot brow'.

120 between in the middle of.

120 unsmirchèd clean, unstained.

124 hedge surround with a defensive hedge or fence.

125 peep...would Continues the image of the hedge. Treason can only peer through, and cannot carry out its plans.

CLAUDIUS Let him demand his fill.
LAERTES How came he dead? I'll not be juggled with. 130
To hell allegiance, vows to the blackest devil,
Conscience and grace to the profoundest pit!
I dare damnation. To this point I stand,
That both the worlds I give to negligence,
Let come what comes, only I'll be revenged 135
Most throughly for my father.
CLAUDIUS Who shall stay you?
LAERTES My will, not all the world.
And for my means, I'll husband them so well,
They shall go far with little.
CLAUDIUS Good Laertes,
If you desire to know the certainty 140
Of your dear father, is't writ in your revenge
That, soopstake, you will draw both friend and foe,
Winner and loser?
LAERTES None but his enemies.
CLAUDIUS Will you know them then?
LAERTES To his good friends thus wide I'll ope my arms, 145
And like the kind life-rendering pelican,
Repast them with my blood.
CLAUDIUS Why now you speak
Like a good child and a true gentleman.
That I am guiltless of your father's death,
And am most sensibly in grief for it, 150
It shall as level to your judgement pierce

137 world] F; worlds Q2 139–40 Good...certainty] F; *as one line* Q2 141 father] Q2; Fathers death F 141 is't] Q2; if F 146 pelican] Q2; Politician F 150 sensibly] Q2; sensible F 151 pierce] F; peare Q2

130 juggled with cheated or deceived as by a juggler or trickster.

132 grace holy disposition.

133–4 I dare damnation...negligence See Introduction, p. 55.

134 give to negligence i.e. disregard, despise.

137 My will,...world 'by my will' is an expression of determination, as in *Love's Labour's Lost* 2.1.99, 'Not for the world, fair madam, by my will'. It is, however, just possible that Laertes is abbreviating the oath 'God's my will'; compare *As You Like It* 4.3.17, 'Od's my will.'

138–9 And for my means...little An interesting comment on the need to be fully equipped and prepared for an act of revenge.

142 soopstake This form, found in both Q2 and F, is evidently what Shakespeare wrote. It is short for 'swoopstake', an alternative form of 'sweepstake', the act of a gambler in taking all stakes at one go.

142 draw draw in.

146 kind...pelican The pelican was supposed to pierce its breast with its bill, and allow its young to feed on the blood.

147 repast feed.

151 level See 4.1.42.

151 pierce So F. Q2 reads 'peare', which Dr Johnson and many later editors have supposed to be an aphetic form of 'appear'. 'pierce' is a stronger and more Shakespearean word, often used for a

As day does to your eye.

A noise within: 'Let her come in'

LAERTES How now, what noise is that?

Enter OPHELIA

O heat dry up my brains, tears seven times salt
Burn out the sense and virtue of mine eye! 155
By heaven, thy madness shall be paid with weight
Till our scale turn the beam. O rose of May,
Dear maid, kind sister, sweet Ophelia –
O heavens, is't possible a young maid's wits
Should be as mortal as an old man's life? 160
Nature is fine in love, and where 'tis fine,
It sends some precious instance of itself
After the thing it loves.

OPHELIA They bore him bare-faced on the bier *Song*
Hey non nonny, nonny, hey nonny, 165
And in his grave rained many a tear –
Fare you well my dove.

LAERTES Hadst thou thy wits, and didst persuade revenge,
It could not move thus.

OPHELIA You must sing a-down a-down, and you call him a-down-a. 170
Oh how the wheel becomes it. It is the false steward that stole his master's daughter.

152 SD] *A noise within. Let her come in* F; *A noyse within* Q2 *(giving* let her come in *to Laertes)* **153** SD *Enter* OPHELIA] Q2, F *(after 152* SD*)* **156** with weight] Q2; by waight F **157** Till] F; Tell Q2 **157** turn] Q2; turnes F **160** an old] F; a poore Q2 **161–3** Nature...loves] F; *not in* Q2 **164** SD *Song*] Q2; *not in* F **165** Hey...nonny] F; *not in* Q2 **166** in] Q2; on F **166** rained] rain'd Q2; raines F **168–9** Hadst...thus] Q2; *as prose* F **170** a-down a-down] a downe a downe Q2; downe a-downe F

communication to the senses, as in the Epilogue to *The Tempest* ('prayer, / Which pierces so...'). Claudius's meaning is 'My innocence will come as sharply home to your judgement as daylight strikes the eye.' I assume Shakespeare wrote 'pearce', and that Q2's 'peare' is a misprint.

155 sense and virtue sensitivity and efficacy.

161–3 Nature...loves Love refines our nature, and this refined nature sends part of itself after the loved one. That is, Ophelia has parted with some of her wits to send to Polonius. This conceit, too absurd even for Laertes, is not in Q2, and is found only in F. Is it possible that for once the Q2 compositor noted a deletion mark overlooked by the playhouse scribe?

164–5 They bore him...hey nonny Ophelia sings a lament, but gives as burden the 'hey nonny no' of a love ditty. Perhaps that is why she then says 'You must sing a-down a-down.'

170 a-down a-down A popular refrain. Two songs, printed in 1600, which use it, have associations suitable for Ophelia's plight. The song at the end of Dekker's *Shoemakers' Holiday* begins 'cold's the wind, and wet's the rain'. 'Let's sing a dirge for St Hugh's soul, / And down it merrily. / Down a down, hey down a down...' In *England's Helicon* (Q2r) is a song about the miseries of love, which maidens are better to avoid; it begins 'Hey down a down did Dian sing.'

171 wheel Unexplained; 'refrain', 'spinning-wheel' and 'the wheel of Fortune' have been suggested.

171–2 It is the false steward...daughter In view of Laertes' next remark, indicating that

LAERTES This nothing's more than matter.

OPHELIA There's rosemary, that's for remembrance – pray you, love, remember – and there is pansies, that's for thoughts. 175

LAERTES A document in madness, thoughts and remembrance fitted.

OPHELIA There's fennel for you, and columbines. There's rue for you, and here's some for me; we may call it herb of grace a Sundays. Oh you must wear your rue with a difference. There's a daisy. I would give you some violets, but they withered all when my father 180 died. They say a made a good end.

[*Sings*]

For bonny sweet Robin is all my joy.

LAERTES Thought and affliction, passion, hell itself,
She turns to favour and to prettiness.

OPHELIA And will a not come again? *Song* 185
And will a not come again?
No, no, he is dead,
Go to thy death-bed,
He never will come again.

174 pray you] Q2; Pray F 175 pansies] Pancies Q2; Paconcies F 178 herb of grace] Q2; Herbe-Grace F 179 Oh you must] F; you may Q2 181 a made] Q2; he made F 182 SD *Sings*] *Capell; not in* Q2, F 183 affliction] F; afflictions Q2 185, 186 will a not] Q2; will he not F 185 SD *Song*] Q2; *not in* F 187–8 No...death-bed] *as one line* Q2, F

Ophelia's disconnected remarks have a special significance, it is embarrassing that no one has been able to throw light on the false steward.

174–5 pray...remember Ophelia obviously gives the rosemary and pansies to Laertes, though (obviously again) Laertes merges in her mind with Hamlet. To whom, Claudius or Gertrude, she gives the fennel and columbines and to whom the rue is much debated. See the long discussion in Jenkins, pp. 536–42.

175 pansies...thoughts The name comes from the French, *pensées*. As elsewhere in this scene, 'thoughts' has the special meaning of *sad* thoughts, melancholy.

176 A document...fitted 'document', not used elsewhere by Shakespeare, means 'instruction'. Ophelia finds a lesson in flowers, and in her interpretation of them Laertes finds a lesson in madness, for a mad person's 'thoughts' are continually 'fitted' (connected) with the 'remembrance' of dark happenings.

177 fennel Widely associated with flattery (see Robert Nares's *Glossary* (1822)). But E. Le Comte points out (*TLS* 22 Oct. 1982) that as a gift to Claudius fennel is appropriate because it was a food much liked by serpents (see *Paradise Lost*, IX, 581).

177 columbines For ingratitude and infidelity (see Nares, *Glossary*, and Jenkins, p. 539).

177 rue For sorrow and repentance.

178 herb of grace Another name for rue (also herb-grace, herby-grass).

179 with a difference A term in heraldry; a mark to distinguish a coat of arms from that of another member or branch of the family.

179 daisy No special symbolism, but, as N. Alexander says, daisies and violets are flowers of springtime and love.

182 bonny sweet Robin Sternfeld gives the music (pp. 68–78) and says 'Bonny Robin songs deal with lovers, unfaithfulness and extra-marital affairs' (58); 'the popularity of this simple ditty excelled by far that of "Greensleeves"'. 'Bonny Robin' is one of the songs which the mad Gaoler's Daughter in *Two Noble Kinsmen* says she can sing (4.1.108). Harry Morris (*PMLA* 73 (1958), 601–3) believes Robin to be a name for the male sex-organ. His best evidence is that one of the common names for *arum maculatum* (lords-and-ladies, cuckoo-pint) is wake-robin.

183 Thought Melancholy.

184 favour beauty.

185 And will a not come again? The words of this song are not otherwise known. The tune traditional in the theatre is given in NV and in Sternfeld, pp. 67–9.

His beard was as white as snow, 190
All flaxen was his poll,
He is gone, he is gone,
And we cast away moan,
God-a-mercy on his soul.

And of all Christian souls, I pray God. God buy you. *Exit* 195

LAERTES Do you see this, O God?

CLAUDIUS Laertes, I must commune with your grief,
Or you deny me right. Go but apart,
Make choice of whom your wisest friends you will,
And they shall hear and judge 'twixt you and me. 200
If by direct or by collateral hand
They find us touched, we will our kingdom give,
Our crown, our life, and all that we call ours,
To you in satisfaction. But if not,
Be you content to lend your patience to us, 205
And we shall jointly labour with your soul
To give it due content.

LAERTES Let this be so.
His means of death, his obscure funeral,
No trophy, sword, nor hatchment o'er his bones,
No noble rite, nor formal ostentation, 210
Cry to be heard, as 'twere from heaven to earth,
That I must call't in question.

CLAUDIUS So you shall.
And where th'offence is, let the great axe fall.
I pray you go with me.

Exeunt

190 was as] Q2; as F **191** All flaxen] F; Flaxen Q2 **191** poll] *Hanmer;* pole Q2, F **192–3** He...moan] *as one line* Q2, F **194** God-a-mercy] God a mercy Q2; Gramercy F **194–5** God-a-mercy...souls] F; *as one line* Q2 **195** Christian] F; Christians Q2 **195** I pray God] F; *not in* Q2 **195** buy you] Q2; buy ye F **195** SD *Exit*] *Exeunt Ophelia* F; *not in* Q2 **196** you see this] F; you this Q2 **196** O God] Q2; you Gods F **197** commune] Q2; common F **208** funeral] Q2; buriall F **210** rite] F; right Q2 **212** call't] Q2; call F

191 flaxen...poll i.e. white-haired.

193 cast away moan i.e. lamenting is useless.

195 SD *Exit.* J. P. Kemble here provided an exit for Gertrude too; a sensible innovation, which became customary.

197 commune Accent on first syllable. I think the meaning here is 'converse', as usually in Shakespeare, not 'share' or 'participate' as Boswell and others suggest. Claudius is insisting on 'getting through' to Laertes' grief, and informing him of the true state of affairs.

199 whom whichever of.

201 collateral indirect.

202 touched concerned, implicated.

208 His means of death The way he died.

208 obscure accent on first syllable.

209 trophy memorial (such as the insignia of his rank and office).

209 hatchment Coat of arms placed over the dead; usually a diamond-shaped tablet.

212 call't in question demand an examination.

[4.6] *Enter* HORATIO *with an* ATTENDANT

HORATIO What are they that would speak with me?
ATTENDANT Seafaring men sir, they say they have letters for you.
HORATIO Let them come in.

[*Exit Attendant*]

I do not know from what part of the world
I should be greeted, if not from Lord Hamlet. 5

Enter SAILORS

1 SAILOR God bless you sir.
HORATIO Let him bless thee too.
1 SAILOR A shall sir, and please him. There's a letter for you sir, it came from th'ambassador that was bound for England, if your name be Horatio, as I am let to know it is. 10

HORATIO (*Reads the letter*) 'Horatio, when thou shalt have overlooked this, give these fellows some means to the king; they have letters for him. Ere we were two days old at sea, a pirate of very warlike appointment gave us chase. Finding ourselves too slow of sail, we put on a compelled valour, and in the grapple I boarded them. On 15 the instant they got clear of our ship, so I alone became their prisoner. They have dealt with me like thieves of mercy, but they knew what they did: I am to do a good turn for them. Let the king have the letters I have sent, and repair thou to me with as much speed as thou wouldest fly death. I have words to speak in thine 20 ear will make thee dumb, yet are they much too light for the bore of the matter. These good fellows will bring thee where I am. Rosencrantz and Guildenstern hold their course for England. Of them I have much to tell thee. Farewell.

He that thou knowest thine, 25
Hamlet.'

Act 4, Scene 6 4.6] *Capell* 0 SD *an* ATTENDANT] F*; others* Q2 2 SH ATTENDANT] *P. Alexander; Gent* Q2*; Ser.* F 2 Seafaring men] Q2; Saylors F 3 SD] *P. Alexander; Exit Ser./ Hanmer; not in* Q2, F 5 SD SAILORS] *Saylers* Q2*; Saylor* F 8 A shall] Q2; Hee shall F 8 and] Q2; and't F 8 came] Q2; comes F 9 ambassador] Q2; Ambassadours F 11 SD *Reads the letter*] F *(as separate line); not in* Q2 15 valour, and in] Q2; *Valour. In* F 18 good turn] F; turne Q2 20 speed] Q2; hast F 20 thine: Q2; your F 21 bore] F; bord Q2

Act 4, Scene 6

4 **what part of the world** i.e. what distant part of the world (involving communication by sea).

8 **and please** if it please.

17 **thieves of mercy** thieves with merciful hearts.

17–18 **they knew what they did** i.e. their mercy was calculated.

21–2 **for the bore of the matter** for the gravity of the substance they speak of. The image is from artillery – the words are too small for the bore of the cannon.

Come, I will give you way for these your letters,
And do't the speedier that you may direct me
To him from whom you brought them.

Exeunt

[4.7] *Enter* CLAUDIUS *and* LAERTES

CLAUDIUS Now must your conscience my acquittance seal,
And you must put me in your heart for friend,
Sith you have heard, and with a knowing ear,
That he which hath your noble father slain
Pursued my life.

LAERTES It well appears. But tell me 5
Why you proceeded not against these feats,
So crimeful and so capital in nature,
As by your safety, wisdom, all things else,
You mainly were stirred up.

CLAUDIUS Oh for two special reasons,
Which may to you perhaps seem much unsinewed, 10
But yet to me they're strong. The queen his mother
Lives almost by his looks, and for myself,
My virtue or my plague, be it either which,
She's so conjunctive to my life and soul,
That as the star moves not but in his sphere, 15
I could not but by her. The other motive,

27 Come] F; *Hor.* Come Q2 27 give] F; *not in* Q2 29 SD *Exeunt*] Q2; *Exit* F **Act 4, Scene 7** 4.7] *Capell* 6 proceeded] F; proceede Q2 7 crimeful] F; criminall Q2 8 safety, wisdom] F; safetie, greatnes, wisdome Q2 10 unsinewed] vnsinnow'd Q2; vnsinnowed F 11 But yet] Q2; And yet F 11 they're] tha'r Q2; they are F 14 She's] F; She is Q2 14 conjunctive] F; concliue Q2

Act 4, Scene 7

1 **my acquittance seal** confirm my discharge; i.e. acknowledge my innocence.

3 **knowing** understanding, intelligent.

6 **feats** exploits. For this pejorative meaning, Schmidt cites also *Macbeth* 1.7.80 and *Henry V* 3.3.17.

8 **safety, wisdom** So F. Q2 inserts 'greatnes' between these words, making the line too long. I assume that once again Q2 preserves a Shakespearean false start. Claudius is 'stirred up' to take action on account of his safety and by persuasion of his wisdom. 'greatness' seems irrelevant.

13–16 **My virtue...but by her** Claudius's profession of his total attachment to Gertrude is deeply important, and suggests something of his motive for murder. But if we are impressed by his candour, we notice that Claudius is concealing from Laertes his real difficulty in proceeding against Hamlet – namely his fear of being exposed – and also the fact that he has (as he supposes) already sent Hamlet to his death.

14 **conjunctive** closely joined.

15 **sphere** one of the series of hollow, transparent globes supposed to encircle the earth and carry the heavenly bodies.

Why to a public count I might not go,
Is the great love the general gender bear him,
Who, dipping all his faults in their affection,
Work like the spring that turneth wood to stone, 20
Convert his gyves to graces, so that my arrows,
Too slightly timbered for so loud a wind,
Would have reverted to my bow again,
And not where I had aimed them.

LAERTES And so have I a noble father lost, 25
A sister driven into desperate terms,
Whose worth, if praises may go back again,
Stood challenger on mount of all the age
For her perfections. But my revenge will come.

CLAUDIUS Break not your sleeps for that. You must not think 30
That we are made of stuff so flat and dull
That we can let our beard be shook with danger
And think it pastime. You shortly shall hear more.
I loved your father, and we love ourself,
And that I hope will teach you to imagine – 35

Enter a MESSENGER *with letters*

How now? What news?

MESSENGER Letters my lord from Hamlet.
This to your majesty, this to the queen.

CLAUDIUS From Hamlet? Who brought them?

MESSENGER Sailors my lord they say, I saw them not;
They were given me by Claudio – he received them 40
Of him that brought them.

20 Work] Q2; Would F 22 loud a wind] F; loued Arm'd Q2 24 And] F; But Q2 24 had] F; haue Q2 24 aimed] aym'd Q2; arm'd F 27 Whose worth] Q2; Who was F 35 SD] Q2; *Enter a Messenger* F 36 How...Hamlet] F; *not in* Q2 37 This] F; These Q2 41 Of...them] Q2; *not in* F

17 count indictment (*OED sb*¹ 8).

18 general gender common people.

20 Work Act, operate.

20 spring...stone Dowden notes that in Harrison's *Description of England* it is stated that the baths at King's Newnham in Warwickshire turn wood to stone (ed. Furnivall, I, 348–9). R. Scot's *Discovery of Witchcraft* (1584; ed. Nicholson, 1886) says 'wood is by the quality of divers waters here in *England* transubstantiated into a stone. (Of late experience near Coventry, etc.)' (p. 238).

21 gyves fetters.

22 Too slightly timbered i.e. too light.

23 reverted returned.

26 desperate terms an extreme or hopeless state.

27 back again i.e. to what she was.

28 on mount of Probably 'mounted above' (= 'placed on high above').

31 flat inert, spiritless. Compare 1.2.133.

32 with danger with dangerous intent, threateningly.

CLAUDIUS Laertes, you shall hear them. –
Leave us.
Exit Messenger

[*Reads*] 'High and mighty, you shall know I am set naked on your kingdom. Tomorrow shall I beg leave to see your kingly eyes, when I shall, first asking your pardon thereunto, recount th'occasion of my sudden and more strange return. 45
Hamlet.'

What should this mean? Are all the rest come back?
Or is it some abuse, and no such thing?
LAERTES Know you the hand?
CLAUDIUS 'Tis Hamlet's character. Naked? 50
And in a postscript here he says alone.
Can you devise me?
LAERTES I'm lost in it my lord. But let him come –
It warms the very sickness in my heart
That I shall live and tell him to his teeth 55
'Thus didest thou!'
CLAUDIUS If it be so, Laertes –
As how should it be so? – how otherwise? –
Will you be ruled by me?
LAERTES Ay my lord,
So you will not o'errule me to a peace.
CLAUDIUS To thine own peace. If he be now returned, 60
As checking at his voyage, and that he means
No more to undertake it, I will work him
To an exploit, now ripe in my device,

42 SD] F; *not in* Q2 43 SD *Reads*] *Capell; not in* Q2, F 45 th'] F; the Q2 45 occasion] Q2; *Occasions* F 47 Hamlet] F; *not in* Q2 49 and] Q2; Or F 52 devise] Q2; aduise F 53 I'm] F; I am Q2 55 shall live] F; liue Q2 56 didest] diddest F; didst Q2 58 Ay my lord] I my Lord Q2; If F 59 you will] Q2; you'l F 61 checking] F; the King Q2

43 **naked** destitute.

49 **abuse** imposition, deception.

49 **no such thing** i.e. no such thing has happened.

50 **character** handwriting.

52 **devise** So Q2. F reads 'advise'. Since Dover Wilson's defence, editors have generally accepted Q2's variant. It is indeed the 'harder reading', but it is not easy to fit any known meaning with the context. *OED* 10 gives a meaning, 'conjecture, guess' and cites *Romeo and Juliet* 3.1.69, 'I do protest I...love thee better than thou canst devise.' So Claudius may mean, 'Can you guess (the meaning of this) for me?' The more regular sense of 'devise' occurs below at 68.

54 **warms** does good to.

54 **very** real.

56 **Thus** Laertes mimes or imagines a sword-thrust. The ferocious retaliation which he relishes in anticipation is completely lost in the unnecessary emendation accepted by Wilson and Jenkins, 'Thus diest thou.'

61 **checking at** A phrase from falconry, used when a hawk is diverted in his pursuit by some new object.

63 **ripe in my device** i.e. a scheme of mine come to maturity.

Under the which he shall not choose but fall,
And for his death no wind of blame shall breathe, 65
But even his mother shall uncharge the practice
And call it accident.

[LAERTES My lord, I will be ruled,
The rather if you could devise it so
That I might be the organ.

CLAUDIUS It falls right.
You have been talked of since your travel much, 70
And that in Hamlet's hearing, for a quality
Wherein they say you shine. Your sum of parts
Did not together pluck such envy from him
As did that one, and that in my regard
Of the unworthiest siege.

LAERTES What part is that my lord? 75

CLAUDIUS A very riband in the cap of youth,
Yet needful too, for youth no less becomes
The light and careless livery that it wears
Than settled age his sables and his weeds
Importing health and graveness.] Two months since 80
Here was a gentleman of Normandy.
I've seen myself, and served against, the French,
And they can well on horseback, but this gallant
Had witchcraft in't. He grew unto his seat,
And to such wondrous doing brought his horse 85
As had he been incorpsed and demi-natured

67–80 LAERTES My lord...graveness] Q2; *not in* F **76** riband] Q 1611; ribaud Q2 **80** Two months] Q2; Some two Monthes F **80** since] Q2; hence F **82** I've] F; I haue Q2 **84** unto] Q2; into F

66 uncharge the practice i.e. not press the accusation that it was a criminal contrivance.

67–80 F omits this, and the cut is sensitive and proper. At 80, F resumes with 'Some two Monthes hence', to make an exact metrical join with 'And call it accident' (67).

68 devise contrive.

69 organ instrument.

75 Of the unworthiest siege Of the least account. Claudius flatters Laertes by saying that the great skill in arms which Hamlet so envied is the least of his virtues.

76 very riband mere ribbon.

77 becomes is in accord with, suits. Really, the subject and object are transposed. The clothes suit the age rather than vice versa.

80 Importing...graveness Which indicates a concern for health and dignity.

82–9 This enthusiastic comment on Lamord's superb horsemanship – even in the midst of plotting Hamlet's death – is an interesting insight into Claudius, perhaps to be compared with Hamlet's enthusiasm for the players, in a scene which has already deepened our perspective on him by his confession of his total love for Gertrude.

83 can well are very skilful.

86 incorpsed of one body. Seemingly a Shakespearean coinage.

86 demi-natured i.e. he, as man, was half of the total nature of a united man–horse creature.

With the brave beast. So far he topped my thought,
That I in forgery of shapes and tricks
Come short of what he did.

LAERTES A Norman was't?

CLAUDIUS A Norman. 90

LAERTES Upon my life Lamord.

CLAUDIUS The very same.

LAERTES I know him well, he is the brooch indeed
And gem of all the nation.

CLAUDIUS He made confession of you,
And gave you such a masterly report 95
For art and exercise in your defence,
And for your rapier most especial,
That he cried out 'twould be a sight indeed
If one could match you. [Th'escrimers of their nation
He swore had neither motion, guard, nor eye, 100
If you opposed them.] Sir, this report of his
Did Hamlet so envenom with his envy
That he could nothing do but wish and beg
Your sudden coming o'er to play with you.
Now out of this –

LAERTES What out of this, my lord? 105

CLAUDIUS Laertes, was your father dear to you?
Or are you like the painting of a sorrow,
A face without a heart?

LAERTES Why ask you this?

CLAUDIUS Not that I think you did not love your father,

87 topped] topt Q2; past F 87 my] F; me Q2 91 Lamord] Q2; *Lamound* F 93 the] Q2; our F 94 made] Q2; mad F 97 especial] Q2; especially F 99–101 Th'escrimers...opposed them] Q2; *not in* F 99 Th'escrimers] th'escrimeurs *White;* the Scrimures Q2 104 you] Q2; him F 105 What] Q2; Why F

87 topped my thought surpassed what I could imagine.

88 in forgery...tricks in imagining displays of horsemanship.

92–3 brooch...gem Dowden compares Jonson, *Staple of News* (1626), 3.2.265, 'The very brooch o'the bench, gem o'the City'.

94 made confession of you revealed the truth about you. Dowden (followed by others) unnecessarily saw this as a grudging acknowledgement by a Norman of a Dane's qualities.

96 art and exercise skilful accomplishments. (A hendiadys.)

99–101 F cuts two lines which interrupt the sweep of Claudius's argument.

99 Th'escrimers Q2, our only authority here, gives 'the Scrimures', and since the quarto of 1611 editions have given 'the scrimers' though there is no such word. The French *escrimeur*, master of fencing, is found in sixteenth-century English (see *OED*). Grant White suggested in 1861 that the MS. reading was 'th'escrimeurs'. More likely it was 'th'escrimures'.

100 motion the skilled movements of the trained fencer.

102 envenom embitter (literally, poison).

But that I know love is begun by time, 110
And that I see, in passages of proof,
Time qualifies the spark and fire of it.
[There lives within the very flame of love
A kind of wick or snuff that will abate it,
And nothing is at a like goodness still, 115
For goodness, growing to a plurisy,
Dies in his own too much. That we would do,
We should do when we would, for this 'would' changes,
And hath abatements and delays as many
As there are tongues, are hands, are accidents; 120
And then this 'should' is like a spendthrift sigh,
That hurts by easing. But to the quick of th'ulcer –]
Hamlet comes back; what would you undertake
To show yourself in deed your father's son
More than in words?

LAERTES To cut his throat i'th'church. 125

CLAUDIUS No place indeed should murder sanctuarize;
Revenge should have no bounds. But, good Laertes,
Will you do this, keep close within your chamber;
Hamlet, returned, shall know you are come home;
We'll put on those shall praise your excellence, 130

113–22 There lives...th'ulcer –] Q2; *not in* F 114 wick] *Rowe*; weeke Q2 121 spendthrift] Q 1676; spend thirfts Q2 124 in deed...son] *Steevens*[2]; indeede your fathers sonne Q2; your Fathers sonne indeed F

110 **by time** by suitable time, by the proper occasion. Love is a creature of time and belongs to time, in that a suitable moment brings it to birth, and the succession of moments, less auspicious, will dull it.

111 **passages of proof** things that have happened which bear me out.

112 **qualifies** reduces, weakens.

113–22 F omits the whole passage. The unkindest cut of all, since the passage is of such great interest thematically, and so illuminating of Claudius's philosophy of life. We cannot think that Shakespeare would delete it unless he were under considerable pressure to shorten the play – which he may have been. Compare the cut at 5.2.100.

114 **snuff** the burnt part of the wick.

115 **still** all the time.

116 **plurisy** (1) excess; (2) the inflammation of the chest (pleurisy) thought to be caused by 'excess' of humours.

121 **spendthrift sigh** The quarto reading (i.e. 'spendthrift's') may possibly be right, but it is really the sigh itself that is a spendthrift – it does harm in the pleasure of indulging itself. Painful breathing is the main feature of pleurisy. Claudius says that if we don't act in due time, our duty becomes painful and difficult.

122 **to the quick of th'ulcer** to the heart of the matter. Claudius moves from one disease-image to another. This one is horrible; no one would ever use it in life.

126 **should murder sanctuarize** should offer sanctuary to murder. Claudius's remark runs in two directions at once. (1) No church should offer sanctuary and protection to a man who like Hamlet has committed murder; (2) no church should be regarded as a sanctuary where the throat-cutting you mention cannot be carried out.

128 **Will you do this** If you are to do this.

128 **keep close** remain confined.

130 **put on those shall praise** arrange for some to praise.

And set a double varnish on the fame
The Frenchman gave you; bring you in fine together,
And wager on your heads. He being remiss,
Most generous, and free from all contriving,
Will not peruse the foils, so that with ease, 135
Or with a little shuffling, you may choose
A sword unbated, and in a pass of practice
Requite him for your father.

LAERTES I will do't,
And for that purpose I'll anoint my sword.
I bought an unction of a mountebank, 140
So mortal that but dip a knife in it,
Where it draws blood no cataplasm so rare,
Collected from all simples that have virtue
Under the moon, can save the thing from death
That is but scratched withal. I'll touch my point 145
With this contagion, that if I gall him slightly,
It may be death.

CLAUDIUS Let's further think of this,
Weigh what convenience both of time and means
May fit us to our shape. If this should fail,
And that our drift look through our bad performance, 150
'Twere better not assayed. Therefore this project
Should have a back or second, that might hold
If this did blast in proof. Soft, let me see.
We'll make a solemn wager on your cunnings –
I ha't! 155

133 on] F; ore Q2 137 pass] passe F; pace Q2 139 that] F; *not in* Q2 141 that but dip] Q2; I but dipt F 149 shape. If] *Rowe*; shape if Q2; shape, if F 153 did] Q2; should F 154 cunnings] Q2; commings F 155 ha't] F; hate Q2

132 in fine in conclusion.

133 remiss 'not vigilant or cautious' (Johnson).

136 shuffling deceit (rather than physically shuffling the foils). See notes to 3.3.61 and 3.1.67.

137 unbated unblunted. (Short for 'unabated'.)

137 a pass of practice 'practice' means a deliberate and malicious stratagem – as in 66 above and 5.2.297. Claudius is speaking of a thrust which is intended to kill. (The other possible meaning is 'a bout intended for exercise'.)

140 unction ointment.

140 mountebank one who travels about selling medicines and cures.

142 cataplasm poultice, medicated dressing.

143 Collected Put together. Compare 3.2.233.

143 simples medicinal plants.

144 Under the moon Probably 'anywhere in the world' rather than a reference to night-gathering.

146 gall injure, wound.

149 fit us to our shape suit us for our design. The predominant meaning of 'shape' here is that which the imagination fashions, as in *Twelfth Night* 1.1.14, 'So full of shapes is fancy.' But there is a strong secondary meaning exploiting the word's theatrical senses (costume, disguise, hence role); i.e. fashion us into the parts we are going to play.

150 drift aim, purpose.

153 blast in proof explode in being tested (like a faulty cannon).

When in your motion you are hot and dry,
As make your bouts more violent to that end,
And that he calls for drink, I'll have preferred him
A chalice for the nonce, whereon but sipping,
If he by chance escape your venomed stuck, 160
Our purpose may hold there. But stay, what noise?

Enter GERTRUDE

How, sweet queen!

GERTRUDE One woe doth tread upon another's heel,
So fast they follow. Your sister's drowned, Laertes.

LAERTES Drowned! Oh where? 165

GERTRUDE There is a willow grows askant a brook,
That shows his hoar leaves in the glassy stream.
Therewith fantastic garlands did she make,
Of crow-flowers, nettles, daisies, and long purples,
That liberal shepherds give a grosser name, 170
But our cold maids do dead men's fingers call them.
There on the pendant boughs her cronet weeds

157 that] Q2; the F 158 preferred] prefard Q2; prepar'd F 161 But...noise] Q2; *not in* F 162 How...queen] F; *not in* Q2 164 they] Q2; they'l F 166 askant] ascaunt Q2; aslant F 166 a brook] F; the Brooke Q2 167 hoar] hore F; horry Q2 168 Therewith] Q2; There with F 168 make] Q2; come F 171 cold] F; cull-cold Q2 172 cronet] Q2, *Ridley*; Coronet F; crownet *Wilson*

158 preferred presented to, offered. The choice between the readings of Q2 and F is very difficult. Q2's spelling is not a problem: 'prefar' is recorded in *OED* for 'prefer' in the sixteenth century. But the 'f' may be a misprint for 'p'. It is impossible to decide whether Claudius thinks of having a chalice *made ready* ('prepared') for Hamlet when occasion demands, or *offered* to him ('preferred').

159 for the nonce for that particular purpose or occasion.

160 stuck thrust.

161–2 But stay...queen! See collation. It seems necessary to conflate Q2 and F at this point.

165 Drowned! Oh where? This much-ridiculed response, looking so much like a clumsy cue for Gertrude's aria, presents an almost impossible task to the actor. Perhaps Laertes is meant to express not so much shock and grief as incredulity and amazement. He has just seen her alive. 'Drowned? Where could she be drowned?' Such disbelief invites us to approve F's 'a brook' rather than Q2's 'the brook'. The queen explains that even in an unconsidered brook a girl who didn't want to live might drown.

166 askant F's 'aslant' gives yet another Q2/F doublet. Both words are normally adverbs meaning 'obliquely' and neither was used, as here, as a preposition.

167 hoar grey.

168 Therewith...make She made garlands from the willow, interwoven with wildflowers and weeds. The playhouse scribe quite misunderstood this, and F reads 'There with fantastic garlands did she come.'

169 crow-flowers 'The crow-flower is called wild williams, marshy gilly-flowers and cuckoo gilly-flowers' (Gerard's *Herbal*). Jenkins supports the view that this is *Lychnis flos-cuculi*, or ragged robin.

169–71 long-purples...call them Generally identified as the wild orchis, *Orchis mascula*, which has a tall flower stem with a spike of purple flowers. The 'grosser name' – something to do with testicles – and 'dead men's fingers' apply to the shape of the roots. (See NV and *OED* sv Dead men's fingers.)

170 liberal free-spoken.

171 cold So F. Q2's 'cull-cold' looks like the remnant of a Shakespearean false start.

172 cronet So Q2. 'cronet', 'crownet' and 'coronet' (which F gives) were all variant forms. Ridley properly restored Q2's form, since the metre

Clamb'ring to hang, an envious sliver broke,
When down her weedy trophies and herself
Fell in the weeping brook. Her clothes spread wide, 175
And mermaid-like awhile they bore her up,
Which time she chanted snatches of old lauds
As one incapable of her own distress,
Or like a creature native and indued
Unto that element. But long it could not be 180
Till that her garments, heavy with their drink,
Pulled the poor wretch from her melodious lay
To muddy death.

LAERTES Alas, then she is drowned?

GERTRUDE Drowned, drowned.

LAERTES Too much of water hast thou, poor Ophelia, 185
And therefore I forbid my tears. But yet
It is our trick; nature her custom holds,
Let shame say what it will. When these are gone,
The woman will be out. Adieu my lord,
I have a speech of fire that fain would blaze, 190
But that this folly douts it. *Exit*

CLAUDIUS Let's follow, Gertrude.

174 her] Q2; the F 177 lauds] laudes Q2; tunes F 181 their drink] Q2; her drinke F 182 lay] Q2; buy F 183 she is] Q2, Q1; is she F 190 of fire] F; a fire Q2 191 douts] *Knight*; doubts F; drownes Q2

requires two syllables. 'cronet weeds' means the garland of willow and weeds which Ophelia had made.

173 **envious** malicious.

173 **sliver** a small branch or twig (though it is not a sliver until it has broken off). Compare *Lear* 4.2.34–5, 'She that will sliver and disbranch / From her material sap'.

177 **lauds** hymns. So Q2; F gives 'tunes', as does Q1, probably an intentional simplification by the playhouse scribe. 'laud' is an unusual word, not frequently used outside its technical reference to the second of the canonical hours in the Catholic breviary. C. J. Sisson objected to 'the picture of Ophelia dying in songs of praise to God' after the improper songs we have heard (*New Readings in Shakespeare,* 1956, II, 226). Perhaps Gertrude is covering up. But crazy hymn-singing might well have marked Ophelia's death.

178 **incapable** uncomprehending.

179 **indued** adapted, conditioned.

180 **But long it could not be** The modern reader cannot suppress his astonishment that Gertrude should have watched Ophelia die without lifting a finger to help her. Shakespeare wrote for a theatre audience before the realistic novel had come into existence: this speech is an impersonal account of Ophelia's death. It has been suggested that the queen's story is something of a 'cover up' of a deliberate act of suicide; the priest (in 5.1.194–7) says there *had* been such a cover-up. In that case, the queen's narrative becomes implausible at this point. In view of Shakespeare's total inconsistency about Horatio's awareness of life in Elsinore (see note to 1.2.176) it is better to say that Gertrude steps out of her role to serve the purpose of the play.

182 **the poor wretch** Gertrude used this phrase for Hamlet at 2.2.166.

187 **our trick** a way we have.

188 **these** i.e. his tears.

189 **The woman...out** The woman in me will have finished.

191 **douts** extinguishes ('folly' being his weeping).

How much I had to do to calm his rage!
Now fear I this will give it start again.
Therefore let's follow.

Exeunt

[5.1] *Enter two* CLOWNS

CLOWN Is she to be buried in Christian burial, when she wilfully seeks her own salvation?

OTHER I tell thee she is, therefore make her grave straight. The crowner hath sat on her, and finds it Christian burial.

CLOWN How can that be, unless she drowned herself in her own defence? 5

OTHER Why, 'tis found so.

CLOWN It must be *se offendendo*, it cannot be else. For here lies the point: if I drown myself wittingly, it argues an act, and an act hath three branches – it is to act, to do, to perform. Argal, she drowned herself wittingly. 10

OTHER Nay, but hear you goodman delver –

CLOWN Give me leave. Here lies the water – good. Here stands the man – good. If the man go to this water and drown himself, it is

Act 5, Scene 1 5.1] Q 1676 1 when she] Q2; that F 3 therefore] Q2; and therefore F 8 *se offendendo*] F; so offended Q2 10 to act] Q2; an Act F 10 to perform] Q2; and to performe F 10 Argal] argall F; or all Q2

Act 5, Scene 1

5.1 There is a clearly marked gap of time between the end of Act 4, in which we hear of Ophelia's death, and the beginning of Act 5, when they are digging her grave. The gap is meant to be short, however; Hamlet spoke in his letter to the king of seeing him 'tomorrow'.

0 SD Both Q2 and F give us the entry for 'two clowns' and refer to them in the speech headings as 'Clown' and 'Other'. This is evidently Shakespeare's designation, and it is interesting that the playhouse scribe did not move towards a less vague appellation, as he had elsewhere (see note to 3.2.120SD). The First Clown, the head gravedigger, calls himself the sexton (137 below).

1–2 wilfully...salvation Could he mean that she is trying to get to heaven before her time, or does he simply confuse salvation and damnation? The Clown's muddle is an ironic presentation of the thin divide which Hamlet finds between salvation and damnation.

3 straight straightaway. But he accidentally implies that if it weren't Christian burial, she would have a crooked grave.

3 crowner Common colloquial form of 'coroner'.

8 *se offendendo* He means *se defendendo*, in self defence, a justifiable plea in case of homicide.

9–10 an act...branches There is general agreement with the suggestion made in the eighteenth century by Sir John Hawkins (see NV) that Shakespeare had in mind the celebrated legal arguments of 1561–2 on the suicide of Sir James Hales, who had walked into the river at Canterbury in 1554. In a suit over whether his lands were thereby forfeit, there was much fine discussion on the nature of the act, including the argument that an act consisted of three parts, the Imagination, the Resolution and the Perfection. See Plowden's *Commentaries*, 1761, p. 259.

10 Argal For *ergo*, 'therefore'.

12 goodman delver master digger.

will he, nill he, he goes – mark you that. But if the water come to him, and drown him, he drowns not himself. Argal, he that is not guilty of his own death shortens not his own life. 15

OTHER But is this law?

CLOWN Ay marry is't, crowner's quest law.

OTHER Will you ha' the truth on't? If this had not been a gentlewoman, she should have been buried out o' Christian burial. 20

CLOWN Why, there thou sayst – and the more pity that great folk should have countenance in this world to drown or hang themselves more than their even-Christen. Come, my spade; there is no ancient gentlemen but gardeners, ditchers, and gravemakers; they hold up Adam's profession. 25

OTHER Was he a gentleman?

CLOWN A was the first that ever bore arms.

OTHER Why, he had none.

CLOWN What, art a heathen? How dost thou understand the scripture? The scripture says Adam digged. Could he dig without arms? I'll put another question to thee. If thou answerest me not to the purpose, confess thyself – 30

OTHER Go to!

CLOWN What is he that builds stronger than either the mason, the shipwright, or the carpenter? 35

OTHER The gallows-maker, for that frame outlives a thousand tenants.

CLOWN I like thy wit well in good faith. The gallows does well, but how does it well? It does well to those that do ill. Now, thou dost ill to say the gallows is built stronger than the church; argal, the gallows may do well to thee. To't again, come. 40

OTHER Who builds stronger than a mason, a shipwright, or a carpenter?

CLOWN Ay, tell me that, and unyoke.

OTHER Marry, now I can tell.

CLOWN To't. 45

20 on't] F; an't Q2 21 o'] a Q2; of F 24 even-Christen] euen Christen Q2; euen Christian F 28 A was] Q2; He was F 29–31 Why...arms] F; *not in* Q2 37 frame] F; *not in* Q2

15 will he, nill he whether he will or no, willy-nilly.

16–17 he that is not guilty...life i.e. only suicides fail to live out their allotted spans; all other accidental deaths must have been foreseen by the Almighty. The Clown's absurd logic is a profound critique of the reasoning of educated men.

19 crowner's quest law coroner's inquest law.

23 countenance permission, authorisation.

24 even-Christen Collective noun for 'fellow Christians' (see *OED* sv 'christen' and 'even-Christian').

24 ancient i.e. of long-standing.

33 confess thyself – 'Confess and be hanged' was proverbial. See *Oxford Dictionary of Proverbs* and Tilley C587.

37 frame structure.

43 unyoke unyoke the oxen; finish the day's work.

OTHER Mass, I cannot tell.

Enter HAMLET *and* HORATIO *afar off*

CLOWN Cudgel thy brains no more about it, for your dull ass will not mend his pace with beating; and when you are asked this question next, say a grave-maker. The houses he makes lasts till doomsday. Go, get thee to Yaughan, fetch me a stoup of liquor. 50

[*Exit Second Clown*]

In youth when I did love, did love, *Song*
Methought it was very sweet
To contract-o the time for-a my behove,
Oh methought there-a was nothing-a meet.

HAMLET Has this fellow no feeling of his business? A sings in grave-making. 55

HORATIO Custom hath made it in him a property of easiness.

HAMLET 'Tis e'en so, the hand of little employment hath the daintier sense.

CLOWN But age with his stealing steps *Song* 60
Hath clawed me in his clutch,
And hath shipped me intil the land,
As if I had never been such.
[*Throws up a skull*]

HAMLET That skull had a tongue in it, and could sing once. How the knave jowls it to th' ground, as if 'twere Cain's jawbone, that did 65

46 SD] F; *Enter Hamlet and Horatio* Q2 *(after 54)* 49 he makes] Q2; that he makes F 50 get thee...fetch] F; get in, and fetch Q2 50 stoup] stoupe F; soope Q2 50 SD] *Rowe; not in* Q2, F 51 SD *Song*] Q2; *Sings.* F 53 contract-o] contract ô Q2; *contract O* F 53 for-a] for a Q2, F 54 there-a] there a Q2; *there* F 54 nothing-a] nothing a Q2; *nothing* F 55 A sings] a sings Q2; that he sings F 55 in] Q2; at F 58 daintier] F; dintier Q2 60 SD *Song*] Q2; *Clowne sings* F 61 clawed] Q2; *caught* F 62 intil] F; into Q2 63 SD] *Capell; not in* Q2, F; *he throwes vp a shouel* Q1 65 th'ground] F; the ground Q2 65 'twere] twere Q2; it were F

46 SD So F. Q2 provides the entry at 60, which is clearly wrong, since Hamlet's first remark indicates that they have been watching and listening.

50 Yaughan An eccentric spelling of 'Johann'. Ben Jonson has a 'Yohan' in *Every Man Out of His Humour* 5.6.48, a London Jew. Q2 could make nothing of this name, it would seem.

50 stoup a large jar or pitcher.

51–54, 60–4, 79–82 In youth when I did love The Clown sings a very free version of a popular song printed, as by Thomas Vaux, in Tottel's Miscellany, 1557, 'I loathe that I did love.' See a full discussion, with the music, in Sternfeld, esp. pp. 130–1, 151–5.

53–4 contract-o...for-a...there-a...nothing -a The Clown is decorating his lyric. For an accommodation to the music, see Sternfeld, p. 155.

53 To contract...behove i.e. to pass away the time to my own advantage.

57 a property of easiness 'a matter of indifference' (N. Alexander). For 'easiness' in this sense, compare current colloquial 'I'm easy.'

62 intil into (F's reading, hardly likely to be scribal).

63 SD ***Throws up a skull*** Capell's SD reflects Q1, '*he throwes vp a shouel*', where 'shouel' is presumably a compositor's misreading of 'skull'.

65 jowls bangs (with a pun on 'jowl' = 'jaw').

65 Cain's jawbone, that did the jawbone of Cain, who did.... A further reminder of the story of Cain and Abel (see Introduction, p. 41). There

the first murder. This might be the pate of a politician which this ass now o'erreaches, one that would circumvent God, might it not?

HORATIO It might my lord.

HAMLET Or of a courtier, which could say 'Good morrow sweet lord, how dost thou sweet lord?' This might be my Lord Such-a-one, 70 that praised my Lord Such-a-one's horse when a meant to beg it, might it not?

HORATIO Ay my lord.

HAMLET Why, e'en so, and now my Lady Worm's, chopless, and knocked about the mazard with a sexton's spade. Here's fine 75 revolution, and we had the trick to see't. Did these bones cost no more the breeding but to play at loggets with 'em? Mine ache to think on't.

CLOWN A pickaxe and a spade, a spade, *Song*
For and a shrowding sheet, 80
Oh a pit of clay for to be made,
For such a guest is meet.
[*Throws up another skull*]

HAMLET There's another. Why may not that be the skull of a lawyer? Where be his quiddities now, his quillets, his cases, his tenures, and his tricks? Why does he suffer this rude knave now to knock him 85 about the sconce with a dirty shovel, and will not tell him of his

66 This] Q2; It F 67 now o'erreaches] Q2; o're Of-/fices F 67 would Q2; could F 70 thou sweet lord] Q2; thou, good Lord F 71 a] Q2; he F 71 meant] F; went Q2 74 chopless] Choples Q2; Chaplesse F 75 mazard] F; massene Q2 76 and] Q2; if F 77 'em] F; them Q2 79 SD *Song*] Q2; *Clowne sings.* F 82 SD] *Capell; not in* Q2, F 83 may] Q2; might F 84 quiddities] Q2; Quiddits F 84 quillets] F; quillites Q2 85 rude] F; madde Q2

is a curious English medieval tradition that Cain killed Abel with the jawbone of an ass (see the Old English *Solomon and Saturn*, ed. J. E. Cross and T. D. Hill, 1982, pp. 101–3). Since Skeat referred to this tradition in 1880 (*N & Q*, 21 Aug.) it has often been supposed that the ass's jawbone is meant here, but of course it is Cain's skull – so contemptuously dropped – that Hamlet means. In view of the widespread appearance of the legend in medieval drama and iconography (see J. K. Bonnell, *PMLA* 39 (1924), 140–6) it seems certain that it was in Shakespeare's mind as he wrote, because of the 'ass' in 67. Both Samson and (it was thought) Cain wielded an ass's jawbone; now an ass wields a human jawbone.

67 **o'erreaches** A politician was a man who o'erreached, in the sense of duped, his pawns and enemies. Now the tables are turned as the gravedigger o'erreaches (i.e. handles) his skull. Jenkins defends F's reading, 'o'er-offices'.

74 **chopless** The chops or chaps are the lower jaw and the flesh about it.

75 **mazard** a drinking-bowl; here used facetiously for the skull or head.

76 **trick** knack.

76–7 **Did these bones...loggets with 'em?** Was the value of bringing up these people so slight that we may justifiably play skittles with their bones?

77 **loggets** A country game in which wooden truncheons about two feet long, bulbous at one end and tapering off to the handle (like the old 'Indian clubs'), were thrown at a fixed stake.

84 **quiddities...quillets** subtle distinctions, quibbles. One would expect a like-sounding pair, either quiddits/quillets, or quiddities/quilleties. F's quiddits could be the true reading.

84 **tenures** suits connected with the holding of land.

86 **sconce** A slang term for 'head'.

action of battery? Hum, this fellow might be in's time a great buyer of land, with his statutes, his recognizances, his fines, his double vouchers, his recoveries. Is this the fine of his fines and the recovery of his recoveries, to have his fine pate full of fine dirt? Will his vouchers vouch him no more of his purchases, and double ones too, than the length and breadth of a pair of indentures? The very conveyances of his lands will scarcely lie in this box, and must th'inheritor himself have no more, ha? 90

HORATIO Not a jot more my lord. 95

HAMLET Is not parchment made of sheepskins?

HORATIO Ay my lord, and of calves' skins too.

HAMLET They are sheep and calves which seek out assurance in that. I will speak to this fellow. Whose grave's this sirrah?

CLOWN Mine sir. 100

(Sings)

Oh a pit of clay for to be made
For such a guest is meet.

HAMLET I think it be thine indeed, for thou liest in't.

CLOWN You lie out on't sir, and therefore 'tis not yours. For my part, I do not lie in't, yet it is mine. 105

HAMLET Thou dost lie in't, to be in't and say 'tis thine. 'Tis for the

89–90 Is this...dirt] F; *not in* Q2 90–1 Will his vouchers] F; will vouchers Q2 91 and double ones too] F; & doubles Q2 93 scarcely] Q2; hardly F 97 calves' skins] Calues-skinnes Q2; Caue-skinnes F 98 which] Q2; that F 99 sirrah] Q2; Sir F 101 SD *Sings*] *Capell; not in* Q2, F 101 Oh] *O* F; or Q2 102 For...meet] F; *not in* Q2 104 'tis] Q2; it is F 105 yet] Q2; and yet F 106 'tis thine] F; it is thine Q2

87 **action of battery** lawsuit dealing with physical violence.

88 **statutes** securities for debts, mortgages.

88–9 **double vouchers...recoveries** Like fines, recoveries were fictitious suits to obtain the authority of a court judgement for the holding of land. A voucher, or *vocatio*, calls in one of the parties necessary in this action – a double voucher rendering the tortuous process even more secure (see the full account in Clarkson and Warren, *The Law of Property in Shakespeare*, pp. 128–30).

88 **recognizances** bonds undertaking to repay debts or fulfil other legal obligations.

89 **fine** conclusion.

90 **fine pate** subtle head.

91 **purchases** Technically this refers to the transfer of property by other means than inheritance. But the word was widely used in Shakespeare's time to indicate, in a pejorative sense, acquisitions and enrichments of any kind. See note to 93 below.

92 **pair of indentures** Two copies of a legal agreement would be made on the same sheet of parchment which was then cut in half by means of an indented or zig-zag line, as a precaution against forgery.

93 **conveyances of his lands** deeds relating to purchases of land for himself. This lawyer has feathered his own nest. See note to 'purchases' above (91).

94 **inheritor** He who has come to own all these lands has in the end only the space of his coffin, which is not big enough even for the deeds of his canny dealings. A subtle joke because this lawyer is not technically an 'inheritor'. Like so many Elizabethan lawyers, he has come to his estates by 'purchase'.

98 **assurance** Parchment documents provide legal proof ('assurance') of material gains, but only fools would seek in them assurance, or security, against mortality.

103–4 'Hamlet uses the familiar *thee* and *thou* to the Sexton, but the Sexton uses the respectful *you* in reply' (Kittredge).

dead, not for the quick, therefore thou liest.

CLOWN 'Tis a quick lie sir, 'twill away again from me to you.

HAMLET What man dost thou dig it for?

CLOWN For no man sir. 110

HAMLET What woman then?

CLOWN For none neither.

HAMLET Who is to be buried in't?

CLOWN One that was a woman sir, but rest her soul she's dead.

HAMLET How absolute the knave is! We must speak by the card, or 115
equivocation will undo us. By the lord, Horatio, this three years
I have took note of it: the age is grown so picked, that the toe of
the peasant comes so near the heel of the courtier, he galls his kibe.
How long hast thou been grave-maker?

CLOWN Of all the days i'th'year, I came to't that day that our last King 120
Hamlet o'ercame Fortinbras.

HAMLET How long is that since?

CLOWN Cannot you tell that? Every fool can tell that. It was the very
day that young Hamlet was born, he that is mad and sent into
England. 125

HAMLET Ay marry, why was he sent into England?

CLOWN Why, because a was mad. A shall recover his wits there, or if
a do not, 'tis no great matter there.

HAMLET Why?

CLOWN 'Twill not be seen in him there. There the men are as mad as 130
he.

HAMLET How came he mad?

116 this] Q2; these F 117 took] Q2; taken F 118 heel of the] Q2; heeles of our F 119 grave-maker] Q2; a Graue-maker F 121 o'ercame] o'recame F; ouercame Q2 123 the very] F; that very Q2 124 is mad] Q2; was mad F 127–8 a...A...a] Q2; he...hee...he F 128 'tis] Q2; it's F 130 him there. There] him there, there Q2; him, there F

107 the quick the living.

115 by the card i.e. with the precision of a sailor, navigating by his compass. 'card' could mean either the seaman's chart, or the face of the compass. It is not clear that Shakespeare meant definitely the one or the other either here or in *Macbeth* 1.3.17. In 5.2.103 below 'card' probably means 'map'.

116 equivocation deliberate playing on language and double meanings to achieve one's ends.

117 picked fastidious, refined.

118 galls his kibe rubs his chilblain.

120 Of all the days i'th'year Shakespeare is echoing himself. He had given this phrase to the Nurse, another reminiscing uneducated comic character, in *Romeo and Juliet* 1.3.25.

121 o'ercame Fortinbras See 1.1.80–95.

123–4 very day...born By making the Clown say later (137–8) that he has been sexton for thirty years, Shakespeare pointedly tells us that Hamlet is thirty. A similar late fixing of the hero's age is in *Lear* 4.7.60 ('fourscore and upward'). Contrast the early mention of Juliet's age (*Romeo and Juliet* 1.3.13): 'she's not fourteen'. Most people think of Hamlet as younger than thirty. It seems unnecessary to speculate, however, that Shakespeare here underlines Hamlet's increasing maturity. But if he *is* thirty, he's an elderly student, and Gertrude must be in her late forties, at least.

CLOWN Very strangely they say.
HAMLET How, strangely?
CLOWN Faith, e'en with losing his wits. 135
HAMLET Upon what ground?
CLOWN Why, here in Denmark. I have been sexton here man and boy thirty years.
HAMLET How long will a man lie i'th'earth ere he rot?
CLOWN Faith, if a be not rotten before a die, as we have many pocky 140 corses nowadays that will scarce hold the laying in, a will last you some eight year, or nine year. A tanner will last you nine year.
HAMLET Why he more than another?
CLOWN Why sir, his hide is so tanned with his trade, that a will keep out water a great while, and your water is a sore decayer of your 145 whoreson dead body. Here's a skull now: this skull hath lien you i'th'earth three and twenty years.
HAMLET Whose was it?
CLOWN A whoreson mad fellow's it was. Whose do you think it was?
HAMLET Nay I know not. 150
CLOWN A pestilence on him for a mad rogue, a poured a flagon of Rhenish on my head once. This same skull sir, was Yorick's skull, the king's jester.
HAMLET This?
CLOWN E'en that. 155
HAMLET Let me see. [*Takes the skull.*] Alas poor Yorick! I knew him Horatio, a fellow of infinite jest, of most excellent fancy, he hath borne me on his back a thousand times – and now how abhorred

137 sexton] Sexten Q2; sixeteene F 140 Faith] Q2; Ifaith F 140 a...a] Q2; he...he F 141 nowadays] now adaies F; *not in* Q2 141 a] Q2; he F 144 a] Q2; he F 146 this skull] F; *not in* Q2 146–7 hath...earth] Q2; has laine in the earth F 147 three and twenty years] F; 23. yeeres Q2 152 This same...Yorick's skull] *Pope (substantially)*; This same skull sir, was sir *Yoricks* skull Q2; This same Scull Sir, this same Scull sir, was *Yoricks* Scull F 156 Let me see] F; *not in* Q2 156 SD *Takes the skull*] *Capell (at 154)*; *not in* Q2, F 158 borne] F; bore Q2 158 now how] Q2; how F

136 ground cause.

140–1 pocky corses nowadays Reflects the frightening spread of syphilis through sixteenth-century Europe.

141 hold the laying in last through the interment. (Compare *OED* Lay v^1 86.)

152 Rhenish Rhine wine.

152 This same...skull This is an eclectic reading put together from Q2 and F, both of which seem to have their own mistakes.

152 Yorick The name is so famous that we may forget that this is where it was born. If Yaughan stands for Johann, possibly Yorick is Shakespeare's version of Jörg.

156 Let me see So F. Q2 omits, and it is likely that the phrase was not in Shakespeare's 'foul-papers' but added during the transcription of his MS. in preparation for stage-performance. The phrase ranks with the earlier entry of Hamlet and Horatio at 46 above (see note) as a necessary tidying of the stage-action, and is for that reason included here. The phrase is also in Q1.

158–9 abhorred...it is i.e. to think of riding on the back of one who is now a mouldy skeleton.

in my imagination it is! My gorge rises at it. Here hung those lips that I have kissed I know not how oft. Where be your gibes now? your gambols, your songs, your flashes of merriment that were wont to set the table on a roar? Not one now, to mock your own grinning? Quite chop-fallen? Now get you to my lady's chamber, and tell her, let her paint an inch thick, to this favour she must come. Make her laugh at that. – Prithee Horatio, tell me one thing. 160 165

HORATIO What's that my lord?

HAMLET Dost thou think Alexander looked o' this fashion i'th'earth?

HORATIO E'en so.

HAMLET And smelt so? Pah! [*Puts down the skull*]

HORATIO E'en so my lord. 170

HAMLET To what base uses we may return, Horatio! Why may not imagination trace the noble dust of Alexander, till a find it stopping a bunghole?

HORATIO 'Twere to consider too curiously to consider so.

HAMLET No faith, not a jot, but to follow him thither with modesty enough, and likelihood to lead it, as thus: Alexander died, Alexander was buried, Alexander returneth to dust, the dust is earth, of earth we make loam, and why of that loam whereto he was converted might they not stop a beer-barrel? 175

Imperious Caesar, dead and turned to clay, 180
Might stop a hole, to keep the wind away.
Oh that that earth which kept the world in awe
Should patch a wall t'expel the winter's flaw!

But soft, but soft! Aside – here comes the king,
The queen, the courtiers.

159 in my imagination it is] Q2; my imagination is F **162** Not one] Q2; No one F **162** grinning] Q2; Ieering F **163** chamber] F; table Q2 **167** o'] F; a Q2 **169** Pah] Q2; Puh F **169** SD] *Collier; not in* Q2, F **172** a] Q2; he F **174** consider too] Q2; consider: to F **176** as thus] F; *not in* Q2 **177** to dust] Q2; into dust F **180** Imperious] Q2, Q1; Imperiall F **183** winter's] F; waters Q2 **184** Aside] F; awhile Q2

159 gorge contents of the stomach; i.e. he retches with disgust.

161 gambols Perhaps jests, practical jokes, rather than anything physical.

162 to mock...grinning i.e. to laugh at the face you're making. 'grinning' is not a smile but a facial distortion, generally of anger (a snarl) or pain, but sometimes of a forced laugh.

163 chop-fallen chap-fallen, with the chops or chaps (the lower jaw) hanging down – figuratively, dismayed or dejected.

164 favour appearance.

173 bunghole pouring hole in a cask or barrel.

174 too curiously with excessive care, over-elaborately.

175 modesty moderation.

178 loam a mortar or plaster made of clay and straw etc.

180 Imperious So Q2 and Q1. F has 'Imperiall'. Shakespeare uses both words interchangeably.

183 flaw squall.

184 but soft! Aside Q2 has 'but soft awhile'. Hamlet has obvious reasons for moving aside and choosing his own time to confront the king. 'soft!' urges caution; see note to 3.1.88.

Enter CLAUDIUS, GERTRUDE, LAERTES, *and a coffin,* [*with* PRIEST] *and* LORDS *attendant*

Who is this they follow? 185
And with such maimèd rites? This doth betoken
The corse they follow did with desperate hand
Fordo it own life. 'Twas of some estate.
Couch we awhile and mark. [*Retiring with Horatio*]

LAERTES What ceremony else? 190

HAMLET That is Laertes, a very noble youth. Mark.

LAERTES What ceremony else?

PRIEST Her obsequies have been as far enlarged
As we have warranty. Her death was doubtful,
And but that great command o'ersways the order, 195
She should in ground unsanctified have lodged
Till the last trumpet. For charitable prayers,
Shards, flints, and pebbles should be thrown on her.
Yet here she is allowed her virgin crants,
Her maiden strewments, and the bringing home 200
Of bell and burial.

LAERTES Must there no more be done?

PRIEST No more be done.
We should profane the service of the dead

185 SD] *Enter K. Q. Laertes and the corse* Q2 *(margin)*; *Enter King, Queene, Laertes, and a Coffin, with Lords attendant* F *(after* king *184)* 185 this] Q2; that F 188 of some] Q2; some F 189 SD] *Capell; not in* Q2, F 193, 202 SH PRIEST] F; *Doct.* Q2 196 have] F; been Q2 197 prayers] Q2; praier F 198 Shards] F; *not in* Q2 199 crants] Q2; Rites F

185 SD Q2 gives us 'the corse' rather than a coffin, and neither text provides the priest. The latter is '*Doct.*' in Q2 speech headings. Dover Wilson argues that Shakespeare had in mind a Protestant 'Doctor of Divinity' (*What Happens in 'Hamlet'*, p. 69).

186 maimèd mutilated, truncated.

188 Fordo Destroy.

188 it its. See note to 1.2.216.

188 some estate considerable social importance.

189 Couch we Let us conceal ourselves ('couch' suggests stooping or crouching to take cover).

191 That is Laertes On this surely unnecessary observation, see note to 1.2.176. Wilson points out, however, that Horatio and Laertes have not met on stage.

194 warranty authorisation.

194 Her death i.e. the manner of her death.

195 great command the commands of great ones.

195 the order the regular proceeding.

197 For Instead of.

198 Shards Broken pottery.

199 crants garlands hung up at funerals, especially those of young girls. An unfamiliar word, too remote for the playhouse scribe, who substituted 'rites'.

200 strewments Another most unusual word, meaning, presumably, flowers strewn on a coffin. See 213 below.

200–1 bringing home / Of bell and burial bringing her to her last home with bell-ringing and proper burial. Verity compares *Titus Andronicus* 1.1.83–4, 'These that I bring unto their latest home, / With burial amongst their ancestors'.

To sing sage requiem and such rest to her
As to peace-parted souls.

LAERTES Lay her i'th'earth, 205
And from her fair and unpolluted flesh
May violets spring. I tell thee, churlish priest,
A ministering angel shall my sister be
When thou liest howling.

HAMLET What, the fair Ophelia!

GERTRUDE Sweets to the sweet, farewell. [*Scattering flowers*] 210
I hoped thou shouldst have been my Hamlet's wife.
I thought thy bride-bed to have decked, sweet maid,
And not t'have strewed thy grave.

LAERTES Oh treble woe
Fall ten times treble on that cursèd head
Whose wicked deed thy most ingenious sense 215
Deprived thee of. Hold off the earth awhile
Till I have caught her once more in mine arms.

Leaps in the grave

Now pile your dust upon the quick and dead
Till of this flat a mountain you have made
T'o'ertop old Pelion or the skyish head 220
Of blue Olympus.

HAMLET [*Advancing*] What is he whose grief
Bears such an emphasis? whose phrase of sorrow
Conjures the wandering stars, and makes them stand
Like wonder-wounded hearers? This is I,

204 sage] F; a Q2 **210** SD] *Johnson; not in* Q2, F **213** t'have] F; haue Q2 **213** treble woe] Q2; terrible woer F **214** treble] F; double Q2 **217** SD] F; *not in* Q2 **220** T'o'ertop] To'retop Q2; to o're top F **221** SD *Advancing*] *Capell; not in* Q2, F **221** grief] Q2; griefes F **223** conjures] Q2; Coniure F

204 sage requiem 'sage' certainly looks odd, and many editors prefer Q2, but the word cannot possibly be a scribal interpolation; it is used to mean 'grave' as well as 'wise'. 'requiem' is funeral music.

204 such rest i.e. invoke or pray for such rest.

205 peace-parted souls those who have departed this life in peace.

209 What, the fair Ophelia! See Introduction, p. 56.

215 most...sense excellent intelligence (?).

217 caught her...in mine arms Since Q2 gives 'a corse' rather than 'a coffin' in the SD at 185 it may be that Shakespeare thought of a bier rather than a closed coffin, but Q1 confirms that the scene as played used a coffin, sealed or not. There is no evidence that Laertes raises the corpse, as in many productions he does.

220 Pelion A mountain in Thessaly. In Greek myth, there was an attempt to climb to heaven by putting Pelion on top of Ossa.

221 Olympus The mountain in Thessaly where in Greek myth the gods lived. 'blue' because it reaches the sky.

222 emphasis...phrase Hamlet accuses Laertes of employing a rhetorician's 'emphasis', and of expressing sorrow in a conventional 'phrase', or formal style.

223 wandering stars planets.

224 wonder-wounded struck with amazement.

Hamlet the Dane.

[*Laertes climbs out of the grave*]

LAERTES The devil take thy soul. [*Grappling with him*] 225

HAMLET Thou pray'st not well.

I prithee take thy fingers from my throat,

For though I am not splenitive and rash,

Yet have I in me something dangerous

Which let thy wisdom fear. Hold off thy hand. 230

CLAUDIUS Pluck them asunder.

GERTRUDE Hamlet, Hamlet!

ALL Gentlemen!

HORATIO Good my lord, be quiet.

[*The Attendants part them*].

HAMLET Why, I will fight with him upon this theme

Until my eyelids will no longer wag.

GERTRUDE O my son, what theme? 235

HAMLET I loved Ophelia; forty thousand brothers

Could not with all their quantity of love

Make up my sum. What wilt thou do for her?

225 SD *Laertes...grave*] *This edn; not in* Q2, F; *Hamlet leapes in after Leartes* Q1 225 SD *Grappling with him*] *Rowe; not in* Q2, F 228 For though] Q2; Sir though F 228 splenitive] spleenatiue Q2, F 228 and] F; *not in* Q2 229 in me something] Q2; something in me F, Q1 230 wisdom] wisedome Q2, Q1; wisensse F *(uncorrected)*; wisenesse F *(corrected)* 230 Hold off] Q2, Q1; Away F 231 ALL Gentlemen] Q2; *not in* F 232 SH HORATIO] *Hora.* Q2; *Gen.* F 232 SD] *Rowe; not in* Q2, F

225 Hamlet the Dane Hamlet asserts his title to the throne: see note to 1.1.15.

225 SD *Laertes...grave* Traditionally, Hamlet jumps into the grave at this point, and the two men struggle. The authority for this is the Bad Quarto, '*Hamlet leapes in after Leartes.*' Q2 and F are silent. Shakespeare cannot have intended Hamlet to leap into the grave and so become the attacker. It is manifest from his words that he is set upon (230, 256). The regret he expresses to Horatio (5.2.75–80) is for his verbal not physical attack. To couple Hamlet's defiant confrontation of Laertes and Claudius with a jump into the grave and a scuffle is unthinkable. Laertes scrambles out of the grave when he sees Hamlet advancing and rushes upon the man who killed his father.

An anonymous elegy on Burbage (who died in 1618) says, 'Oft have I seen him leap into the grave / Suiting the person which he seemed to have / Of a sad lover with so true an eye / That there I would have sworn he meant to die' *(Shakespere Allusion-Book,* 1932, I, 273). This is assumed to refer to Hamlet, but the sad lover meaning to die sounds more like Romeo. The evidence of Q1 certainly indicates stage practice in 1603, however, whether at the Globe or not. Neither Irving nor Booth observed the business of leaping into the grave. Granville Barker, in his *Preface* to *Hamlet* (1937), argued eloquently that Shakespeare intended Laertes to leap out of the grave and attack Hamlet. See the drawing by C. Walter Hodges, p. 57.

228 splenitive quick-tempered, irascible.

230 wisdom F's 'wiseness' is an attractive reading here, conveying a certain contempt or irony. But 'wisdom' is supported by Q1, and I think 'wiseness' is an error of the later scribe or the Folio compositor.

234 wag Simply 'move' or 'open and close'; the word now in such a context would be absurd. Hamlet means he will fight while he has any muscular strength left, even if only to blink.

236–38 I loved Ophelia...my sum Laertes' brotherly love may have expressed itself (in 1.3) priggishly and pompously and now his grief emerges in extravagant language, but he never behaved as cruelly to her as Hamlet did. Has Hamlet any right to be angry with Laertes for expressing his love for Ophelia? MacDonald says 'Perhaps this is the speech in all the play of which it is most difficult to get into a sympathetic comprehension.'

CLAUDIUS Oh he is mad Laertes.
GERTRUDE For love of God forbear him. 240
HAMLET 'Swounds, show me what thou't do.
Woo't weep, woo't fight, woo't fast, woo't tear thyself?
Woo't drink up eisel, eat a crocodile?
I'll do't. Dost thou come here to whine,
To outface me with leaping in her grave? 245
Be buried quick with her, and so will I.
And if thou prate of mountains, let them throw
Millions of acres on us, till our ground,
Singeing his pate against the burning zone,
Make Ossa like a wart. Nay, and thou'lt mouth, 250
I'll rant as well as thou.
GERTRUDE This is mere madness,
And thus awhile the fit will work on him;
Anon, as patient as the female dove
When that her golden couplets are disclosed,
His silence will sit drooping.
HAMLET Hear you sir, 255
What is the reason that you use me thus?
I loved you ever – but it is no matter.
Let Hercules himself do what he may,
The cat will mew, and dog will have his day. *Exit*
CLAUDIUS I pray thee good Horatio wait upon him. 260
Exit Horatio

241 'Swounds] Q2; Come F **241** thou't] th'owt Q2; thou'lt F **242** woo't fast] Q2; *not in* F **243** eisel] *Theobald*[2]; Esill Q2; *Esile* F **244** Dost thou] F; doost Q2 **251** SH GERTRUDE] *Quee.* Q2; *Kin.* F **252** thus] F; this Q2 **259–60** SD *Exit / Exit Horatio*] *Pope*; *Exit Hamlet / and Horatio* Q2; *Exit* F *(259)* **260** pray thee] Q2; pray you F

242 Woo't Colloquial for 'wilt thou'.

243 eisel vinegar (to increase his bitterness).

243 eat a crocodile i.e. to increase the flow of hypocritical tears.

249 the burning zone the sun's orbit between the tropics.

250 Ossa See note to 220 above.

250 and if.

251–5 This is mere madness...drooping F gives this speech to Claudius, most inappropriately, and is supported by Q1. It looks as though this was an error on the part of the playhouse scribe which was carried over into performance.

254 her golden couplets are disclosed 'The pigeon lays two eggs, and the young, when *disclosed* or hatched...are covered with yellow down' (Dowden).

255 silence...drooping i.e. his quietness resembles that of the patient dove not moving from her young and 'drooping' with lack of food for herself.

256 What is the reason...thus? It is hard to believe that Hamlet would have the audacity to ask this if he had in fact given the provocation of leaping in the grave after Laertes. See note to 225 above.

258–9 Let Hercules...day Hamlet recovers his poise sufficiently to depart with one of his riddles. Does Hamlet mean, contemptuously, that even Hercules couldn't stop Laertes having his petty triumph? Or does the contempt go into calling Laertes not a dog but a Hercules? i.e. 'Let this little Hercules carry on, but my turn will come.'

(*To Laertes*) Strengthen your patience in our last night's
speech;
We'll put the matter to the present push. –
Good Gertrude, set some watch over your son. –
This grave shall have a living monument.
An hour of quiet shortly shall we see, 265
Till then in patience our proceeding be.

Exeunt

[5.2] *Enter* HAMLET *and* HORATIO

HAMLET So much for this sir, now shall you see the other.
You do remember all the circumstance?
HORATIO Remember it my lord!
HAMLET Sir, in my heart there was a kind of fighting
That would not let me sleep. Methought I lay 5
Worse than the mutines in the bilboes. Rashly,
And praised be rashness for it – let us know,
Our indiscretion sometime serves us well
When our deep plots do pall, and that should learn us
There's a divinity that shapes our ends, 10

265 shortly] F; thirtie Q2 *(uncorrected)*; thereby Q2 *(corrected)* **266** Till] F; Tell Q2 **Act 5, Scene 2** 5.2] *Rowe* 1 shall you see] Q2; let me see F 5 Methought] me thought F; my thought Q2 6 bilboes] Bilboes F; bilbo Q2 7 praised] praysd Q2; praise F 8 sometime] Q2; sometimes F 9 deep] Q2; deare F 9 pall] Q2 *(uncorrected)*, paule F; fall Q2 *(corrected)* 9 learn] Q2; teach F

261 in our last night's speech i.e. by remembering what we planned last night.

262 present push immediate operation.

264 living enduring – with a grim secondary meaning that Hamlet's death will be the memorial for Ophelia.

Act 5, Scene 2

1 So much...other A mid-conversation entry, 'this' referring presumably to the first part of the story and 'the other' to the rest of it.

2 circumstance details.

6 the mutines in the bilboes mutineers in their shackles.

6–7 Rashly...rashness 'rash' (etc.) in Shakespeare means as often 'hasty', 'sudden' as it does 'unconsidered' or 'ill-advised'. The sense here is of a sudden, impulsive act without forethought.

7 let us know let us recognise, acknowledge.

8 indiscretion want of prudence and forethought (rather than a misguided act).

9 pall grow flat and stale, like wine that has gone off.

9 learn teach.

10–11 a divinity...we will i.e. there is a higher power in control of us, directing us towards our destination, however much we have blundered in the past and impeded our own progress. This recognition drastically modifies Hamlet's earlier assessment of his freedom and power to direct his own course. 'Rough-hew' is given by Florio in a definition of *Abbozzare*: 'to rough-hew or cast any first draught, to bungle up ill-favouredly'. (See NV.) Shakespeare here uses it to mean a crude botching. Hamlet feels the guiding hand of heaven in his own impulsive and unpremeditated actions, after the failure of his own willed efforts. Compare the tenth of the 39 Articles, 'Of Free-Will', which argues that 'we have no power to do good works' until we have the 'good will' given by 'the grace of God by Christ', after which that grace will be 'working with us'.

Rough-hew them how we will –

HORATIO That is most certain.

HAMLET Up from my cabin,
My sea-gown scarfed about me, in the dark
Groped I to find out them, had my desire,
Fingered their packet, and in fine withdrew 15
To mine own room again, making so bold,
My fears forgetting manners, to unseal
Their grand commission; where I found, Horatio –
O royal knavery! – an exact command,
Larded with many several sorts of reasons, 20
Importing Denmark's health, and England's too,
With ho! such bugs and goblins in my life,
That on the supervise, no leisure bated,
No, not to stay the grinding of the axe,
My head should be struck off.

HORATIO Is't possible? 25

HAMLET Here's the commission, read it at more leisure.
But wilt thou hear now how I did proceed?

HORATIO I beseech you.

HAMLET Being thus benetted round with villainies,
Or I could make a prologue to my brains, 30
They had begun the play. I sat me down,
Devised a new commission, wrote it fair.
I once did hold it, as our statists do,
A baseness to write fair, and laboured much
How to forget that learning; but sir, now 35

17 unseal] F; vnfold Q2 19 O] Oh F; A Q2 20 reasons] Q2; reason F 27 hear now] Q2; heare me F 29 villainies] *Capell;* villainy *Theobald*[2]; villaines Q2; Villaines F 30 Or] Q2; Ere F

13 **sea-gown** seaman's coat of coarse cloth, a duffle-coat.

13 **scarfed** wrapped loosely.

15 **Fingered** Filched, stole.

15 **in fine** in conclusion.

17 **forgetting** neglecting; i.e. causing him to forget.

20 **Larded** See 4.5.37.

21 **Importing** Appertaining to.

22 **bugs...life** monstrosities to be feared from my continued existence.

23 **supervise** viewing (of the commission).

23 **no leisure bated** i.e. no free time was to abate, or soften, the rigour of the execution.

29 **benetted round** i.e. trapped.

29 **villainies** Both F and Q2 agree in reading 'villains' and that is presumably what stood in Shakespeare's MS. But this leaves the line metrically lame, and the abstract is so much more apt here than the concrete that it is usually assumed that 'villainies' was what Shakespeare meant to write.

30 **Or** before, ere. See note to 1.2.147.

30–1 **Or I could...begun the play** i.e. his brains had put things in motion before he had set them to work.

33 **statists** statesmen.

34 **baseness** something befitting people of low rank.

It did me yeoman's service. Wilt thou know
Th'effect of what I wrote?

HORATIO Ay good my lord.

HAMLET An earnest conjuration from the king,
As England was his faithful tributary,
As love between them like the palm might flourish, 40
As peace should still her wheaten garland wear,
And stand a comma 'tween their amities,
And many suchlike as-es of great charge,
That on the view and knowing of these contents,
Without debatement further, more, or less, 45
He should those bearers put to sudden death,
Not shriving time allowed.

HORATIO How was this sealed?

HAMLET Why, even in that was heaven ordinant.
I had my father's signet in my purse,
Which was the model of that Danish seal; 50
Folded the writ up in the form of th'other,
Subscribed it, gave't th'impression, placed it safely,
The changeling never known. Now, the next day
Was our sea-fight, and what to this was sequent
Thou know'st already. 55

HORATIO So Guildenstern and Rosencrantz go to't.

HAMLET Why man, they did make love to this employment.
They are not near my conscience. Their defeat

37 Th'effect] Q2; The effects F 40 like] Q2; as F 40 might] Q2; should F 43 as-es] Assis F; as sir Q2 44 knowing] Q2; know F 46 those] Q2; the F 48 ordinant] Q2; ordinate F 51 in the form of th'other] Q2; in forme of the other F 52 Subscribed] Subscrib'd F; Subscribe Q2 54 sequent] Q2; sement F 55 know'st] F; knowest Q2 57 Why...employment] F; *not in* Q2 58 defeat] Q2; debate F

36 **yeoman's service** the service of a faithful attendant ('yeoman' in its earlier sense of a servant in a royal household).

38 **conjuration** solemn entreaty.

42 **a comma 'tween their amities** An odd phrase, but the language is meant to be affected. *OED* points to the definition of a comma given by Puttenham (*Art of English Poesy*, 1589, II.iv) as 'the shortest pause or intermission' between sections of speech. So the kingdoms are meant to be as near together as separate institutions can be, and what is between them is peace, not discord.

43 **charge** burden (punning on 'as-es' = asses).

45 **debatement further, more, or less** Continued ridicule of official verbiage.

47 **shriving time** time for confession and absolution. Compare Hamlet's attitude to the death of Claudius, 3.3.73–95.

48 **ordinant** directing.

49 **signet** seal.

50 **model** copy.

50 **that Danish seal** The official seal of Denmark on the commission which Hamlet has handed to Horatio (26 above).

52 **Subscribed it** Signed it (with Claudius's name).

57 **Why man...employment** This line is found only in F. I argue in the Introduction that this, with a passage in Hamlet's next speech, was part of a crucial Shakespearean revision. See pp. 14–19.

58 **defeat** destruction. Compare 2.2.523.

Does by their own insinuation grow.
'Tis dangerous when the baser nature comes 60
Between the pass and fell incensèd points
Of mighty opposites.

HORATIO Why, what a king is this!

HAMLET Does it not, think thee, stand me now upon –
He that hath killed my king, and whored my mother,
Popped in between th'election and my hopes, 65
Thrown out his angle for my proper life,
And with such cozenage – is't not perfect conscience
To quit him with this arm? And is't not to be damned
To let this canker of our nature come
In further evil? 70

HORATIO It must be shortly known to him from England
What is the issue of the business there.

HAMLET It will be short. The interim's mine,
And a man's life's no more than to say 'one'.
But I am very sorry, good Horatio, 75
That to Laertes I forgot myself,

59 Does] Q2; Doth F 63 think thee] Q2; thinkst thee F 68–80 To quit...comes here] F; *not in* Q2 73–5 It...mine,/And...'one'./But...Horatio,] *Hanmer*; It...short,/The...no more/Then...*Horatio*, F 73 interim's] F; interim is *Hanmer*

59 **insinuation** i.e. between Hamlet and Claudius.

60 **baser** inferior in rank. See note to 34 above.

61 **pass** thrust. Compare 4.7.137.

61–2 **pass...opposites** Hendiadys and transferred epithet. The fell (deadly) pass of the sword-points of incensed opposites (opponents).

63 **Does it not...stand me now upon** Is it not now incumbent upon me.

63 **think thee** bethink thee, please consider. F's 'thinkst thee' is a difficult impersonal construction, meaning 'does it appear to thee'.

65 **Popped in** This is meant to be contemptuous, but probably not as comic as we now feel it to be. 'pushed in' might be our equivalent. For Hamlet's accusation, compare 3.4.99–101.

66 **angle** fishing-line.

66 **my proper life** my very life.

67 **cozenage** cheating, fraud.

67 **is't not perfect conscience** is it not absolutely in accord with what is right.

68–80 This whole passage is not found in Q2. See Introduction, pp. 17–19.

68 **quit** requite, punish.

68 **is't not to be damned** See Introduction, pp. 56–8. Hamlet sees a prospect of damnation not, as before, in obeying a possibly fraudulent ghost (2.2.556) nor in opting out by suicide (3.1.78), but in failing to rid the world of the evil represented by Claudius.

69 **canker of our nature** a cancerous growth in humankind.

69–70 **come / In** enter into.

71–2 Horatio, whose replies are guarded in this scene, does not answer Hamlet directly, but warns him that if he is going to act he hasn't much time, because Claudius will soon hear of the death of Rosencrantz and Guildenstern and is then bound to act swiftly and decisively against Hamlet.

73 **The interim's mine** Deeply ironic, in view of the plot against his life which has been prepared by Claudius and Laertes, and which is now about to be sprung.

The line is a syllable short. Editions universally mend it by printing 'The interim is mine', but there is no authority for this.

74 **And a man's life...one** And in any case one's whole life is only a short space of time. One's death is never very far away. It is in this spirit that he turns to regret his outburst to Laertes.

For by the image of my cause, I see
The portraiture of his. I'll court his favours.
But sure the bravery of his grief did put me
Into a towering passion.

HORATIO Peace, who comes here? 80

Enter young OSRIC

OSRIC Your lordship is right welcome back to Denmark.
HAMLET I humbly thank you sir. – Dost know this water-fly?
HORATIO No my good lord.
HAMLET Thy state is the more gracious, for 'tis a vice to know him. He hath much land and fertile; let a beast be lord of beasts, and 85 his crib shall stand at the king's mess. 'Tis a chough, but as I say, spacious in the possession of dirt.
OSRIC Sweet lord, if your lordship were at leisure, I should impart a thing to you from his majesty.
HAMLET I will receive it sir with all diligence of spirit. Put your bonnet 90 to his right use, 'tis for the head.
OSRIC I thank your lordship, it is very hot.
HAMLET No believe me, 'tis very cold, the wind is northerly.
OSRIC It is indifferent cold my lord, indeed.
HAMLET But yet methinks it is very sultry and hot for my complexion. 95
OSRIC Exceedingly my lord, it is very sultry, as 'twere – I cannot tell how. But my lord, his majesty bade me signify to you that a has laid a great wager on your head. Sir, this is the matter –

78 court] *Rowe;* count F 80 SD *Enter young* OSRIC] F; *Enter a Courtier* Q2 81 SH OSRIC] *Osr.* F; *Cour.* Q2 *(& so throughout)* 82 humbly] F; humble Q2 86 say] Q2; saw F 88 lordship] Q2; friendship F 90 sir] Q2; *not in* F 90 Put] F; *not in* Q2 92 it is] Q2; 'tis F 95 But yet] Q2; *not in* F 95 sultry] soultry F; sully Q2 95 for] F; or Q2 97 But] F; *not in* Q2 97 a has] Q2; he ha's F

77–8 by the image...of his i.e. I recognise in my situation the essential features of his. (As a bereaved son, I should have remembered that grief makes one act strangely.) 'my cause' cannot mean his vengeance, because it is clear that (as Jenkins points out) he simply does not recognise himself as a proposed victim of Laertes' revenge. Presumably he cannot equate his accidental killing of Polonius with the premeditated murder of his father.

79 bravery extravagant display.

80 SD young OSRIC '*young Osricke*' (F) is only '*a Courtier*' in Q2. F brings forward his name from 171 and 231 below (where Q2 gives it as 'young *Ostricke*').

82 water-fly 'the proper emblem of a busy trifler' (Johnson).

85–6 let a beast...mess i.e. if you own a lot of livestock, even though you are an animal yourself you'll have a place at the king's table. 'crib' = manger.

86 chough Pronounced 'chuff'. A big black cliff bird, but the name seems to have been used for the jackdaw as well, and that is probably what is meant here. Jenkins has revived the old arguments of Caldecott and Furness (see NV) that the word should be 'chuff', a country bumpkin, a coarse, rough fellow.

91 his its.

94 indifferent moderately.

95 complexion temperament.

HAMLET I beseech you remember.

[*Hamlet moves him to put on his hat*]

OSRIC Nay good my lord, for my ease in good faith. Sir, [here is newly come to court Laertes; believe me an absolute gentleman, full of most excellent differences, of very soft society and great showing. Indeed, to speak feelingly of him, he is the card or calendar of gentry, for you shall find in him the continent of what part a gentleman would see. 100 105

HAMLET Sir, his definement suffers no perdition in you, though I know to divide him inventorially would dozy th'arithmetic of memory, and yet but yaw neither in respect of his quick sail. But in the verity of extolment, I take him to be a soul of great article, and his infusion of such dearth and rareness as, to make true diction of him, his semblable is his mirror, and who else would trace him, his umbrage, nothing more. 110

OSRIC Your lordship speaks most infallibly of him.

HAMLET The concernancy, sir? Why do we wrap the gentleman in our more rawer breath? 115

OSRIC Sir?

HORATIO Is't not possible to understand in another tongue? You will to't sir, really.

99 SD] *Johnson; not in* Q2, F **100** good my lord] Q2*;* in good Faith F **100** my ease] Q2*;* mine ease F **100–25** here is...Well sir] Q2*; not in* F **101** gentleman] Q 1611*;* gentlemen Q2 **103** feelingly] Q 1611*;* fellingly Q2 *(corrected);* sellingly Q2 *(uncorrected)* **107** dozy] *Kittredge;* dosie Q2 *(uncorrected);* dazzie Q2 *(corrected);* dizzie Q 1611 **108** yaw] Q2 *(uncorrected);* raw Q2 *(corrected)* **118** to't] too't Q2 *(uncorrected);* doo't Q2 *(corrected)*

99 remember *OED* (1d) cleverly associates this with the rather odd use of 'remember your courtesy' or 'be remembered' to request someone to put on his hat or cover his head. Perhaps this is right; but perhaps Hamlet just asks him to remember what he has said.

100–25 F here imposes a swingeing cut. Like the cutting out of the Lord's part, 171–82 below, this is clearly an attempt to shorten this very long build-up to the final scene by cutting out material not essential to the plot. These lines are almost entirely fun at the expense of Osric's diction.

102 excellent differences i.e. he excels in a variety of different accomplishments. Delius suggested the ingenious gloss 'different excellences' (NV).

102 soft society easy sociability.

102 great showing excellent appearance.

103 card or calendar map or guide.

104 gentry gentility.

104–5 the continent...would see he contains whatever quality a gentleman would wish to find.

106 perdition loss.

107 inventorially by means of an inventory of his qualities.

107 dozy make dizzy. Kittredge restored this quite common variant of 'dizzy' in 1939.

108 yaw swing off course.

108 neither after all.

108 in respect of in comparison with.

108–9 in the verity of extolment to praise him truthfully.

109 of great article i.e. there would be many articles to list in his inventory.

109 his infusion what is poured into him, his nature.

110 dearth dearness, high price.

111 trace him follow him closely.

111 umbrage shadow.

114 The concernancy sir? What's all this about? The word seems to be Hamlet's invention.

114–15 wrap...breath i.e. attempt to dress him in the crudity of language.

117–18 Is't not possible...really Paradoxically, Horatio's interjection is more obscure than the

HAMLET What imports the nomination of this gentleman?
OSRIC Of Laertes? 120
HORATIO His purse is empty already, all's golden words are spent.
HAMLET Of him sir.
OSRIC I know you are not ignorant –
HAMLET I would you did sir, yet in faith if you did, it would not much approve me. Well sir?] 125
OSRIC You are not ignorant of what excellence Laertes is.
[HAMLET I dare not confess that, lest I should compare with him in excellence, but to know a man well were to know himself.
OSRIC I mean sir for his weapon; but in the imputation laid on him by them, in his meed he's unfellowed.] 130
HAMLET What's his weapon?
OSRIC Rapier and dagger.
HAMLET That's two of his weapons, but well.
OSRIC The king sir hath wagered with him six Barbary horses, against the which he has impawned, as I take it, six French rapiers and 135 poniards, with their assigns, as girdle, hangers, and so. Three of the carriages in faith are very dear to fancy, very responsive to the hilts, most delicate carriages, and of very liberal conceit.
HAMLET What call you the carriages?
HORATIO I knew you must be edified by the margent ere you had done. 140

126 Laertes is.] Q2; *Laertes* is at his weapon. F 127–30 HAMLET I dare...unfellowed] Q2; *not in* F 129 his weapon] Q 1676; this weapon Q2 134 king...wagered] Q2; sir King ha's wag'd F 135 he has impawned] hee has impaund Q2; he impon'd F 136 hangers] F; hanger Q2 136 and so] Q2; or so F 140 HORATIO I knew...done] Q2; *not in* F

ridiculous colloquy which he interrupts. Some think he asks Osric if he can't understand his own jargon when another person speaks it. Perhaps it is an appeal to start again in a simpler language. 'You will to't' may mean (to Osric) 'You will get there eventually.'

119 What imports...gentleman? What is the purpose of naming this gentleman?

124–5 not much approve me i.e. it would be little to my credit to have such a testimony from you.

127–8 I dare...know himself This is not meant to have much meaning. The tenor is that for Hamlet to admit Laertes' excellence would be to claim that excellence for himself, since to *know* such excellence you would need to be able to *perform* such excellence.

129–30 in the imputation...by them in what people attribute to him.

130 meed merit (*OED* 3).

133 but well but never mind.

134 Barbary horses Arab horses, much prized, and soon to be bred in England by James I.

135 impawned wagered (F's spelling, 'impon'd', may indicate pronunciation). This is now Laertes' stake set up against the king's.

136 poniards daggers.

136 assigns appurtenances.

136 hangers the straps to hold the sword, attached to the girdle or sword-belt.

136 and so and so on.

137 dear to fancy i.e. they please one's taste.

137 very responsive All he means is that they are well adjusted.

138 liberal conceit imaginative design.

140 edified by the margent made wiser by a marginal gloss.

OSRIC The carriages sir are the hangers.

HAMLET The phrase would be more germane to the matter if we could carry a cannon by our sides; I would it might be hangers till then. But on, six Barbary horses against six French swords, their assigns, and three liberal-conceited carriages – that's the French bet against (145) the Danish. Why is this impawned, as you call it?

OSRIC The king sir, hath laid sir, that in a dozen passes between yourself and him, he shall not exceed you three hits. He hath laid on twelve for nine. And it would come to immediate trial, if your lordship would vouchsafe the answer. (150)

HAMLET How if I answer no?

OSRIC I mean my lord, the opposition of your person in trial.

HAMLET Sir, I will walk here in the hall. If it please his majesty, it is the breathing time of day with me. Let the foils be brought, the gentleman willing, and the king hold his purpose, I will win for (155) him and I can. If not, I will gain nothing but my shame and the odd hits.

OSRIC Shall I redeliver you e'en so?

HAMLET To this effect sir, after what flourish your nature will.

OSRIC I commend my duty to your lordship. (160)

HAMLET Yours, yours.

[*Exit Osric*]

He does well to commend it himself, there are no tongues else for's turn.

HORATIO This lapwing runs away with the shell on his head.

HAMLET A did comply with his dug before a sucked it. Thus has he, (165)

141 carriages] F; carriage Q2 143 a cannon] Q2; Cannon F 143 it might be] F; it be might Q2 *(uncorrected)*; it be Q2 *(corrected)* 145 bet] Q2; but F 146 impawned] impon'd F; all Q2 147 laid sir] Q2; laid F 147 yourself] Q2; you F 148–9 laid...nine] Q2; one twelue for mine F 149 it would] Q2; that would F 153 it is] Q2; 'tis F 156 and I can] Q2; if I can F 156 I will] Q2; Ile F 158 redeliver...so] F; deliuer you so Q2 161 Yours, yours] F; Yours Q2 161 SD] *Capell, following Rowe; not in* Q2, F 162 He does] F; doo's Q2 163 turn] Q2; tongue F 165 A did] Q2; He did F 165 comply] F; so sir Q2 *(corrected)*; sir Q2 *(uncorrected)* 165 a sucked] Q2; hee suck't F 165 has] Q2; had F

147–9 The king sir...twelve for nine There are those who claim to understand this wager, and those who, like Dr Johnson and the present editor, do not. There are to be twelve bouts, and the bet is that Laertes will not lead by more than three wins. As soon as Laertes has got eight hits, he can't lose; as soon as Hamlet registers five hits, *he* can't lose. But what is this 'twelve for nine'? It has never been satisfactorily explained.

150 vouchsafe the answer offer yourself as an opponent.

154 breathing exercising.

154 Let Conditional. 'If the foils are brought, if Laertes is willing, if the king maintains his purpose, then I will play the match and win for the king if I can.'

158 redeliver you report back what you say.

159 after what flourish conforming to whatever embellishment.

160 commend my duty See note to 1.5.184. Hamlet takes up the routine word 'commend' in its meaning 'recommend'.

164 This lapwing...head A proverb for juvenile forwardness (Tilley L69).

165 his dug his mother's (or his nurse's) nipple.

and many more of the same bevy that I know the drossy age dotes on, only got the tune of the time and outward habit of encounter, a kind of yesty collection, which carries them through and through the most fanned and winnowed opinions; and do but blow them to their trial, the bubbles are out. 170

[*Enter a* LORD

LORD My lord, his majesty commended him to you by young Osric, who brings back to him that you attend him in the hall. He sends to know if your pleasure hold to play with Laertes, or that you will take longer time.

HAMLET I am constant to my purposes, they follow the king's pleasure. 175 If his fitness speaks, mine is ready; now or whensoever, provided I be so able as now.

LORD The king and queen, and all, are coming down.

HAMLET In happy time.

LORD The queen desires you to use some gentle entertainment to 180 Laertes, before you fall to play.

HAMLET She well instructs me.]

[*Exit Lord*]

HORATIO You will lose, my lord.

HAMLET I do not think so. Since he went into France, I have been in

166 many] Q2; mine F 166 bevy] Beauy F; breede Q2 167 outward] F; out of an Q2 168 yesty] F; histy Q2 169 fanned and winnowed] *Warburton*; prophane and trennowed Q2; fond and winnowed F 170 trial] Q2; tryalls F 170–82 *Enter a* LORD...instructs me] Q2; *not in* F 171 Osric] *Rowe*; *Ostricke* Q2 182 SD] *Theobald*[2]; *not in* Q2 183 lose] Q2; lose this wager F

166 the drossy age the people of these rubbishy times.

167 got the tune of the time The sense is of listening attentively to what other people sing and learning to copy them.

168 yesty yeasty, frothy. A regular form of the word. Compare *Macbeth* 4.1.53, 'the yesty waves'.

168 collection mixture, brew (see notes to 3.2.233, 4.7.143).

169 fanned and winnowed Synonyms for blowing the chaff off the grain. 'fanned' is Warburton's emendation for F's 'fond'. Probably Shakespeare wrote 'fand'. The Q2 compositor saw this as 'fane'. The MS. must have been dirty or tattered; he thought he had the end of the word 'profane'. He could not read 'winnowed' either, and came out wildly with 'prophane and trennowed'.

The image is of a frothy mass working its way through refined material to the top, where it appears as mere bubbles which can be blown away. The superficial qualities of people like Osric take them through the society of superior people, but they cannot last, and when they are tested, their hollowness reveals itself.

170 SD–182 SD Enter a LORD... This passage is not found in F, which thus dispenses with an additional character not necessary to the play.

171 commended him to you sent his compliments to you (see note to 1.5.184).

175 I am constant to my purposes A grim double meaning here: Hamlet must also be thinking of his deeper resolve.

176 If his fitness speaks When his convenience names a time.

179 In happy time It is an opportune time.

180 use...entertainment give a courteous reception.

continual practice; I shall win at the odds. But thou wouldst not 185
think how ill all's here about my heart – but it is no matter.

HORATIO Nay good my lord –

HAMLET It is but foolery, but it is such a kind of gaingiving as would
perhaps trouble a woman.

HORATIO If your mind dislike anything, obey it. I will forestall their 190
repair hither, and say you are not fit.

HAMLET Not a whit, we defy augury. There is special providence in
the fall of a sparrow. If it be now, 'tis not to come; if it be not to
come, it will be now; if it be not now, yet it will come – the
readiness is all. Since no man of aught he leaves knows, what is't 195
to leave betimes? Let be.

A table prepared, with flagons of wine on it. Trumpets, Drums and Officers with cushions. Enter CLAUDIUS, GERTRUDE, LAERTES *and* LORDS, *with other Attendants with foils, daggers and gauntlets*

CLAUDIUS Come Hamlet, come and take this hand from me.
[*Hamlet takes Laertes by the hand*]

HAMLET Give me your pardon sir, I've done you wrong;
But pardon't as you are a gentleman.
This presence knows, 200
And you must needs have heard, how I am punished

185 But thou] F; thou Q2 **185** wouldst] Q2; wouldest F **186** how ill all's] Q2; how all F **188** gaingiving] F; gamgiuing Q2 **190** obey it] Q2; obey F **192** There is] Q2; there's a F **193** If it be now] F; if it be Q2 **195** of aught...what is't] of ought he leaues, knowes what ist Q2; ha's ought of what he leaues. What is't F **196** Let be] Q2; *not in* F **196** SD] *This edn; A table prepared, Trumpets, Drums and officers with Cushions, King, Queene, and all the state, Foiles, daggers, and Laertes.* Q2; *Enter King, Queene, Laertes and Lords, with other Attendants with Foyles, and Gauntlets, a Table and Flagons of Wine on it.* F **197** SD *Hamlet...hand*] *This edn; not in* Q2, F; *Gives him the hand of Laertes / Hanmer* **198** I've] F; I haue Q2 **199–200** But...knows] F; *as one line* Q2

185 at the odds given these particular odds.

188 gaingiving foreboding, presentment of evil. Perhaps stronger than 'misgiving': Shakespeare thinks of 'gain' as in 'gainsay' – indicating opposition. This is a singular use of an uncommon word.

192–3 we defy...sparrow Hamlet rejects 'augury', the attempt to read signs of future events and to take steps accordingly. All occurrences show God's immediate concern and control, and he will therefore accept the circumstances which present themselves and not try to avoid them. 'special providence' is a theological term for a particular act of divine intervention. 'the fall of a sparrow' alludes to Matthew 10.29.

193 If it be now i.e. his own death. He knows the king will be making a second attempt to murder him. He must also have in mind the final confrontation when he will 'quit' Claudius, even if it costs him his life.

195–6 Since no man...betimes? I follow Q2 fairly closely, regarding F as a deliberate simplification (you can't take it with you). 'Since no one has any knowledge of the life he leaves behind him, what does it matter if one dies early?' An early death may be a blessing.

196 Let be Do not try to alter the course of things.

196 SD This is a conflation of Q2 and F. F does not provide for trumpets and drums (i.e. trumpeters and drummers), nor the cushions, nor the daggers. Q2, on the other hand, does not have gauntlets. It is quite possible that the book-keeper had ideas different from Shakespeare about staging the fight, but Wilson's view that F represents later developments in fencing customs cannot be maintained if this edition's view of the provenance of F is correct.

200 presence assembly (suggesting a formal court occasion).

With a sore distraction. What I have done,
That might your nature, honour and exception
Roughly awake, I here proclaim was madness.
Was't Hamlet wronged Laertes? Never Hamlet. 205
If Hamlet from himself be tane away,
And when he's not himself does wrong Laertes,
Then Hamlet does it not, Hamlet denies it.
Who does it then? His madness. If't be so,
Hamlet is of the faction that is wronged, 210
His madness is poor Hamlet's enemy.
Sir, in this audience,
Let my disclaiming from a purposed evil
Free me so far in your most generous thoughts,
That I have shot my arrow o'er the house 215
And hurt my brother.

LAERTES I am satisfied in nature,
Whose motive in this case should stir me most
To my revenge; but in my terms of honour
I stand aloof, and will no reconcilement
Till by some elder masters of known honour 220
I have a voice and precedent of peace
To keep my name ungored. But till that time
I do receive your offered love like love,
And will not wrong it.

HAMLET I embrace it freely,
And will this brother's wager frankly play. 225

202 a sore] Q2; sore F **212** Sir...audience] F; *not in* Q2 **215** my arrow] Q2; mine Arrow F **216** brother] Q2; Mother F **222** keep] F; *not in* Q2 **222** ungored] vngord Q2; vngorg'd F **222** till] F; all Q2 **224–5** I embrace...play] F; *as prose in* Q2 **224** I embrace] Q2; I do embrace F

204–11 I here proclaim...enemy This is certainly disingenuous. Hamlet was not mad when he killed Polonius. He is making a public declaration to an audience, one of whom, Claudius, knows perfectly well why he killed Polonius. The furthest he dare go in apologising to Laertes is to say that he never intended to kill his father – there was no 'purposed evil' (213). In blaming his madness, he knows that his audience (apart from Claudius) will believe him; he is continuing to play his part, and keeping up the long battle of wits with Claudius. But beneath all this, now that Hamlet is revaluing all his past actions, he must consider his behaviour intolerable, a 'sore distraction' indeed, when he was not himself. It *was* madness, of a kind, to kill Polonius, and his regret is entirely genuine, even if his expression of it is considerably less than candid.

206 tane taken.

210 faction party.

216 in nature so far as natural feeling goes.

217 motive prompting.

221 voice judgement.

221 of peace for reconciliation.

222 my name ungored my reputation undamaged.

224 And will not wrong it Laertes is preparing to kill Hamlet. His whole speech is pretence and deceit.

225 frankly freely, with an unburdened mind.

Give us the foils, come on.

LAERTES Come, one for me.

HAMLET I'll be your foil Laertes. In mine ignorance
Your skill shall like a star i'th'darkest night
Stick fiery off indeed.

LAERTES You mock me sir.

HAMLET No, by this hand. 230

CLAUDIUS Give them the foils, young Osric. Cousin Hamlet,
You know the wager?

HAMLET Very well my lord.
Your grace has laid the odds a'th'weaker side.

CLAUDIUS I do not fear it, I have seen you both.
But since he is bettered, we have therefore odds. 235

LAERTES This is too heavy, let me see another.

HAMLET This likes me well. These foils have all a length?

OSRIC Ay my good lord.

Prepare to play

CLAUDIUS Set me the stoups of wine upon that table.
If Hamlet give the first or second hit, 240
Or quit in answer of the third exchange,
Let all the battlements their ordnance fire.
The king shall drink to Hamlet's better breath,
And in the cup an union shall he throw
Richer than that which four successive kings 245
In Denmark's crown have worn. Give me the cups,

226 come on] F; *not in* Q2 **233** has] Q2; hath F **235** betterd] better'd F; better Q2 **238** SD] F *(237)*; *not in* Q2 **242** ordnance] Q2; Ordinance F **244** union] vnion F; Vnice Q2 *(uncorrected)*; Onixe Q2 *(corrected)*

227 foil material used to set off or display some richer thing, as a jewel.

229 Stick fiery off Stand out brilliantly.

233 laid the odds A puzzling phrase, which has generated much discussion. It *must* mean either that Claudius has backed the weaker contestant, or, more probably, that he has kindly provided an advantage for Hamlet in the handicap he has given Laertes.

234–5 An extremely politic reply. Claudius says he does *not* think Hamlet is weaker, but because Laertes has *improved*, he has arranged a handicap for him.

236 let me see another Wilson supposes that Osric is an accomplice. It is quite incredible that Claudius and Laertes should have admitted anyone else into their plot – least of all the young waterfly! Whatever 'shuffling' is done to get the poisoned and unbated foil into Laertes' hand is done by himself.

237 likes me pleases me.

239 stoups The flagons mentioned in 196SD.

241 Or quit...exchange Or, having lost the first two bouts, gets his revenge in fighting the third bout.

243 better breath i.e. he will drink to the increase of Hamlet's energy or power.

244 union a pearl of special quality and high value. F's reading. Q2 printed first 'Vnice', which could be a misreading of 'Vniõ'; the press-corrector, using his wits rather than the MS., changed this to 'Onixe'. When F again has 'Vnion', at 305, Q2 again prints 'Onixe'.

246 Give me the cups The cups, or goblets, are not mentioned in 196SD. At the beginning of the speech (239), Claudius has the wine brought before him. He now asks for the goblets. (There is a good deal of ceremonial fetching and carrying in this

And let the kettle to the trumpet speak,
The trumpet to the cannoneer without,
The cannons to the heavens, the heaven to earth,
'Now the king drinks to Hamlet!' Come, begin, 250
And you the judges bear a wary eye.

Trumpets the while

HAMLET Come on sir.

LAERTES Come my lord.

They play

HAMLET One.

LAERTES No. 255

HAMLET Judgement.

OSRIC A hit, a very palpable hit.

LAERTES Well, again.

CLAUDIUS Stay, give me drink. Hamlet, this pearl is thine.
Here's to thy health.

Drum, trumpets sound, and shot goes off

Give him the cup. 260

HAMLET I'll play this bout first, set it by awhile.
Come.

[*They play*]

Another hit. What say you?

LAERTES A touch, a touch, I do confess't.

CLAUDIUS Our son shall win.

GERTRUDE He's fat and scant of breath.
Here Hamlet, take my napkin, rub thy brows. 265
The queen carouses to thy fortune, Hamlet.

HAMLET Good madam.

247 trumpet] Q2; Trumpets F 250 'Now...Hamlet.'] *as reported speech in Capell; not differentiated in* Q2, F 251 SD] Q2; *not in* F 253 Come my lord] Q2; Come on sir F 260 SD] *This edn; Drum, trumpets and shot. Florish, a peece goes off* Q2 *(257): Trumpets sound, and shot goes off* F 261 set it by] Q2; set by F 262 SD *They play*] *They play again* / *Rowe; not in* Q2, F 263 A touch, a touch] F; *not in* Q2 263 confess't] Q2; confesse F 265 Here...brows] Q2; Heere's a Napkin, rub thy browes F

scene.) Claudius then explains just how his toast will be given. He does not drink until after the first bout (259).

247 kettle kettle-drum.

259–60 give me drink...health The king drinks to Hamlet's health while holding the 'pearl' aloft. He then deposits the poisoned pellet in the goblet while the drum, trumpet and shot are sounding off.

264 fat...breath It is hard indeed to think of Hamlet as a fat man – and if Burbage was corpulent, all the less reason for calling attention to it. 'sweaty' has been suggested as the meaning of 'fat' but it is not properly attested. Probably the queen means that he is soft, out of condition, in poor trim. It is interesting that the word 'fat' is associated with shortness of breath at 3.4.154, in the phrase, 'the fatness of these pursy times' (see the note).

265 napkin handkerchief.

266 carouses drinks a health.

CLAUDIUS Gertrude, do not drink!
GERTRUDE I will my lord, I pray you pardon me.
[*Drinks*]
CLAUDIUS [*Aside*] It is the poisoned cup. It is too late. 270
HAMLET I dare not drink yet madam, by and by.
GERTRUDE Come, let me wipe thy face.
LAERTES My lord, I'll hit him now.
CLAUDIUS I do not think't.
LAERTES And yet it is almost against my conscience.
HAMLET Come, for the third, Laertes. You do but dally. 275
I pray you pass with your best violence.
I am afeard you make a wanton of me.
LAERTES Say you so? Come on.
Play
OSRIC Nothing neither way.
LAERTES Have at you now! [*Wounds Hamlet*] 280
In scuffling they change rapiers
CLAUDIUS Part them. They are incensed.
HAMLET Nay, come again. [*Wounds Laertes*]
[*Gertrude falls*]
OSRIC Look to the queen there, ho!
HORATIO They bleed on both sides. How is it my lord?
OSRIC How is't Laertes? 285
LAERTES Why, as a woodcock to mine own springe, Osric.
I am justly killed with mine own treachery.

269 SD *Drinks*] *Hanmer; not in* Q2, F **270** SD *Aside*] *Rowe; not in* Q2, F **274** it is almost against] Q2; 'tis almost 'gainst F **275** You do but] Q2; you but F **277** afeard] affear'd F; sure F **278** SD] F; *not in* Q2 **280** SD *Wounds Hamlet*] *Laertes wounds Hamlet…/ Rowe; not in* Q2, F **280.1** SD *In scuffling…rapiers*] F; *not in* Q2 **282** SD *Wounds Laertes*] *Rowe (substantially); not in* Q2, F **282.1** SD *Gertrude falls*] *Queen falls / Capell; not in* Q2, F **284** is it] Q2; is't F **286** mine own springe] Q2; mine Sprindge F

274 And yet…conscience Rowe made this an aside, and many editions follow. But it is possible that Laertes is speaking directly to the king. The reader, actor or director must make his own decision, and an editor's stage direction ought not to restrict his freedom.

276 pass thrust.

277 make a wanton of me indulge me as though I were a child.

279 Nothing neither way This is presumably the end of the third bout.

280 Have at you now! There is no indication in Q2, and therefore presumably no indication in Shakespeare's MS., how he wanted the crisis of the play to be managed. The exchange of rapiers, given in F's stage direction, is confirmed by Q1, '*They catch one anothers Rapiers.*' The usual stage practice is that at the beginning of the fourth bout, Laertes lunges at Hamlet before he is ready, and wounds him slightly with the unbated and poisoned foil. Realising that there is some malpractice, Hamlet fights violently with Laertes, disarms him, picks up the deadly rapier and sees its unbated point. Sometimes he grimly offers Laertes his own practice-foil. The fight resumes until Hamlet succeeds in wounding Laertes.

286 as a woodcock…springe i.e. caught in my own trap. See 1.3.115.

HAMLET How does the queen?
CLAUDIUS She sounds to see them bleed.
GERTRUDE No, no, the drink, the drink – O my dear Hamlet –
The drink, the drink – I am poisoned. [*Dies*] 290
HAMLET Oh villainy! – Ho, let the door be locked!
Treachery! Seek it out!
[*Laertes falls*]
LAERTES It is here Hamlet. Hamlet, thou art slain,
No medicine in the world can do thee good,
In thee there is not half an hour of life – 295
The treacherous instrument is in thy hand,
Unbated and envenomed. The foul practice
Hath turned itself on me; lo, here I lie,
Never to rise again. Thy mother's poisoned –
I can no more – the king, the king's to blame. 300
HAMLET The point envenomed too! Then, venom, to thy work!
Hurts the king
ALL Treason, treason!
CLAUDIUS Oh yet defend me friends, I am but hurt.
HAMLET Here, thou incestuous, murderous, damnèd Dane,
Drink off this potion. Is thy union here? 305
Follow my mother. *King dies*
LAERTES He is justly served,
It is a poison tempered by himself.
Exchange forgiveness with me, noble Hamlet.
Mine and my father's death come not upon thee,
Nor thine on me. *Dies* 310
HAMLET Heaven make thee free of it! I follow thee.

290 SD *Dies*] *Queen dies* / *Rowe; not in* Q2, F **292** SD *Laertes falls*] *Capell; not in* Q2, F **293** Hamlet. Hamlet, thou] F; *Hamlet,* thou Q2 **295** hour of life] F; houres life Q2 **296** thy hand] F; my hand Q2 **301** SD] F; *not in* Q2 **304** Here] Heere F; Heare Q2 **304** murderous] F; *not in* Q2 **305** thy union] F; the Onixe Q2 **306** SD] F; *not in* Q2 **306–7** He...himself] F; *as one line* Q2 **310** SD] F; *not in* Q2

288 sounds swoons.

297 envenomed poisoned.

297 practice plot.

302 Treason, treason! This reaction is some indication of what Hamlet has all along had to face in planning to kill the king for a crime unknown to the people. Notice also his concern (323–4) at not having been able to explain the reasons for his action.

305 Drink off this potion Some commentators (including Capell and Kittredge) think this is figurative, and that 'this potion' is a second sword-stab. Kittredge doesn't like the savagery of forcing the drink down the dying man's throat. Like it or not, that, it seems, is what we are given.

305 thy union In a double sense: the fake pearl, and the 'incestuous' marriage. Hamlet sends him to continue this latter false union – in death. 'Follow my mother.'

307 tempered mixed, prepared.

309 come not upon thee This is a wish or prayer, not a statement: 'Let not these deaths be visited upon, or charged to thee!'

311 make thee free absolve thee.

I am dead, Horatio. Wretched queen adieu.
You that look pale, and tremble at this chance,
That are but mutes or audience to this act,
Had I but time, as this fell sergeant death 315
Is strict in his arrest, oh I could tell you –
But let it be. Horatio, I am dead,
Thou livest; report me and my cause aright
To the unsatisfied.

HORATIO Never believe it.
I am more an antique Roman than a Dane. 320
Here's yet some liquor left.

HAMLET As th'art a man,
Give me the cup. Let go, by heaven I'll ha't.
O God, Horatio, what a wounded name,
Things standing thus unknown, shall live behind me!
If thou didst ever hold me in thy heart, 325
Absent thee from felicity awhile,
And in this harsh world draw thy breath in pain
To tell my story.

March afar off, and shot within

What warlike noise is this?

OSRIC Young Fortinbras, with conquest come from Poland,
To the ambassadors of England gives 330
This warlike volley.

HAMLET Oh I die, Horatio,
The potent poison quite o'ercrows my spirit.
I cannot live to hear the news from England.

318 cause aright] Q2; causes right F **322** ha't] hate Q2; haue't F **323** O God] O god Q2; Oh good F **324** shall live] F; shall I leaue Q2 **328** SD] *Steevens; March afarre off, and shout within* F; *A marche a farre off* Q2 *(Q2 and F then give / Enter Osrick)* **330** To the] *Pope;* To th' Q2, F **330–1** To...volley] *as one line* Q2, F

313 chance mischance.

314 mutes Characters in a play with no speaking parts. Hamlet's remarkable view of himself as he dies, as being at the centre of a theatre-performance, is discussed by Anne Righter, *Shakespeare and the Idea of the Play*, 1962, at the end of ch. 6.

315 sergeant Officer who summoned persons to appear before a court.

319 unsatisfied i.e. those who will need to be satisfied with an explanation. It is to be remembered that Polonius, Laertes and Ophelia all die without knowing of Claudius's crime and the reason for Hamlet's conduct.

320 antique Roman i.e. for whom suicide might be noble rather than damnable. Cato is the person the Elizabethans would chiefly have in mind in a context like this. Compare *Julius Caesar* 5.1.100–7. When in his reply Hamlet calls death 'felicity' (332) he does not think of the possible sufferings awaiting those who take their own lives, as he does in his great soliloquy in 3.1.

329 OSRIC Both Q2 and F give an entry for Osric at this point. But it doesn't appear that he has left the stage. Perhaps Shakespeare meant him to go to the door as if to investigate, then return?

332 o'ercrows triumphs over (an image from cockfighting).

But I do prophesy th'election lights
On Fortinbras; he has my dying voice. 335
So tell him, with th'occurrents more and less
Which have solicited – the rest is silence. *Dies*

HORATIO Now cracks a noble heart. Good night sweet prince,
And flights of angels sing thee to thy rest. –
Why does the drum come hither? 340

Enter FORTINBRAS *and* ENGLISH AMBASSADORS, *with drum, colours and Attendants*

FORTINBRAS Where is this sight?

HORATIO What is it you would see?
If aught of woe or wonder, cease your search.

FORTINBRAS This quarry cries on havoc. O proud death,
What feast is toward in thine eternal cell
That thou so many princes at a shot 345
So bloodily hast struck?

I AMBASSADOR The sight is dismal,
And our affairs from England come too late.
The ears are senseless that should give us hearing,
To tell him his commandment is fulfilled,
That Rosencrantz and Guildenstern are dead. 350
Where should we have our thanks?

HORATIO Not from his mouth,
Had it th'ability of life to thank you;
He never gave commandment for their death.
But since, so jump upon this bloody question,

336 th'] Q2; the F 337 silence.] Q2; silence. O, o, o, o. F 337 SD] F; *not in* Q2 338 cracks] Q2; cracke F 340 SD] F *(Ambassador); Enter Fortenbrasse, with the Embassadors* Q2 341 you] Q2; ye F 343 This] Q2; His F 345 shot] Q2; shoote F 346 SH I AMBASSADOR] I. E. *Capell; Embas.* Q2; *Amb.* F

334–5 th'election...Fortinbras i.e. Fortinbras will be chosen as the next king. See 65 above, and the note to 1.2.109.

335 voice vote.

336 occurrents more and less i.e. all the happenings.

337 solicited – prompted, brought forth (his own actions, presumably).

338 cracks a...heart The heart-strings were supposed to snap at the moment of death. Compare *Richard III* 4.4.365, 'till heart-strings break', and Massinger, *Duke of Milan* 3.3.157, 'though my heart-strings crack for't'.

340 SD ENGLISH AMBASSADORS The F direction gives us only one ambassador, again reflecting the theatre's scaling down of Shakespeare's generous provisions.

343 This quarry cries on havoc This heap of bodies proclaims a massacre. A 'quarry' is literally a heap of dead animals after a hunt. For 'cries on', compare *Othello* 5.1.48, 'Whose noise is this that cries on murder?'

344 toward Monosyllable, 'to'ard'.

344 eternal Shakespeare occasionally uses this word as if it meant 'damnable' or 'infernal'. See *Othello* 4.2.130, 'some eternal villain'. (See *OED* 7, and Schmidt.)

354 jump immediately.

354 question quarrel, dispute (compare 4.4.26).

You from the Polack wars, and you from England, 355
Are here arrived, give order that these bodies
High on a stage be placèd to the view,
And let me speak to th'yet unknowing world
How these things came about. So shall you hear
Of carnal, bloody, and unnatural acts, 360
Of accidental judgements, casual slaughters,
Of deaths put on by cunning and forced cause,
And in this upshot, purposes mistook
Fallen on th'inventors' heads. All this can I
Truly deliver.

FORTINBRAS Let us haste to hear it, 365
And call the noblest to the audience.
For me, with sorrow I embrace my fortune.
I have some rights of memory in this kingdom,
Which now to claim my vantage doth invite me.

HORATIO Of that I shall have also cause to speak, 370
And from his mouth whose voice will draw on more.
But let this same be presently performed,
Even while men's minds are wild, lest more mischance
On plots and errors happen.

FORTINBRAS Let four captains
Bear Hamlet like a soldier to the stage, 375
For he was likely, had he been put on,
To have proved most royal; and for his passage,

358 to th'yet] F; to yet Q2 362 forced cause] F; for no cause Q2 364 th'inventors] Q2; the Inuentors F 368 rights] Q2; Rites F 369 now] Q2; are F 370 also] Q2; alwayes F 371 on more] F; no more Q2 373 while] Q2; whiles F 377 royal] royall Q2, Q1; royally F

360 carnal...acts Claudius's deeds.

361 accidental judgements punishments brought about fortuitously. Horatio no doubt has Laertes in mind.

362 put on arranged, set up.

362 forced cause A cause where the truth has been wrested and constrained into falsehood (compare *Winter's Tale* 3.3.79, the 'forced baseness' which Leontes has put upon Perdita). Horatio probably means the lies to the English king by which Hamlet would have been executed. Some editors wrongly suppose 'forced' = 'compelled'.

363 this upshot the final issue, visible here. ('upshot' is the deciding shot in an archery contest.)

368 rights of memory ancient rights (?). We do not know what these are. What we do know is that the throne of Denmark now goes to a foreigner who at the beginning of the play was preparing to gain that throne by force of arms.

369 my vantage my present advantageous situation.

371 whose voice...more i.e. whose vote is likely to influence other electors.

372 presently immediately.

373 wild lacking order, bewildered.

374 On Arising from.

376 put on put to the test.

377 royal Nosworthy argues that F gives the true reading and that Q2 followed Q1 (*Shakespeare's Occasional Plays*, p. 137). F's reading ('royally') is metrically better, but it gives the phrase a different meaning, and I think the wrong one. Q2 means that Hamlet, if he had become king, would have turned

The soldier's music and the rite of war
Speak loudly for him.
Take up the bodies. Such a sight as this 380
Becomes the field, but here shows much amiss.
Go bid the soldiers shoot.
Exeunt marching, after the which a peal of ordnance are shot off

378 rite] right Q2; rites F 380 bodies] Q2; body F 382 SD] F; *Exeunt* Q2

out to be truly royal. F means that Hamlet would have thrived in true royal fashion.

377 passage i.e. from this world.

378 rite of war F gives 'rites', but Shakespeare frequently uses the singular, e.g. 'the rite of May', *Midsummer Night's Dream* 4.1.133, 'rite of love', *All's Well* 2.4.41.

382 a peal of ordnance a salute of guns.

READING LIST

Among the voluminous writings on *Hamlet* there is so much that is good and important that any manageable list of recommended titles is bound to appear capricious and invidious. There are however many guides which can help the reader to find the studies he needs. In the selection which follows, the order of entry in each section is chronological.

BIBLIOGRAPHIES

Jaggard, W. *Shakespeare Bibliography,* 1911, pp. 306–18

Ebisch, W. and Schücking, L. L. *A Shakespeare Bibliography,* 1931, pp. 224–38
Supplement for the Years 1930–1935, 1937, pp. 80–5

Raven, A. A., *A 'Hamlet' Bibliography and Reference Guide, 1877–1935,* 1936, reprinted 1966

Bateson, F. W. (ed.). *The Cambridge Bibliography of English Literature,* 1940, I, 564–8.

Watson, G. (ed.). *Supplement* to *The Cambridge Bibliography of English Literature,* 1957, pp. 267–70

Smith, Gordon Ross. *A Classified Shakespeare Bibliography, 1936–1958,* 1963, pp. 665–99

Watson, G. (ed.). *The New Cambridge Bibliography of English Literature*, 1974, I, 1515–23

HISTORIES AND ANALYSES OF CRITICISM

Waldock, A. J. A. *'Hamlet': A Study in Critical Method,* 1931

Conklin, P. S. *A History of 'Hamlet' Criticism, 1601–1821*, 1947, reprinted 1957

Leech, C. 'Studies in *Hamlet*, 1901–1955', *Shakespeare Survey* 9 (1956), 1–15

Hunter, G. '*Hamlet* criticism', *Critical Quarterly* 1 (1959), 27–32

Spencer, T. J. B. 'The decline of *Hamlet*', in '*Hamlet*' (Stratford-upon-Avon Studies 5), ed. J. R. Brown and B. Harris, 1963, pp. 185–99

Wells, S. 'A reader's guide to *Hamlet*', in *ibid.*, pp. 200–7

Weitz, M. *'Hamlet' and the Philosophy of Literary Criticism,* 1964

Jenkins, H. '*Hamlet* then till now', *Shakespeare Survey* 18 (1965), 34–45

Gottschalk, P. *The Meanings of 'Hamlet': Modes of Literary Interpretation since Bradley,* 1972

Jump, J. '*Hamlet*', in *Shakespeare* (Select Bibliographical Guides), ed. S. Wells, 1973, pp. 144–58

ANTHOLOGIES OF CRITICISM

Furness, H. H. *Hamlet* (A New Variorum Edition of Shakespeare), 1877, reprinted 1963, II, 143–393
Williamson, C. C. H. *Readings on the Character of Hamlet, 1661–1947*, 1950
Hoy, C. *Hamlet* (Norton Critical Edition), 1963, pp. 145–266
Hubler, E. *The Tragedy of Hamlet, Prince of Denmark* (The Signet Classic Shakespeare), 1963, pp. 189–264
Jump, J. *Shakespeare: 'Hamlet': A Casebook*, 1968
Bevington, D. M. *Twentieth-century Interpretations of 'Hamlet'*, 1968

STAGE HISTORY

Winter, W. *Shakespeare on the Stage: First Series*, 1911, reprinted 1969
Odell, G. C. D. *Shakespeare from Betterton to Irving*, 2 vols., 1920, reprinted 1966
Spencer, H. *Shakespeare Improved: The Restoration Versions in Quarto and on the Stage*, 1927
Child, H. 'The stage-history of *Hamlet*', in *Hamlet* (New Shakespeare), ed. J. D. Wilson, 1934, pp. lxix–xcvii
Sprague, A. C. *Shakespeare and the Actors: The Stage Business in his Plays, 1660–1905*, 1944, reprinted 1963, ch. 3
Hogan, C. B., *Shakespeare in the Theatre, 1701–1800*, 2 vols., 1952, 1957
Mander, R. and Mitchenson, J. *'Hamlet' through the Ages: A Pictorial Record from 1709*, 1952
Sprague, A. C. *Shakespearian Players and Performances*, 1953, ch. 1 (Betterton as Hamlet), ch. 3 (Kemble)
Browne, E. Martin. 'English Hamlets of the twentieth century', *Shakespeare Survey* 9 (1956), 16–23
Shattuck, C. H. *The Shakespeare Promptbooks: A Descriptive Catalogue*, 1965, pp. 91–127
Buell, W. A. *The Hamlets of the Theatre*, 1968